Law Office Technology

Aspen College Series

Law Office Technology

▶ **George E. Guay, III**

Wolters Kluwer
Law & Business

Printed in the United States of America.

1 2 3 4 5 6 7 8 9 0

ISBN   978-0-7355-8316-0

Library of Congress Cataloging-in-Publication Data

Guay, George E., III.

Law office technology / George E. Guay III.
    pages cm. — (Aspen College Series)
Includes index.
ISBN-13: 978-0-7355-8316-0 (alk. paper)
ISBN-10: 0-7355-8316-1 (alk. paper)
1.   Law offices—United States—Automation. 2.   Law offices—United States—Automation—Equipment and supplies. 3.   Law offices—United States—Software. 4.   Law offices—United States—Computer network resources. 5.   Law offices—United States—Data processing. 6.   Legal assistants—United States—Handbooks, manuals, etc. 7.   Law offices—Automation.   I. Title.

    KF320.A9G83 2013
    340.0285—dc23

                                                                2013008736

About Wolters Kluwer Law & Business

Wolters Kluwer Law & Business is a leading global provider of intelligent information and digital solutions for legal and business professionals in key specialty areas, and respected educational resources for professors and law students. Wolters Kluwer Law & Business connects legal and business professionals as well as those in the education market with timely, specialized authoritative content and information-enabled solutions to support success through productivity, accuracy and mobility.

Serving customers worldwide, Wolters Kluwer Law & Business products include those under the Aspen Publishers, CCH, Kluwer Law International, Loislaw, ftwilliam.com and MediRegs family of products.

CCH products have been a trusted resource since 1913, and are highly regarded resources for legal, securities, antitrust and trade regulation, government contracting, banking, pension, payroll, employment and labor, and healthcare reimbursement and compliance professionals.

Aspen Publishers products provide essential information to attorneys, business professionals and law students. Written by preeminent authorities, the product line offers analytical and practical information in a range of specialty practice areas from securities law and intellectual property to mergers and acquisitions and pension/benefits. Aspen's trusted legal education resources provide professors and students with high-quality, up-to-date and effective resources for successful instruction and study in all areas of the law.

Kluwer Law International products provide the global business community with reliable international legal information in English. Legal practitioners, corporate counsel and business executives around the world rely on Kluwer Law journals, looseleafs, books, and electronic products for comprehensive information in many areas of international legal practice.

Loislaw is a comprehensive online legal research product providing legal content to law firm practitioners of various specializations. Loislaw provides attorneys with the ability to quickly and efficiently find the necessary legal information they need, when and where they need it, by facilitating access to primary law as well as state-specific law, records, forms and treatises.

ftwilliam.com offers employee benefits professionals the highest quality plan documents (retirement, welfare and non-qualified) and government forms (5500/PBGC, 1099 and IRS) software at highly competitive prices.

MediRegs products provide integrated health care compliance content and software solutions for professionals in healthcare, higher education and life sciences, including professionals in accounting, law and consulting.

Wolters Kluwer Law & Business, a division of Wolters Kluwer, is headquartered in New York. Wolters Kluwer is a market-leading global information services company focused on professionals.

To the four binding forces in my life — Anne, Jane, Octavia, and Ramona — without whom nothing is possible.

▶ Summary of Contents

▶ Contents

 Hardware and Software 1

Office Productivity Software   13

3   Practice-Specific Software   113

Practice Management and
Case Management Software   189

5 Internet-Based Legal Research 241

Telecommunications and Data Management   311

▶ List of Illustrations

▶ Preface

Changes in technology have contributed to improvements in the practice of law. This text shows many of the ways that technology has increased the efficacy and efficiency of those who work in the legal field.

Chapter One describes how the growing use of hardware and software have helped to transform how people practice the law. Software can harness a computer's processing power, going beyond the efficient retrieval, modification, and use of information about the law to reducing the risk of mistake in the timely completion of formal documents like a petition for bankruptcy. Hardware, which describes the machinery of technology, can improve office functionality.

Office productivity software, the focus of Chapter Two, expands upon the effective preparation and management of letters, briefs, and pleadings. For example, the software can generate standardized forms from fee agreements to requests for the production of documents for quick modification and use. Spreadsheet software can help a lawyer satisfy an ethical obligation to keep accurate records about clients' funds. During a trial about damages from an automobile accident, slide show software can direct a jury's attention to visual details about the vehicles and road conditions to make a point about who had obeyed the traffic laws.

A legal practice can increase the volume of business it can handle through the use of specialized software, like that reviewed in Chapter Three. Software that can automatically adjust the totals in the RESPA form for a real estate closing, perhaps due to a change in the fees kept in an escrow account, increases the likelihood of completing the sale on time. For a bankruptcy proceeding or a divorce settlement, revising the list of a client's assets can help to resolve the legal issues faster. When incorporating a client's business, software can generate documents critical to the operation of the business, like changes to the Articles of Incorporation. To guide a client about how to manage assets in case of incapacitation, a comprehensive software package can generate an array of important documents, like a durable power of attorney or a healthcare proxy.

Practice-management software can help improve the operations of a law office, as shown in Chapter Four. For example, it can keep track of business expenditures while monitoring the time employees spend working on client matters. Case management software, synchronized with practice management software, can record time spent preparing materials for discovery on a client's case, making it easy to generating a monthly bill.

Access to sophisticated databases and search engines, as discussed in Chapter Five, has improved legal research. Besides not having to set aside space for a law library, conducting Internet-based research also simplifies the process of trying out different research strategies without having to search and thumb through law books.

Using the Internet can pose risks for a legal practice. Chapter Six explores issues related to preserving the integrity of computers and networks to meet ethical obligations about safeguarding client information.

This text looks at how technology has positively improved the practice of law. By looking at how hardware and software can lead to greater efficiency and effectiveness, paralegals and lawyers can better use the law.

▶ Acknowledgments

It might seem that an author alone can generate a text, but that would downplay the involvement of others without whom the manuscript would never achieve printed form. Among the many whose contributions made it possible for the manuscript of this text to become a textbook, David Herzig's vision for such a text has guided the manuscript from initial discussions about its creation to its final publication. Betsy Kenny has served as the primary overseer of the preparation from the manuscript; without her diligence the manuscript would not appear in the form of this particular text. Consultation with Faith Sherlock made clear exactly how this text would benefit those who purchase it. As project manager for Progressive Publishing Alternatives, Sylvia Rebert managed the transformation of manuscript into a text. Many thanks as well to librarians in general, especially those at the Thomas Crane Public Library in Quincy, Massachusetts, and the Maxwell Library of Bridgewater State University, in Bridgewater, Massachusetts.

I would also like to thank those who provided valuable input through the review process on the manuscript:

Stephen Barnes, Coastline Community College
Loretta Calvert, Volunteer State Community College
Regina Dowling Graziani, University of Hartford
Ruth Harrison, Yavapai College
June McLaughlin, Irvine Valley College
Deborah Vinecour, SUNY-Rockland Community College
Deborah Walsh, Middlesex Community College

Thank you to the following rights owners for permission to use their illustrations in the text:

Figures 2.1–2.40.   Used with permission from Microsoft.
Figures 2.41–2.54.   Apache and Apache OpenOffice Writer are trademarks of The Apache Software Foundation. Used with permission. No endorsement by The Apache Software Foundation is implied by the use of these marks.
Figures 2.55–2.58; 5.96–5.101   Google and the Google logo are registered trademarks of Google Inc., used with permission.
Figures 3.1–3.13; 3–58–3.63.   Reprinted with permission from National Law Forms.

Figures 3.14–3.21.   Reprinted with permission of Business Entity Software.

Figures 3.22–3.57.   Reprinted with permission of Easysoft.

Figures 4.1, 4.2, 4.5, 4.6, 4.19–4.26, 4.37–4.39, 5.3–5.37.   Copyright 2013 LexisNexis, a division of Reed Elsevier Inc.   All Rights Reserved. LexisNexis and the Knowledge Burst logo are registered trademarks of Reed Elsevier Properties Inc. and are used with the permission of LexisNexis.

Figures 4.3, 4.7–4.9.   Reprinted with permission of Abacus Law.

Figures 4.4, 4.15–4.18.   Reprinted with permission of Tabs3.

Figure 4.10.   Reprinted with permission of Amicus Attorney.

Figures 4.11–4.14.   Reprinted with permission of Needles.

Figures 4.27, 4.32, 4.43–4.44, 5.38–5.72.   Reprinted with permission of Thomson Reuters.

Figures 4.28–4.31.   Reprinted with permission of Clarity Legal Software.

Figure 4.33.   Reprinted with permission of EDRM (edrm.net).

Figures 4.34–4.36.   Reprinted with permission of Intella.

Figures 4.40–4.42.   Reprinted with permission of Masterfile.

Figure 4.45.   Reprinted with permission of Daegis eDiscovery.

Figures 5.73–5.87, 6.4–6.6.   Reprinted with permission of Wolters Kluwer.

Figures 5.88–5.92.   Reprinted with permission of FastCase.

Figures 5.93–5.95   Reprinted with permission of Casemaker.

George E. Guay, III
February 2013

Hardware and Software

Objectives

▶ **Investigate** those components common to personal computers.

▶ **Identify** the role that the CPU plays.

▶ **Review** the ways to store data for use with a personal computer.

▶ **Survey** the different types of printers used with personal computers.

▶ **Examine** the types of computing devices, other than PCs, commonly used in a business environment.

▶ **Explore** different types of software, from operating systems to applications and from drivers to utilities.

▶ **Review** a checklist of considerations for deciding whether to acquire software.

▶ **Examine** the limitations that could exist when using free software.

Introduction

The introduction of personal computers has dramatically boosted office productivity. Computer programs, called software, have made it possible to achieve increased efficiency and effectiveness.

An exploration of hardware related to telecommunications, including but not limited to networks and Internet connectivity, takes place in Chapter 6.

Hardware

Personal Computers

Two basic hardware configurations dominate the personal computing market: the **PC** and the **Mac.** Primarily, because of IBM's ability to manufacture its computers on a large scale, and the early availability of Microsoft's **operating system** (OS), most personal computers are PCs. Their ubiquity means that most software creators write code for that OS, but then, so do those who create viruses.

When Apple created the Mac, it designed the hardware and software as part of a whole, so as to maximize the functionality of both.

1. Components

a. Common features

Personal computers typically have:

▶ A **mouse,** for greater flexibility using the cursor;

▶ A **keyboard,** with Alt, Ctrl, and Function keys, that can effectively triple the usefulness of each key; some have an ergonomic design, with keys positioned at an angle to reduce the risk of workplace-related injuries, such as carpal tunnel syndrome; and

▶ **Ports,** for connecting an external device; PCs have USB ports and Macs have **FireWire. Ethernet ports** can connect a computer to a network and/or directly to the World Wide Web.

▶ **Monitors,** which graphically display the product of the interaction between the hardware and software, usually have to be purchased separately.

b. Common accessories

Accessories may include:

▶ A **scanner,** which can work like a photocopier by scanning printed copy to record it into a digital format.

▶ A **camera,** which when connected to the PC can capture an image for use in a digital format. Some monitors may come with a camera embedded in them.

2. CPU

The central processing unit (CPU), sometimes called the chip, a core, or the **microprocessor,** works as the brain of the computer. Embedded in the motherboard, which connects it to the other parts of the computer, the CPU can perform multiple computing tasks accurately and efficiently. Recent design innovations include having multiple cores, allowing it to do the work of two or four computers simultaneously.

3. Storage

Accessing data for the CPU to use may depend on where the data gets stored. The following represent storage locations, in order in terms of ease of access:

▶ Information for using operating system (OS) software and software applications may get stored in read-only memory (ROM), which can be changed only with great difficulty.

▶ A CPU may have space to set aside on it, called a **cache.** Because the CPU will need that information frequently, it might hold the data currently in use or a software application in the cache.

▶ Next, a CPU would use a random access memory (RAM) module to store information temporarily. This type of memory can easily get rewritten by the CPU. For example, if data changes in an Excel spreadsheet document containing client expenses, that data will get stored here until it is time to store it to a more permanent location. Computer manufacturers may include expansion slots for adding more RAM modules, which will provide the CPU with more space for fast access to more data.

▶ The hard drive serves as the primary storage medium for most software and data. It is a small copper disk set on a spindle which rotates when the CPU has to access the data kept there, in predetermined locations known as **sectors.** Hard drives store data wherever the CPU can find an empty sector or one that could be overwritten. For example, data used to generate a client's bill might lie in different sectors. **Defragmentation** can group data from different sectors more closely together, making it easier and faster to get to the data. It can also identify bad sectors to avoid them in the future.

Over the next few years, the hard drive with a spinning copper disk will be replaced with a solid-state drive, a kind of very large memory chip, which will dramatically increase the speed with which the CPU can get information, since it will not require any mechanical movement to get access to data.

▶ A **flash drive,** sometimes called a jump drive or a thumb drive, offers solid-state memory that connects to the computer via a **Universal Serial Bus (USB) port.** This drive's portability makes it convenient for carrying large files, but poses a potential security risk because its size makes it vulnerable to theft.

Figure 1-1. Flash drive
Paul Williams/www.wpclipart.com

▶ Although different, a secured digital (SD) card can have the storage capacity of a flash drive. This memory card can be used with many types of electronic devices, such as cameras. Many computers now come with a port designed to receive this card, making an upload of pictures quite simple.

Figure 1-2. SD card
Paul Williams/www.wpclipart.com

Users might wish to encrypt all data on a flash drive to reduce the risk of unintended disclosure of client information if the drive was lost or stolen.

▶ **CDs** and **DVDs** offer permanent, high-capacity data storage on portable media. Accidental erasure of data on a CD or DVD will not happen due to the proximity of a magnet, as would happen with older storage media, like floppy disks. Instead, a laser inscribes data on the metal disk, encased in plastic, making it potentially a more stable storage environment. Although easily accessible, since most computers have disk drives, drive motors do fail, which might limit access to data stored in this format. Increasingly, laptops (see below) do not have drives for reading CDs and DVDs, which add weight and draw heavily on battery power, but use a solid-state flash drive for data storage.

4. Printers

The primary output device, a printer, generates a paper copy of data. Types of printers include:

▶ A laser printer, which works like a photocopier, and can print quickly and cheaply.

▶ An inkjet printer, which has a spray nozzle mounted on a crossbar. It can generate quality color printouts, although cheap color printers may eventually replace these.

All-in-one printers can also work as photocopiers, scanners, and fax machines. Having this type of printer may reduce office clutter, but a breakdown could mean that an office loses the benefit of having any of these functions.

Portable Computing

Advances in technology have helped to make computing more portable, with devices such as:

▶ **Notebooks,** also called laptops, which may most closely match the experience of using a PC. Notebooks typically have smaller displays and may rely on battery power. Their portability makes them more vulnerable to theft, which raises an ethical issue about preserving the confidentiality of data stored on them.

▶ **Netbooks** are often lighter than notebooks, because they typically do not have a hard drive. Even though they may have smaller keyboards, it still may be possible to touch-type.

▶ **Tablets** lack a keyboard, although they have touchscreen displays. They may be most appealing to counsel in court who would need to call up a document quickly without having to carry paper versions of all documents to court.

Software

Software, encoded electrical information, makes it possible to exploit a personal computer's processing capacity. Federal **copyright** law protects software from unauthorized copying and use. It recognizes the creator's interest in receiving compensation for using the software via a license. A common form of licensing agreement for software is known as the **End User Licensing Agreement (EULA).**

Essential Software

Types of essential software include:

▶ The **basic information operating system (BIOS),** which tells the computer how to perform basic operations, like what should happen when a user turns on the computer; and

▶ The **operating system (OS),** which makes it possible for the computer to use common software applications, such as for word processing. Microsoft's **Windows OS** dominates the marketplace since it exploited the processing power of the Intel microprocessor that IBM used in its PCs. Apple's OS has historically made better use of a computer's CPU, because the software and hardware were specifically designed for one another. Free operating systems exist, such as Linux. Such an OS might not need expensive, periodic upgrades; technical assistance will have to be purchased separately.

Software makers might periodically distribute computer code, known as **patches,** to fix a problem with the software. A software maker might send along a series of patches. Microsoft refers to these as **service packs.**

Preloaded Software

Commonly preloaded software includes:

▶ **Drivers** (also sometimes called device drivers) that allow the computer to use peripherals, such as a printer. For example, when the user sends a document to a printer, the driver translates the print request into language that the printer's processor understands in order to print the document.

▶ **Utilities** consist of software that can maintain the computer's functionality. For example, the utilities could automatically generate backup copies of the OS and installed software, so that if the OS fails, the copy could be used to reinstall the OS and installed software.

▶ **Synchronization** ensures that, for example, a laptop and desktop computer have exact copies of data on each device.

Licensed Software

Users might like to purchase a license for a copy of software because:

▶ The software has gained such widespread use that most people would have already learned how to use it, like a word processing application that has become a *de facto* standard in a professional field;

▶ The documents generated with a licensed copy may come in a format that a client can easily use;

▶ No free software may exist that has as many features;

▶ It might work well with the operating system of a user's personal computer;

▶ It offers 24-hour support;

▶ Training is included in the form of tutorials; and

▶ It has **scalability,** where the software creator has made different versions that could run on a Microsoft and a Mac OS platform.

Licensed software, in the form of **Software as a Service (SaaS),** sometimes referred to as **cloud computing,** will be discussed in the next chapter. SaaS involves the storage of data and software on a **server** (a type of computer), which is accessible over the World Wide Web. This raises, however, ethical concerns about preserving the confidentiality of client information.

Figure 1-3. Server
Paul Williams/www.wpclipart.com

Pirated Software

Complying with ethical standards would mean not using unauthorized, or pirated, copies of software. Using an unauthorized copy flouts the legal protections accorded to copyrighted material under federal law. Software providers typically require users to register a copy of the software in order to send users information about fixing a problem with the software or to help a user with a technical problem. The user of an illegal copy would lose out on this. A pirated copy might not have safeguards to prevent unauthorized access to data on a computer, including information that a lawyer has an ethical obligation to keep confidential. Finally, an unauthorized copy of software may lack supporting materials.

Free Software

Free software seems like the ideal first consideration when seeking out a specialized software application.

1. Advantages and Disadvantages

Consider the following points:

▶ Free software might be **open source,** which involves making the basic code of the software, often called a **kernel,** freely available, so that people can design applications that use the kernel. For example, Linux is a type of open-source OS. Linus Thorvalds made the Linux kernel available for free in the hope that software makers would create different applications for use with that kernel. Governments have come to use the Linux kernel because they could not justify to their constituents the costs of paying for regular updates of a proprietary OS.

A community of users might make, as in the case of Linux, training, support, and upgrades available from members of that community. That community might also modify the kernel without violating any copyright protections.

▶ Free software may offer no training or support services.

▶ Free software might carry a hidden cost, in terms of the time spent installing the software on a personal computer, as the software creator might not have invested the time and effort in making installation an easy, seamless process, unlike with licensed software such as Microsoft's Office Suite (more on this in the next chapter).

▶ Free software might not work well with other software platforms, which might mean that a word processing document created on free software may be inaccessible on commonly used licensed software, such as Microsoft's Word.

▶ A cloud computing or SaaS version might not exist, which might increase the time spent installing an upgrade of the free software on every personal computer that uses the free software.

Making software free, like an OS such as Linux, might present an opportunity for a sale. For example:

▶ A software creator could build a graphic user interface that would make it easier to use the free software, and sell this.

▶ A business could offer, for a fee, guidance on how best to use the features of the free software.

▶ A business could build an operating system off of a kernel, then offer it for free, while selling software applications (or apps) that would exploit the advantages in their particular operating system.

Microsoft effectively used that strategy as a way to gain market dominance because, early in the development of a market for PCs, manufacturers of personal computers could load the Microsoft OS for free on their products as an added sales incentive. Then Microsoft began to sell apps such as Word and Excel, and OS upgrades that made it easier to use a PC.

▶ A software creator could, for example, make simplified word processing software available for free, but then offer for sale an advanced version with more features.

▶ A software creator could make the software free for a limited period of time, so that a user would grow to appreciate the benefits of the free software, demonstrating to a user why it would make sense to buy a license without such a time limit. For example, the makers of the popular file compression software WinZip use this strategy. (File compression software makes data files smaller, so that they can get passed along faster on the Internet.) In fact, this marketing strategy contributed to making it the *de facto* standard for file compression software. Users could, after the expiration of the trial period, merely uninstall and then reinstall the trial version of WinZip, but the makers of the software thought that for some it would make more sense just to buy a license instead of having to periodically uninstall and reinstall the limited-time version.

▶ The free version could contain advertising and the licensed version might not have it; at worst, then, the software creator has a chance to sell the advertising.

Even sites that offer downloads of free software, such as www.download.com or www.tucows.com, could sell advertising on their sites.

▶ A software creator might offer free software just to get users to visit the creator's website, which could have advertising and/or other software available for purchase.

▶ Free software might contain malicious software (malware) that would compromise the security of a computer. While sites like www.download.com recognize this danger and examine all software before making it available for download, other sites might not. Or, simply, the software creator makes the software available only through its site, without having any independent review regarding its safety.

2. Examples

a. Microsoft OS platform

A short list of free software that works on the Microsoft OS platform includes:

▶ Podcasting: www.easypodcast.com

▶ Internet
  ▷ Apache web server (transforms computer into a web server): www.apache.org
  ▷ Bit torrent (allows peer-to-peer file sharing): www.bittorrent.com
  ▷ Filezilla (FTP client for windows): http://sourceforge.net/projects/filezilla/?source=directory
  ▷ Mozilla Webmaker (a web page authoring system): http://www.mozilla.org/en-US/webmaker/
  ▷ NVU (web page creating software, akin to FrontPage, Dreamweaver): www.nvu.com
  ▷ OsCommerce (on-line shopping cart): www.oscommerce.com
  ▷ Perl (programming language for web functions): www.cpan.org
  ▷ PHP (programming language for web functions): www.php.net
  ▷ Pidgin (handles multiple IM messaging platforms): www.pidgin.im
  ▷ TightVNC (remote access to desktop): www.tightvnc.com

▶ Graphics
  ▷ Inkscape (akin to Adobe Illustrator): www.inkscape.org
  ▷ QCad (computer-aided drafting software): http://www.ribbonsoft.com/en/qcad
  ▷ Wings 3D (three-dimensional modeling tool): www.wings3d.com

b. Mac OS platform

A short list of free software that works on the Mac OS platform includes:

▶ Fastest Free YouTube Downloader to MP3 Converter (Media converter): http://www.fastestvideodownloader.com/

▶ Adobe Reader (to read files in PDF format): http://www.adobe.com/

▶ Adobe Flash Player (to view Flash animations): http://www.adobe.com/

▶ OpenOffice (office productivity): http://www.openoffice.org/

▶ MacZip (file compression): http://www.haase-online.de/dirk/maczip/

▶ HotSpot Shield (encryption for public Wi-Fi hot spots): http://anchorfree.com

▶ Handbrake for Mac (video converter to put into MPEG-4 format): http://handbrake.m0k.org/

Conclusion

The personal computer has enhanced office productivity by managing data better, increasing accuracy, and reducing costs for a firm. The interaction of the hardware, from the central processing unit working as the computer's "brain," to the printer generating tangible results of a user's efforts, has changed the way a law firm can meet a client's needs. Computer code, as software, exploits the power and flexibility of the computer's CPU, making it easy to produce updated financial statements for a divorce settlement, as well as making a slideshow presentation that can show a jury why a client should avoid liability for accidental injury.

Terms

Application

Basic information operating system (BIOS)

Cache

Central processing unit (CPU)

Cloud computing

Compact discs (CDs)

Copyright

Core

Defragmentation

Digital video disks (DVDs)

Diskettes

Driver

End User Licensing Agreement (EULA)

Ethernet port

Firewire

Flash drive

Hard drive

Inkjet printers

Kernel

Laser printers

License

Linux

Mac

Malicious software (malware)

Microprocessor

Monitor

Motherboard

Mouse

Netbooks

Notebooks

Open source:

Operating system (OS)

Patches

PC

Peripherals

Ports

Printer

RAM (random access memory)

ROM (read-only memory)

Scalability

Scanner

Sectors

Server

Service packs

Software as a Service (SaaS)

Synchronization

Tablet

USB

Utilities

Hypotheticals

1. Having used software that can make a will for a client, a legal assistant has now modified it. In light of the discussion in this chapter about different types of memory, talk about each kind of memory or storage media that could be used, then explain which one the legal assistant should use for saving the modified will.

2. Talk about the advantages and disadvantages of using free software.

3. Present arguments as to why a law firm should buy software that is licensed, free, or open source.

4. Explain the strengths and weaknesses of each of the types of personal computers mentioned in this chapter.

Office Productivity Software

Objectives

▶ **Survey** types of office productivity software that can increase the effectiveness of a legal practice.

▶ **Examine** Microsoft's Word in detail and compare it with other word processing software, especially for generating and managing legal documents like pleadings and briefs.

▶ **Determine** how **spreadsheet** software like Microsoft's Excel can make it easier for a legal practice to manage numerical data efficiently and accurately, such as for tracking time spent on a client's case.

▶ **Evaluate** slide show presentation software, like Microsoft's PowerPoint or OpenOffice.org's Impress, for use in a legal practice.

▶ **Assess** the utility of free office productivity software such as OpenOffice. Org and Google Docs in a law office.

Introduction

Software commonly used in a law office can increase productivity by simplifying the steps needed to create and edit documents. This, in turn, can generate savings that could be passed along to clients in the form of reduced fees.

Common Features of Software

Bars and Ribbons and Pulldowns

The **graphic user interface (GUI)** of software describes how information will look on a computer screen. One approach to organizing those visual cues (sometimes called **buttons**) involves grouping them in a **toolbar** (or a **ribbon**), particularly by function. Users can often customize the number and kind of features available with a toolbar or ribbon. A user in a law firm could, for example, include a button for quick access to software used for a real estate closing or for generating a petition for bankruptcy.

Suites

Software makers appreciate that customers might prefer to have software applications that mesh well with one another. For example, Microsoft's suite, MS Office, integrates software that has, among other features, word processing, spreadsheets, Internet browsing, and the creation of slide shows. Of course, a suite, or bundle, of applications will cost less than if a law firm had to buy a license for each application.

Microsoft Office Suite

The preeminent office productivity suite, Microsoft Office, has an array of software most commonly used in any business. While Microsoft updates Office every few years, the company tends to have the same features in its software. This review will use the 2007 version of Office.

Word 2007

A common feature of Office software is the Microsoft graphic in the upper left-hand corner of the screen.

1. Office Button

In Word, clicking on the Office button will reveal a pulldown submenu of commonly used functions, such as to close a document, or the following:

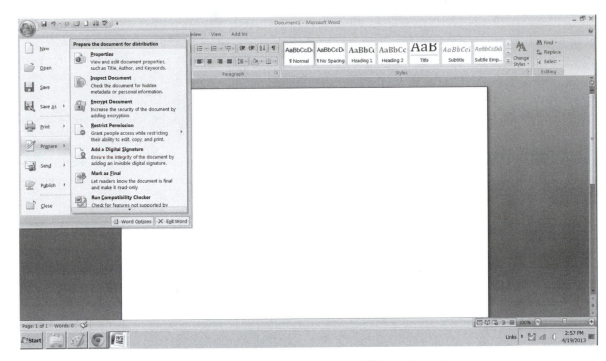

Figure 2-1. Microsoft Word—Microsoft Word with submenu

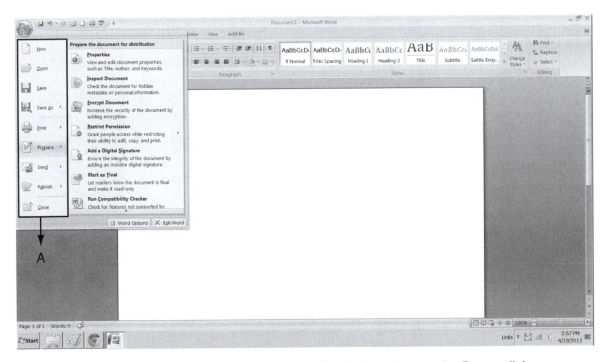

Figure 2-1a. Microsoft Word—Microsoft Word with submenu: the Prepare link

▶ **New:** Not only can a user create a blank document, but Word also provides templates for different types of documents. For example, a law firm could create a template that contains standard language in a services contract for a new client. A link to Microsoft Office Online provides access to additional templates.

▶ **Open:** Here the user obtains access to documents by file name or in a particular folder.

▶ **Save, Save As:** Not only can a user save a copy of a document, but via Save As the user can save it in a different format, such as PDF (protected document format), which limits options for subsequently altering it.

▶ **Print:** Options for printing a document include being able to select printers, like those in a firm's networked computers.

▶ **Prepare:** Before a user distributes a document, like a non-compete agreement, the user can select who can access the agreement or limit changes that recipients can make.

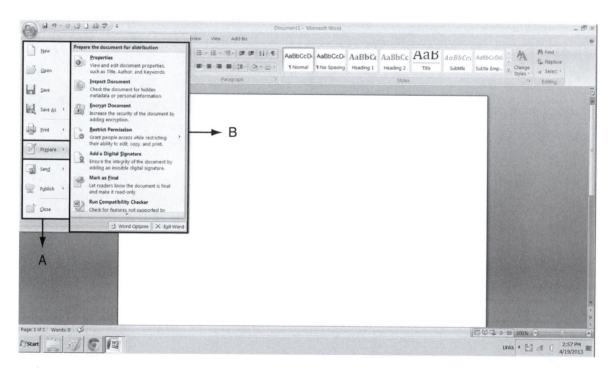

Figure 2-1b. Microsoft Word—Prepare options in Word

▶ **Send:** In addition to the opportunity to send a document as an e-mail, a user could also send it as a fax via the web (where that service is available).

▶ **Publish:** Here, for example, the user could post a commentary about a recent U.S. Supreme Court decision on a blog, or store a document on a server so that others may access it.

▶ **Word Options:** Clicking this button, on the bottom of the menu, opens a submenu where a user may personalize a copy of Word, like adding or deleting features, such as for proofreading.

2. Tabs

Tabs, like those along the top of manila folders, serve as the way of using particular features of the software. Under each tab, options get sorted in labeled subsections, as seen in the boxes entitled Editing or Font, under the Home tab.

a. Home tab

A user will find, under the Home tab, the following boxes: Clipboard, Font, Paragraph, Styles, and Editing.

i. Clipboard

The Clipboard box contains buttons for cutting and pasting material. Via a submenu, a user could, for example, open a box on the side that contains material that has been cut, like a disclaimer of warranty. To insert that disclaimer later in the document, a user needs only to move the browser arrow onto the disclaimer and click it to insert it.

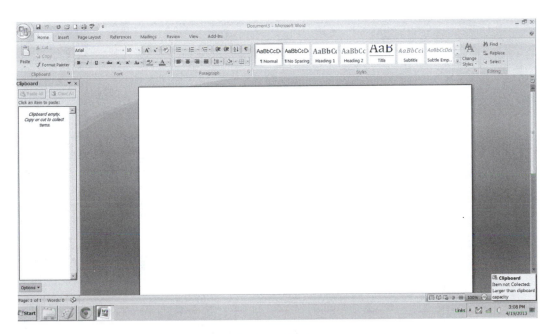

Figure 2-2. Microsoft Word—Home tab

Figure 2-2a. Microsoft Word—Home tab: Clipboard option

Figure 2-2b. Microsoft Word—Clipboard option submenu

ii. Font

The Font box allows the user to manipulate the appearance of the typeface. Some courts only accept documents that use the Courier typeface, with a font size of 12, and the user can easily change the typeface and font here. Using the bottom row's buttons means putting content into italics or underlining. Clicking the double-headed arrow in the corner will open a submenu with other options, such as inserting double-strike lines over typed material.

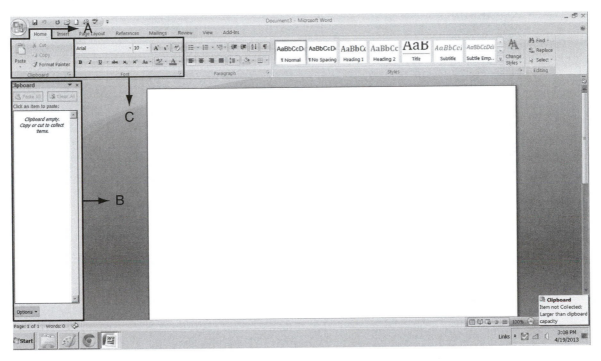

Figure 2-2c. Microsoft Word—Home tab: Font box

iii. Paragraph

The adjacent Paragraph box provides users with buttons, along the top, for inserting bullet points or numbers, as well as to indent and sort text. Buttons on the bottom make it easy for a user to center, justify content, or have text run flush to either margin. Also, a user can change the line spacing of the text, as well as add different types of borders.

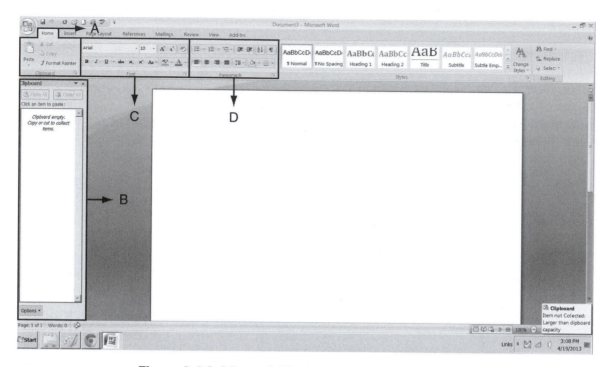

Figure 2-2d. Microsoft Word—Home tab: Paragraph box

iv. Styles

Over the past few decades, courts have established requirements regarding aspects of a legal brief. This might mean using only 8 1/2″ x 11″ paper (because the old 8 1/2″ x 14″ "legal size" required special file cabinets), with one-inch margins. Briefs might have a page limit and require a certain typeface or font.

An easy way to meet these requirements would involve setting up a style. The Styles box provides users with a way to create styles that can be applied with a click of a button. Style templates called Quick Style come as presets which the user can quickly modify.

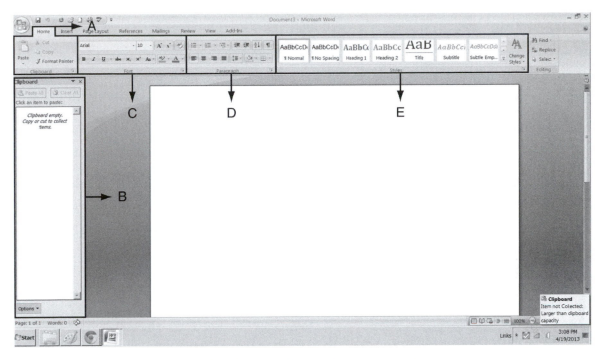

Figure 2-2e. Microsoft Word—Home tab: Styles box

v. Editing

A user will want the freedom to move around the document quickly. The last box, Editing, contains links to go to a page in the document and to find and/or replace content.

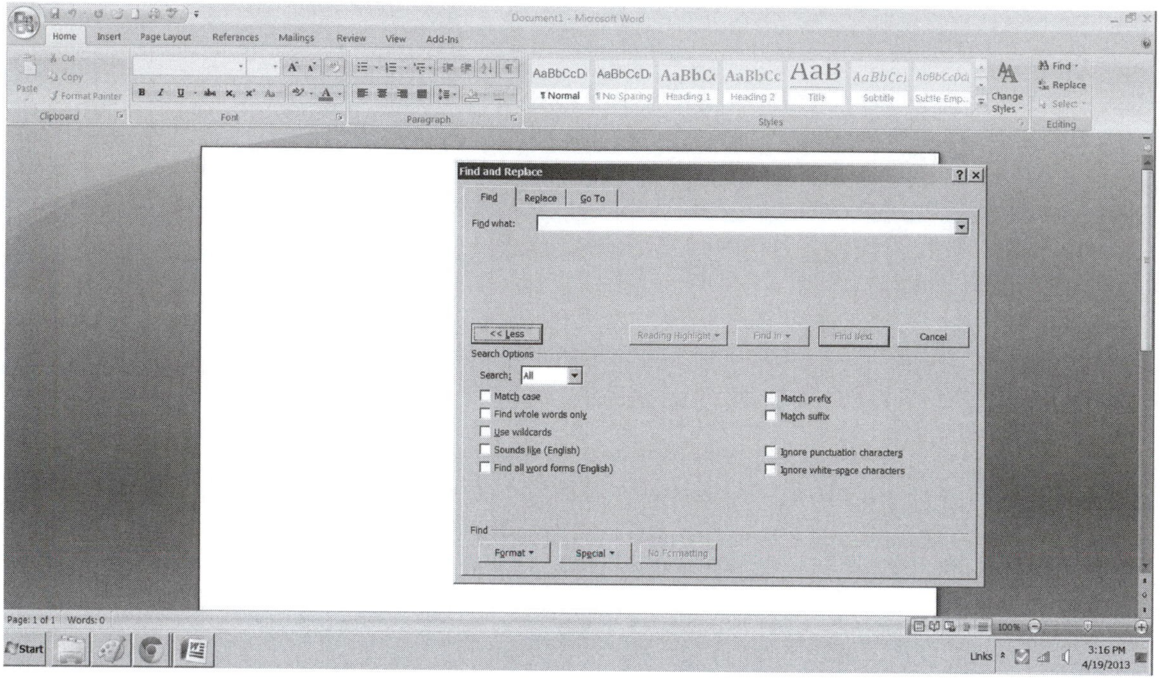

Law Office Technology

Figure 2-3. Microsoft Word—Home tab: Editing box

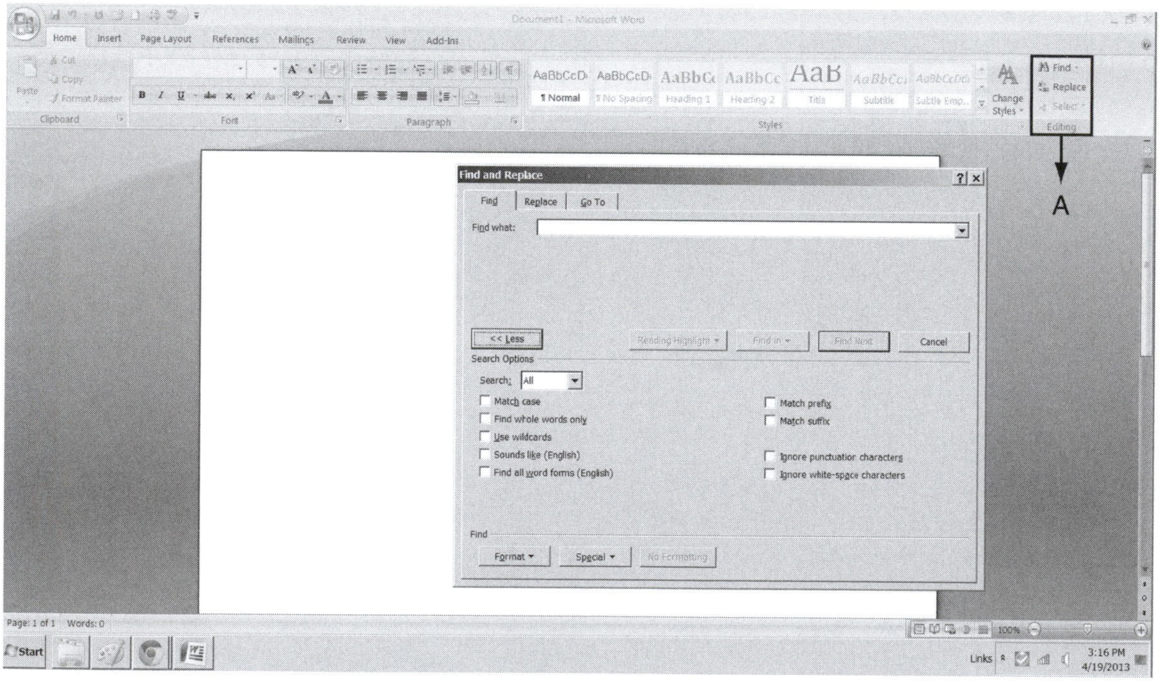

Figure 2-3a. Microsoft Word—Home tab: Editing box

The Find link, when clicked, opens to a submenu with Find, Replace, and Go To tabs, as well as buttons. The user can find and/or replace letters, numbers, punctuation, functions (like a page break), or special characters (like the section symbol §). The Go To tab allows the user to move around the document, whether to a page, heading, or predesignated location, called a bookmark.

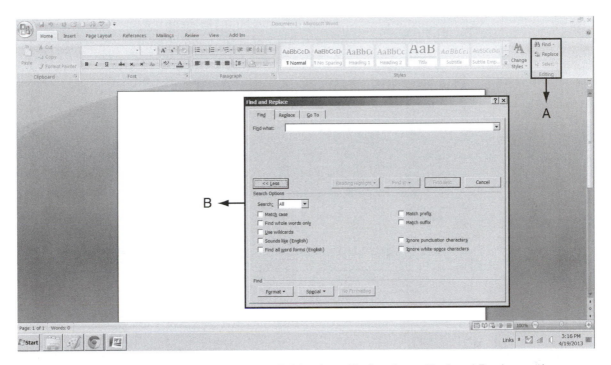

Figure 2-3b. Microsoft Word—Home tab: Editing box, Find options, Find and Replace submenu

b. Insert tab

The Insert tab provides a user with the chance to add a number of nontextual features, such as tables, pictures, or hyperlinks, as well as allowing the editing of headers and footers.

i. Pages

Here, the user can insert a blank page or a page break and use templates to create a cover page.

ii. Tables

This box makes it possible to create and insert tables, including Excel spreadsheets. If a plaintiff will suffer reduced earnings in the future because of an injury, a table could describe how much that plaintiff will not earn in successive years. Also, a user can convert text into a table.

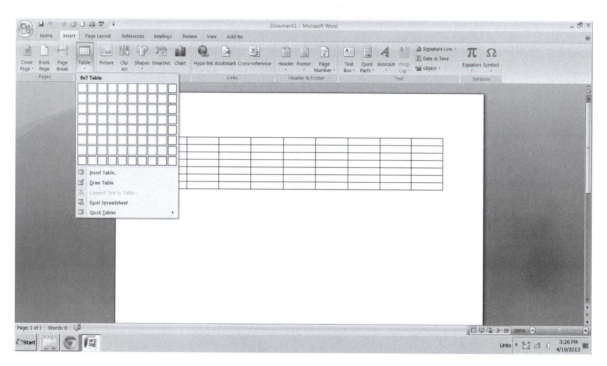

Figure 2-4. Microsoft Word—Insert tab: Table box, Table button options, Insert Table submenu, 9x7 table displayed

iii. Illustrations

Illustrations can make it easier to describe, for example, the layout of an intersection where cars collided. Here, a user can insert:

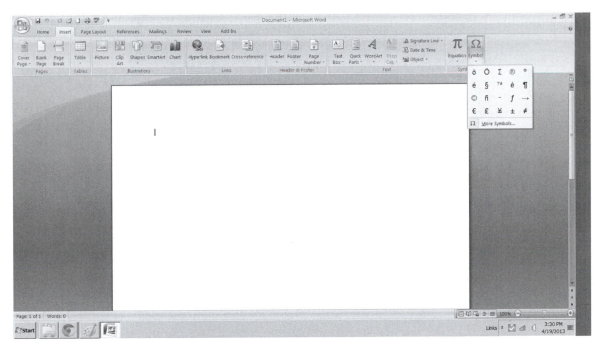

Figure 2-5. Microsoft Word—Insert tab

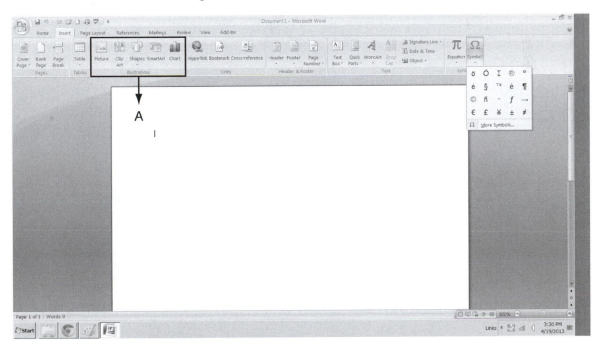

Figure 2-5a. Microsoft Word—Insert tab: Illustrations box

▶ Pictures in formats such as a bitmap and JPEG, depicting the post-accident condition of the vehicle in which that plaintiff was riding;

▶ **Clip art:** small, simple graphics that come with Word;

▶ Shapes such as lines, arrows, and other figures, with an option to create effects like shadowing;

▶ Smart art: additional graphic styles that show how a process unfolds, such as the flow of traffic on a highway; and

▶ Charts, using columns, lines, bars, or a pie chart, perhaps to show how to apportion damages among multiple defendants.

iv. Links

In this box, a user can insert a:

▶ **Hyperlink,** a connection to a web page;

▶ **Bookmark,** so that a user can go instantly to a predetermined point in a document, like an appendix that breaks down the medical expenses of an injured plaintiff; and

▶ **Cross-reference,** so that a user can go to predetermined headings in a document, such as an introduction or conclusion.

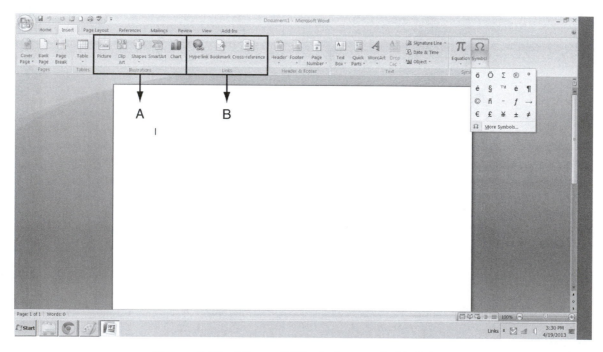

Figure 2-5b. Microsoft Word—Insert tab: Links box

v. Header and footer

By running a header on a multipage letter, a reader can figure out instantly the sequence of the pages. For a brief, a footer contains the information about the order of the pages. The real benefit of the software occurs when a paralegal inserts or deletes content, because the software will automatically adjust headers and footers to accommodate such a change.

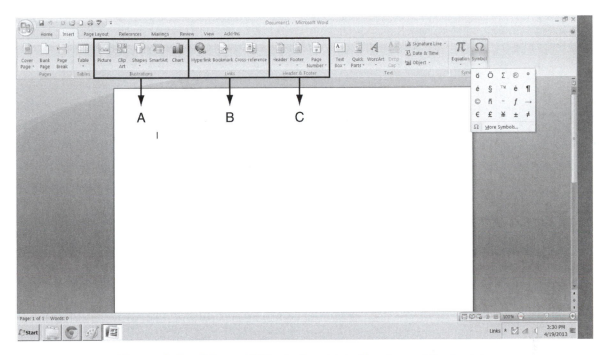

Figure 2-5c. Microsoft Word—Insert tab: Header and Footer box

vi. Text

This box allows the user to insert different, specialized kinds of content in order to reflect the date and time, and to have it update over several days as changes are made. Or, in a trademark dispute, a user may need to insert the art for the trademark, even when the art came from a different type of document.

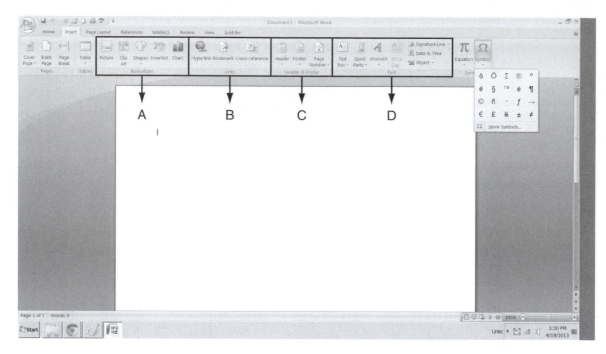

Figure 2-5d. Microsoft Word—Insert tab: Text box

vii. Symbols

Symbols such as ™ or © immediately alert a reader to a claim of legal right in a trademark or a copyright. Buttons, here, make it possible to insert those and other symbols into the text. Also, if needed, the user could include letters used in the Cyrillic alphabet, commonly used in Eastern European languages. For sales made with a business located in a member state of the European Union (EU), the user can insert the symbol for the monetary unit, the euro: € .

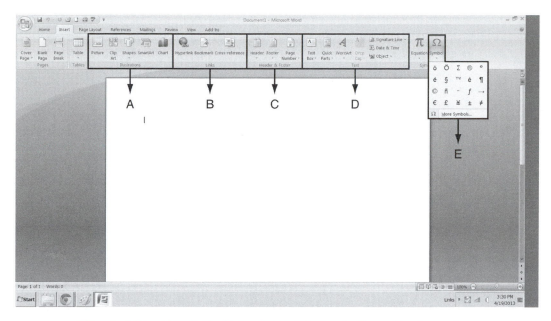

Figure 2-5e. Microsoft Word—Insert tab: Symbol box, Symbol button

c. Page layout tab

A law firm might want to keep its client current about changes in the firm. Because a newsletter can convey that information, the software contains options for presenting that information in a more appealing format.

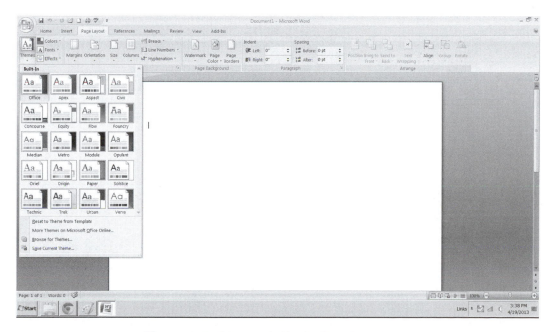

Figure 2-6. Microsoft Word—Page Layout tab

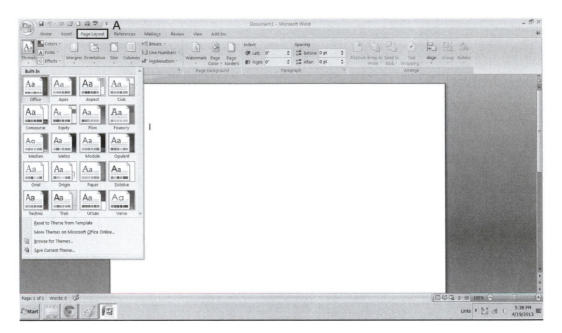

Figure 2-6a. Microsoft Word—Page Layout tab

i. Themes

Here, a user could choose a theme for such a newsletter. A theme allows the user to select a specific color scheme for the material and adjust the size and nature of the words, known as the font. Also, a user could choose graphics that alert the reader to the importance of the information.

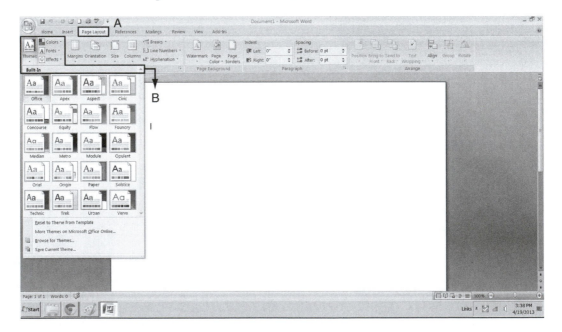

Figure 2-6b. Microsoft Word—Page Layout tab: Themes box, Themes button, Built-in

ii. Page setup

When people created letters using a typewriter, they could adjust the margins or insert tabs manually. Here the user can make similar adjustments to the image on the monitor. That means not just adjusting margins, but also:

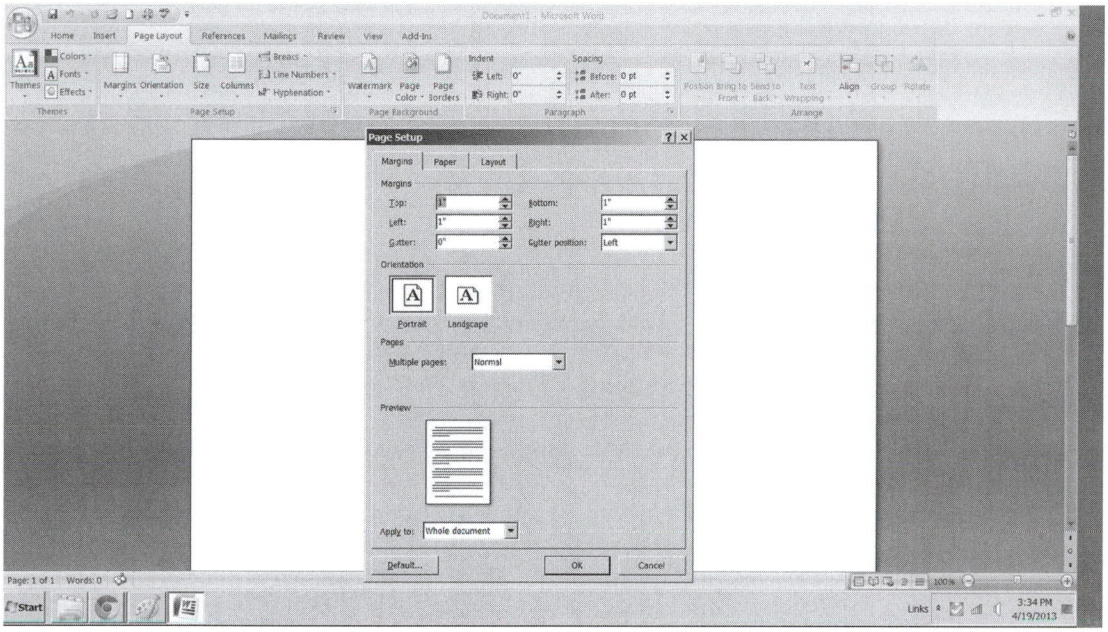

Figure 2-7. Microsoft Word—Page Layout tab: Page Setup

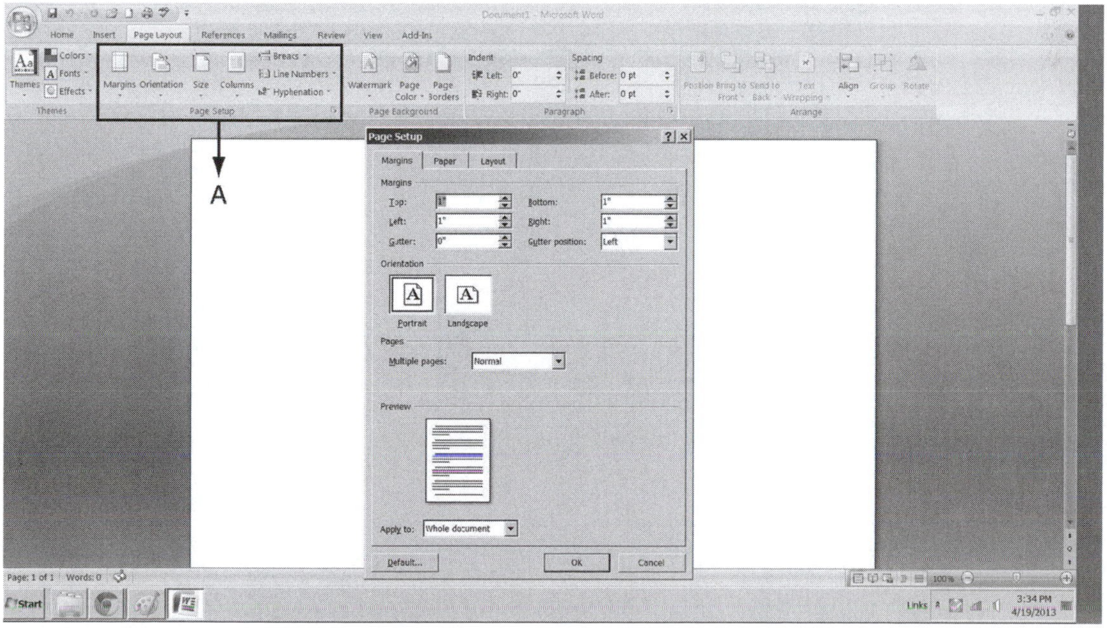

Figure 2-7a. Microsoft Word—Page Layout tab: Page Setup box

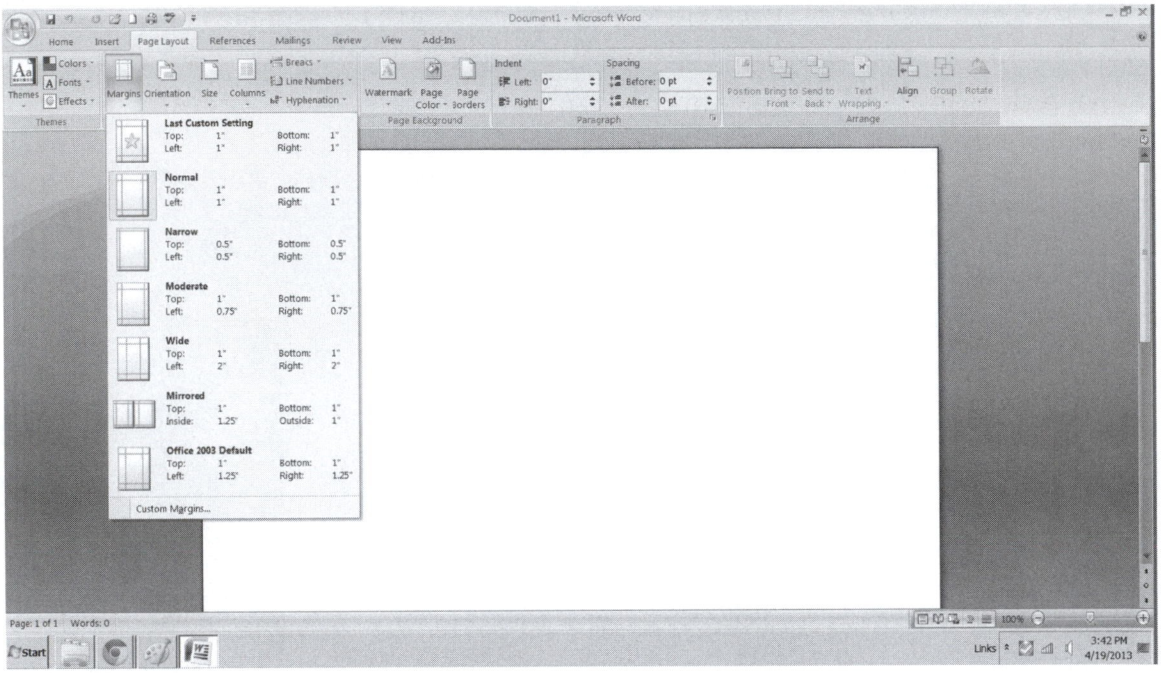

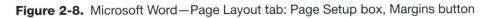

Figure 2-8. Microsoft Word—Page Layout tab: Page Setup box, Margins button

▶ Selecting the size of the electronic page in a documents, such as 8 ½″ x 11″;

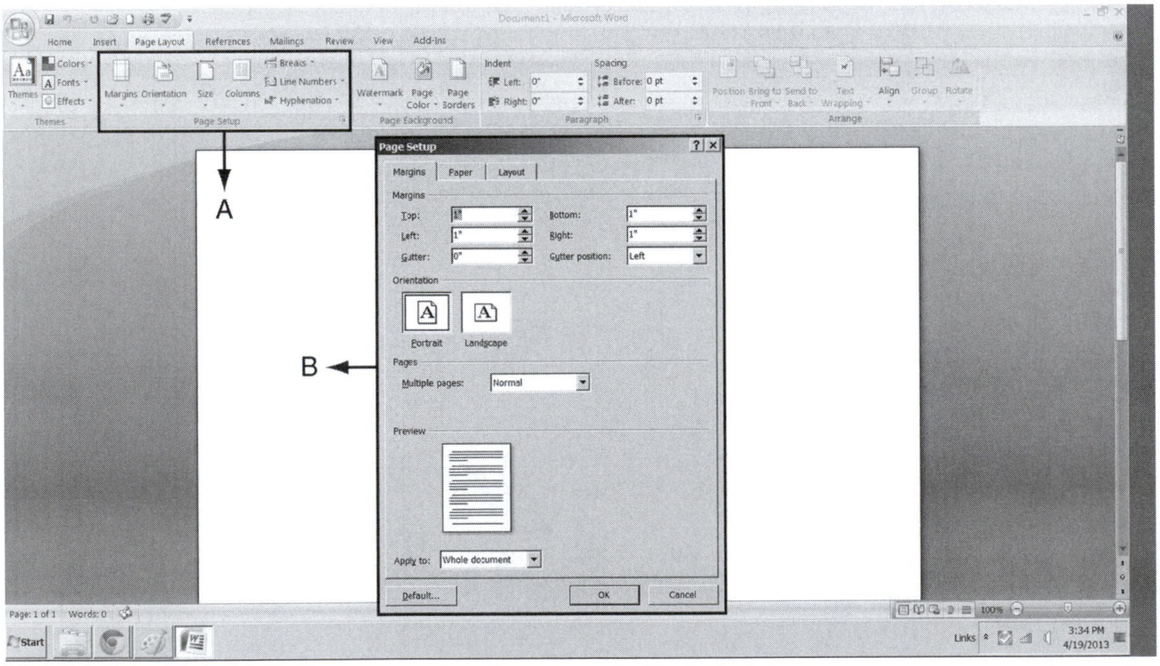

Figure 2-7b. Microsoft Word—Page Layout tab: Page Setup box, Margins button, Custom Margins link, Paper tab

▶ Choosing the orientation of the electronic page, such as portrait or land-scape;

▶ Inserting columns, including an option for multiple columns, such as the annual change in an injured plaintiff's earnings;

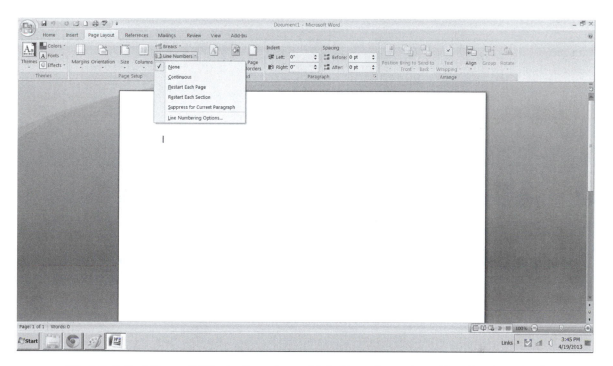

Figure 2-9. Microsoft Word—Page Layout tab: Page Setup box, Line Numbers link

▶ Making page or section breaks;

▶ Using line numbers; and

▶ Adjusting hyphenation.

iii. Page background

A client might ask a firm to draft a contract. As the firm and client make changes to the contract, using a watermark could identify the document as a "Draft," so as to reflect this process while not obscuring the provisions of the contract. The user may also select a page color and borders.

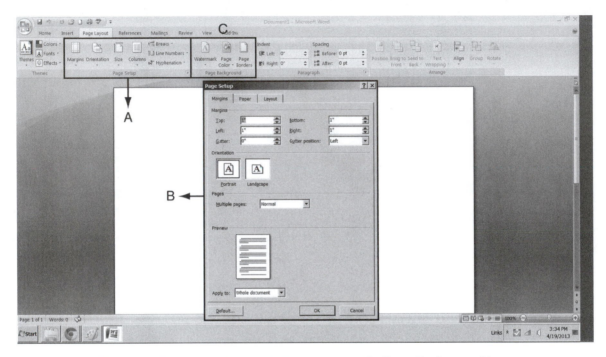

Figure 2-7c. Microsoft Word—Page Layout tab: Page Background box

iv. Paragraph

Here, a user can insert a large amount of quoted material, known as a block quote, and set the format for that quote. This might happen in a dispute about a specific provision in a contract. Options here include setting indents, and whether to insert spaces, of varying length, before and after a paragraph.

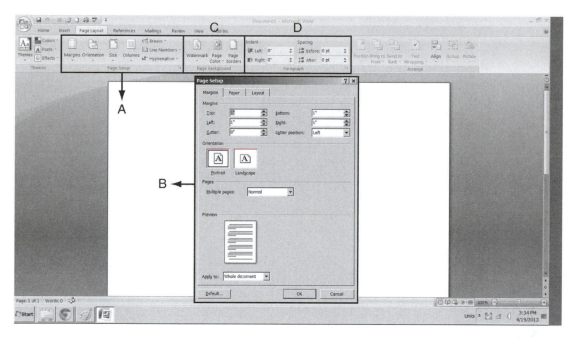

Figure 2-7d. Microsoft Word—Page Layout tab: Paragraph box

v. Arrange

The presentation, or layout, of material can make it easier for a reader to understand what a user wants to say. Here, the user can arrange the layout of text, so that in a newsletter to clients text can wrap around an image, for example.

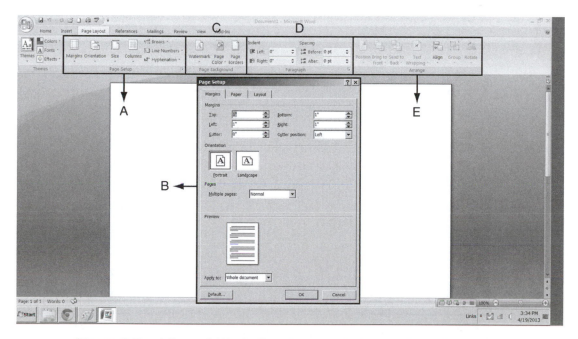

Figure 2-7e. Microsoft Word—Page Layout tab: Arrange box, Align button

d. References tab

To make a legally persuasive argument, an attorney may need to refer to the case law, statutory law, or regulations that support the point that the lawyer wants to make. This tab allows the user to manage those references.

Figure 2-10. Microsoft Word—References tab

Figure 2-10a. Microsoft Word—References tab

i. Table of Contents

Especially with appellate briefs, a table of contents has to show where certain important information, such as the case law used in the brief, appears in the document.

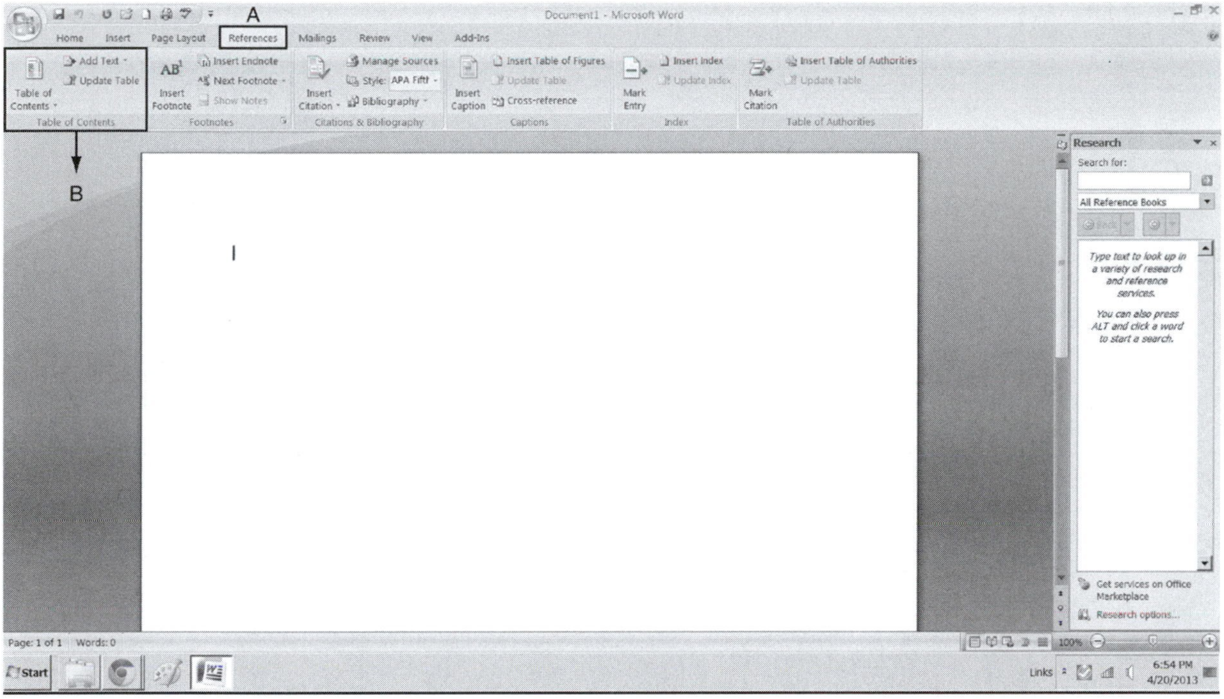

Figure 2-10b. Microsoft Word—References tab: Table of Contents box

ii. Footnotes

Where an attorney is making a legally persuasive argument in a brief, but wants to make a point not directly related to the argument, the lawyer will use a footnote. Because one of the benefits of software involves making the work of a user easier, the buttons here will properly place a footnote. Best of all, the software will automatically adjust the placement of a footnote if the attorney wants to add or delete material, an otherwise time-consuming process if done manually, such as before the advent of word processing software.

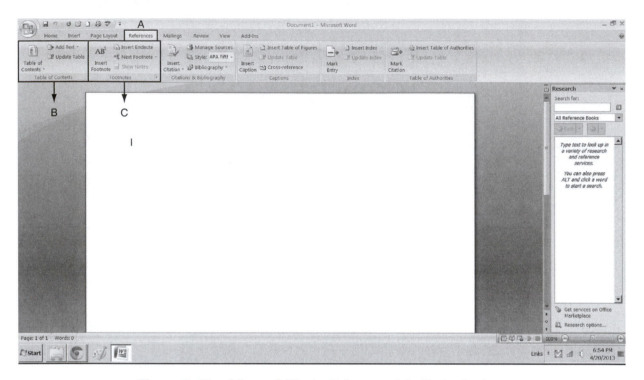

Figure 2-10c. Microsoft Word—References tab: Footnotes box

iii. Citations and bibliography

One way to make an argument more persuasive in a brief involves referring to appropriate case law, statutes, regulations, or other authority, by including a citation. Critically, the citation for the legal reference has to conform to the specific style commonly used in the American legal field, the "Blue Book" format. Although this software can style a citation into a format used in research papers or periodicals, it will not automatically put a case citation into "Blue Book" format. It can, however, compile a list of references, in the form of a bibliography.

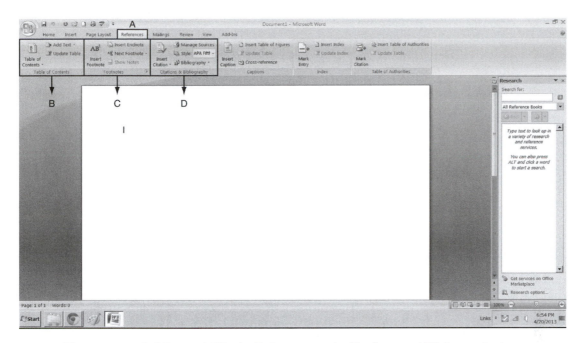

Figure 2-10d. Microsoft Word—References tab: Citations and Bibliography box

The user can also search for references from sources such as Microsoft's Bing search engine.

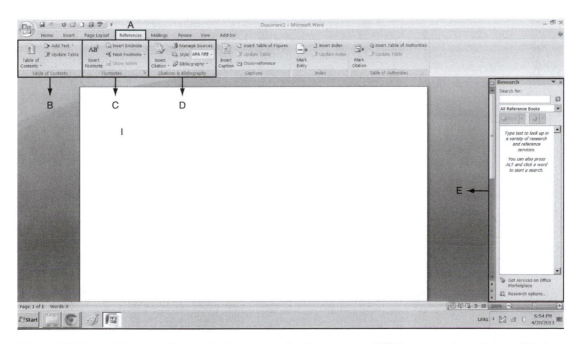

Figure 2-10e. Microsoft Word—References tab: Citations and Bibliography box, Insert Citation button, Search Libraries submenu

iv. Captions

In a dispute regarding a patent, often a question arises about "original art" which relates to important graphic information. This box offers options to:

▶ Generate captions for such graphics;

▶ Insert a table of figures;

▶ Update the table; and

▶ Make a cross-reference.

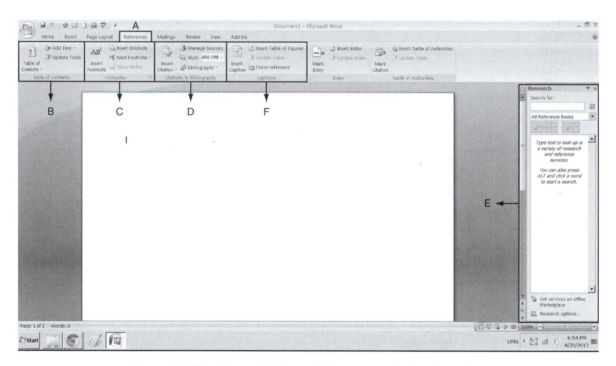

Figure 2-10f. Microsoft Word—References tab: Captions box

v. Index

One way that a lawyer could share his or her expertise would involve writing a text. The author could use this option to create an index. This involves going through the manuscript and designating the level of importance of information, so that the software can generate an index. For example, the index for this book has as a heading Microsoft Office, with subordinate headings for Word and for Excel.

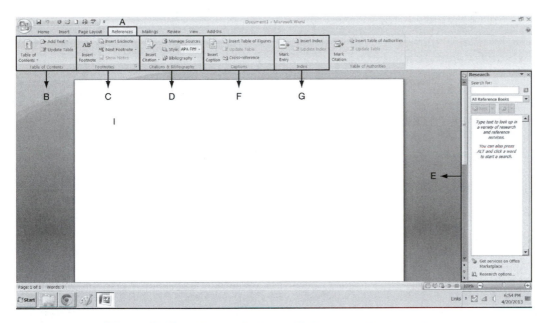

Figure 2-10g. Microsoft Word—References tab: Index box

vi. Table of Authorities

Rules of appellate courts generally require that an appellate brief include a listing of all sources of law mentioned in a brief, called a table of authorities. The last box makes it possible to create a table of authorities.

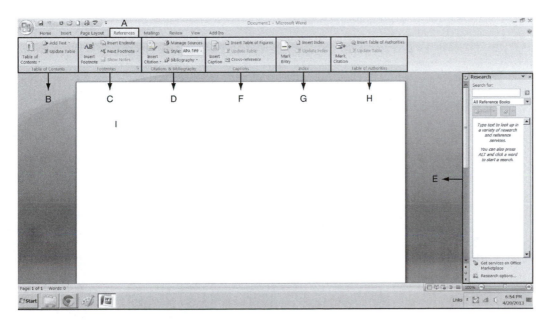

Figure 2-10h. Microsoft Word—References tab: Table of Authorities box

a. Mark Citation

When the user clicks this option, a submenu entitled Mark Citation opens with the following features to:

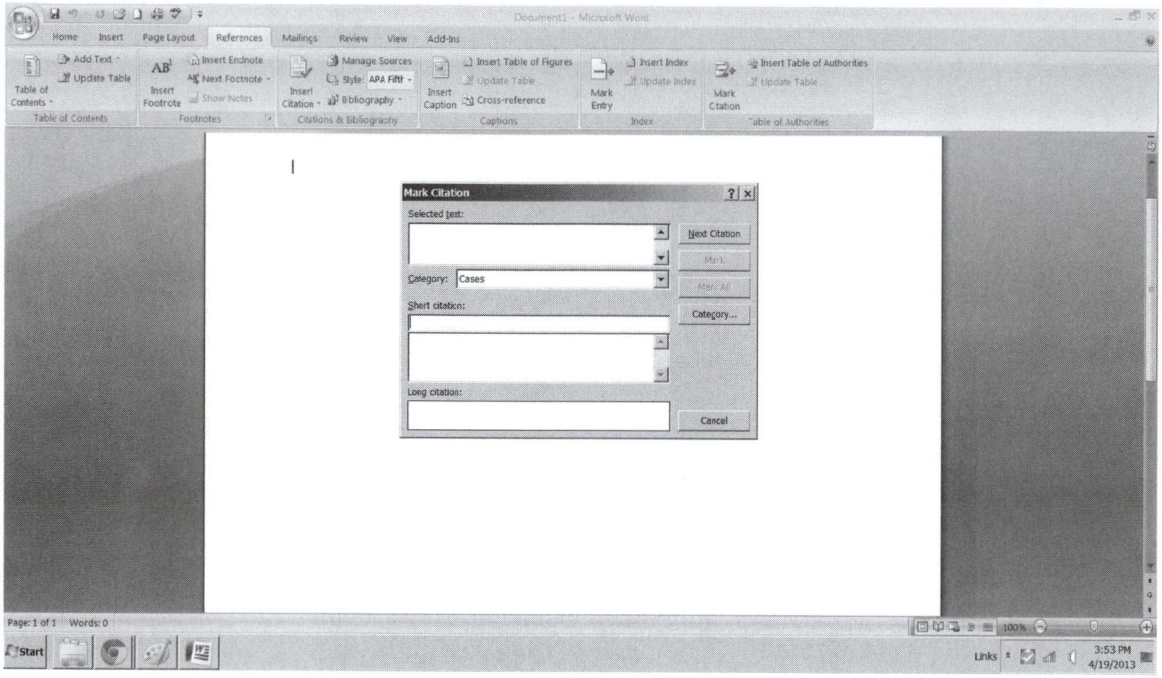

Figure 2-11. Microsoft Word—References tab: Table of Authorities box, Mark Citation submenu

▶ Select the text that will be included in a table of authorities;

▶ Categorize this citation (also possible using an adjacent button);

▶ Provide a short citation; and

▶ Provide a long citation.

The user will find a button that continues this type of citation process.

b. Insert Table of Authorities

When the user clicks this option, a submenu entitled Table of Authorities opens to a tab by that name; several other inactive tabs also appear. These are accessible in other boxes, such as the one for generating an index.

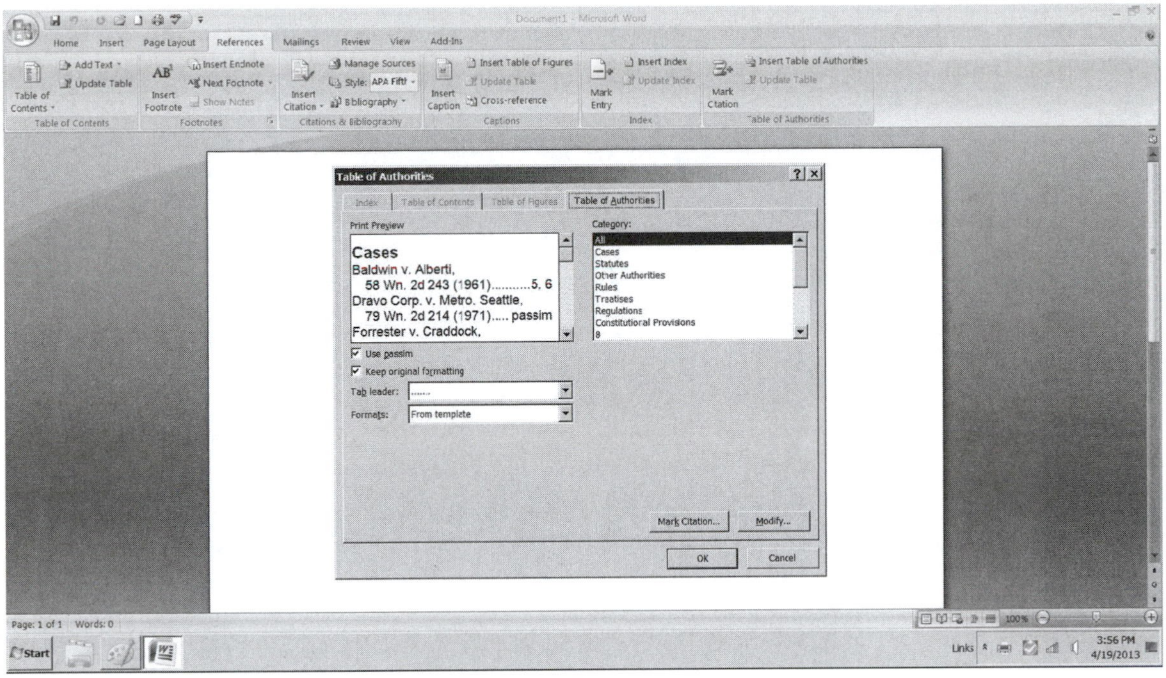

Figure 2-12. Microsoft Word—References tab: Table of Authorities box, Table of Authorities submenu

This submenu provides the user with:

▶ The ability to see how a table of authorities will look;

▶ Another opportunity to categorize authorities;

▶ The chance to note whether an authority is mentioned *passim* (that is, in passing);

▶ The choice to keep original formatting;

▶ The option to select a tab header (with choices just like those mentioned above); and

▶ The option to determine the formatting header (with choices just like those mentioned above).

Here the user has buttons to Mark Citations and to Modify. This box also contains an option to update the table of authorities automatically when changes occur in the text of the document.

e. Mailings tab

Under this tab heading, a user can generate different types of mailings. For example, this could mean drawing client names and addresses from a database to print out envelopes for a mailing about the addition of a new attorney to a firm.

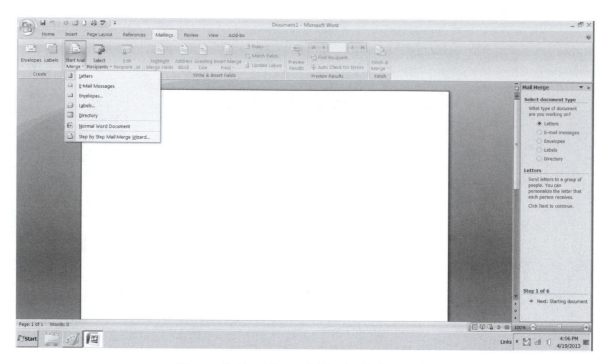

Figure 2-13. Microsoft Word—Mailings tab

Figure 2-13a. Microsoft Word—Mailings tab

i. Create

Here, the user can draw on a list of names and addresses to generate envelopes and labels. Options can include setting the position of the envelopes in the printer and generating a single label or a sheet of labels.

Figure 2-13b. Microsoft Word—Mailings tab: Create box

ii. Mail merge

The software can guide a user, via a Mail Merge **Wizard,** on how to generate envelopes and labels from an existing list of addresses. In addition to making it possible to generate labels and envelopes, a user could merge a list of clients' e-mail addresses with an announcement of the addition of a new employee in order to notify clients instantly about this significant change to a law firm.

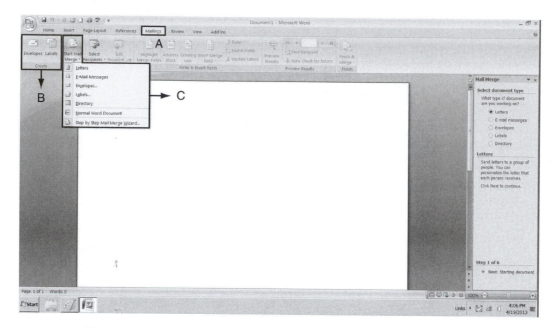

Figure 2-13c. Microsoft Word—Mailings tab: Start Mail Merge box

f. Review tab

Because documents issued by a law firm can have a significant impact, the software provides options to improve upon the quality of a document's content.

Figure 2-14. Microsoft Word—Review tab

Figure 2-14a. Microsoft Word—Review tab

i. Proofing

Software can simplify the checking of spelling and even identify potential mistakes in grammar. Other options include generating a word count, determining whether a document will exceed a court's page-length requirements for a brief, or translating text.

Figure 2-14b. Microsoft Word—Review tab: Proofing

ii. Comments

Members of a law firm might need to review a document to offer their insights or opinions. Here, they can insert comments without altering the document's appearance. Given the possibility of input from several reviewers, the user can assign a particular color for each reviewer's input or indicate where to place the comments, such as in a marginal area of the document.

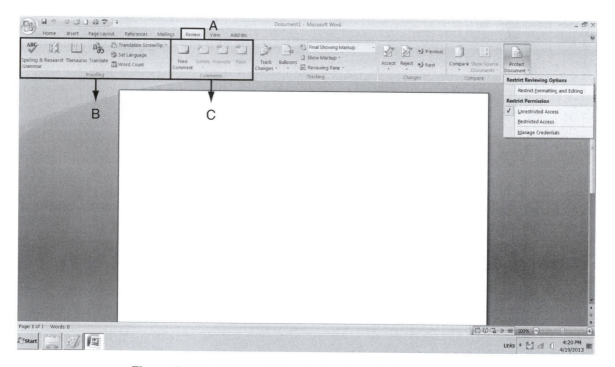

Figure 2-14c. Microsoft Word—Review tab: Comments box

iii. Tracking changes

Because a document might undergo numerous revisions and changes, this feature helps the user to see the history and types of changes made.

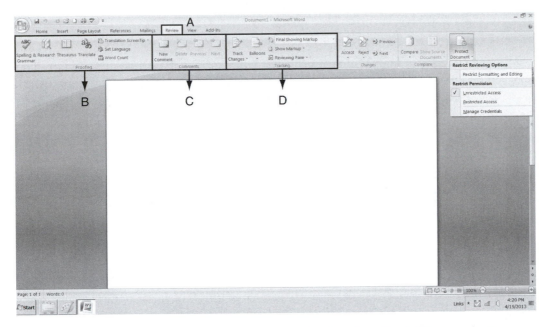

Figure 2-14d. Microsoft Word—Review tab: Tracking box, Track Changes button

iv. Changes

Here, the option exists to accept or reject a change, such as whether to include a disclaimer in a document regarding the title to property for sale.

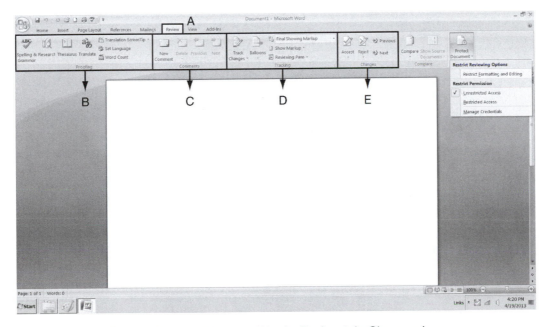

Figure 2-14e. Microsoft Word—Review tab: Changes box

v. Compare

a. Compare and combine

Another way to look at changes involves comparing versions of a document. The software can quickly identify differences in otherwise similar documents. Doing this manually, by underlining differences between versions of a document in red or black ink, is called **blacklining** or **redlining.**

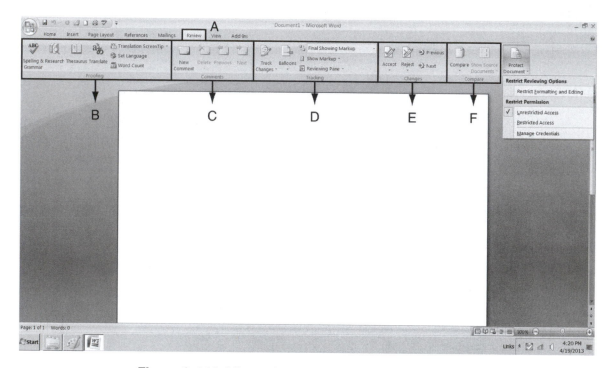

Figure 2-14f. Microsoft Word—Review tab: Compare box

b. Using Compare

To start this process, clicking the button will open up the following submenu.

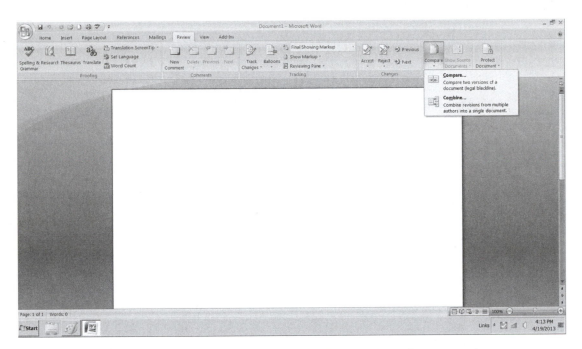

Figure 2-15. Microsoft Word—Review tab: Compare box, Compare submenu

Clicking on the Compare link will produce this submenu.

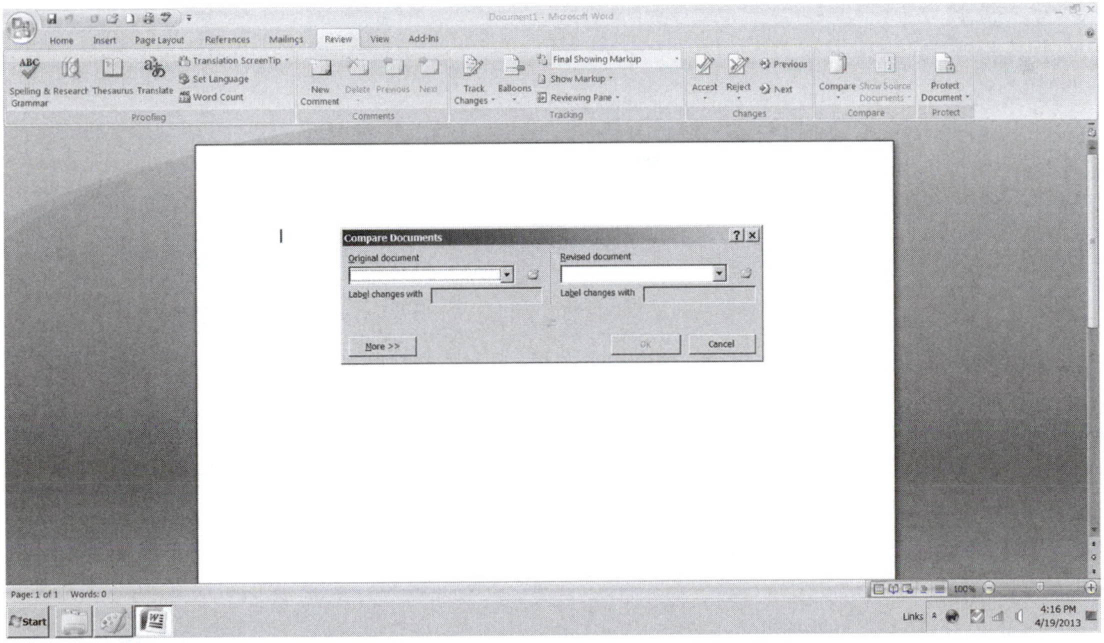

Figure 2-16. Microsoft Word—Review tab: Compare box, Compare submenu, Compare link, Compare documents

Here, the user has the option to:

▶ Select an original and revised version of the baseline document;

▶ Choose how to identify changes in the two;

▶ Determine the criteria to be used in the comparison from a long list that may, for example, include looking at tables or commas;

▶ Indicate where to put the results—in the baseline or other documents, or into a new document—with indications identifying the changes.

The user then can combine changes made by reviewers into one document and have the same options available as with the Compare function.

vi. Protect document

A law firm could send a client a draft of a prenuptial agreement without allowing the client to make a change to the electronic version of the agreement. The software can protect the agreement or portions of it from alteration.

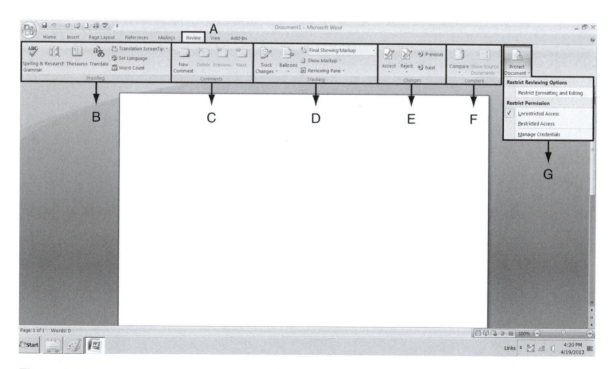

Figure 2-14g. Microsoft Word—Review tab: Protect Document box, Protect Document button, submenu

Consider this possibility: for the sake of speed, a firm and a client could each make revisions to a purchase and sale agreement stored in a central location on a Microsoft **server.** By activating the free Information Rights Management service available through Microsoft, the firm could limit access to the agreement, or provide limited access to portions of this contract.

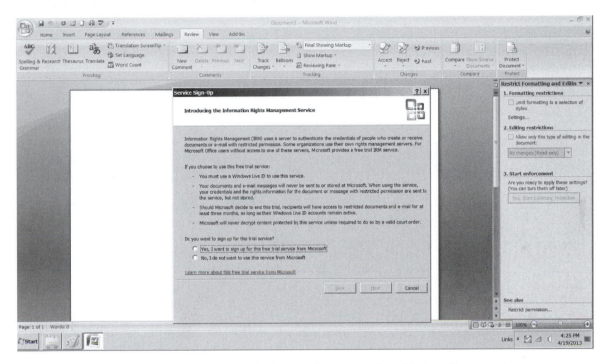

Figure 2-17. Microsoft Word—Review tab: Protect Document box, Protect Document button, submenu Restrict Formatting and Editing options, Information Rights Management service option

g. View tab

Understanding how a document, like a newsletter, might look to clients, could make it more appealing for clients to read. The last tab on the standard Word screen makes it possible to see, but not change, how content will look.

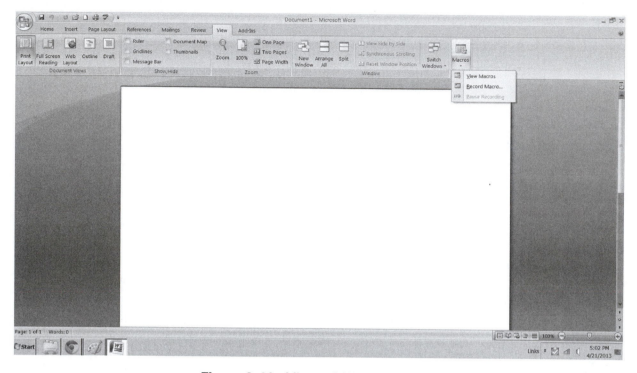

Figure 2-18. Microsoft Word—View tab

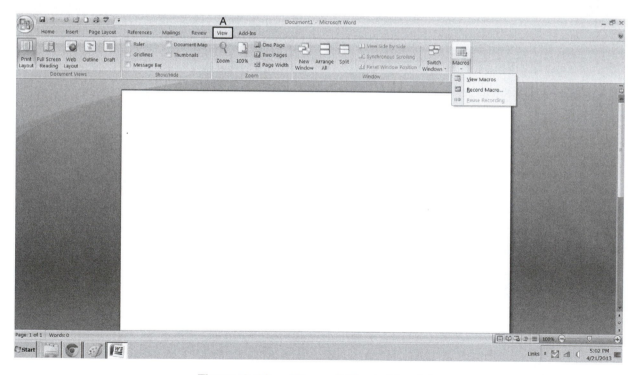

Figure 2-18a. Microsoft Word—View tab

i. Document views

Here, the views reveal how different content will look when printed out as a book or posted on the Web. Submenus, accessible via a toolbar, allow the user to look up words while reading or page through the document.

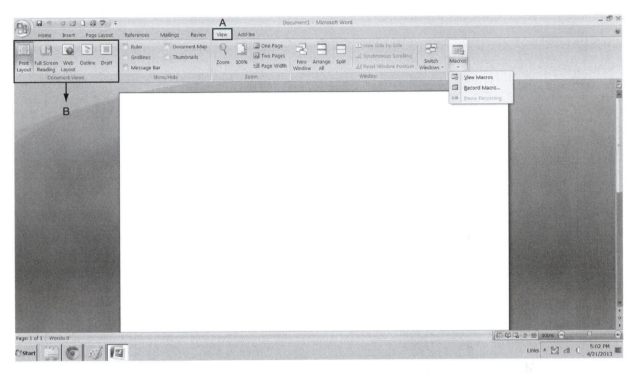

Figure 2-18b. Microsoft Word—View tab: Document Views box

ii. Show/Hide

With this box, a user can have a ruler appear at the top of the screen to show the placement of tabs and margins, impose gridlines on the text, or provide small graphic images, called **thumbnails,** which represent the placement of pages in a document.

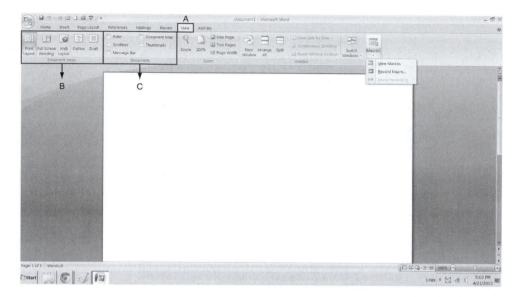

Figure 2-18c. Microsoft Word—View tab: Show/Hide box

iii. Zoom

This box allows a user to magnify the screen image, have it expand, or adjust its layout to fit on adjacent pages.

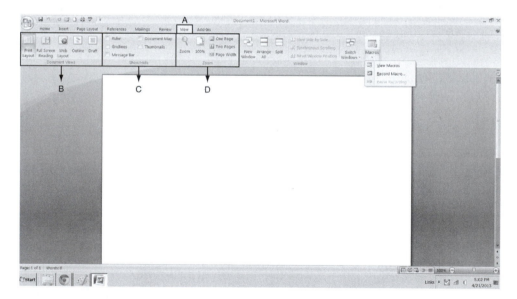

Figure 2-18d. Microsoft Word—View tab: Zoom box

iv. Window

One way to look at multiple documents simultaneously would involve opening them in multiple windows. Using the options in this box makes it possible to arrange those multiple windows on the screen.

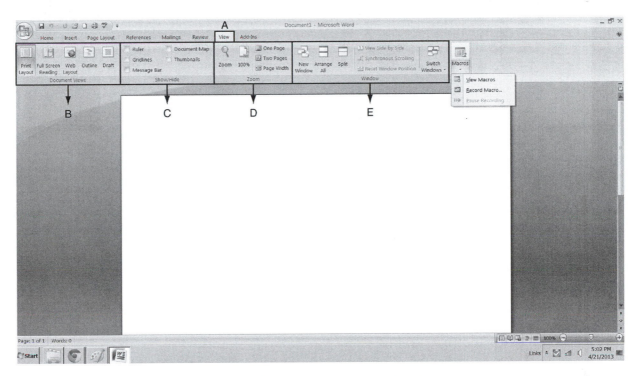

Figure 2-18e. Microsoft Word—View tab: Window box

v. Macros

A **macro,** in this context, is a very simple computer program. By creating a macro, a user could automate the performance of an activity. For example, since clients who get billed by the hour need to get accurate expense statements, a user could create a macro that lists those expenses typically associated with a client's case. The user also can find and edit macros.

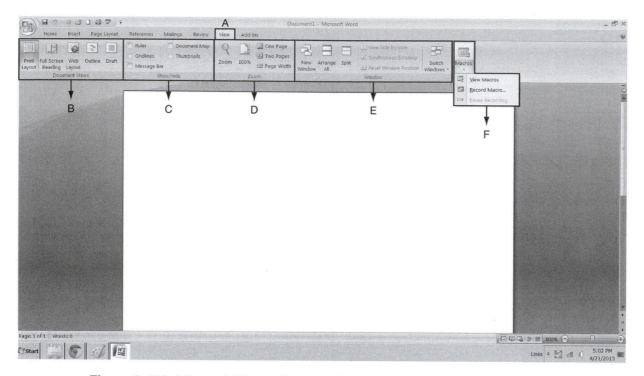

Figure 2-18f. Microsoft Word—View tab: Window box, Macros button, submenu

Excel

Software that took advantage of the speed and accuracy of a personal computer's microprocessor demonstrated the benefit of having computers in the workplace. For example, spreadsheet software could perform calculations and eliminate errors. Even better, a user could change data and see the results instantly. So, if a client wants a firm to create a trust fund for the client's child, the firm could show how changing the amount of money put into the fund would change the amount that a child would receive as a monthly payment.

1. Features

a. Grids, cells, and sheets

The Excel screen has a gridwork of lines like that of graphing paper.

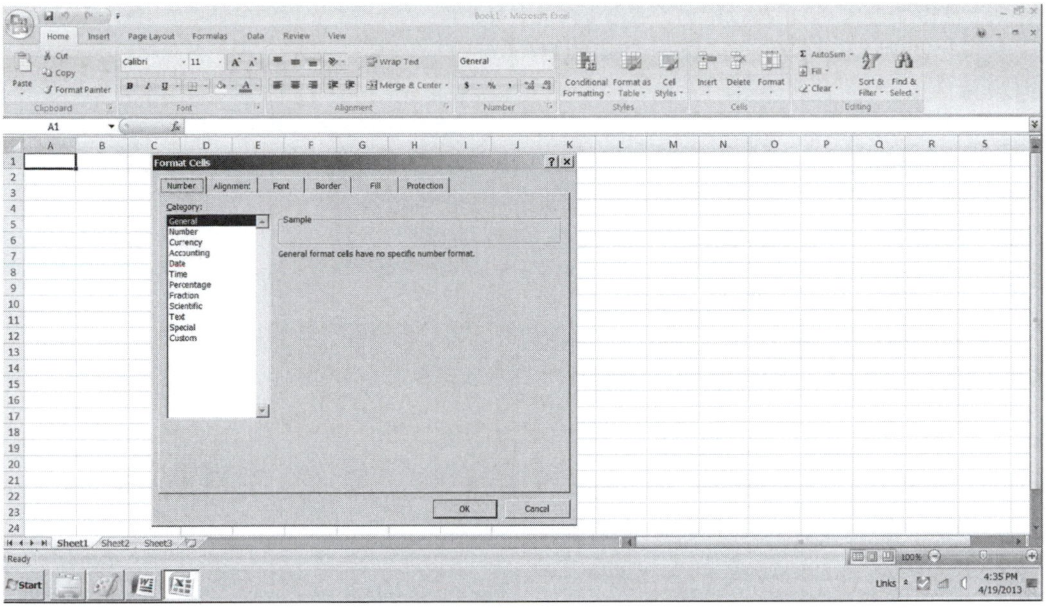

Figure 2-19. Microsoft Excel—Home tab: gridwork of cells

The **cell** serves as the basic unit of operation in Excel. When preparing a divorce agreement, a user could take a year's worth of electrical bills, enter them into individual cells, and calculate an average, to estimate some of the cost for running a household where children will reside.

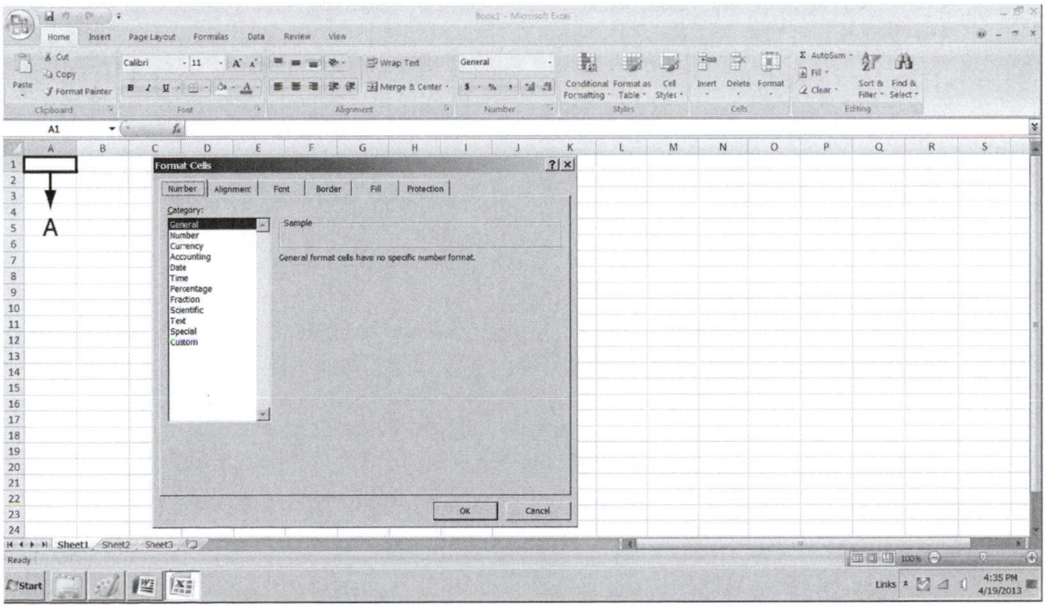

Figure 2-19a. Microsoft Excel—Home tab: cell

The grids exist on sheets. **Sheets** are the Excel version of a page in Word. A collection of sheets is called a **workbook.**

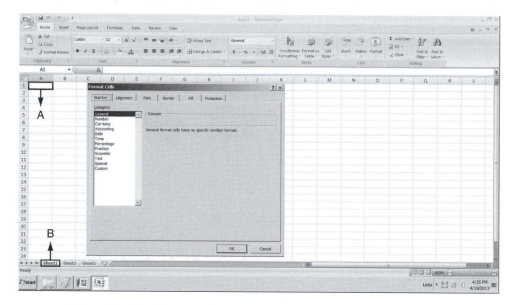

Figure 2-19b. Microsoft Excel—Sheet 1 tab: bottom of start page

b. Function box

The function box may best demonstrate what spreadsheet software can do. By using the function box, users can create their own formula for manipulating information in cells. For example, the user could create and insert a formula that makes it possible to project a business's growth based on information contained in cells, such as anticipated expenses.

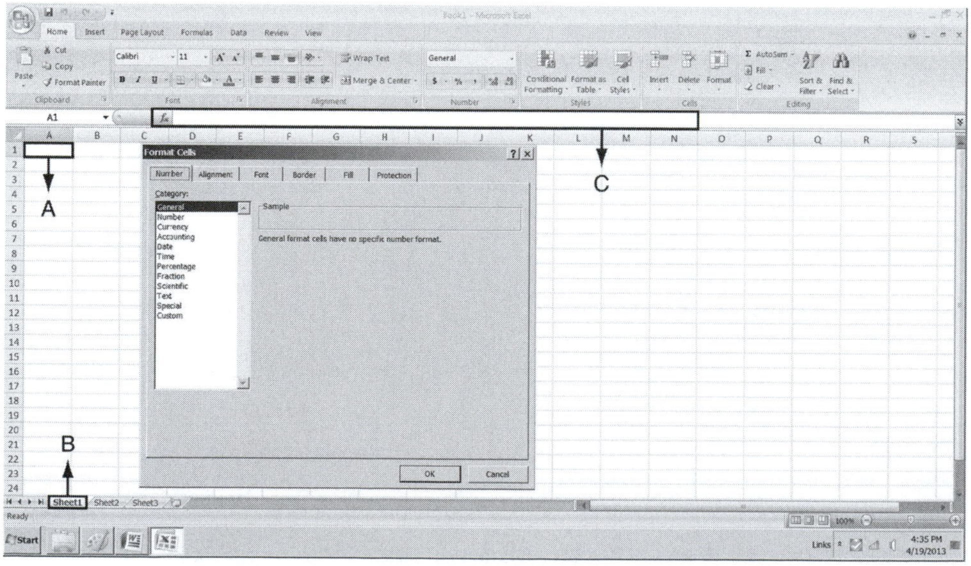

Figure 2-19c. Microsoft Excel—Function box

2. Tabs

Microsoft uses the metaphor of a manila folder's tab to organize different software functions. Not surprisingly, then, many of the same tab headings appear for organizing functions, like in other Microsoft software.

a. Home tab

Like the Home tab in Word, this contains similar boxes for further organizing applications. The first two—Clipboards and Font—have the identical buttons, links, and functions as in Word.

Boxes unique to Excel contain the following:

i. Alignment

a. Positioning material in a cell

By using buttons in this box, a user can align content in a cell relative to a margin, putting the data at the top, middle, or bottom.

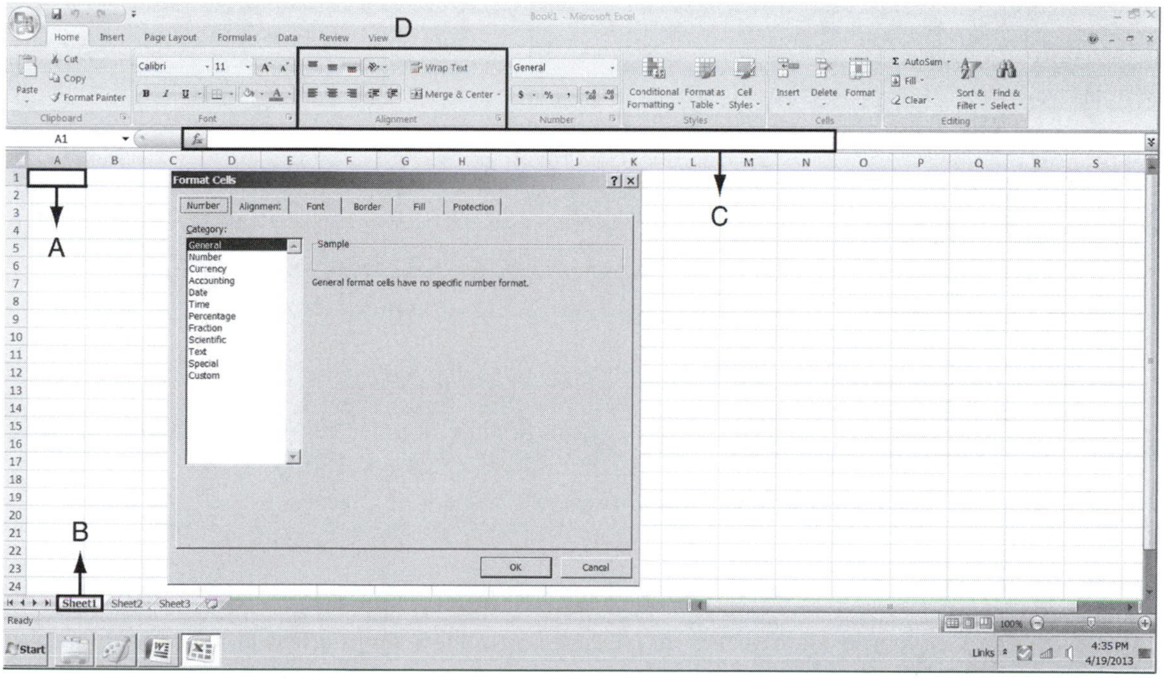

Figure 2-19d. Microsoft Excel—Home tab: Alignment box

The user can also rotate that data at an angle, such as a right angle. This would give the user another way of identifying characteristics of data, like monthly bills that fall closest to the end of a month, if a law firm needed to generate projections about the annual costs for running a business.

b. Formatting of a cell

Formatting data in a cell allows the user to make adjustments quickly to the data. If a firm doing business in the European Union needed to determine its costs, a user could switch between those costs expressed as Euros or American dollars.

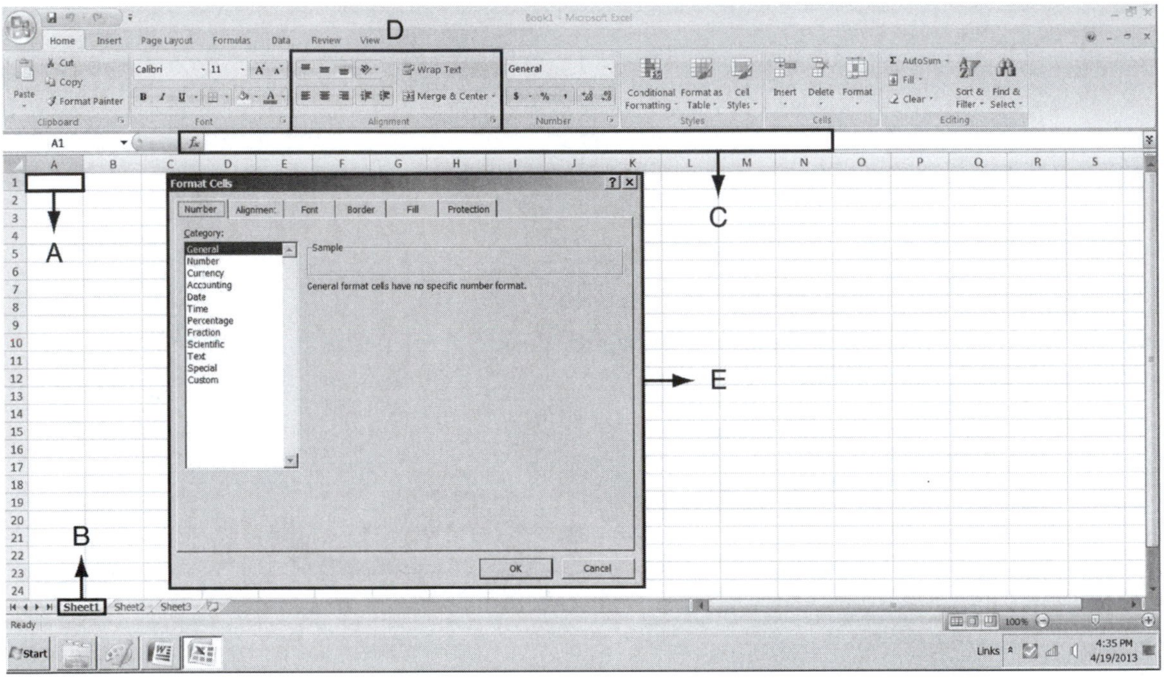

Figure 2-19e. Microsoft Excel—Home tab: Alignment box, top row, Angle of Content button submenu, Format Cells options

Also, a user can alter the font, create or alter a border, fill in cells with colors so as to quickly show the costs of operating a law office in different parts of the world, and password-protect data to prevent subsequent alteration.

c. Combining cells

The Merge and Center link makes it possible to combine information in cells. This could allow a user, for example, to show cumulative changes in business costs over different intervals.

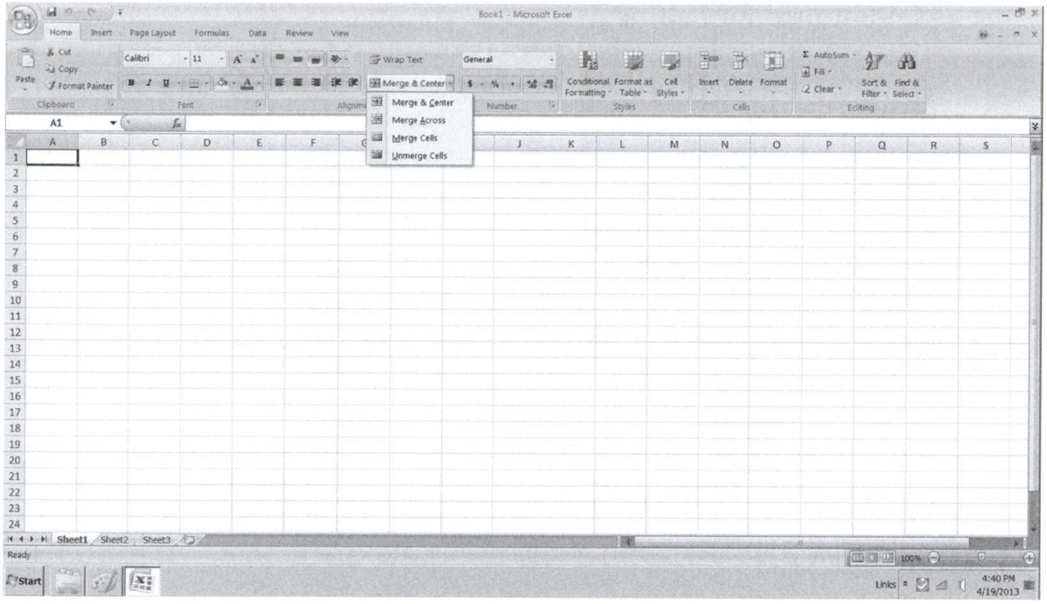

Figure 2-20. Microsoft Excel—Home tab: Alignment box, bottom row, Merge and Center button submenu

ii. Styles

Manipulating the way that data appears in cells could make it easier to show changes in operating costs for a client's different business offices. Options in the Styles box let the user alter the presentation of data in cells.

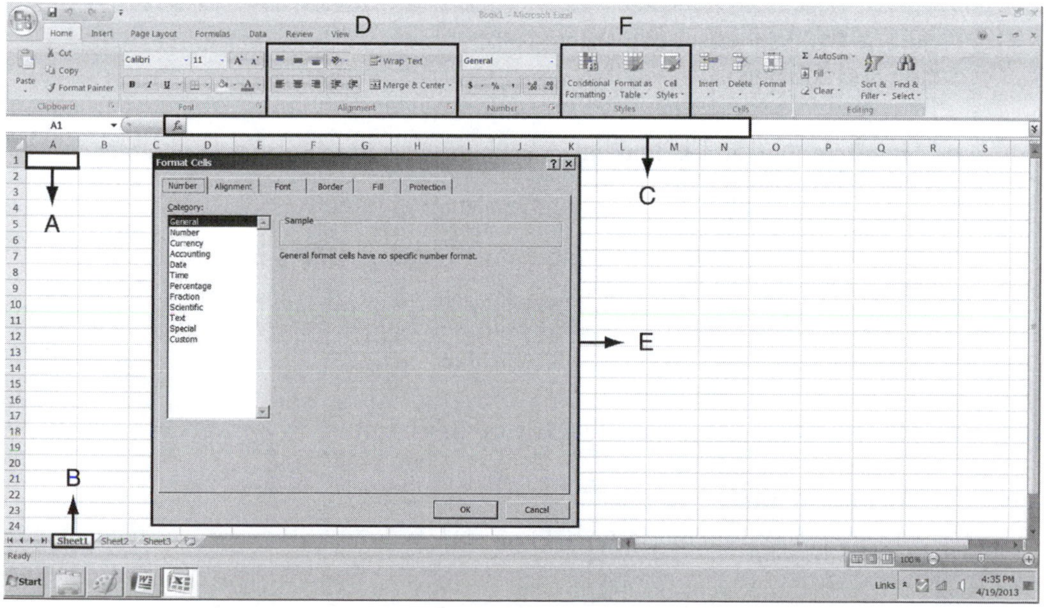

Figure 2-19f. Microsoft Excel—Home tab: Styles box

a. Conditional formatting

Excel makes it possible to apply different rules to cells. For example, a business may not have the option to deduct from annual income taxes the complete cost of acquiring equipment in a year, but must do that over time. Conditional formatting gives the user the ability to apply different rates of deducting the costs for different classes of equipment over time. Given the volatility of tax law, the user can adjust those rules when Congress votes to change the rate at which a business may deduct the expense of purchasing the equipment on the business's annual tax returns. In addition to presenting data graphically, some of the following affect the presentation of data.

Figure 2-21. Microsoft Excel—Home tab: Styles box, Conditional Formatting button and submenu

▶ Highlight Cell Rules, making clear the nature of rules that apply to cells;

▶ Top/Bottom Rules, about sorting information in cells;

▶ Data Bars, to depict information in cells in the form of bars on a graph;

▶ Icon sets, to select the color and shape of icons that will reflect certain values (as a number or percentage), using a graphic image in a "traffic light" pattern; and

▶ Manage Rules, which would apply to the cells.

b. Format as table

As with the Styles option available in Word, here the user can set styles for the table or portions of the table. Different styles could represent the different types of annual expenses that a firm has.

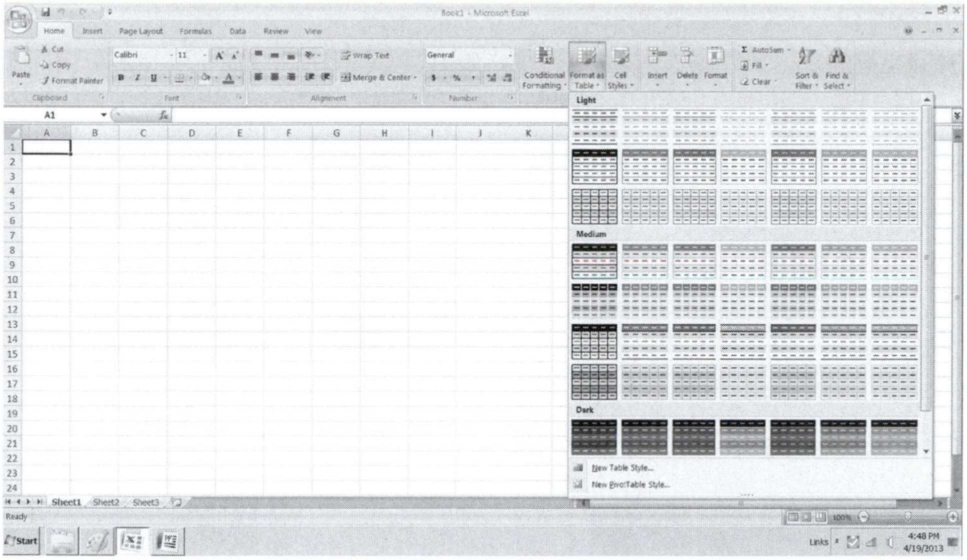

Figure 2-22. Microsoft Excel—Home tab: Styles box, Format as Table button and submenu

Also, the user can assign a new **Pivot table** style to data. Pivot table is a proprietary application of Microsoft, designed for changing the presentation of data.

c. Cell styles

Similarly, the user can select features of a cell, such as title or headings. For example, titles could identify different firm-related expenses, like salary or rent.

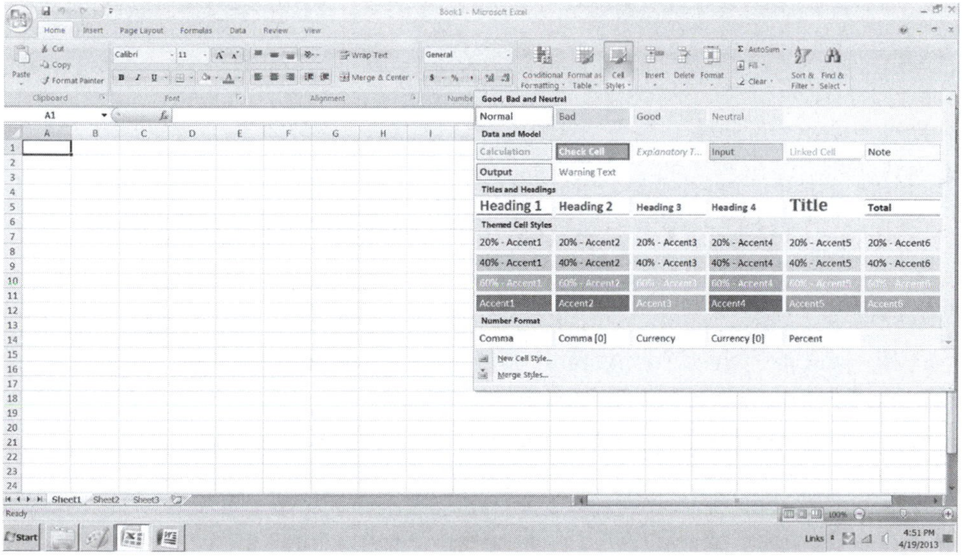

Figure 2-23. Microsoft Excel—Home tab: Styles box, Format as Table, Cell styles

iii. Cells

This box allows the user to alter portions of a table, like having to combine a year's average expenditures on computer technology, with other years. Other operations available here include:

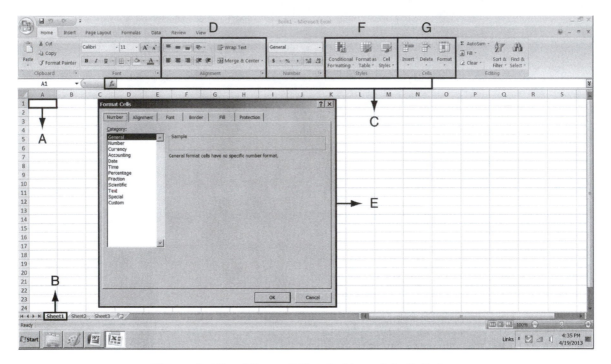

Figure 2-19g. Microsoft Excel—Home tab: Cells box

▶ Inserting or deleting cells, rows, columns, or a sheet;

▶ Formatting of cells;

▶ Hiding or making visible cells; and

▶ Organizing sheets, such as moving them or renaming them.

iv. Editing

In Word, clicking the Σ (the capital Greek letter sigma) button makes it possible to add up figures. This button, in Excel, also allows a user to perform mathematical calculations and to:

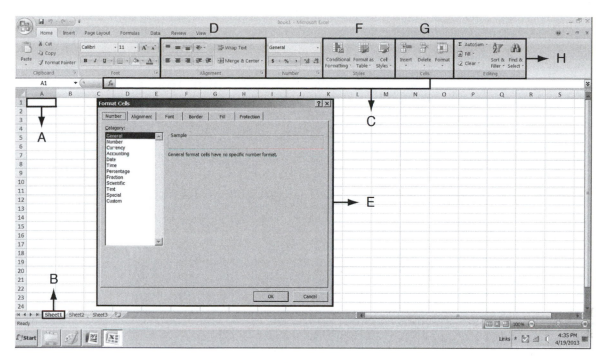

Figure 2-19h. Microsoft Excel—Home tab: Editing box

▶ Continue a pattern among cells;

▶ Clear formatting, content, and comments;

▶ Sort and filter information; and

▶ Find and select, such as looking for differences or formulas.

b. Insert tab

i. Content

As in Word, the user can insert illustrations, a Pivot table, or a chart.

ii. Charts

This box makes it possible for a user to depict cell data as:

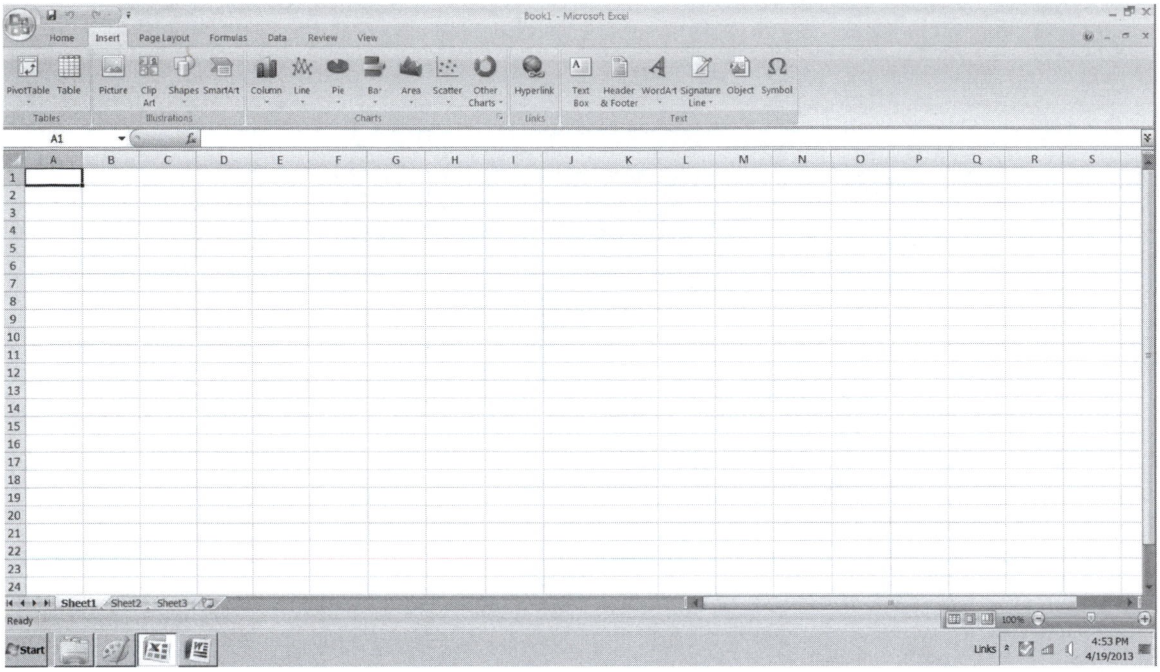

Figure 2-24. Microsoft Excel—Insert tab: Charts box

▶ Columns;

▶ Lines;

▶ Pie charts;

▶ Bar graphs;

▶ An area, or;

▶ Scattergrams.

Taking a client's projections for growth, the user could present this data graphically as lines or columns.

c. Page layout tab

Here, much like in Word, the user can adjust the:

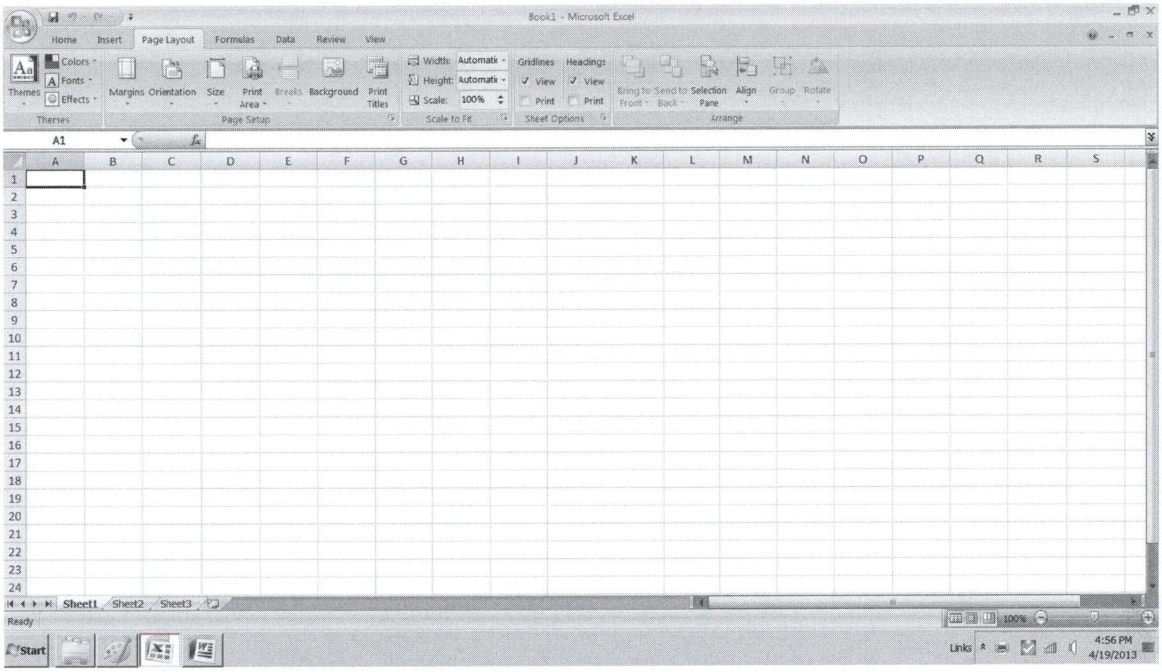

Figure 2-25. Microsoft Excel—Page Layout tab

▶ Page Setup, regarding the presentation of data on sheets;

▶ Scale to Fit, to adjust the width and height of a printout; or

▶ Sheet Options, including whether to include gridlines on the printout.

d. Formulas tab

Under this tab, a user can create or use existing formulae. For example, if a business's assets decline in value at a particular rate, a user could create a formula that can show the pace at which physical assets like equipment lose their value over time.

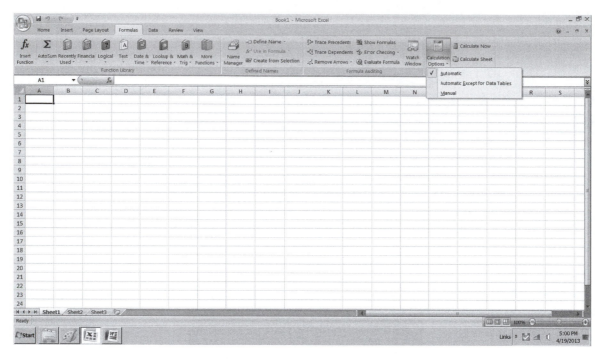

Figure 2-26. Microsoft Excel—Formulas tab

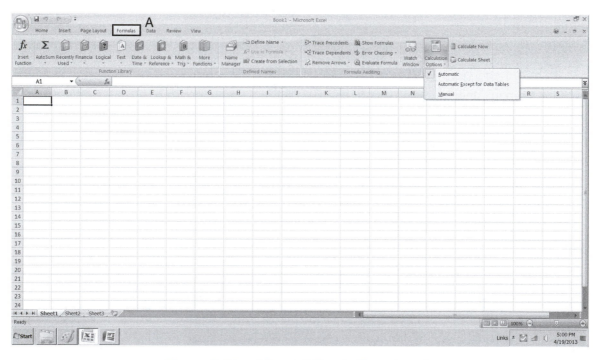

Figure 2-26a. Microsoft Excel—Formulas tab

i. Function Library

This box provides a user with different types of functions, such as financial formulae. Once selected, the function shows up in the function bar, adjacent to the *fx* symbol in the bar just below the ribbon, as seen in Figure 2-26b.

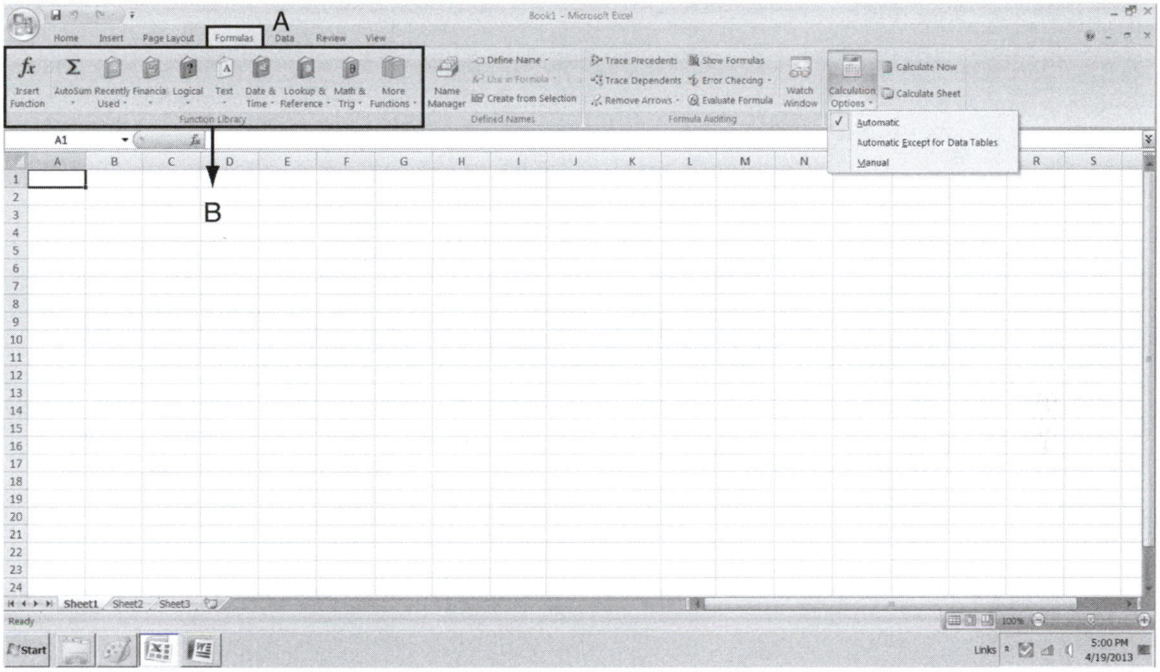

Figure 2-26b. Microsoft Excel—Formulas tab: Function Library box

Buttons under this tab allow a user to:

▶ Calculate the percentage yield of a bond daily, weekly, or annually, using Financial;

▶ Add up information, via Auto Sum (Σ);

▶ Calculate financial formulae, such as yield, price, or rate;

▶ Engage logical functions, such as those involving "if-then" statements, via Logical;

▶ Manage text strings, in order to be able to convert content to text;

▶ Convert information into the date-time code used by Excel;

▶ Obtain information about the location of a cell or areas of cells, under Lookup and Reference;

▶ Perform mathematical calculations or trigonometric functions like sine or cosine; and

▶ Employ functions related to statistics and engineering, among others.

For example, a law firm representing a joint enterprise created for a large public works project might need to use many of these in order to predict expenses or estimate costs.

ii. Defined Names

This box allows the user to manipulate names in a document, such as for associating a value for a name, like the fixed rate of decline in value of a class of assets over time.

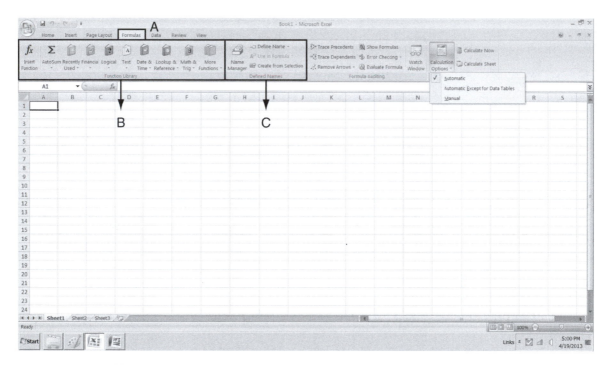

Figure 2-26c. Microsoft Excel—Formulas tab: Defined Names box

iii. Formula Auditing

If a firm created a formula to project an average increase in rent for office space, the result might be wildly beyond what was expected. To check why the software produced this clearly erroneous outcome, a user has buttons here for helping to figure out why a formula did not produce the expected results.

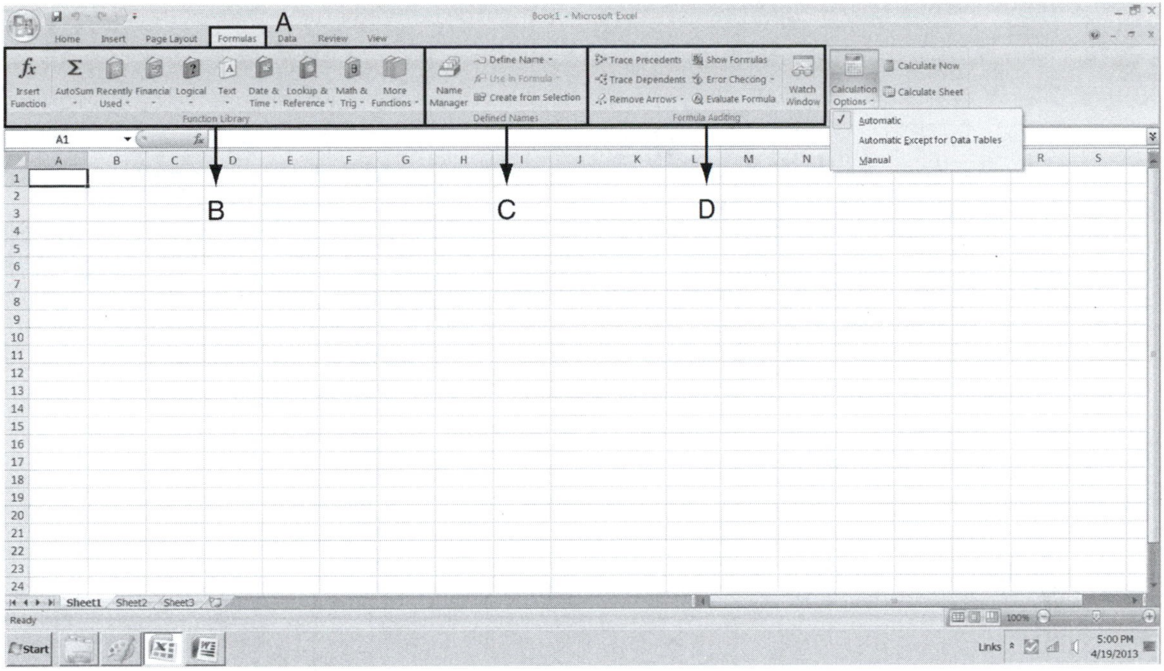

Figure 2-26d. Microsoft Excel—Formulas tab: Formula Auditing box

Another available function in this box, called Watch Window, allows a user to open a separate window that remains open no matter where in the workbook the user is. This way, a user can monitor the results in a window on selected cells when the user changes values elsewhere on a sheet.

iv. Calculation

The user can instruct the software, via buttons in this box, how to do calculations in order to run:

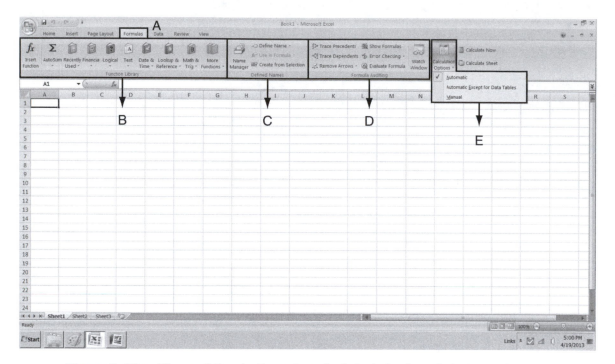

Figure 2-26e. Microsoft Excel—Formulas tab: Calculation box, Calculation Options button submenu

▶ Automatically or manually;

▶ Without data tables; and

▶ Only for a sheet.

This could allow a firm, representing a grievously injured client, to project cost-of-living increases needed for a lifetime of the client's care because of the severity of the client's injuries.

e. Data tab

Here, a user can use and manage data.

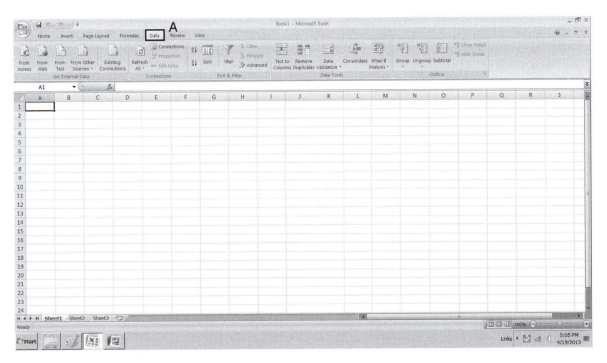

Figure 2-27. Microsoft Excel—Data tab

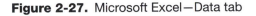

Figure 2-27a. Microsoft Excel—Data tab

i. Get External Data

The data can come from an array of sources, like:

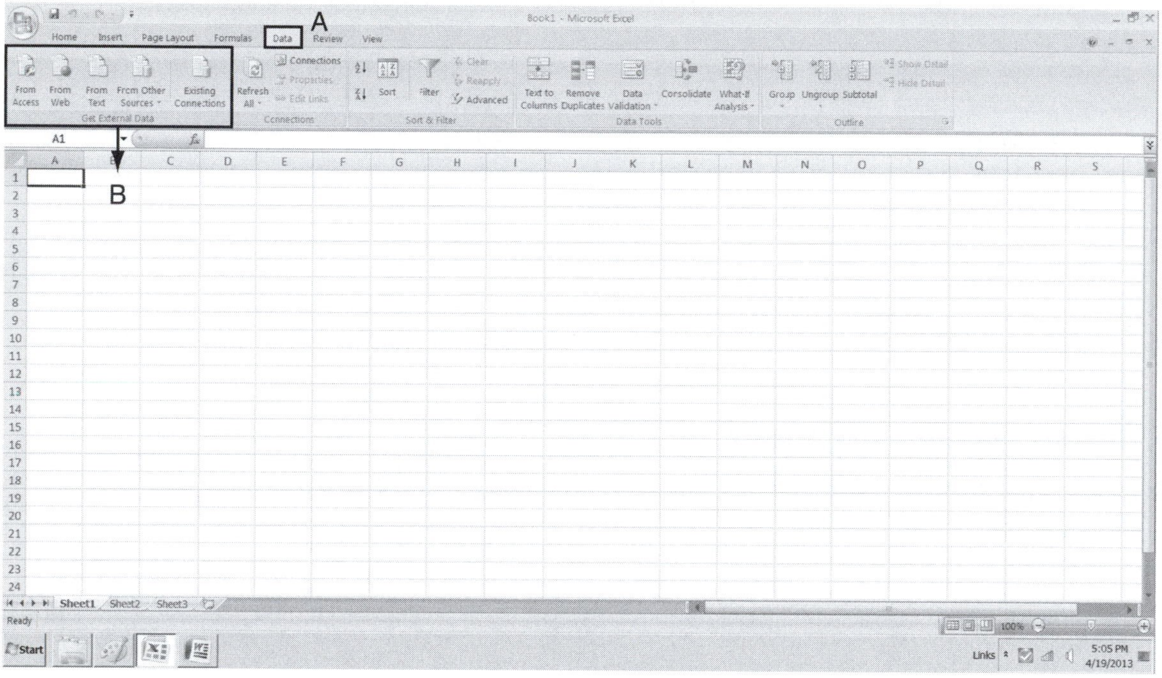

Figure 2-27b. Microsoft Excel—Data tab: Get External Data box

▶ **Access,** Microsoft's database software;

▶ The web; and

▶ An **SQL** server.

ii. Connections

The user can adjust or manage cell connections in the workbook. For example, this would allow a firm to show how changes in the design of a client's new house will increase the projected costs of construction.

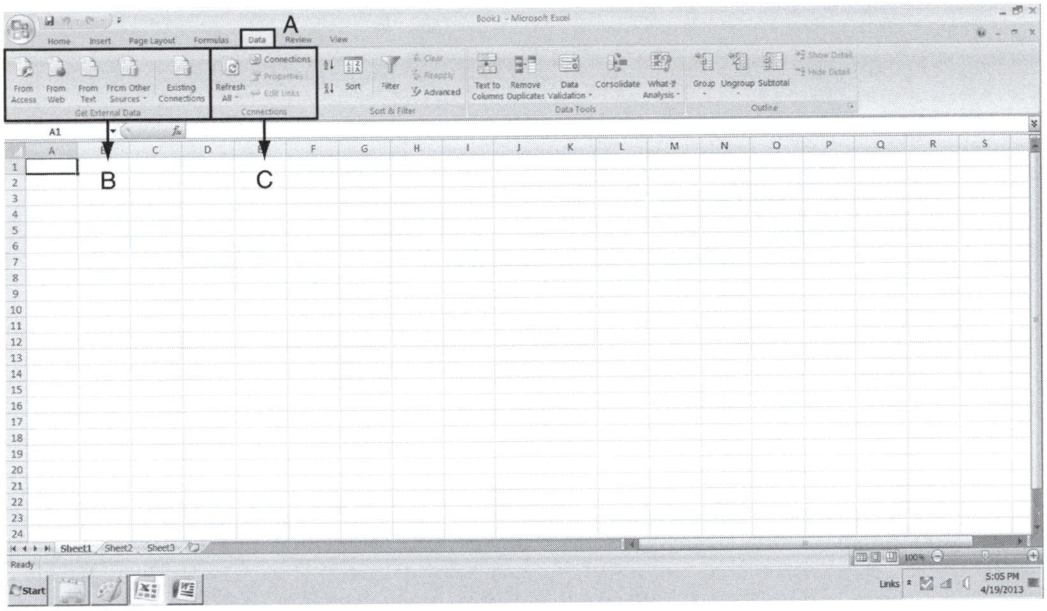

Figure 2-27c. Microsoft Excel—Data tab: Connections box

iii. Sort & Filter

Not only can a user organize data here, but a user could sort a corporation's projected expenses for a year, whether a one-time cost or an annual cost.

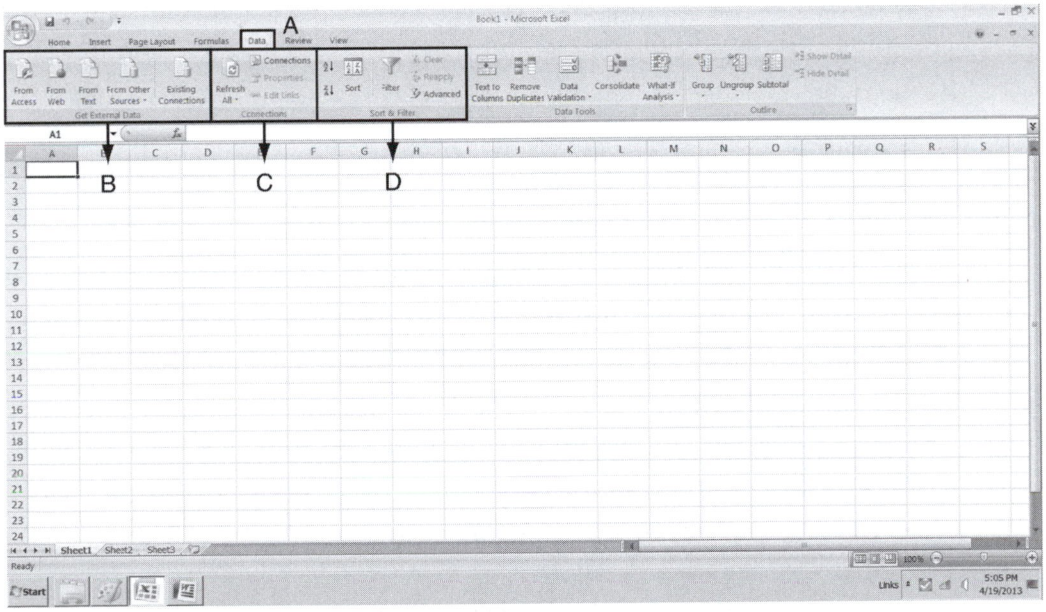

Figure 2-27d. Microsoft Excel—Data tab: Sort and Filter box

iv. Data Tools

Buttons in the Data Tools box make it possible for a user to:

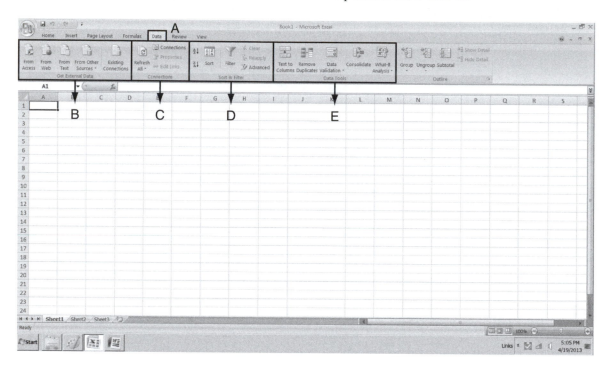

Figure 2-27e. Microsoft Excel—Data tab: Data Tools box

▶ Separate the contents of a cell into columns (similar to a feature in Word for putting text into columns);

▶ Consolidate values from multiple ranges of cells into a single, new range;

▶ Validate data, which can:

▷ Prevent the entry of invalid data into a cell;
▷ Check that the correct values were used; and
▷ Identify invalid data.

Because a business's operating costs can change with the addition of a new client or a loss of business, these tools allow a user to:

▶ Conduct a "what if" analysis, so that a firm could anticipate an increase in the costs of employment if it signs on a big, multinational communications firm, for example;

▶ Use a scenario manager, in order to predict costs if there is a sudden economic downturn; and

▶ Alter data tables, to reflect a change in a firm's policy about how to calculate billable hour rates.

v. Outline

A question of law may exist of whether a client's expenses can be deducted from income taxes for a single business year. Via the buttons here, expenses can be grouped with similar kinds of expenditures depending on whether they can be deducted over time or in a year.

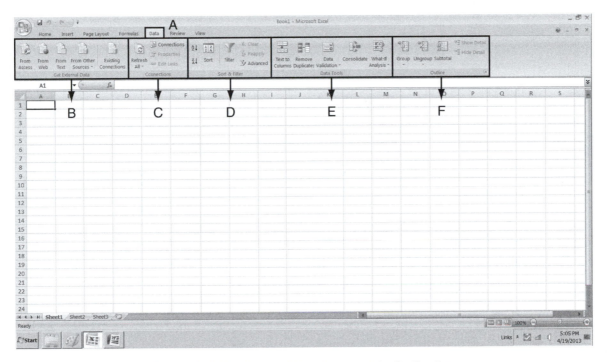

Figure 2-27f. Microsoft Excel—Data tab: Outline box

f. Review tab

In addition to allowing a user to choose actions like those in the corresponding box in Word, the user can:

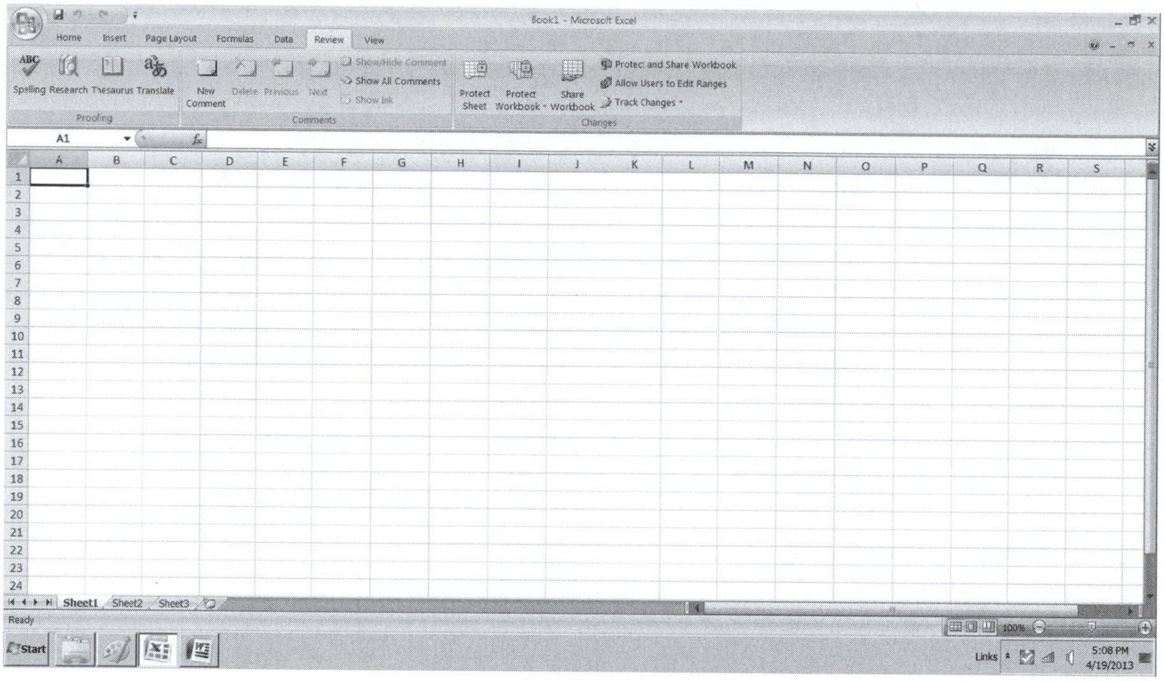

Figure 2-28. Microsoft Excel—Review tab: Changes box

▶ Password-protect the contents of a sheet or a workbook;

▶ Designate those with the authority to alter data; and

▶ Accept or reject changes.

PowerPoint

A slide show presentation can visually convey to a client the impact of an adverse court ruling in a client's case. Because of the difference in impact that graphic information has over text, Microsoft's slide show presentation software, Power-Point, may get used as often as Word or Excel.

Using tabs like those in Word and Excel across the top of the screen, the user can select a title and subtitle for a slide, such as "annual expenditures," and then a "breakdown of costs" by month.

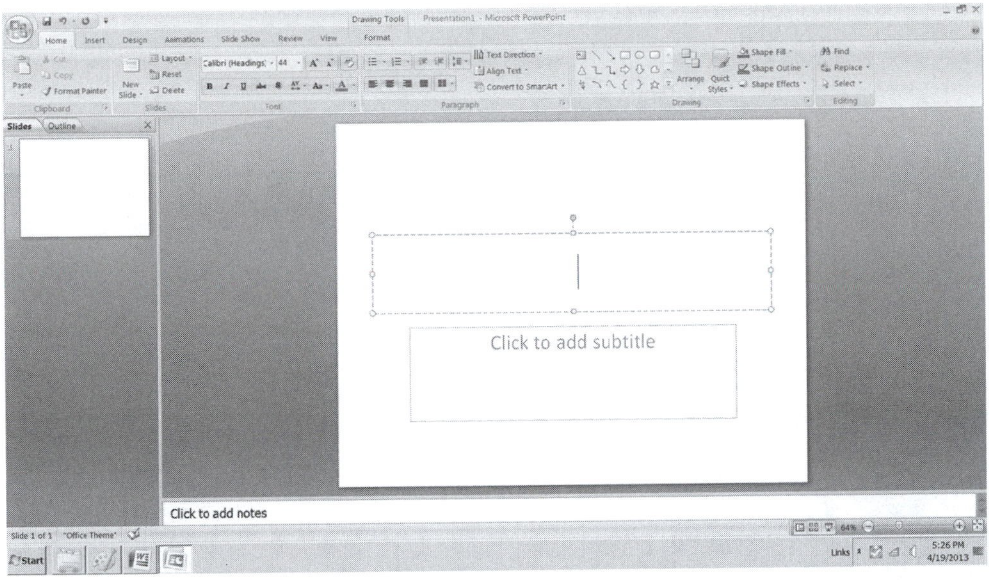

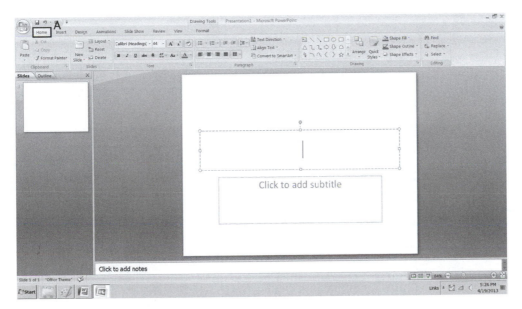

Figure 2-29. Microsoft PowerPoint

On the left-hand screen, the user has a box that shows the positioning of the slides. This allows a user to change the sequence of the slides via a drag-and-drop option or to see how the slides will look in an outline format.

1. Home Tab

The Home tab, here, has many of the same boxes in Word and Excel. For example, the Editing box has the same features as that box in Word and Excel.

Figure 2-29a. Microsoft PowerPoint—Home tab

Some boxes might differ slightly:

▶ The Clipboard box has a link to Format Painter, for preserving the formatting of content when cut or copied for use elsewhere in the slide show.

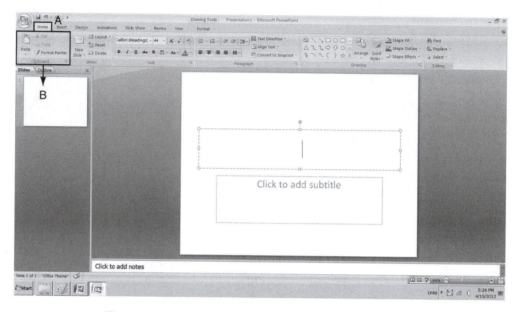

Figure 2-29b. Microsoft PowerPoint—Clipboard box

▶ The Font box has a button for adding a shadow to text, so that it can stand out on the slide.

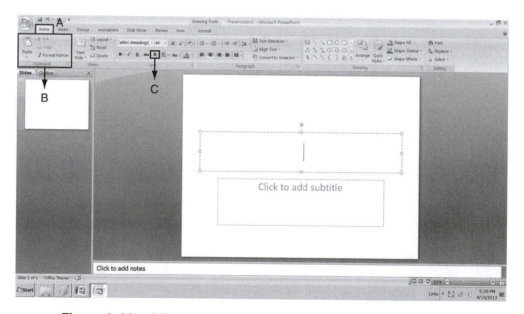

Figure 2-29c. Microsoft PowerPoint—Font box: Text Shadow button

▶ The Paragraph box has a link to convert text in a slide into SmartArt.

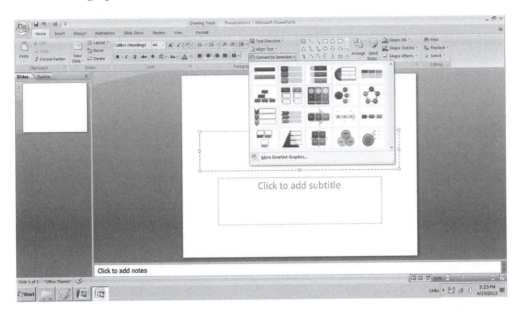

Figure 2-30. Microsoft PowerPoint—Paragraph box: Convert to SmartArt button

Some boxes reflect the unique possibilities for creating a slide show.

a. Slides

The Slides box, to the immediate right of the Clipboard box, has buttons for generating and for altering features of slides.

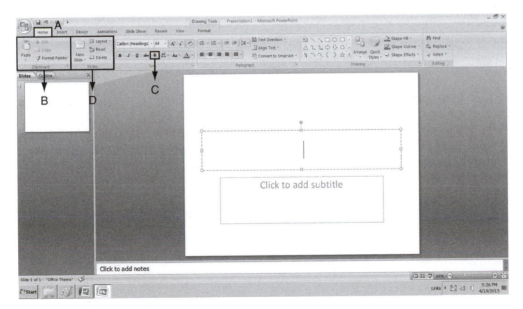

Figure 2-29d. Microsoft PowerPoint—Home tab: Slides box

For example, when creating a slide, a user can choose different layouts for presenting the content of a slide. These can include Two Content, which has a narrow header at the top and adjacent blocks for inserting text. Using a Picture with Caption layout allows a user, for example, to present the image of a house along with its square footage and the size of the house's lot. Links at the bottom allow for easy duplication and reuse of slides, as well as to take slides from saved outline files. Other links make it easy for the user to start over, to delete a slide, or to alter the layout of its content.

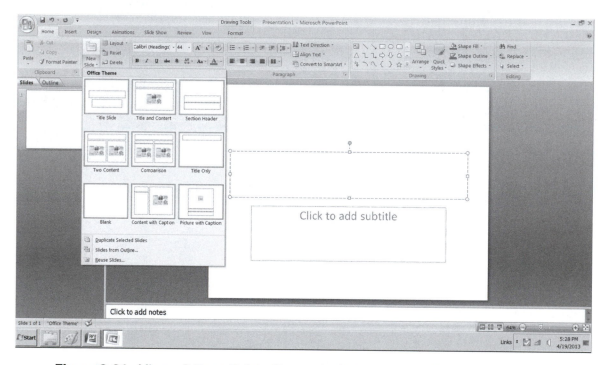

Figure 2-31. Microsoft PowerPoint—Home tab: Slides box, New Slide button submenu

b. Drawing

Because the presentation of information visually can have a significant impact, a user has options for the use of graphic images which can involve inserting ready-made shapes, like those available in Word. A submenu offers a host of other such shapes.

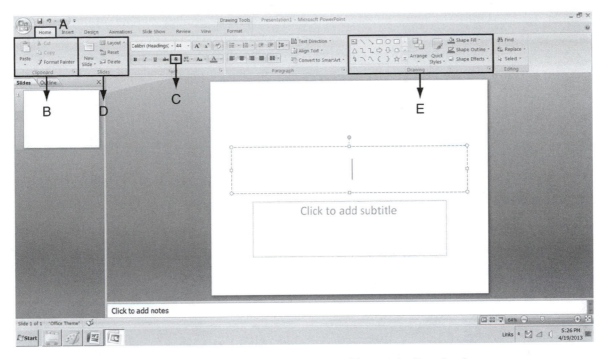

Figure 2-29e. Microsoft PowerPoint—Home tab: Drawing box

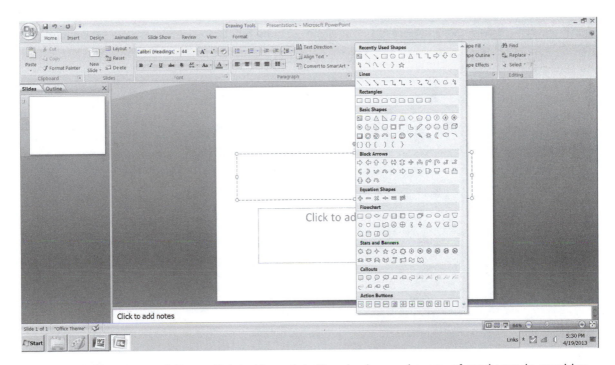

Figure 2-32. Microsoft PowerPoint—Home tab: Drawing box, submenu of ready-made graphics

Options allow a user to change the capacity of a shape to hold an image, and to vary the lighting and texture of the content of a shape. This could highlight differences to an arrow shape depicting a range of cost increases, based upon different rates of inflation, that a firm could anticipate having to make.

Via the Shape Fill submenu, a user could adjust the texture of the fill.

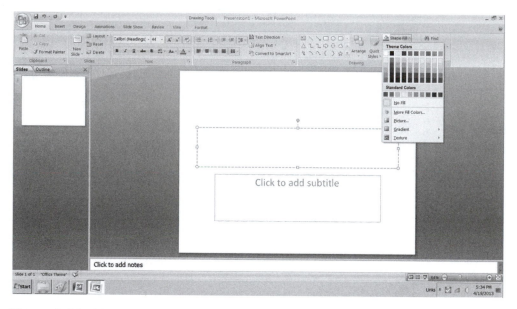

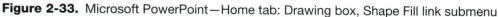

Figure 2-33. Microsoft PowerPoint—Home tab: Drawing box, Shape Fill link submenu

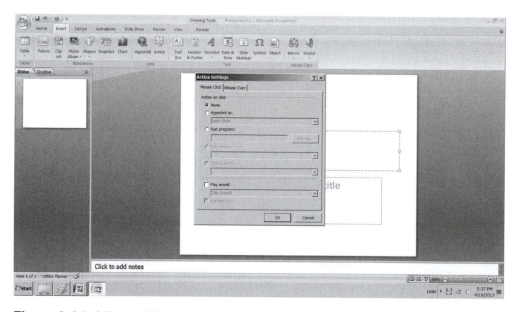

Figure 2-34. Microsoft PowerPoint—Home tab: Drawing box, Shape Fill link submenu, Texture link

The user could also, through the link at the bottom of the previous submenu, further edit the nature of the fill used in order to:

▶ Select the type of material to fill a shape;

▶ Decide to vary the width of a line, or to depict it as dashes;

▶ Use effects like shadowing or 3-D;

▶ Adjust the transparency of a shape; or

▶ Insert a picture or text.

2. Insert Tab

In addition to being able to insert material as in Word and Excel, such as pictures or text, a user can include images that can enhance the quality of the presentation.

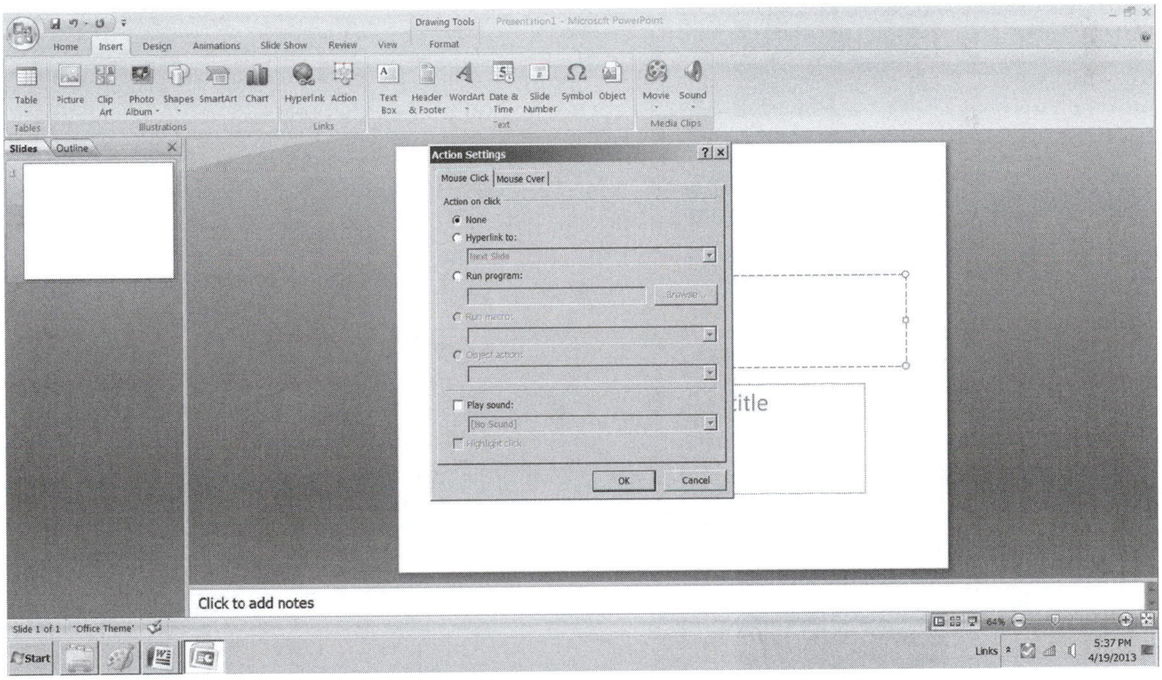

Figure 2-35. Microsoft PowerPoint—Insert tab

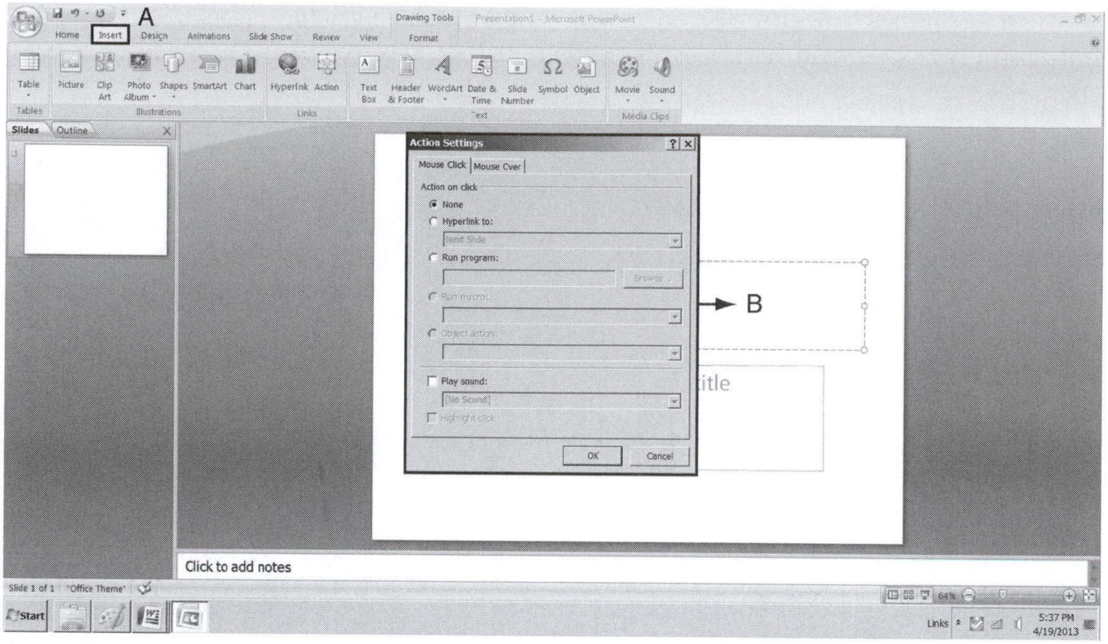

Figure 2-35a. Microsoft PowerPoint—Insert tab

For a presentation to a jury, where a plaintiff is suing an insurance company for breach of the terms of an insurance policy, a user could insert animation, such as a graphic of a car crash, and the sound of the crash.

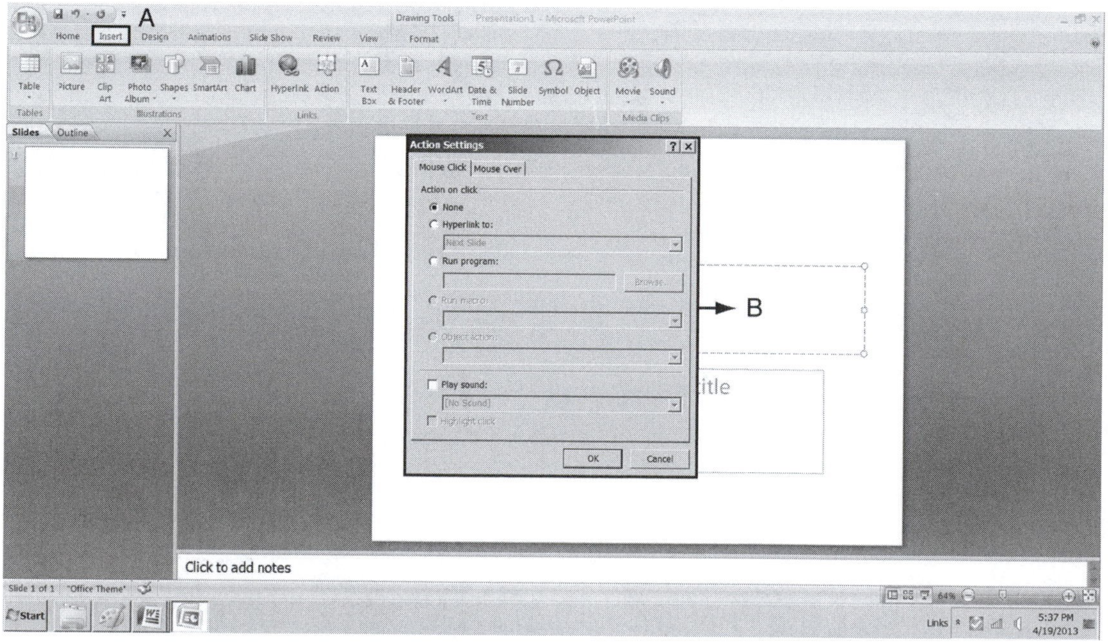

Figure 2-35b. Microsoft PowerPoint—Insert tab: Links box, Action button submenu

Also, a user can insert media clips, such as a segment from a local television news program that talks about the number of accidents that have happened at a bad curve in a road.

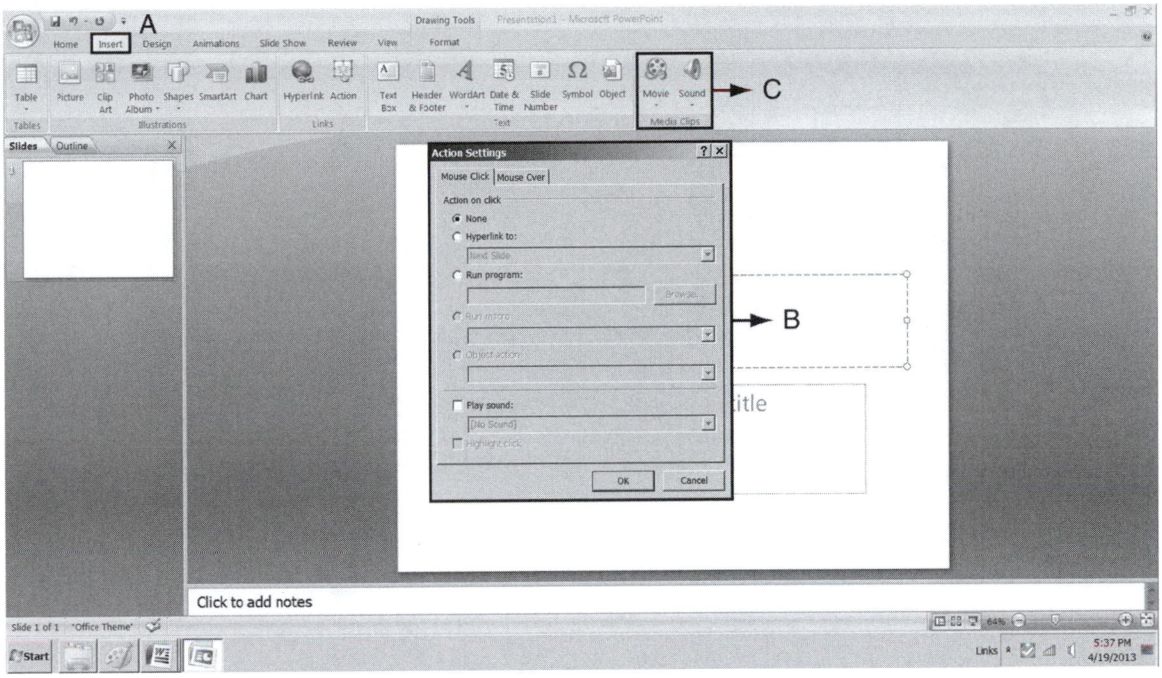

Figure 2-35c. Microsoft PowerPoint—Insert tab: Media Clips box

3. Design Tab

Just as in Word, the user can orient a slide to the portrait or landscape positions. In landscape, a user would have more room to magnify the text of a specific provision in a contract in a lawsuit about a breach of that contract.

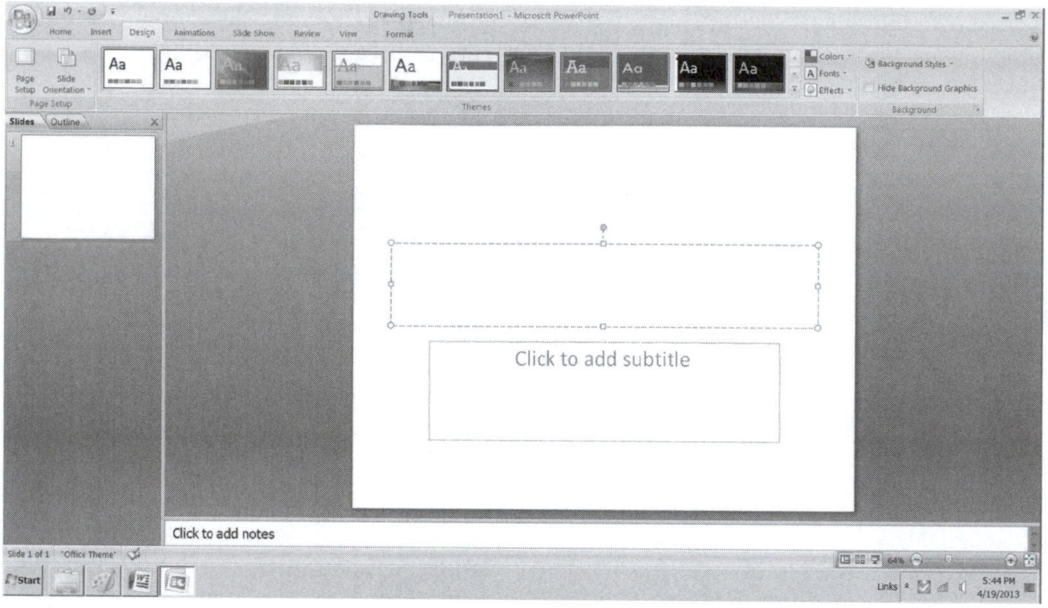

Figure 2-36. Microsoft PowerPoint—Design tab

4. Animations Tab

The use of animation allows a user to tap into the full power of the software, making a presentation more dynamic than if the slide merely contained text and graphics.

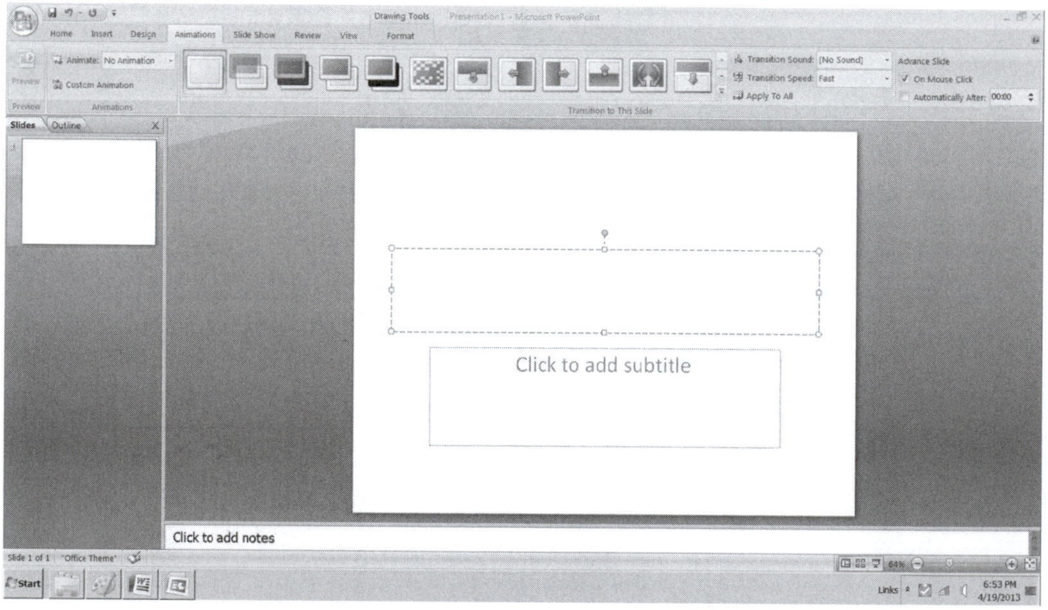

Figure 2-37. Microsoft PowerPoint—Animations tab

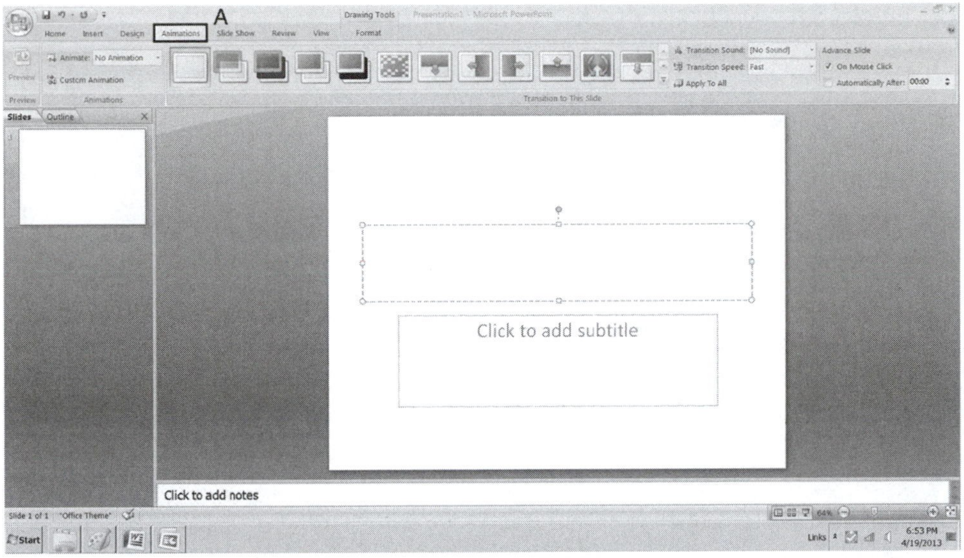

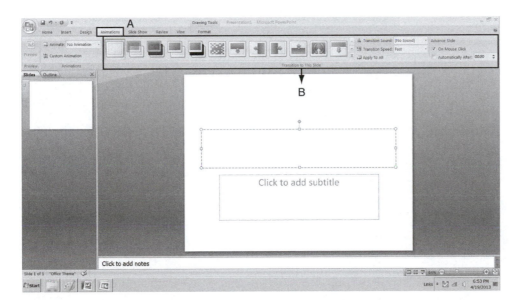

Figure 2-37a. Microsoft PowerPoint—Animations tab

The user can also:

▶ Modify the animation, controlling when it should start and end, as when to begin a video clip of the beating of a plaintiff at the hands of a defendant;

▶ Adjust the transition, so that one slide may fade away as another appears; and

▶ Select sounds that play during a transition, such as applause or a drumroll.

Figure 2-37b. Microsoft PowerPoint—Animations tab: Translation to This Slide box

5. Slide Show Tab

Options in the Start the Slide Show box allow the user to have the slide show loop continuously or run without narration.

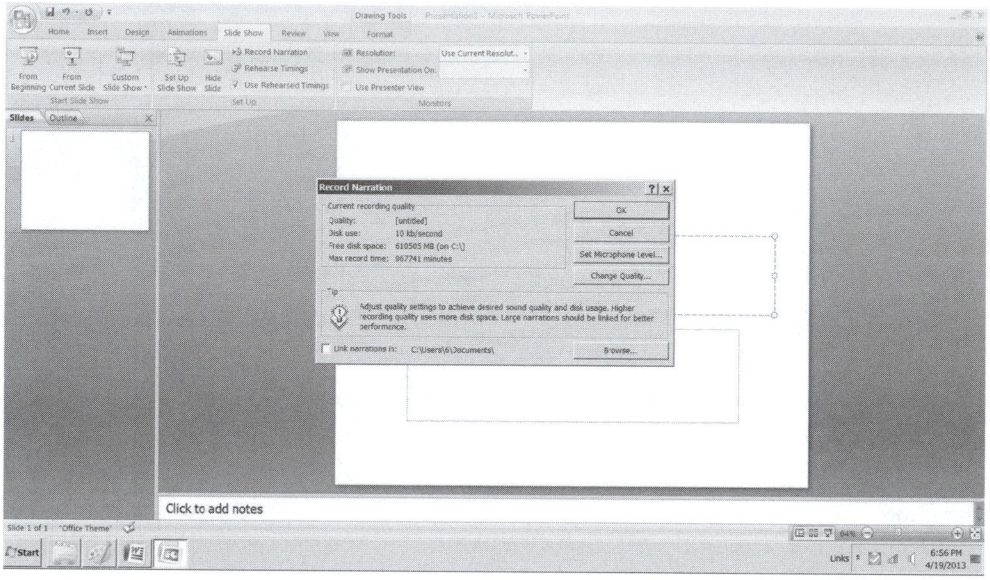

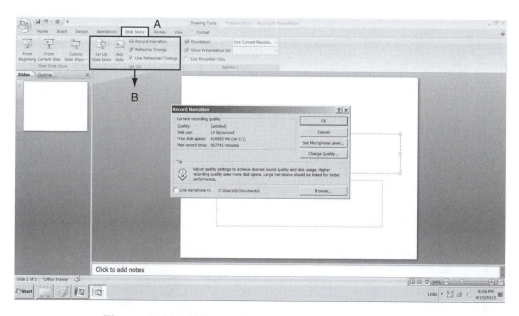

Figure 2-38. Microsoft PowerPoint—Slide Show tab

Figure 2-38a. Microsoft PowerPoint—Slide Show tab

The next box provides the user with options for setting up the slide show. Those options include recording narration that will run during the slide show. For example, when presenting a slide show about a plaintiff's injuries from a car crash, the plaintiff can talk about the pain associated with those injuries.

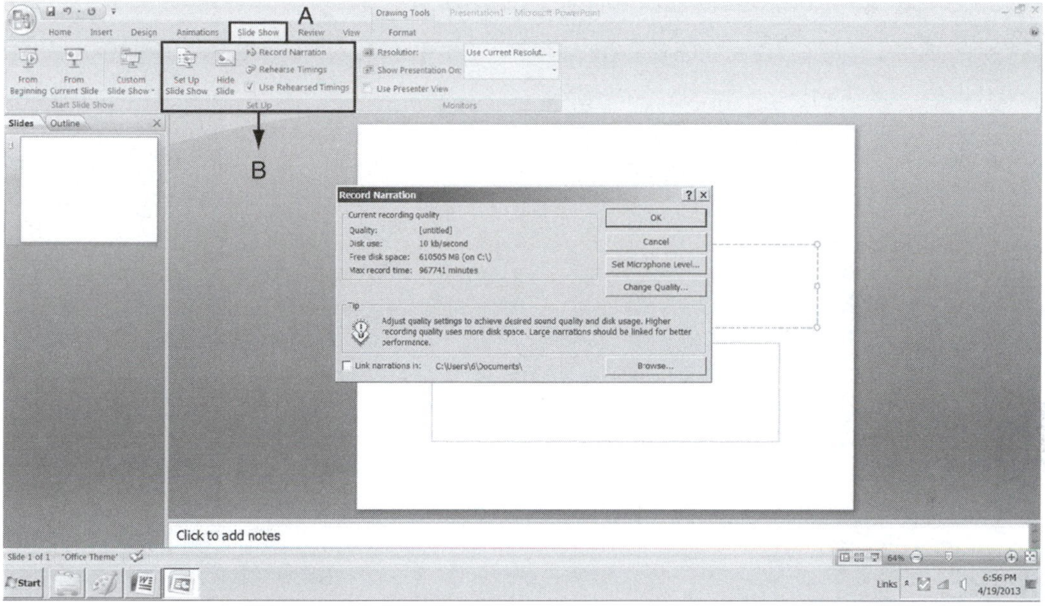

Figure 2-38b. Microsoft PowerPoint—Slide Show tab: Setup box

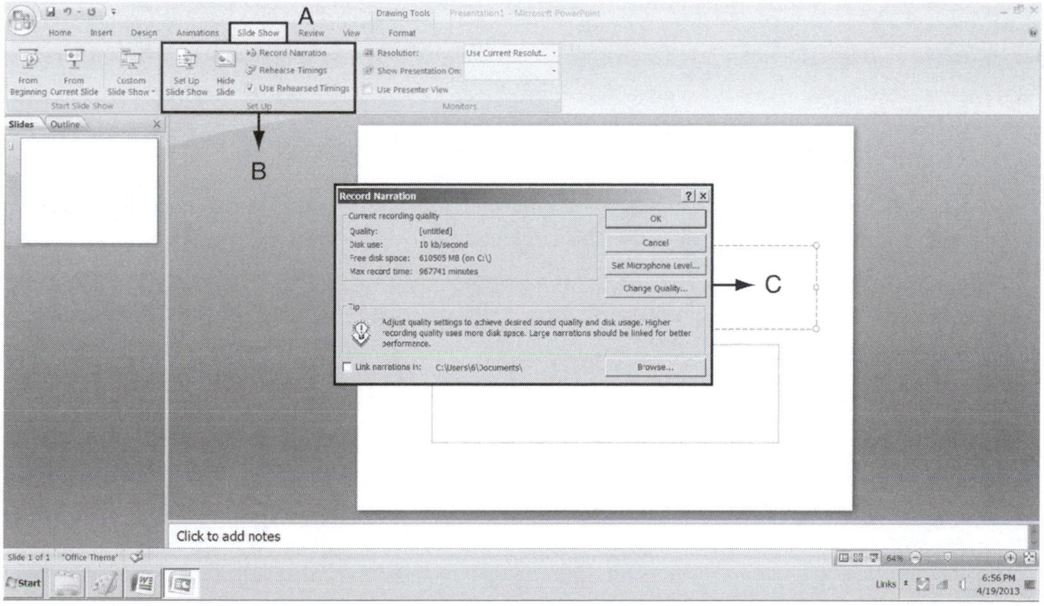

Figure 2-38c. Microsoft PowerPoint—Slide Show tab: Setup box, Record Narration link submenu

6. Review Tab

As with the Review tab in Word, a user can proofread text and insert comments. Also, the user can protect the contents from unauthorized alteration.

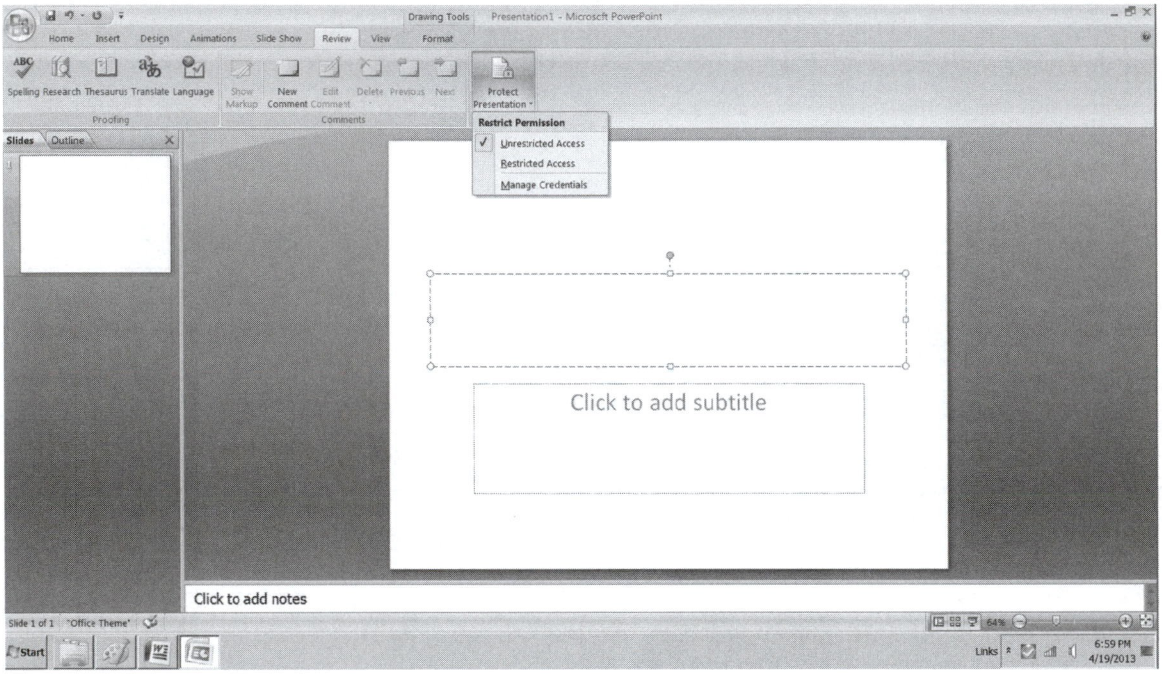

Figure 2-39. Microsoft PowerPoint—Review tab: Changes box, Protect Presentation button submenu

7. View Tab

In addition to having the same options as the View tab in Word, like Show/Hide and Zoom, a user can see how the presentation will look.

Buttons allow the user to:

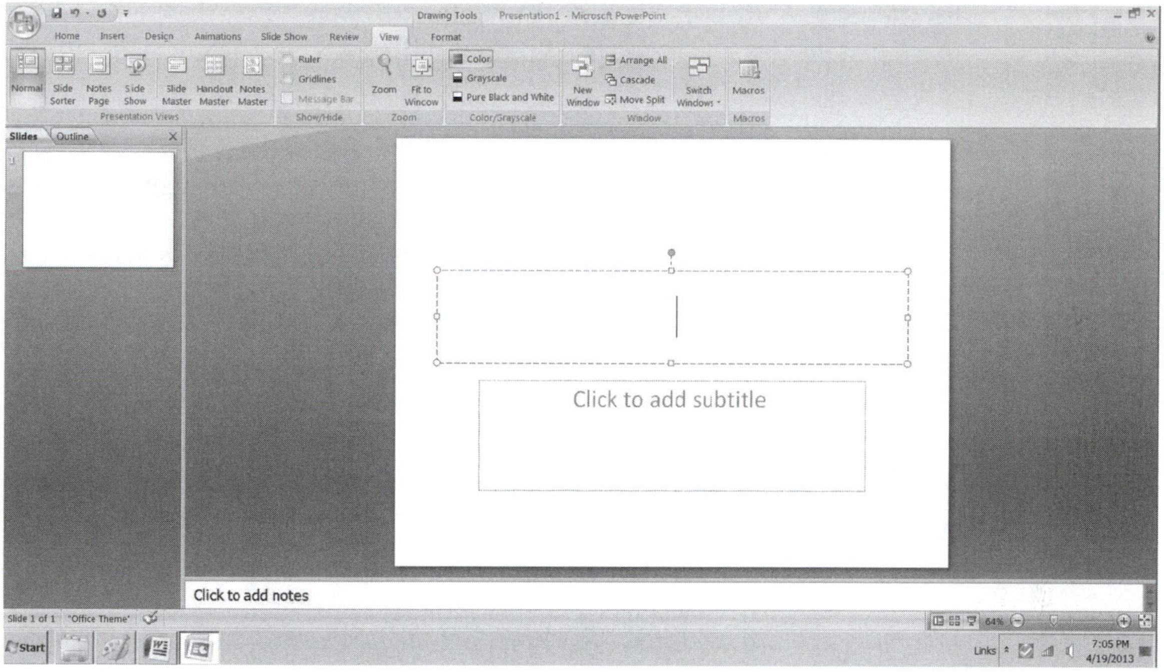

Figure 2-40. Microsoft PowerPoint—View tab: Presentation Views box

▶ Look at a normal presentation of the show;

▶ Use a slide sorter to rearrange the sequence of slides;

▶ Edit the notes that only the presenter will see during the presentation, such as a reminder to a presenter about the elements that make up a tort for negligence;

▶ Select the style for the slides, including the design and layout of master slides, which serve as a style template for subsequent slides; and

▶ Choose the design and layout of the slides when printed as a handout.

OpenOffice.Org

The free software suite put out by OpenOffice.org, which uses the open-source Unix operating system, has many of the same features available in the Microsoft Office suite. One trend in the creation of free software involves making it "open source," where the creators disclose all the underlying computer code that makes the software work. As a result, people might create different, free versions of, for example, office productivity software. Often, users might provide revisions and fixes to correct occasional glitches in the free software. Also, the community of users may modify the software to run on different OSs, including Microsoft's Windows and Apple's Mac OS.

A legal practice might want to use free software to manage costs, since updates could also be free. Given the wide base of users for many types of free software, it likely will ensure the continuing accessibility of the content with newer versions of the software.

Because the software applications available at OpenOffice.org approximately correspond to those in Microsoft's Office suite, an Office user might quickly learn how to use this free software. Freeware like OpenOffice.org may not come with technical support, something available with Office. People may provide such support for a fee, or, some might provide free support.

Writer

Writer, the word processing software in the OpenOffice.org suite, shares many of the features of Word. For example, this suite uses tabs, like those in Word, to sort out categories of software functions. Writer has toolbars instead of the ribbon used in Word, with rows of similar buttons, as well as a drop-down link for customizing the toolbar.

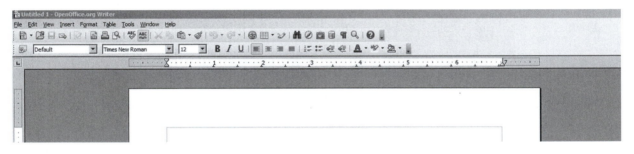

Figure 2-41. Writer default view

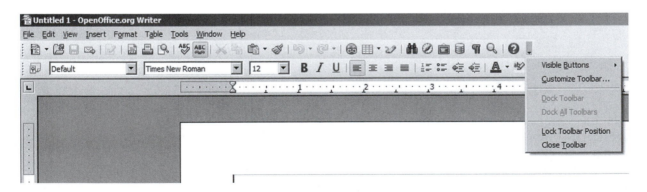

Figure 2-42. Writer Toolbar—top level, drop-down link

Familiar tabs and functions in Writer include:

▶ Edit, as well as the option to block the undo or restore features;

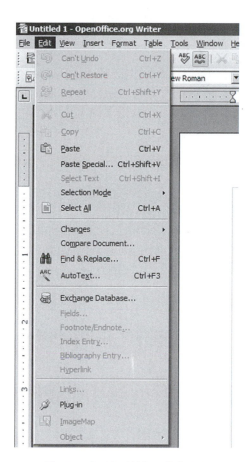

Figure 2-43. Writer Edit tab

▶ View, which also can control the addition of content;

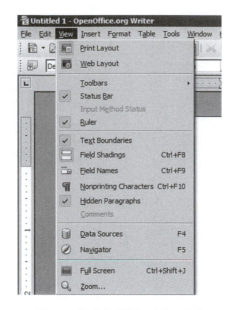

Figure 2-44. Writer View tab

▶ Insert, including the ability to add a movie or a sound;

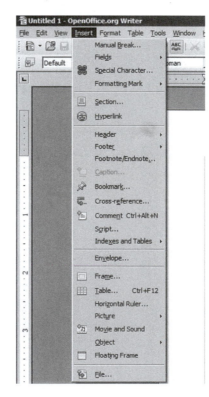

Figure 2-45. Writer Insert tab

▶ Table;

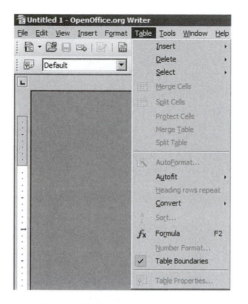

Figure 2-46. Writer Table tab

▶ Tools, including spelling and grammar checking; and

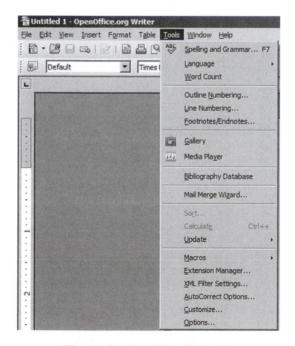

Figure 2-47. Writer Tools tab

▶ Help.

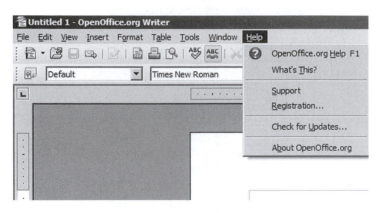

Figure 2-48. Writer Help tab

Writer also uses wizards, which provide step-by-step guidance in using a feature of the software. For example, these could make it possible to use an address book for generating an e-mail using Microsoft **Outlook** or Mozilla's **Thunderbird.**

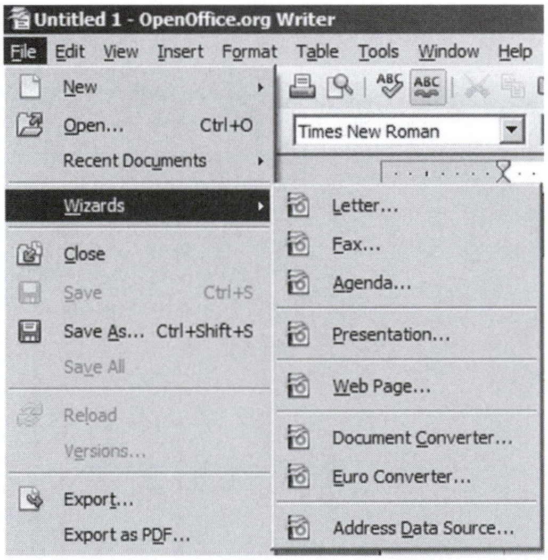

Figure 2-49. Writer File Tab—Wizards link submenu

Many of the keyboard shortcuts available in Word, such as CTRL-S (to save), will also work in Writer.

Base

The database software for OpenOffice.org is Base. A law office's database could include all data associated with representing clients, such as client contact information. It roughly corresponds to the Access database application in the Microsoft Office suite.

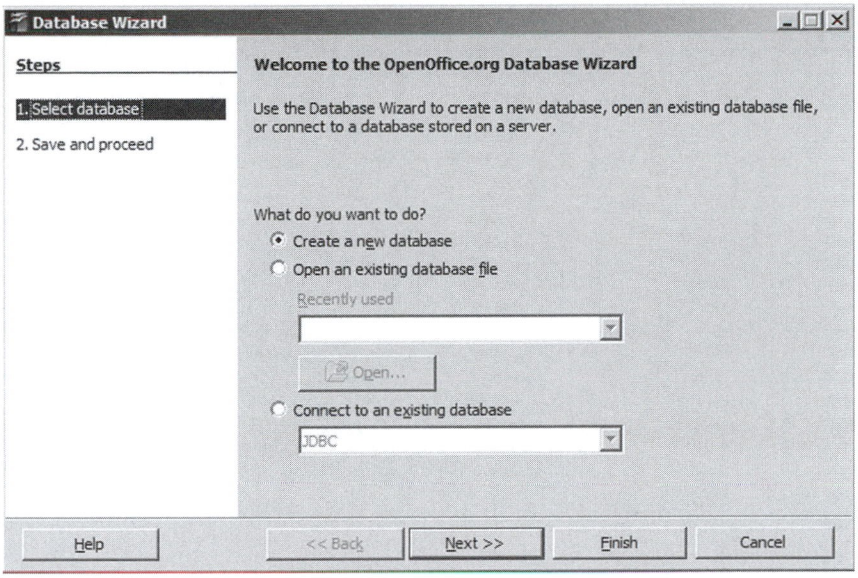

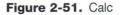

Figure 2-50. Base—Database Wizard page

Calc

Calc, OpenOffice.org's spreadsheet software, roughly corresponds to the Excel software in the Microsoft Office suite. For example, a user might find it just as easy to add up litigation expenses for inclusion in a bill to a client as when using Excel.

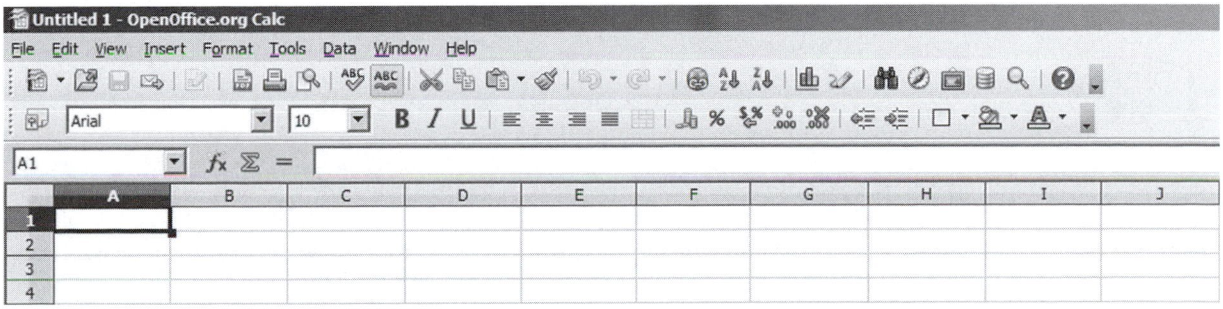

Figure 2-51. Calc

Math

With Math, OpenOffice.org gives a user the option to do calculations without the grid used in Calc. Math users can insert formula elements, such as operators or functions, with a single click. Using a formula makes it easy to generate a graphic representation of the math process for subsequent insertion into any of the other applications available in OpenOffice.org.

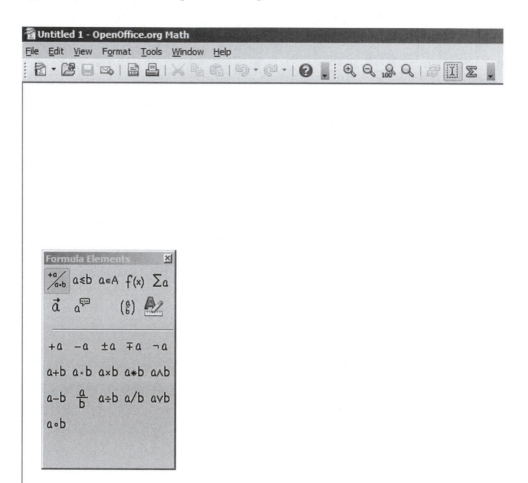

Figure 2-52. Math start page

Impress

Impress, the OpenOffice.org version of Microsoft's PowerPoint software, contains many of the same options for the creating and editing of a slide show. Slight differences include an option to enter data points on a slide and to keep the data points at a specific position in the slide.

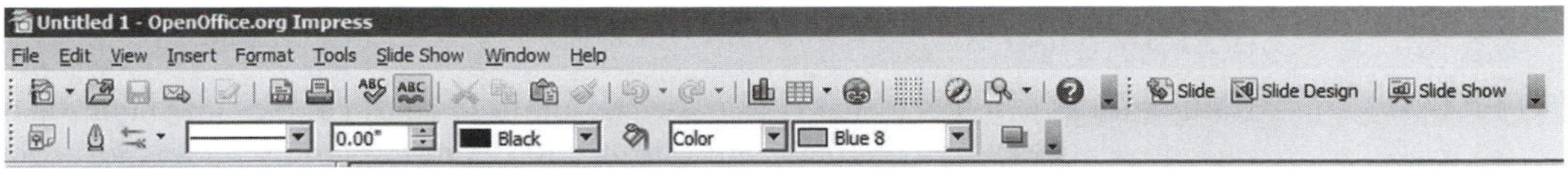

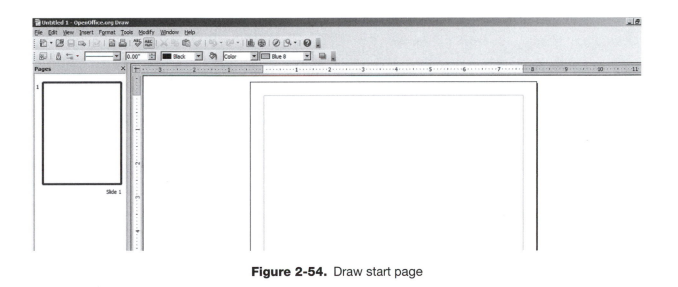

Figure 2-53. Impress start page

Draw

OpenOffice.org has Draw, software that allows for drawing. It approximately corresponds to the Microsoft Word application, Paint.

Figure 2-54. Draw start page

Google Docs

Software in the Cloud

Google Docs is a type of free software that involves **cloud computing.** As noted earlier, the concept of **Software as a Service (SaaS),** also known as cloud computing, allows a user to edit and save documents using software stored on a server. This would allow a lawyer to obtain and/or modify a brief or pleading stored online by using any computer with Internet access. Google Docs comes with one gigabyte of free storage, with the option to buy more storage for an annual fee.

Features

Google Docs has features akin to those in Microsoft's Office suite and OpenOffice.org's business productivity software, such as presentation and spreadsheet software. Microsoft's Office Suite and OpenOffice.org may have an advantage over Google Docs because of the wider array of applications they contain.

1. Access

Typing www.google.com/docs into a browser brings the user to the log-in to a free Google Account.

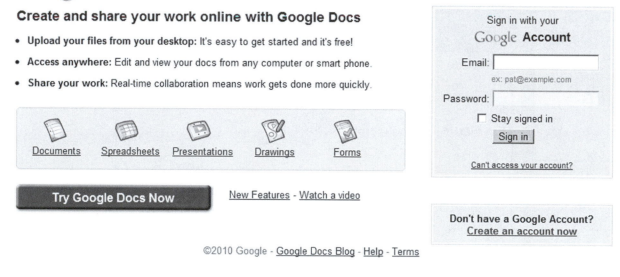

Figure 2-55. Google Docs sign in

2. The First Screen

The first screen of Google Docs shows a menu of documents stored there. From here, a user could create a new word processing document, slide show presentation, or spreadsheet.

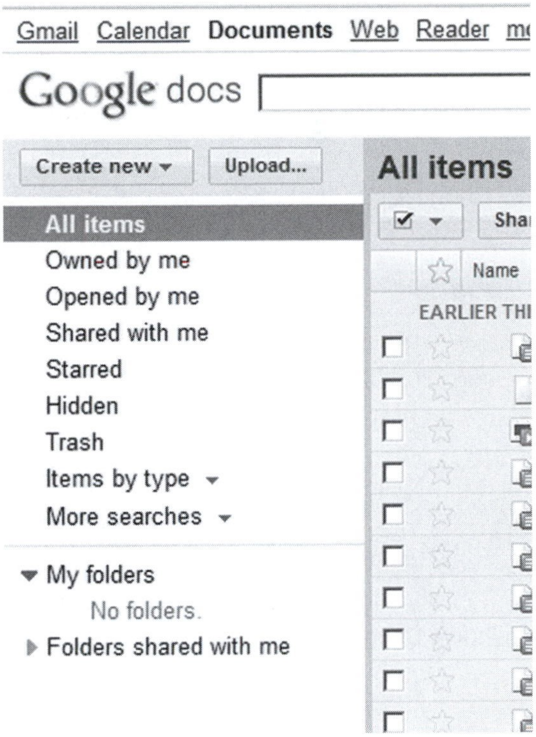

Figure 2-56. Google Docs start page

3. Search

Because this is from Google, a user has the option to search for documents. A lawyer could find, among a series of briefs, one that mentions a particular statute.

Figure 2-57. Google Docs start page—Search Docs box

4. Link

Along the top of the web page, Google Docs also has links to applications like Gmail.

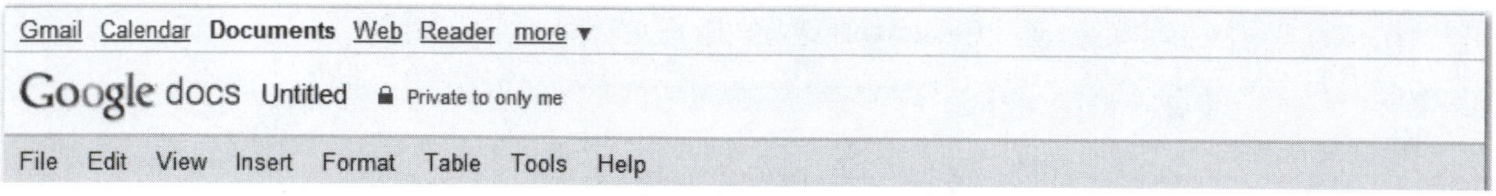

Gmail Calendar **Documents** Web Reader more ▼

Google docs Untitled 🔒 Private to only me

File   Edit   View   Insert   Format   Table   Tools   Help

Figure 2-58. Google Docs start page—links

5. Toolbar and Tabs

Beneath this row appears a toolbar with tabs that correspond to those in Word and OpenOffice.org, such as File, Edit, View, Insert, Format, Table, Tools, and Help.

Figure 2-59. Google Docs start page—toolbar

Conclusion

Office productivity software can make a business operate more efficiently. Suites, which are integrated bundles of such software, make it easier for a user to exploit the full processing capacity of a computer, regardless of the nature of the license or operating system. Word processing technology goes beyond mere typing to provide a number of options on how to design and use a document. Spreadsheet software increases the ease with which a business can assess a range of information often related to the efficient operation of a business. Slide show software can more effectively convey information in a presentation to enhance clarity. A user can purchase a license to the very popular Microsoft Office suite, with frequent updates and readily available help, or use free software like OpenOffice.org or Software as a Service, like Google Docs.

Terms

Access	Servers
Blacklining	Sheet
Buttons	Slide
Cell	Software as a Service (SaaS)
Clip art	Spreadsheet software
Cloud computing	SQL
Graphic user interface (GUI)	Suite
Hyperlink	Tabs
Macro	Thumbnails
Outlook	Thunderbird
PDF (protected document format)	Toolbar
Pivot table	Wizard
Redlining	Workbook
Ribbon	

Hypotheticals

1. Generating a table of cases

Have students generate a table of cases from the following quote, from *Citizens United v. Federal Election Commission*, 130 S. Ct. 876, 886-890 (2010):

> Limits on electioneering communications were upheld in *McConnell v. Federal Election Comm'n*, 540 U.S. 93, 203-209, 124 S. Ct. 619, 157 L. Ed. 2d 491 (2003). The holding of *McConnell* rested to a large extent on an earlier case, *Austin v. Michigan Chamber of Commerce*, 494 U.S. 652, 110 S. Ct. 1391, 108 L. Ed. 2d 652 (1990). *Austin* had held that political speech may be banned based on the speaker's corporate identity.

In this case, we are asked to reconsider *Austin* and, in effect, *McConnell.* It has been noted that *"Austin* was a significant departure from ancient First Amendment principles," *Federal Election Comm'n* v. *Wisconsin Right to Life, Inc.*, 551 U.S. 449, 490, 127 S. Ct. 2652, 168 L. Ed. 2d 329 (2007) *(WRTL)* (Scalia, J., concurring in part and concurring in judgment). [. . .]

Citizens United is a nonprofit corporation. [. . .]

In January 2008, Citizens United released a film entitled *Hillary: The Movie.* We refer to the film as *Hillary.* It is a 90-minute documentary about then-Senator Hillary Clinton, who was a candidate in the Democratic Party's 2008 Presidential primary elections. *Hillary* mentions Senator Clinton by name and depicts interviews with political commentators and other persons, most of them quite critical of Senator Clinton. *Hillary* was released in theaters and on DVD, but Citizens United wanted to increase distribution by making it available through video-on-demand.

[. . .]

Before the Bipartisan Campaign Reform Act of 2002 (BCRA), federal law prohibited—and still does prohibit—corporations and unions from using general treasury funds to make direct contributions to candidates or independent expenditures that expressly advocate the election or defeat of a candidate, through any form of media, in connection with certain qualified federal elections. 2 U.S.C. § 441b (2000 ed.); see *McConnell, supra,* at 204 and n. 87, 124 S. Ct. 619, 157 L. Ed. 2d 491; *Federal Election Comm'n* v. *Massachusetts Citizens for Life, Inc.*, 479 U.S. 238, 249, 107 S. Ct. 616, 93 L. Ed. 2d 539 (1986) *(MCFL).* [. . .]

Citizens United contends that § 441b does not cover *Hillary*, as a matter of statutory interpretation, because the film does not qualify as an "electioneering communication." § 441b(b)(2). Citizens United raises this issue for the first time before us, but we consider the issue because "it was addressed by the court below." *Lebron* v. *National Railroad Passenger Corporation*, 513 U.S. 374, 379, 115 S. Ct. 961, 130 L. Ed. 2d 902 (1995).

[. . .]

Prolix laws chill speech for the same reason that vague laws chill speech: People "of common intelligence must necessarily guess at [the law's] meaning and differ as to its application." *Connally* v. *General Constr. Co.*, 269 U.S. 385, 391, 46 S. Ct. 126, 70 L. Ed. 322 (1926).

[. . .]

On what we might call conventional television, advertising spots reach viewers who have chosen a channel or a program for reasons unrelated to the advertising. With video-on-demand, by contrast, the viewer selects a program after taking "a series of affirmative steps": subscribing to cable; navigating through various menus; and selecting the program. See *Reno* v. *ACLU*, 521 U.S. 844, 867, 117 S. Ct. 2329, 138 L. Ed. 2d 874 (1997).

While some means of communication may be less effective than others at influencing the public in different contexts, any effort by the Judiciary to decide which means of communications are to be preferred for the particular type of message and speaker would raise questions as to the courts' own lawful authority. Substantial questions would arise if courts were to begin saying what means of speech should be preferred or disfavored. And in all events, those differentiations might soon prove to be irrelevant or outdated by technologies that are in rapid flux. See *Turner Broadcasting System, Inc.* v. *FCC*, 512 U.S. 622, 639, 114 S. Ct. 2445, 129 L. Ed. 2d 497 (1994).

2. Using the compare function in Word

A prospective client seeks legal advice over a possible copyright infringement. This prospective client says that an unscrupulous agent passed along a first draft of a chapter on word processing software, who then published a book allegedly containing content from the first draft. The lawyer has doubts that a well-established publishing firm would do that and wants to see whether the prospective client's claim has any merit. In particular, the lawyer has asked you to compare a paragraph in the prospective client's manuscript with that of the publication, using Word.

A. Here's the prospective client's original paragraph:

Since an office may use software for word processing, for generating financial reports or for communication, some such as Microsoft have bundled together the software that a business might have a need to use. Microsoft Office's suite, for example, integrates software that does word processing, spreadsheets, Internet access, and slide show presentations, at a minimum. An integrated bundle or suite of software, then, may mean having information in a format that lends itself to easy use by other software from the software manufacturer. Of course, the bundle as a group will cost less than if the office would separately buy a license to each application.

B. Here's a paragraph from the publication:

Software makers understand how customers might prefer to have software that meshes well with one another. For example, Microsoft's suite, MS Office, integrates software that does word processing, spreadsheets, Internet browsing, and the creation of slide shows, at a minimum. Of course, the bundle as a group will cost less than if the business would separately buy a license for each application.

Show the results, explaining what they mean.

3. Prepare a PowerPoint slide show. For each bullet-pointed item, create a separate slide, using appropriate graphics, appearing below the content.

[Aside: to copy a graphic from a Microsoft document, have the image on the screen. Using CTRL-PrtSc will capture the image. Paste the image into

Painter, usually available with a Microsoft OS. In Painter, options exist for cropping out that information not part of the graphic to be saved.]

Like a typewriter, word processing software will, at a minimum, have the capacity to manipulate:

- ▶ Spacing
- ▶ Font
- ▶ Style
- ▶ Margins
- ▶ Italics, bold face, underlining (or any combination of the three)
- ▶ Subscript
- ▶ Superscript
- ▶ Insert a symbol
- ▶ Indent
- ▶ Center
- ▶ Flush left or right
- ▶ Insert bullet points or numbers
- ▶ Generating page numbers, headers, or footers

4. As part of a divorce, the couple will maintain the marital residence, for the raising of children. The following constitutes the financial information that you have available, for a six month period:

   Gas: February, $292.41; March, $314.13; April, $209.91; May, $163.15; June, $77.36

   Electric: January, $78.24; February, $81.24; March, $37.18; April, $62.32; May, $65.92; June, $89.07

   Water: March, $124.45; June, $149.34

   Cable: January, $174.72, February, $167.44; March, $167.44; April, $174.72; May, $174.72; June, $174.72

Using Excel, answer the following:

   a. What are average costs for electricity, per month?
   b. What are average costs for cable, per month?
   c. What are average costs for water, per month?
   d. For gas, used for heating and to heat water, you do not have information for January. What are average costs for gas, for those five months? Use that figure as an estimate for gas costs for January. What are average costs for gas, for those six months?

5. Create company letterhead, using Google Docs. This is for the firm Cahoone, Lamb and Murray, LLP, with offices at 1 Beacon Street, Suite 101, Peabody, Massachusetts 01960. They have a website, www.CahooneLambLLP.com, and

a telephone number, 978-555-1212. The lawyers are David Cahoone, Scott Lamb, and Susan Murray. Identify yourself on the letterhead as a paralegal.

Use one of the graphics available after doing a search for "legal graphics," at the top of the letterhead. The software will automatically annotate the source for the image, although using such a graphic would not typically be appropriate without having paid a licensing fee for its use.

When done composing this document, download a copy of it as a PDF file.

Practice-Specific Software

3

Objectives

▶ **Review** the process involved in generating appropriate documents for a bankruptcy filing so that a debtor/petitioner can reach a settlement with creditors for a discharge of debts in order to obtain a fresh start.

▶ **Examine** the documents used in creating and operating a corporation, such as Articles of Incorporation, resolutions, and the appropriate reports that would have to be filed with the state.

▶ **Proceed** through the steps involved for completing a federal HUD-1 form, used when financing a purchase of residential property.

▶ **Determine** what assets and obligations a court would need to consider to arrive at a financial settlement in a divorce.

▶ **Identify** and process information needed to generate an accurate accounting of a trust.

▶ **Gather** information necessary for estate planning and for the generation of additional useful documents.

Introduction

Upon graduation from law school, lawyers may have the ability to practice any kind of law but might find it easier to have a specialty. Increasingly, areas of law have developed such complexity that a lawyer has to watch for daily changes in the law so as to serve the interests of clients diligently and conscientiously. Software about a specific legal topic can make it easier to operate a legal practice. This chapter showcases types of practice-specific software.

Bankruptcy

Bankruptcy can mean that a client, whether individually (and a spouse) or as a business, has more debts than **assets** (**property** or savings) and seeks help, under federal law, to get a fresh start. A court-approved distribution of debtor/petitioner's assets to the **creditors** likely means that the creditors typically will get only partial payment of the debt. Bankruptcy software can help a lawyer gather and organize the client's information to prepare a petition in bankruptcy so that a client can get relief from those debts.

In General

1. Terms

The client, as the **debtor/petitioner,** owes money to creditors. To obtain a fresh start, the client has to request, or petition, for bankruptcy protection. A **trustee,** appointed by the bankruptcy court, will oversee the distribution of the debtor/petitioner's assets to creditors. Upon completion of that process, the debtor/petitioner obtains a **discharge in bankruptcy.** This means that the debtor/petitioner no longer has a legal obligation to repay creditors beyond what they had received from the bankruptcy court. All assets that the debtor/petitioner has available for distribution to creditors are known as the **estate.**

A discharge in bankruptcy, involving the distribution of all of a debtor/petitioner's assets, save for some exemptions, is known as **liquidation.** Alternatively, the debtor/petitioner could ask for **reorganization,** which involves setting a schedule to repay some or all debts. If the debtor/petitioner has a job, reorganization could mean that part of the paycheck goes toward paying off the debt; creditors could get more of the moneys owed would have to wait to get that money.

2. Type of Petition

A debtor/petitioner would start by filing a voluntary petition for a discharge in bankruptcy. Sometimes creditors, like suppliers to a department store, can force the department store, as debtor, into bankruptcy by filing an involuntary petition. This increases the chances that the creditors will get some payment for the debt, avoiding the possibility that the debtor uses up all the assets before filing for bankruptcy. Software will generate a completed version of a petition for voluntary bankruptcy, available at: http://www.uscourts.gov/uscourts/RulesAndPolicies/rules/BK_Forms_Current/B_001.pdf.

3. Software

This exploration of software for filing for bankruptcy uses National LawForms Bankruptcy Case Software, available at www.nationallawforms.com. All images taken from this software are copyrighted by the creator of such images and inclusion of such images in this text does not constitute any claim of copyright in them. Other such software comes from the publisher of this text, Wolters Kluwer, at www.bestcase.com/, as well as from www.ezfiling.com/ and www.bankruptcy-software.com/, among others.

4. Electronic Filing

Courts increasingly prefer to receive documents as electronic files because this:

▶ Cuts down on the space used for storing paper documents;

▶ Makes it easier to search the data files; and

▶ Can make it easy to generate copies.

Because the client has to file a paper version of the petition, the output generated by the software can come in the form of a text or a PDF, per the requirements of the federal court. Blank versions of these forms also appear at http://www.uscourts.gov/FederalCourts/Bankruptcy.aspx.

Content

Information in support of the petition appears in documents called **pages, schedules,** and **exhibits.**

1. Familiar Tabs

The makers of this software created an interface similar to the ribbon used with Microsoft's Office Suite. This includes familiar tabs such as File, Edit, and Help.

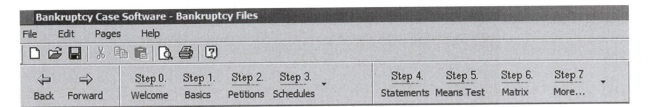

Figure 3-1. National LawForms Bankruptcy Case Software—start screen

2. Pages Tab

The Pages tab contains links to begin the preparation of a petition for bankruptcy protection.

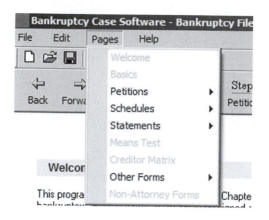

Figure 3-2. National LawForms Bankruptcy Case Software—Pages tab

a. Voluntary petition link

i. Page 1

Via the Petitions link, a law firm preparing a voluntary petition for a client needs to indicate the:

Figure 3-3. National LawForms Bankruptcy Case Software—Pages tab: Petitions link, Voluntary petition, Page 1

- Type of debtor, since the debts and assets of a person can dramatically differ from that of a business;
- Type of petition, for
  - Reorganization (**Chapter 11** of the **Bankruptcy Code** for a business or **Chapter 13** for an individual); or
  - Liquidation (**Chapter 7**);
- Type of **liabilities,** like a **mortgage** or credit card debt; and

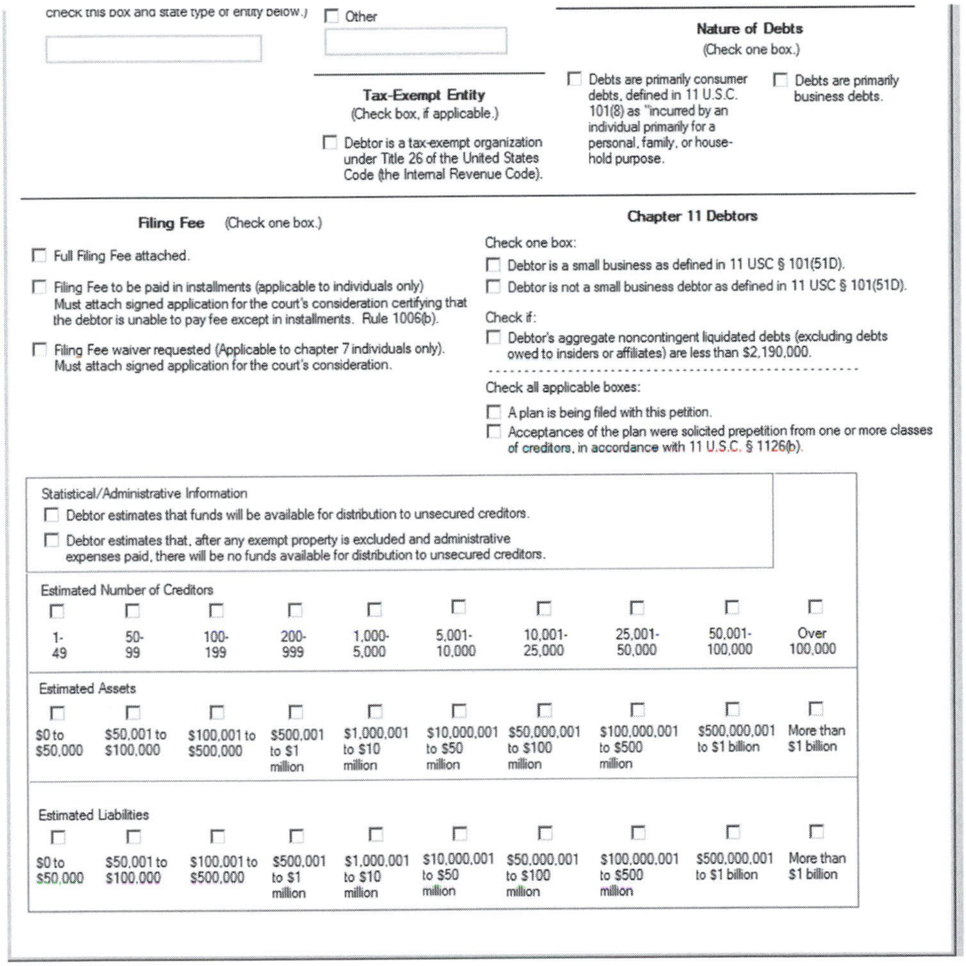

check this box and state type of entity below.) ☐ Other

Nature of Debts
(Check one box.)
☐ Debts are primarily consumer debts, defined in 11 U.S.C. 101(8) as "incurred by an individual primarily for a personal, family, or household purpose.
☐ Debts are primarily business debts.

Tax-Exempt Entity
(Check box, if applicable.)
☐ Debtor is a tax-exempt organization under Title 26 of the United States Code (the Internal Revenue Code).

Filing Fee (Check one box.)
☐ Full Filing Fee attached.
☐ Filing Fee to be paid in installments (applicable to individuals only) Must attach signed application for the court's consideration certifying that the debtor is unable to pay fee except in installments. Rule 1006(b).
☐ Filing Fee waiver requested (Applicable to chapter 7 individuals only). Must attach signed application for the court's consideration.

Chapter 11 Debtors
Check one box:
☐ Debtor is a small business as defined in 11 USC § 101(51D).
☐ Debtor is not a small business debtor as defined in 11 USC § 101(51D).
Check if:
☐ Debtor's aggregate noncontingent liquidated debts (excluding debts owed to insiders or affiliates) are less than $2,190,000.
Check all applicable boxes:
☐ A plan is being filed with this petition.
☐ Acceptances of the plan were solicited prepetition from one or more classes of creditors, in accordance with 11 U.S.C. § 1126(b).

Statistical/Administrative Information
☐ Debtor estimates that funds will be available for distribution to unsecured creditors.
☐ Debtor estimates that, after any exempt property is excluded and administrative expenses paid, there will be no funds available for distribution to unsecured creditors.

Estimated Number of Creditors

☐	☐	☐	☐	☐	☐	☐	☐	☐	☐
1-49	50-99	100-199	200-999	1,000-5,000	5,001-10,000	10,001-25,000	25,001-50,000	50,001-100,000	Over 100,000

Estimated Assets

☐	☐	☐	☐	☐	☐	☐	☐	☐	☐
$0 to $50,000	$50,001 to $100,000	$100,001 to $500,000	$500,001 to $1 million	$1,000,001 to $10 million	$10,000,001 to $50 million	$50,000,001 to $100 million	$100,000,001 to $500 million	$500,000,001 to $1 billion	More than $1 billion

Estimated Liabilities

☐	☐	☐	☐	☐	☐	☐	☐	☐	☐
$0 to $50,000	$50,001 to $100,000	$100,001 to $500,000	$500,001 to $1 million	$1,000,001 to $10 million	$10,000,001 to $50 million	$50,000,001 to $100 million	$100,000,001 to $500 million	$500,000,001 to $1 billion	More than $1 billion

Figure 3-4. National LawForms Bankruptcy Case Software—Pages tab: Petitions link, Voluntary petition, Page 1, Preliminary information

- Identity of creditors, like banks, individuals, credit card companies, or a government.

ii. Page 2

Additional necessary information includes:

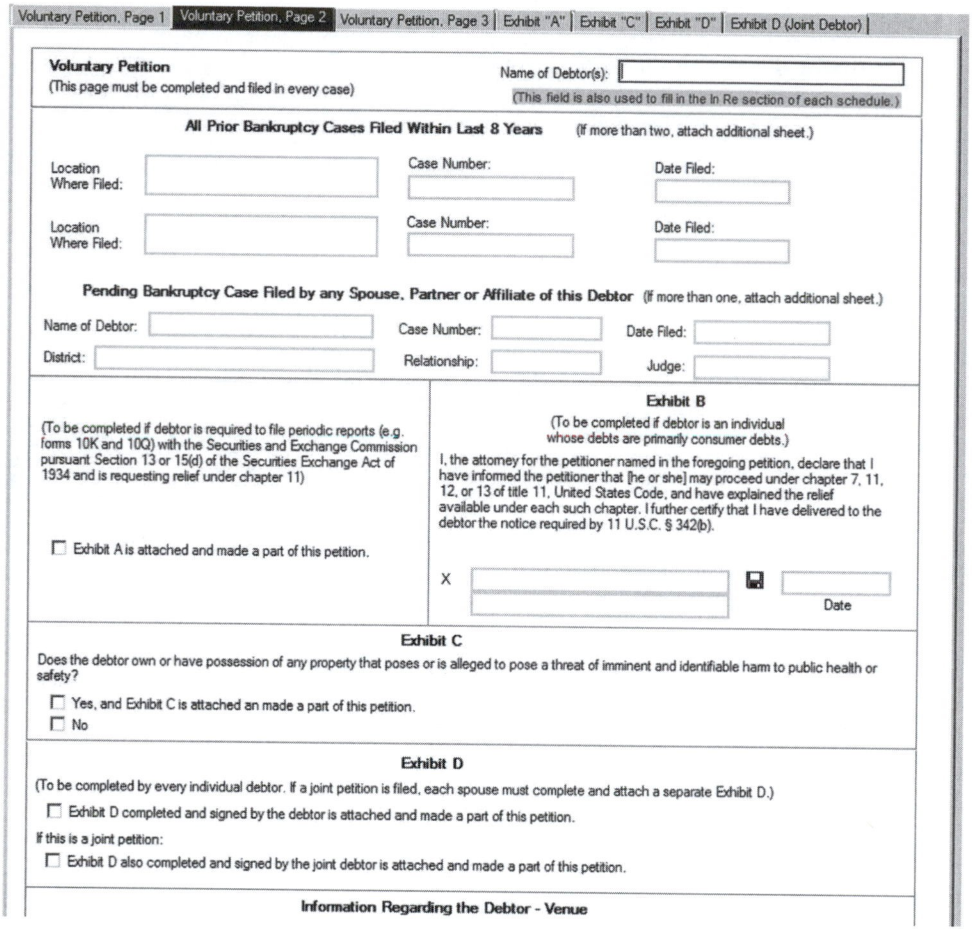

Voluntary Petition, Page 1 | Voluntary Petition, Page 2 | Voluntary Petition, Page 3 | Exhibit "A" | Exhibit "C" | Exhibit "D" | Exhibit D (Joint Debtor)

Voluntary Petition
(This page must be completed and filed in every case)

Name of Debtor(s):
(This field is also used to fill in the In Re section of each schedule.)

All Prior Bankruptcy Cases Filed Within Last 8 Years (If more than two, attach additional sheet.)

Location Where Filed: Case Number: Date Filed:

Location Where Filed: Case Number: Date Filed:

Pending Bankruptcy Case Filed by any Spouse, Partner or Affiliate of this Debtor (If more than one, attach additional sheet.)

Name of Debtor: Case Number: Date Filed:

District: Relationship: Judge:

(To be completed if debtor is required to file periodic reports (e.g. forms 10K and 10Q) with the Securities and Exchange Commission pursuant Section 13 or 15(d) of the Securities Exchange Act of 1934 and is requesting relief under chapter 11)

☐ Exhibit A is attached and made a part of this petition.

Exhibit B
(To be completed if debtor is an individual whose debts are primarily consumer debts.)

I, the attorney for the petitioner named in the foregoing petition, declare that I have informed the petitioner that [he or she] may proceed under chapter 7, 11, 12, or 13 of title 11, United States Code, and have explained the relief available under each such chapter. I further certify that I have delivered to the debtor the notice required by 11 U.S.C. § 342(b).

X Date

Exhibit C
Does the debtor own or have possession of any property that poses or is alleged to pose a threat of imminent and identifiable harm to public health or safety?

☐ Yes, and Exhibit C is attached an made a part of this petition.
☐ No

Exhibit D
(To be completed by every individual debtor. If a joint petition is filed, each spouse must complete and attach a separate Exhibit D.)

☐ Exhibit D completed and signed by the debtor is attached and made a part of this petition.

If this is a joint petition:

☐ Exhibit D also completed and signed by the joint debtor is attached and made a part of this petition.

Information Regarding the Debtor - Venue

Figure 3-5. National LawForms Bankruptcy Case Software—Pages tab: Petitions link, Voluntary petition, Page 2

- Whether and what other bankruptcy cases the client might be involved with;
- If the federal Securities and Exchange Commission (SEC), which oversees corporations that have made available **stock** for sale to the public, has been notified;
- Identifying property that could pose an imminent public safety threat, like propane tanks (as noted in Exhibit C); and
- A statement where an individual debtor/petitioner (and a spouse, if married and filing jointly) **attests** to the accuracy of the information in this petition (Exhibits B and D).

iii. Page 3

Besides learning about all debtors/petitioners, the bankruptcy court judge will need to know whether a non-attorney completed the petition for the client, an option available under the law.

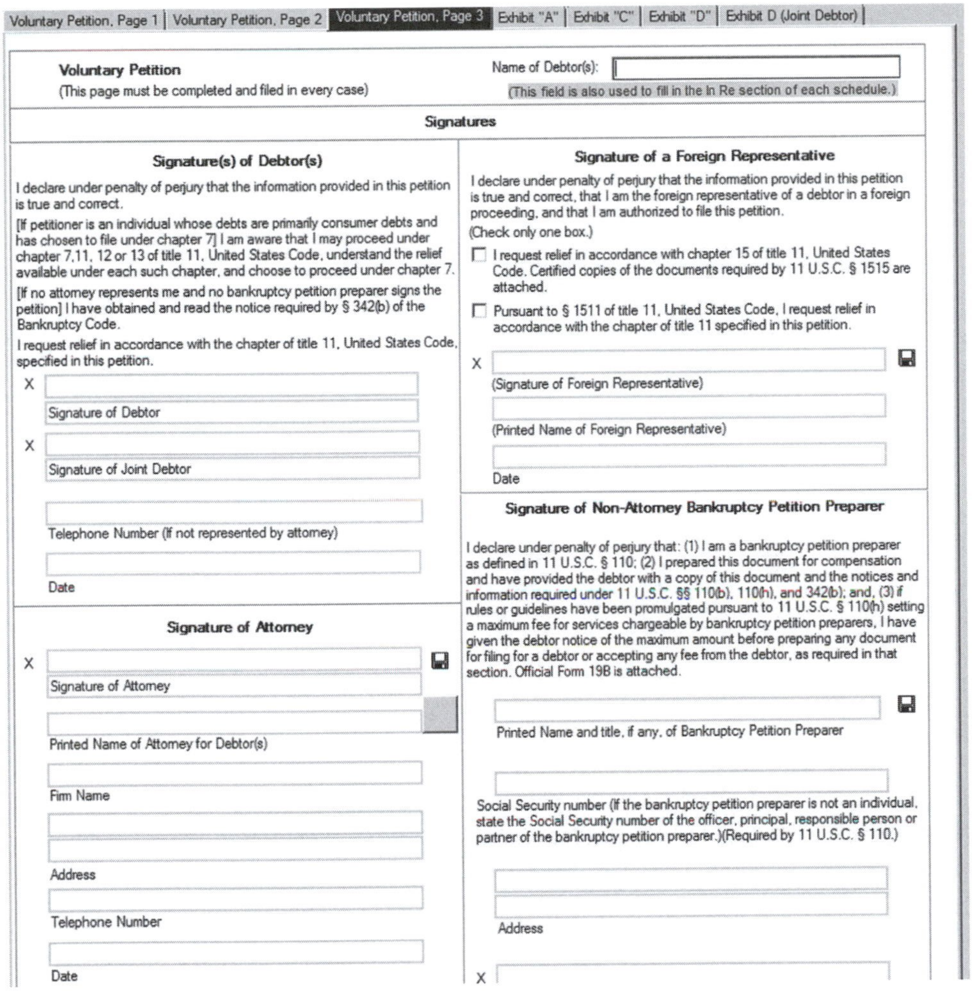

Figure 3-6. National LawForms Bankruptcy Case Software—Pages tab: Petitions link, Voluntary petition, Page 3

iv. Exhibits A through D

These documents, which would accompany the petition, would include:

▶ A list of assets, such as stock (Exhibit A);

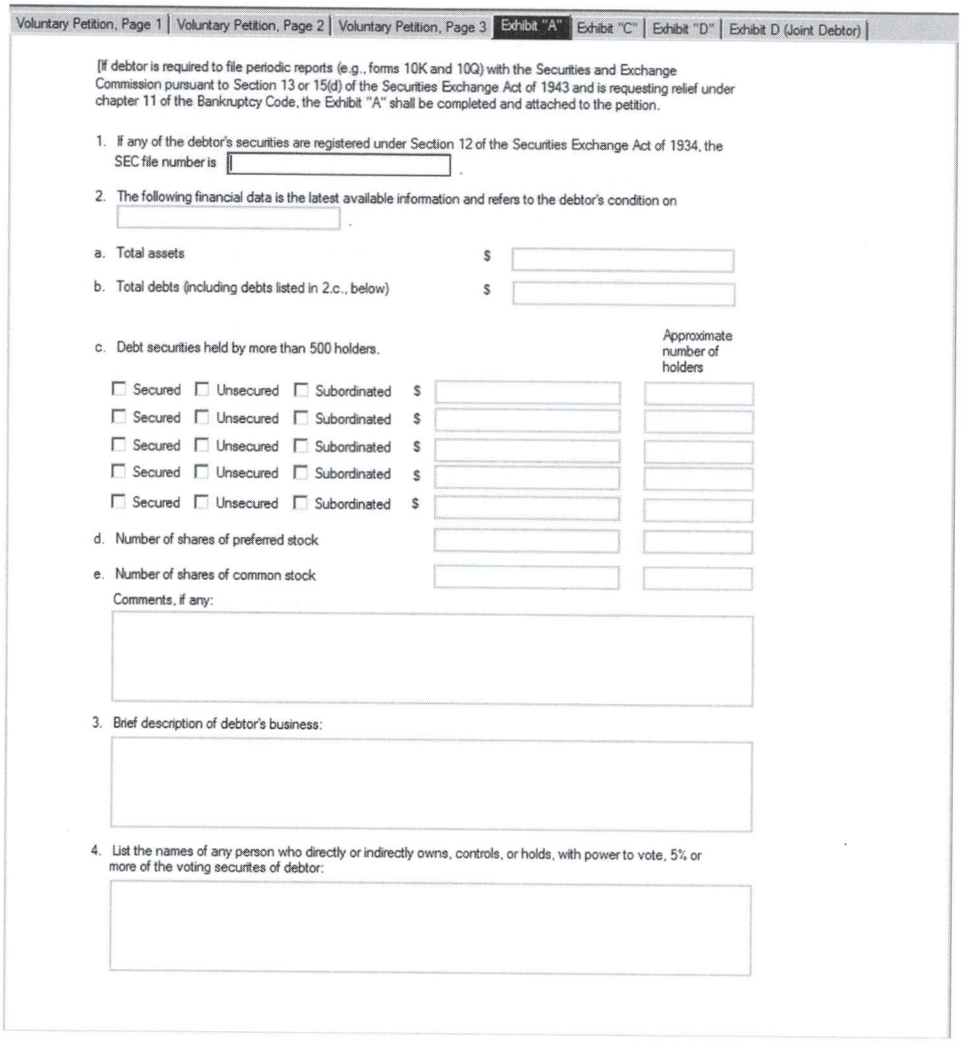

| Voluntary Petition, Page 1 | Voluntary Petition, Page 2 | Voluntary Petition, Page 3 | Exhibit "A" | Exhibit "C" | Exhibit "D" | Exhibit D (Joint Debtor) |

[If debtor is required to file periodic reports (e.g., forms 10K and 10Q) with the Securities and Exchange Commission pursuant to Section 13 or 15(d) of the Securities Exchange Act of 1943 and is requesting relief under chapter 11 of the Bankruptcy Code, the Exhibit "A" shall be completed and attached to the petition.

1. If any of the debtor's securities are registered under Section 12 of the Securities Exchange Act of 1934, the SEC file number is

2. The following financial data is the latest available information and refers to the debtor's condition on

a. Total assets $

b. Total debts (including debts listed in 2.c., below) $

c. Debt securities held by more than 500 holders.

Approximate number of holders

☐ Secured ☐ Unsecured ☐ Subordinated $
☐ Secured ☐ Unsecured ☐ Subordinated $
☐ Secured ☐ Unsecured ☐ Subordinated $
☐ Secured ☐ Unsecured ☐ Subordinated $
☐ Secured ☐ Unsecured ☐ Subordinated $

d. Number of shares of preferred stock

e. Number of shares of common stock

Comments, if any:

3. Brief description of debtor's business:

4. List the names of any person who directly or indirectly owns, controls, or holds, with power to vote, 5% or more of the voting securites of debtor:

Figure 3-7. National LawForms Bankruptcy Case Software—Pages tab: Petitions link, Voluntary petition, Exhibit A

▶ Interests in real estate, such as land, and personal property, such as an automobile (Exhibit C); and

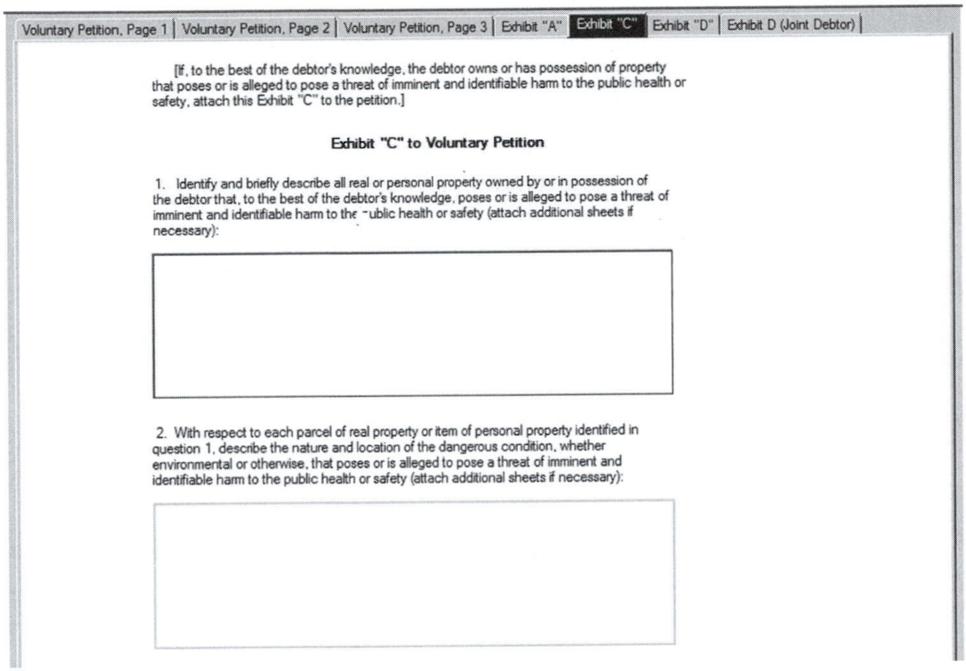

Figure 3-8. National LawForms Bankruptcy Case Software—Pages tab: Petitions link, Voluntary petition, Exhibit C

▶ A statement by the debtor/petitioner of meeting the educational requirements for filing for bankruptcy (Exhibit D), since federal law requires a debtor/petitioner to take classes on debt management before qualifying for a discharge in bankruptcy.

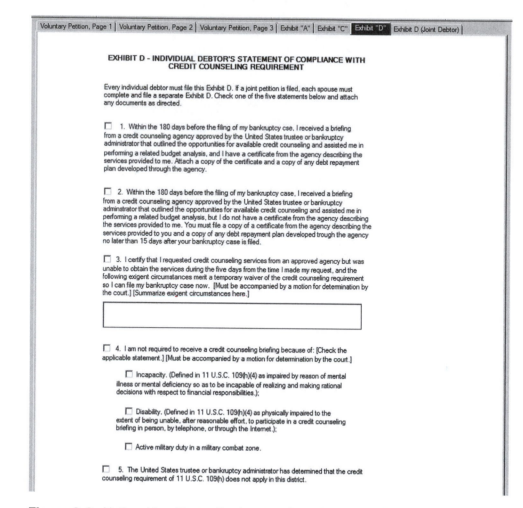

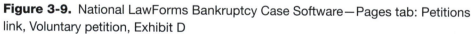

Figure 3-9. National LawForms Bankruptcy Case Software—Pages tab: Petitions link, Voluntary petition, Exhibit D

b. Schedules

In addition to the petition and its exhibits, the debtor/petitioner will need to file these as well, which identify:

▶ Property, such as land or automobiles (Schedules A and B);

▶ **Exempt** property (Schedule C), because federal law might exclude some assets, like a pension, from inclusion in the debtor/petitioner's estate; and

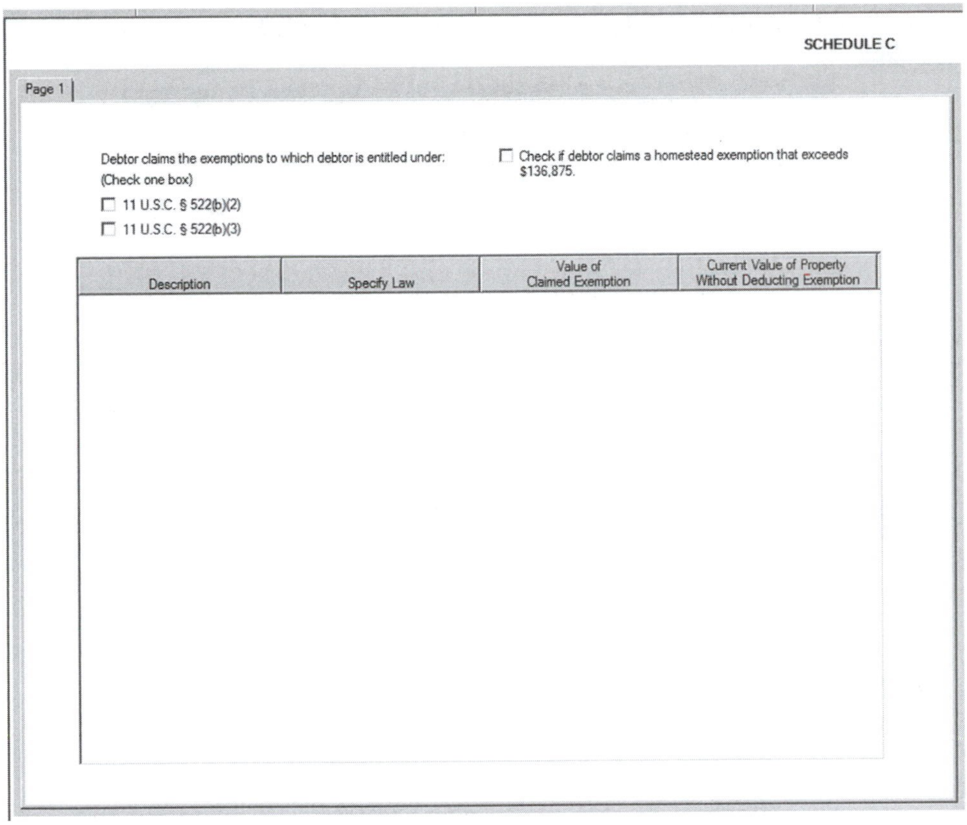

Figure 3-10. National LawForms Bankruptcy Case Software—Pages tab: Petitions link, Schedule C

▶ Debts, like **unsecured loans** (Schedule E), such as a personal loan, or **secured loans** (Schedule D), such as a car loan, where the lender will have the right to sell the car at auction if the debtor does not make a monthly payment, because secured loans may not be discharged in bankruptcy.

The debtor/petitioner also needs to list such essential information as:

▶ Sources of income (Schedule I) and expenditures (Schedule J);

▶ Co-debtors (Schedule H), like a spouse; and

▶ All uncompleted contracts, like an employment contract (Schedule G).

c. Statements

Completing these questions helps to get a better sense of the nature of assets, such as if they include income from employment.

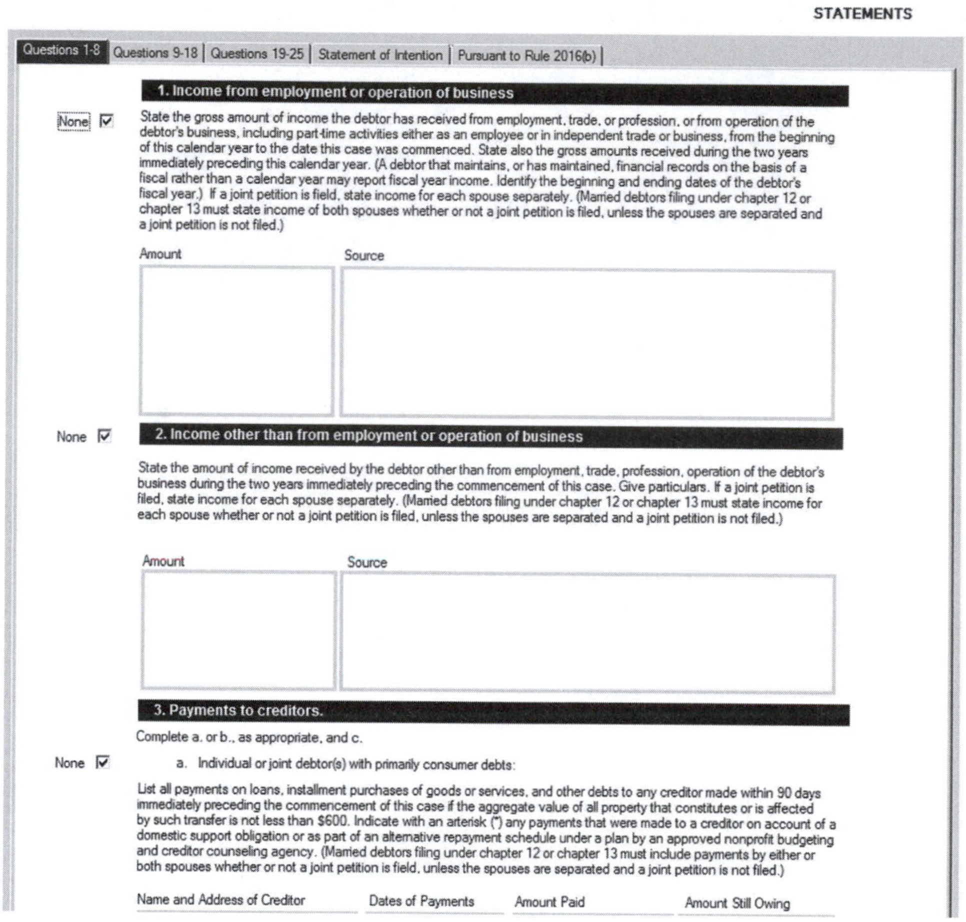

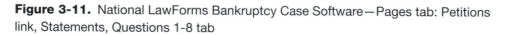

Figure 3-11. National LawForms Bankruptcy Case Software—Pages tab: Petitions link, Statements, Questions 1-8 tab

i. Means test

Only those debtor/petitioners with a certain amount of debt qualify for a discharge in bankruptcy. Using the information provided here, the trustee in bankruptcy can determine whether the petitioner has enough debt. This process of evaluation is called a means test. This test varies, depending upon whether the debtor/petitioner seeks:

▶ Liquidation (Chapter 7); or

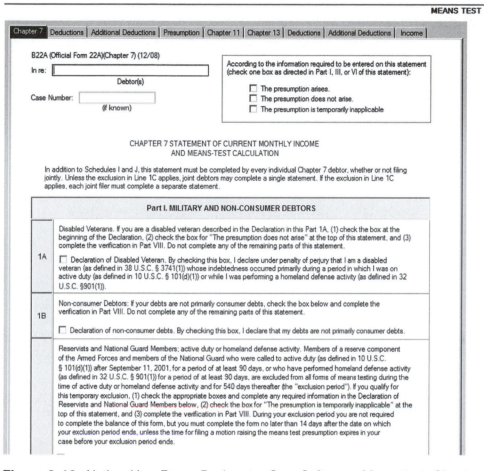

Figure 3-12. National LawForms Bankruptcy Case Software—Means test: Chapter 7 tab

▶ Reorganization, whether for a business (Chapter 11) or an individual (Chapter 13).

d. Creditor matrix

This listing contains information about creditors, such as:

▶ A mailing list of creditors, for example; and

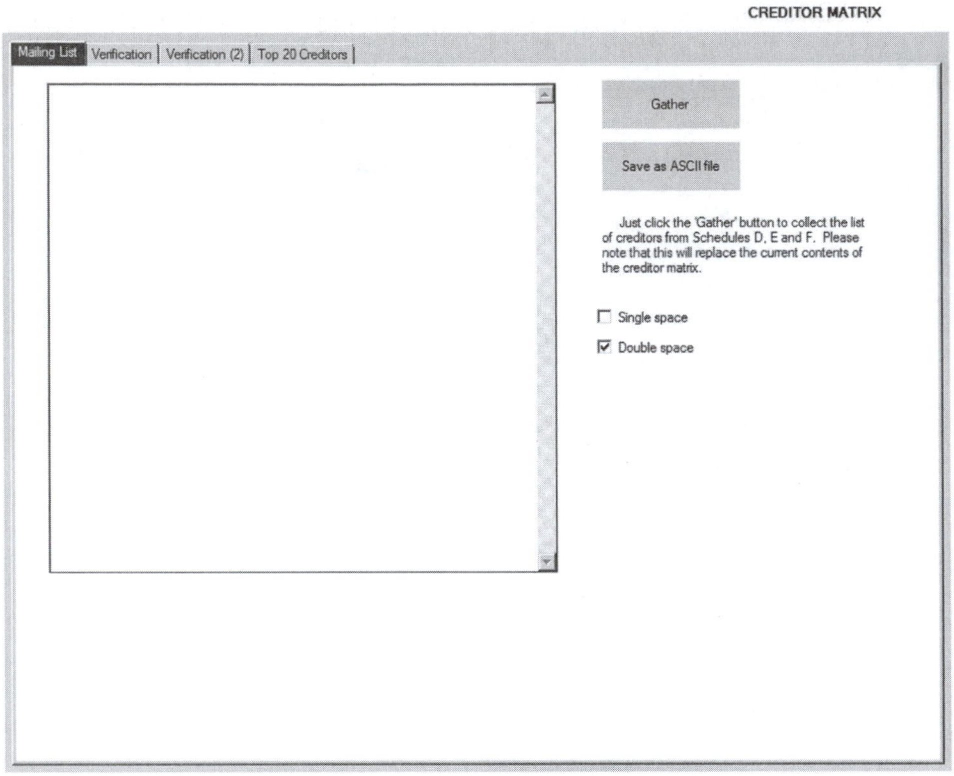

CREDITOR MATRIX

Figure 3-13. National LawForms Bankruptcy Case Software—Creditor Matrix test: Mailing list of creditors tabs

▶ A list of the top twenty unsecured creditors (often, those who have made personal loans to the debtor/petitioner).

e. Other helpful information

Other helpful information may include the fees charged for completing and filing the petition and the social security number(s) of all debtor/petitioners, as well as tax identification numbers for businesses.

Software for Managing a Corporation

What Is a Corporation?

Corporations are business entities created primarily under state law. Unlike with a partnership, the owners of the corporation are not personally liable for corporate debts. This means that if the business files for bankruptcy, individuals involved in the creation and/or management of the corporation will not personally lose their assets, and those people can try again. While they might fail a dozen times to create a thriving business, freeing those people from the debts of those failed businesses makes it possible for them to try again to create a successful business that leads to job creation and tax revenues.

While a corporation will have officers, such as a president and secretary/treasurer to start, it might subsequently sell stock publicly. Stockholders will then be able to elect directors, who then have the primary responsibility for corporate governance. The board of directors will hire the people who manage the corporation daily, such as a chief executive officer.

States require the filing of specific documents for the creation and operation of the corporation. Also, the federal government may require a corporation with publicly traded stock to file financial reports about the corporation's fiscal status.

Software

1. Type

The software used to illustrate what corporate compliance software can do is known as BizDoc. A trial version can be downloaded from https://www.businessentitysoftware.com/ BizDoc_setup.exe. A web version will be available in 2014. The publisher's webpage at https://businessentitysoftware.com/ includes tutorial movies. All images taken from this software are copyrighted by Instructional Software, Inc., and inclusion of such images in this text does not constitute any copyright interest or claim in them.

Another program that can perform some of the same functions is from www.nationallawfirms.com. Also, http://www.standardlegal.com/ Merchant2 / merchant.mvc?Screen=PROD&Product_Code=SLS511 offers forms related to incorporation. All states require documents, like articles of incorporation, resolutions, and meeting minutes. Any quality word processor can generate the documents needed to keep a business entity legally compliant.

2. Features

a. Tabs

Upon opening the software, familiar tab headings—File, Edit, Windows, Help, and Edit—appear in the top left corner of the screen.

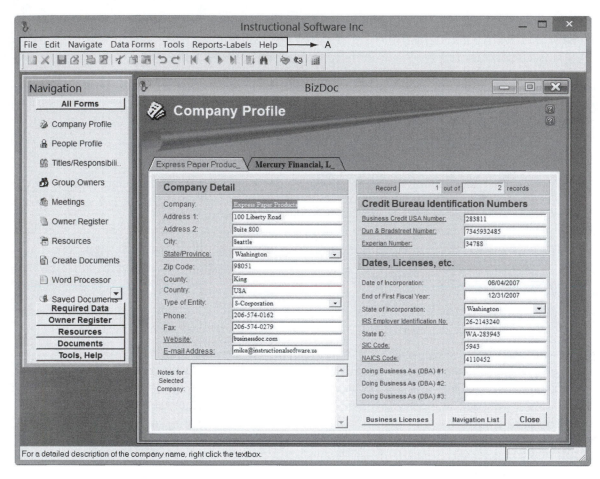

Figure 3-14a. BizDoc Software—Company Profile: tabs

b. Toolbar

A toolbar beneath the tabs contains buttons for performing many of the operations common to a Microsoft Office application, from file and save to indent and search.

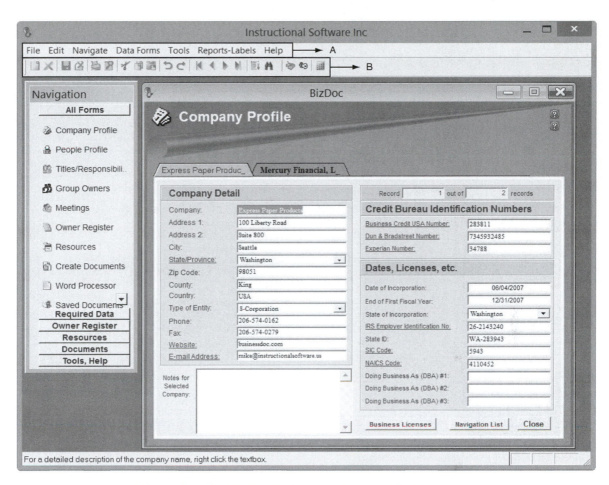

Figure 3-14b. BizDoc Software—Company Profile: toolbar

c. Sidebar menu

The sidebar menu, entitled Navigation, on the left of the screen provides access to topics related to the operation of a corporation, via tabs and links.

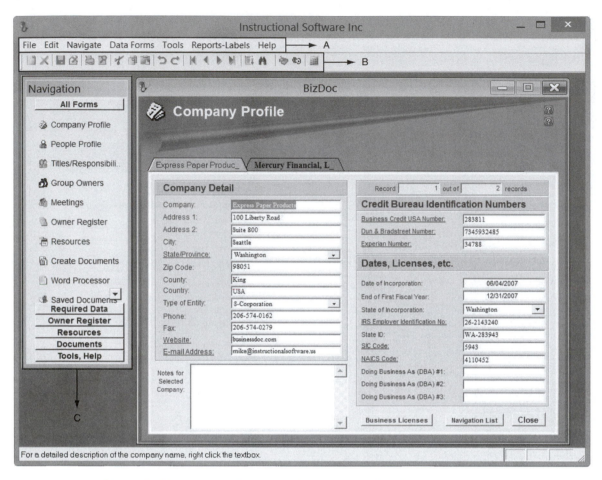

Figure 3-14c. BizDoc Software—Company Profile: Navigation toolbar

The first link under the Navigation toolbar on the left of the screen, Company Profile, provides the opportunity for recording information related to operating the corporation. For example, the Company Profile link opens to a screen for entering critical information, such as the nature of the corporation and credit bureau identification numbers.

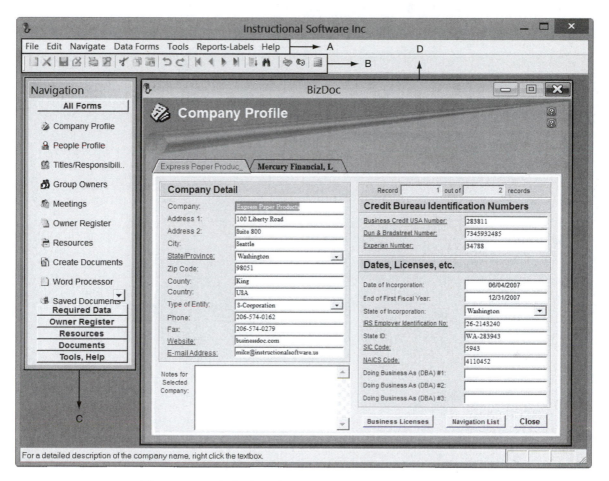

Figure 3-14d. BizDoc Software—Company Profile Form

The option exists to include additional information such as:

▶ The date and state of incorporation, as part of the Company Profile;

▶ The identity and responsibilities of corporate personnel;

▶ Who will serve as **Officers**, like president and secretary/treasurer, and as **Directors**; and

▶ Who serves as the corporation's attorneys, accountants and resident agent or agents.

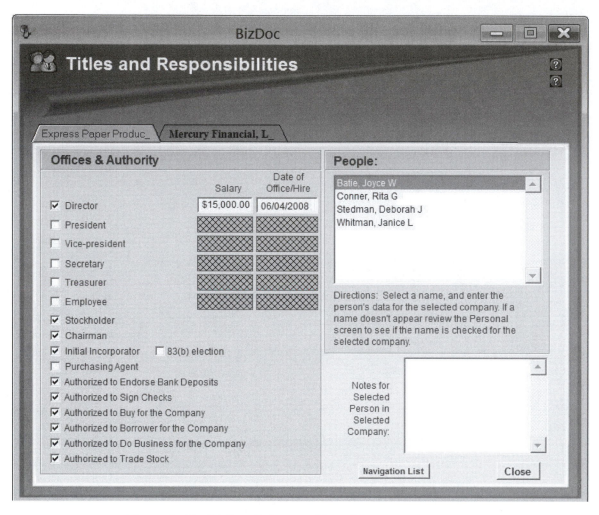

Figure 3-15. BizDoc Software—Titles/Responsibilities Form

The corporation needs to designate a **resident agent**, who will serve as the corporation's representative to state government when filing reports regarding corporate activity.

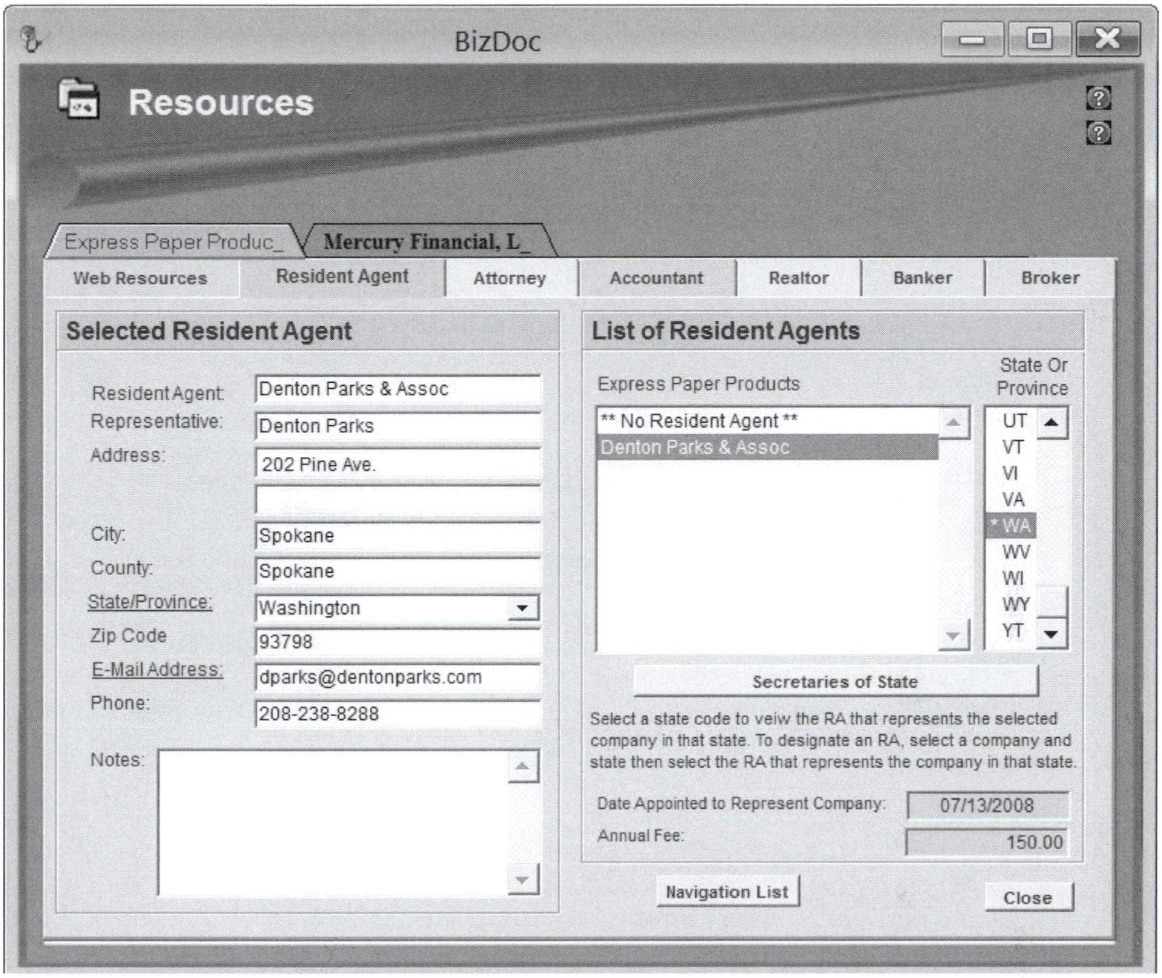

Figure 3-16. BizDoc Software—Company Profile: Data Forms submenu, Resources link, Resident Agent

Essential Corporate Documents

State law will require that a corporation provide a range of documents.

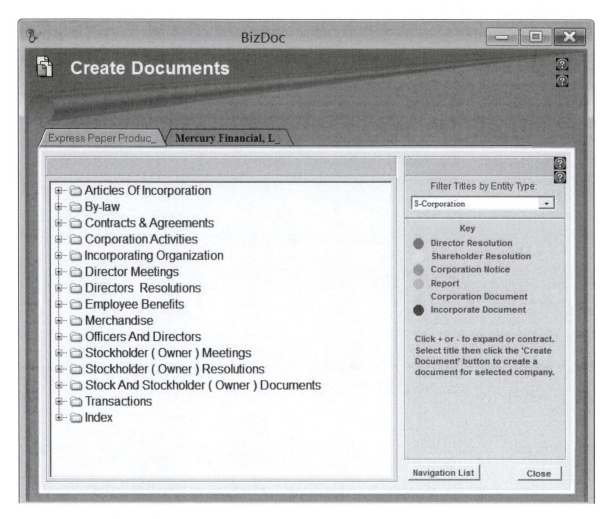

Figure 3-17. BizDoc Software—Create Documents for Corporations

These include **Articles of Incorporation,** to start the corporation, which need to:

▶ Describe the purpose of the corporation;

▶ Identify the role officers will play;

▶ Address issues regarding directors, such as:

    ▷ Their scope of authority for setting corporate policy; and
    ▷ Their appointment or resignation, compensation, and benefits, such as stock options.

▶ Issue stock, which represents an ownership interest in the corporation, and stock options, where someone can buy stock at a fixed price by a specific date (often used to reward managers and workers, in addition to employment compensation);

▶ Establish what happens at stockholder meetings, such as:

▷ Voting for who will serve on the Board of Directors;
▷ Passing **resolutions;**
▷ Scheduling different types of meetings; and
▷ Dealing with procedural concerns, such as issuing notices, waivers, and **proxies,** which contain authorization granted by the stockholder to someone to cast the stockholder's vote.

▶ Indicate what happens at director meetings, such as:

▷ Hiring personnel, such as a corporate executive officer;
▷ Passing resolutions, such as whether the corporation should issue stock for public purchase;
▷ Scheduling different types of meetings; and
▷ Recording what happens and making those **meeting minutes** available.

▶ Enact and modify **bylaws,** which involve the daily operation of the corporation;

▶ Change the type of the business from a traditional corporation into a **limited liability** or **Subchapter S** corporation, so as to gain certain tax advantages;

▶ Pay out money, or **dividends,** on each share; and

▶ Keep track of the certificates representing the shares, via a **stock register,** of the type and number issued and the shares traded.

For example, upon notice of a new stock transaction, the software can generate an updated stock register to reflect the certificate owner, date of transaction, identity of new owner, number of shares, who previously owned the stock, and the amount paid, among other information. This creates an audit trail, from initial offering of stock to who currently owns shares.

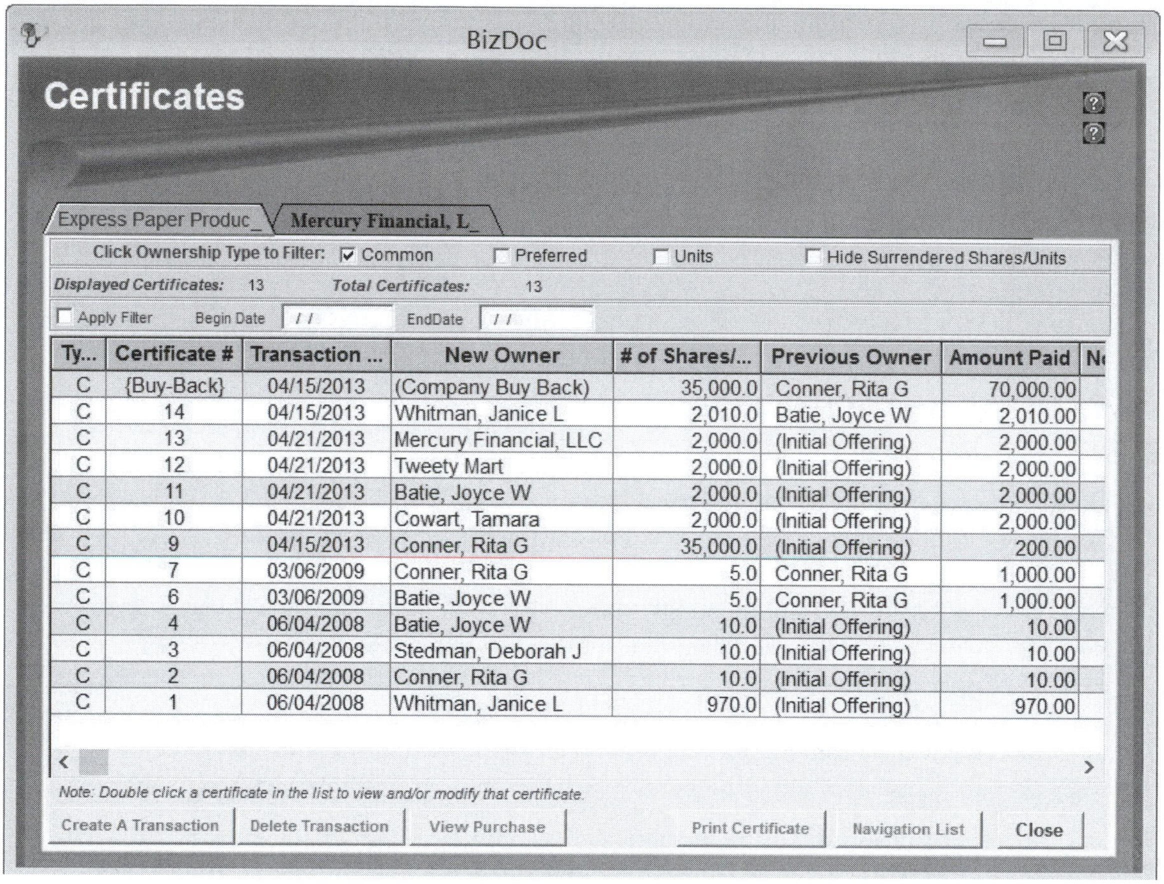

Ty...	Certificate #	Transaction ...	New Owner	# of Shares/...	Previous Owner	Amount Paid	N
C	{Buy-Back}	04/15/2013	(Company Buy Back)	35,000.0	Conner, Rita G	70,000.00	
C	14	04/15/2013	Whitman, Janice L	2,010.0	Batie, Joyce W	2,010.00	
C	13	04/21/2013	Mercury Financial, LLC	2,000.0	(Initial Offering)	2,000.00	
C	12	04/21/2013	Tweety Mart	2,000.0	(Initial Offering)	2,000.00	
C	11	04/21/2013	Batie, Joyce W	2,000.0	(Initial Offering)	2,000.00	
C	10	04/21/2013	Cowart, Tamara	2,000.0	(Initial Offering)	2,000.00	
C	9	04/15/2013	Conner, Rita G	35,000.0	(Initial Offering)	200.00	
C	7	03/06/2009	Conner, Rita G	5.0	Conner, Rita G	1,000.00	
C	6	03/06/2009	Batie, Joyce W	5.0	Conner, Rita G	1,000.00	
C	4	06/04/2008	Batie, Joyce W	10.0	(Initial Offering)	10.00	
C	3	06/04/2008	Stedman, Deborah J	10.0	(Initial Offering)	10.00	
C	2	06/04/2008	Conner, Rita G	10.0	(Initial Offering)	10.00	
C	1	06/04/2008	Whitman, Janice L	970.0	(Initial Offering)	970.00	

Figure 3-18. BizDocs Software—Certificates Form

- Additional important documents that this particular software generates relate to:
- Assignments, which involve a transfer of rights in something that the corporation owns or possesses;
- Ownership of real estate and/or **leases;**
- **Contracts,** which are legally binding agreements, such as for the purchase of land;
- Inventories, receipts, and bills of sale, when needed;
- Credit and notes, which relate to a corporation's economic resources;

▶ Employee records, regarding hiring, firing, training, compensation and benefits, like pensions; and

▶ An index for all documents generated with this software.

For example, a client might prefer to incorporate as a limited liability corporation (LLC), which offers certain tax advantages. The software can generate about 350 documents related to the creation and operation of this type of corporation, such as an easily edited proof copy.

Divorce—Financials

Introduction

A critical issue with the dissolution of a marriage involves the division of assets held by the couple. Beyond a simple division of property, another issue upon dissolution of a marriage involves making regular disbursements, such as **alimony** or **child support.**

Software

1. Type

The software used here comes from EasySoft, LLC, http://www.easysoft-usa. com/divorce-settlement-software.html, which also makes software for real estate closings, as seen in the next section. All documents generated through the use of this software will end with the suffix .cis.

According to EasySoft, the forms generated here meet the requirements of the law in all states.

All images taken from this software are copyrighted by the creator of such images and inclusion of such images in this text does not constitute any copyright interest or claim in them. Other sources for forms related to a divorce include http:// www.familylawsoftware.com/ and http://divorce-forms.com/, among others.

2. Features

Information recorded here can make up part of an annual income tax filing, since a change in marital status will have an impact on each of the couple's annually filed federal tax returns.

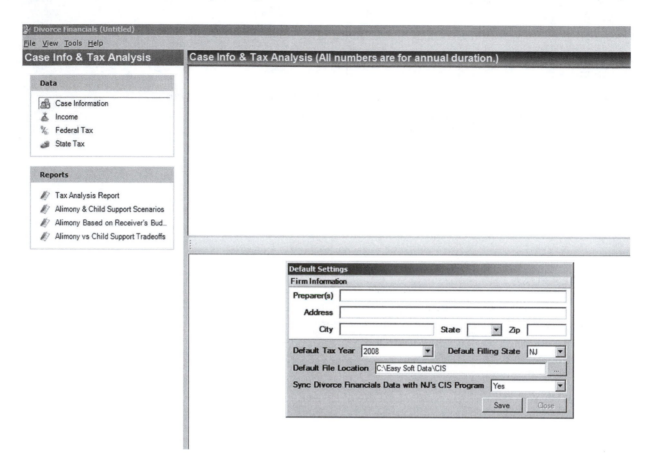

Figure 3-19. Divorce—Financials software: Case Info and Tax Analysis screen

a. Tabs

Familiar tabs appear across the top: File, View (providing quick access to critical documents, such as Tax Info Case Analysis), Tools, and Help (including a PDF-formatted help manual).

b. Menu

A sidebar menu allows for the recording of data and the generation of reports.

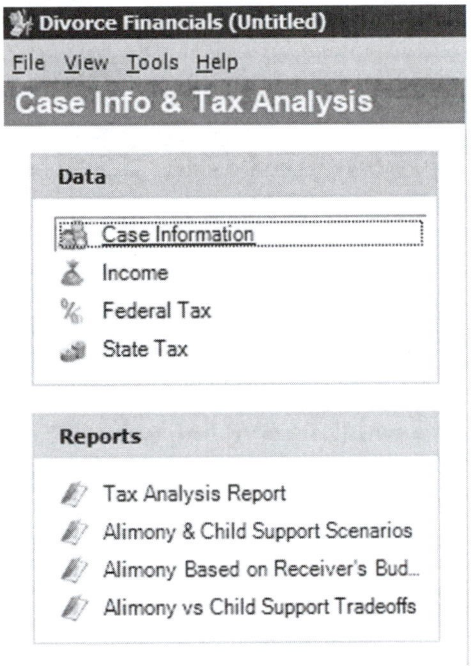

Figure 3-20. Divorce—Financials software: Sidebar menu

Critical Information

1. Case Information

Information about the divorce case, which will appear on documents generated by the software includes the:

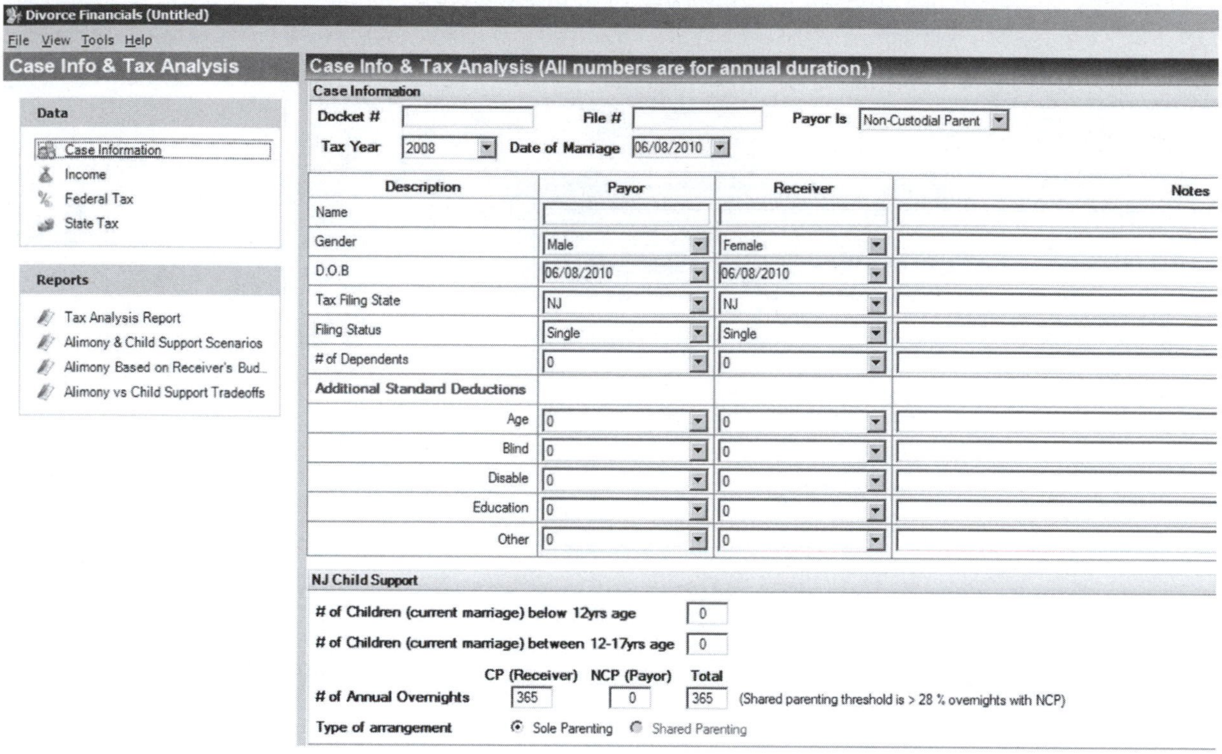

Figure 3-21. Divorce—Financials software: Sidebar menu, Data subsection, Case information link

▶ **Docket number** for the case; and

▶ **Payor** and recipients of funds periodically distributed, like alimony.

Toward the bottom, this software prompts the user for information that a state, which in this example is New Jersey, needs for purpose of identifying relevant custody laws.

2. Assets and Liabilities

a. Income

Identifying sources of income can make it easier to determine who should pay, and receive, monthly payments such as alimony and child support.

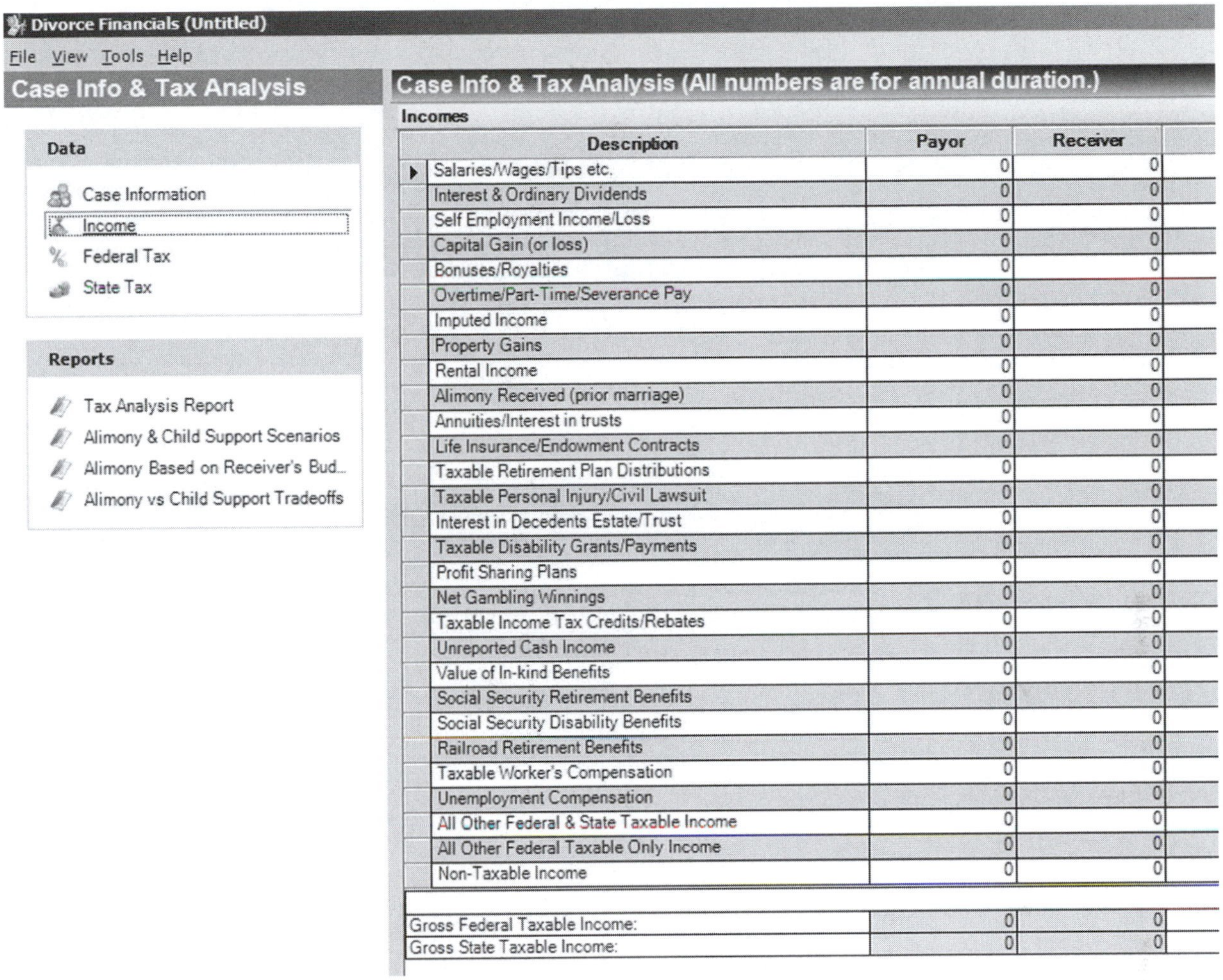

Figure 3-22. Divorce—Financials software: Sidebar menu, Data subsection, Income link

b. Additional assets and liabilities

Clicking a button makes it possible to identify and list such assets as:

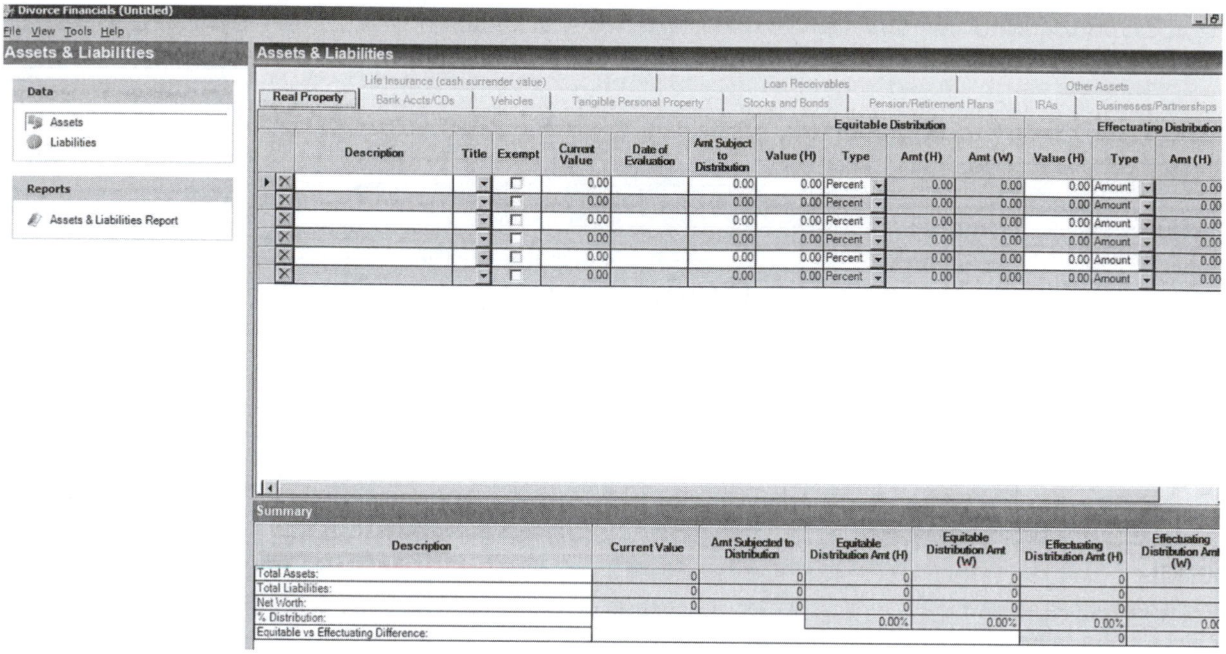

Figure 3-23. Divorce—Financials software: Sidebar menu, Assets and Liabilities link

- ▶ Bank accounts and certificates of deposit;

- ▶ Vehicles;

- ▶ Tangible personal property, such as jewelry;

- ▶ Stocks and bonds;

- ▶ Pensions, including the current value of the pension, as well as of expected pension payments;

- ▶ IRAs (individual retirement accounts);

- ▶ An interest in a business, such as a **partnership;**

- ▶ Life insurance policies, at current cash surrender values (the amount that the policyholder would receive upon immediately ending the insurance policy);

- ▶ The present value of any interest in land (like a lease);

- ▶ Loan receivables (payments owed from a loan);

- ▶ An inheritance; and

- ▶ Other assets which were not otherwise identified in the previous tabs.

  These documents should also account for:

- ▶ Alimony recapture, where an ex-spouse remarries and would no longer need alimony;

▶ The present value of alimony payments, including the amount needed to cover all projected alimony payments; and

▶ An alimony buyout amount which, if paid, would discharge all alimony obligations.

The software will also generate a summary regarding liabilities, such as a mortgage on a house, for the total value of all assets.

Summary						
Description	Current Value	Amt Subjected to Distribution	Equitable Distribution Amt (H)	Equitable Distribution Amt (W)	Effectuating Distribution Amt (H)	Effectuating Distribution Amt (W)
Total Assets:	0	0	0	0	0	
Total Liabilities:	0	0	0	0	0	
Net Worth:	0	0	0	0	0	
% Distribution:			0.00%	0.00%	0.00%	0.00
Equitable vs Effectuating Difference:					0	

Figure 3-24. Divorce—Financials software: Sidebar menu, Assets and Liabilities link, Summary box

3. Tax Information

Having income data may make it easy to determine the taxable income for annual tax filings, especially in light of monthly transfer payments like alimony and child support.

a. Federal

In addition to income, the federal government will want tax information about:

▶ **Adjustments,** which reflect a transfer of funds, like payments into a pension account;

▶ **Personal exemptions,** such as the standard tax deduction, which changes annually;

▶ **Itemized deductions,** where listing deductions could produce a number greater than the standardized tax deduction;

▶ **Tax credits,** like the earned income tax credit; and

▶ The **Alternative Minimum Tax,** a minimum tax owed, regardless of credits and deductions.

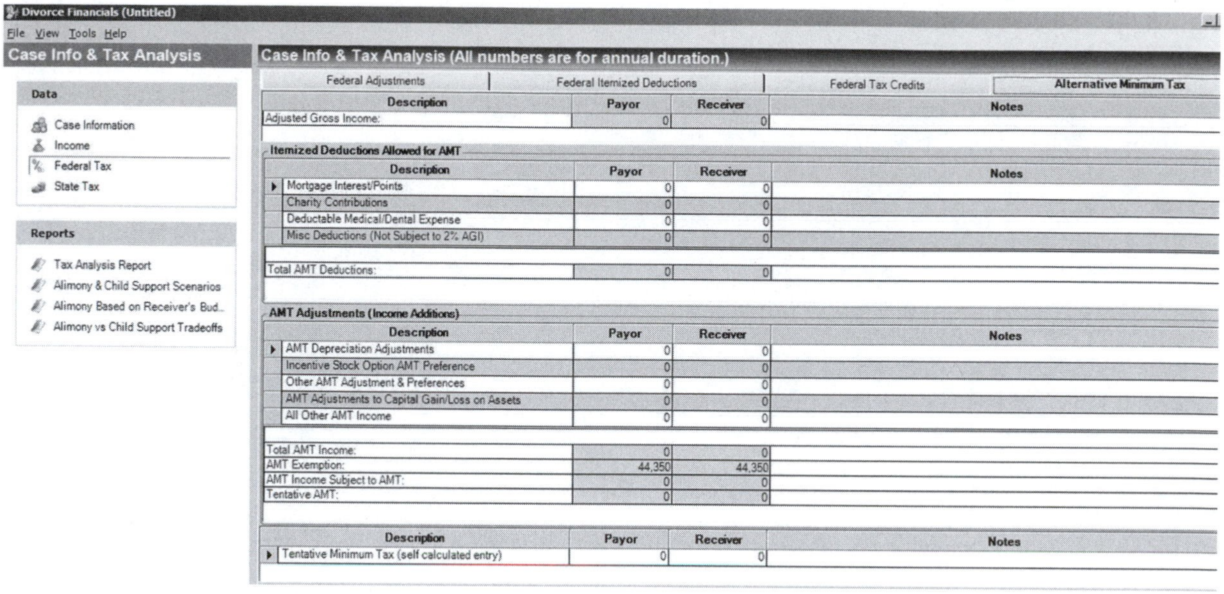

Figure 3-25. Divorce—Financials software: Sidebar menu, Data subsection, Federal Tax link

b. State

State tax law generally offers different kinds of credits and deductions than those allowed under federal tax law.

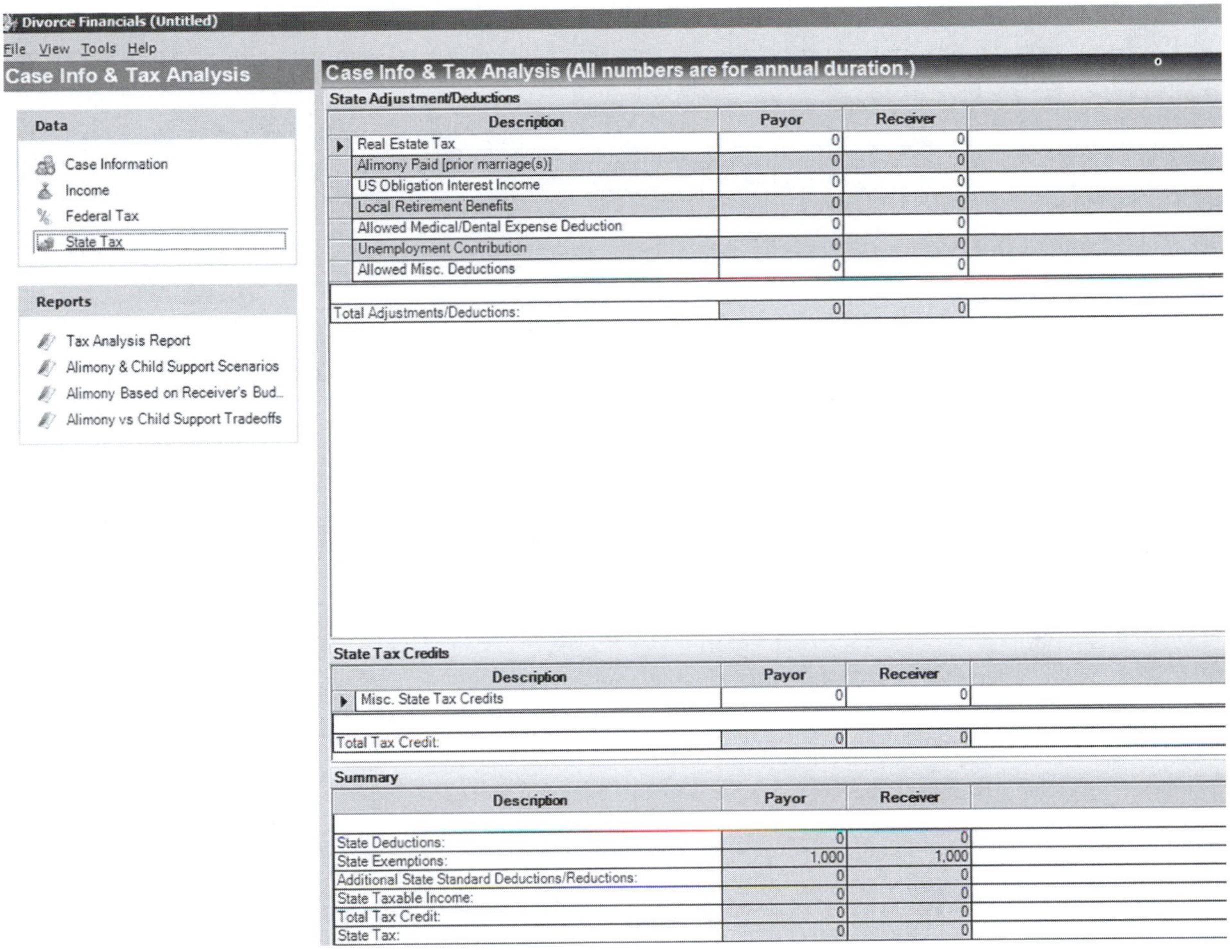

Figure 3-26. Divorce—Financials software: Sidebar menu, Data subsection, State Tax link

c. Reports

The software can generate reports or charts about the tax consequences for a proposed divorce financial settlement. These can quickly change under different scenarios involving alimony and child support payments, taking into account:

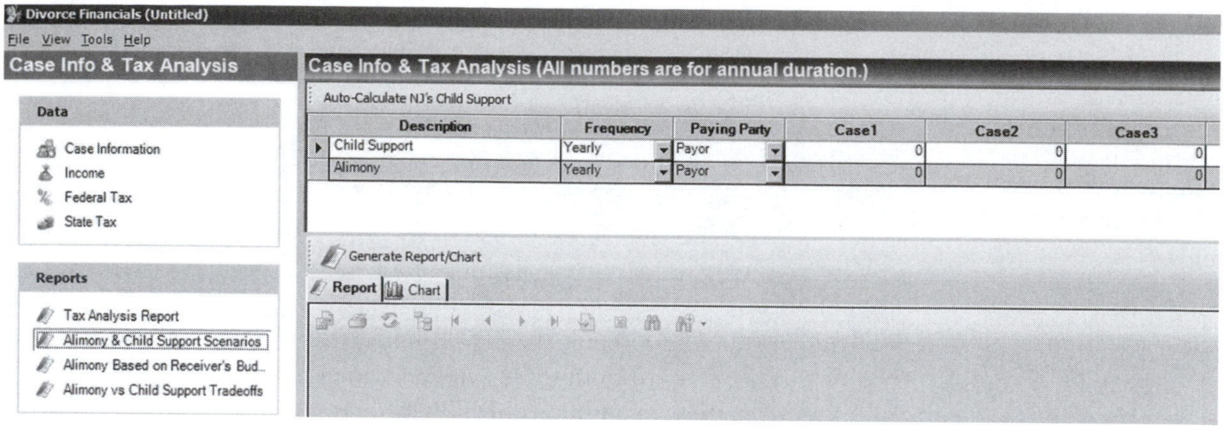

Figure 3-27. Divorce—Financials software: Sidebar menu: Reports subsection, Alimony and Child Support Scenarios link

▶ Educational expenses for offspring of the marriage;

▶ Changes in the expenses of the recipient of any support payments; and

▶ Consequences from altering child support or alimony payments.

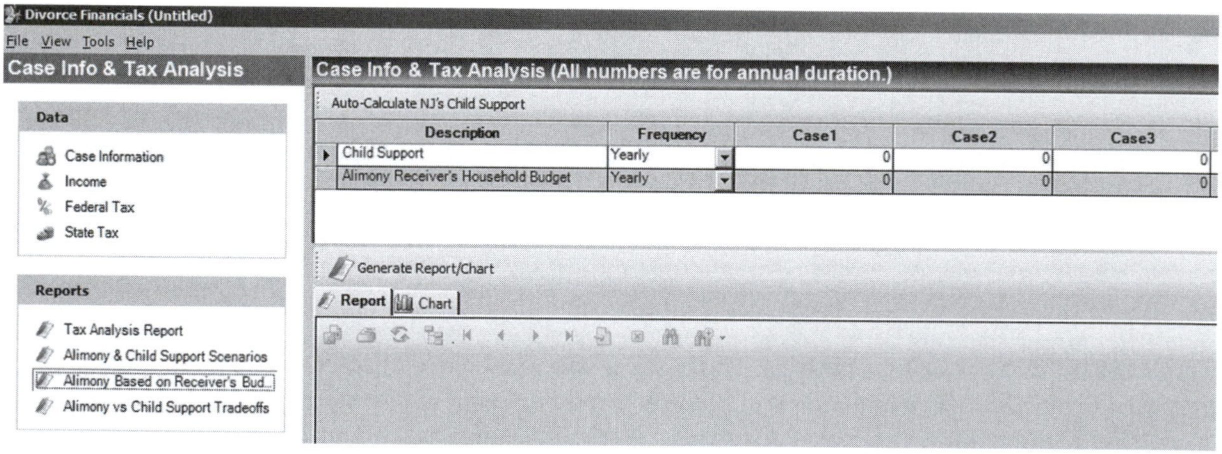

Figure 3-28. Divorce—Financials software: Sidebar menu: Reports subsection, Alimony versus Child Support Tradeoffs

Real Estate

Real Estate Concepts

1. Overview

Because a significant part of the American dream involves home ownership, buying a house can be the most significant legal transaction for a client. After considering some basic real estate concepts, the discussion will shift to the proper completion of that critical financial document, the **HUD-1.**

2. Property

Real property, commonly called **real estate,** involves land and everything permanently attached to it, like a home. Personal property is everything else.

a. Ownership and possession

An **owner** has an unqualified right to use the land. This includes entering into a lease with a **tenant,** who could then use the land. This renter's rights in the land are limited only by the owner's superior rights.

b. Deeds and title searches

A **deed** represents ownership in land. It is also called a **title.** It will:

▶ Include a detailed description of the property;

▶ Identify the previous owner;

▶ State when that owner obtained the property; and

▶ Describe where to find a copy of the deed at the **registry of deeds,** typically a county building that has copies of all deeds for property in that county.

Checking that the seller actually owns the property involves researching the history of the land's ownership. This process, a **title search,** means reviewing prior deeds for a property to see that when a transfer of the land occurred, on the date of the transfer, the buyer received all of the rights that the seller promised to provide.

c. Mortgages

i. Definition

Most people need to borrow money to purchase land. A borrower will pay back the loan over time, with interest, and will provide the lender with a mortgage. The mortgage gives the lender the authority to seize and sell the property at auction if the borrower fails to make the monthly loan payment.

ii. Second mortgage

Another reason for doing a title search arises if the owner needs to take out an additional loan on the property. Anyone lending money will want a mortgage and will want to know whether the borrower has already granted a mortgage. If the owner fails to make a monthly loan payment, forcing the sale of the property at auction, the second lender, who has received a second mortgage, will be repaid only after the first lender has received a full repayment of its loan. Because the price paid at auction to the first lender may not leave much, if any, money to pay off the second loan, second lenders usually charge higher interest rates on their loans to reflect the higher risk of not getting paid.

iii. Liens

A mortgage is a specialized type of **lien.** Someone files a lien on property to collect payment on a debt so that upon a sale of the property, the lienholder will then have the right to collect on the debt out of the moneys transferred during the sale. A carpenter could file a lien on a property to guarantee payment for services rendered, such as making and installing kitchen cabinets. Governments could file liens for nonpayment of taxes.

d. Closing

i. Definition

The actual handing over of the deed to the buyer, the **closing,** may take place anywhere. A buyer might want this to happen at the registry of deeds, so that the new owner can immediately record the transfer and reduce the risk that a seller might fraudulently try to sell the land twice.

ii. Closing documents

To make it easier to buy and sell a home, the federal government requires that those borrowing money for such a purchase complete a standardized form, the HUD-1.

Software

1. Easy HUD Real Estate Software

Software for completing the HUD-1 can reduce the likelihood of mistakes while speeding up the completion of the form. The HUD-1 form is available at the following website: http://portal.hud.gov/hudportal/documents/huddoc?id=1.pdf.

The copyrighted software used here to show how the software works to generate the HUD-1 and all necessary supporting documents, the Easy HUD v.4.0.02, is available through EasySoft LLC at http://www.easysoft-usa.com/hud-software.

html. A partial list of other providers of real estate closing software includes www.nationallawforms.com and http://www.lawfirmsoftware.com/software/closing.htm. Other closing software might ask for information in a different sequence and use different types of graphics, but they all must generate a properly formatted HUD-1.

All images taken from this software are copyrighted by the creator of the software used to generate such images. Inclusion of such images in this text does not constitute any claim of copyright in them.

2. Features

a. Tabs: top row

i. Familiar headings

This software uses the system of tabs and toolbars common to many Microsoft products, such as File, for document management, and View, for access to the HUD-1 Form.

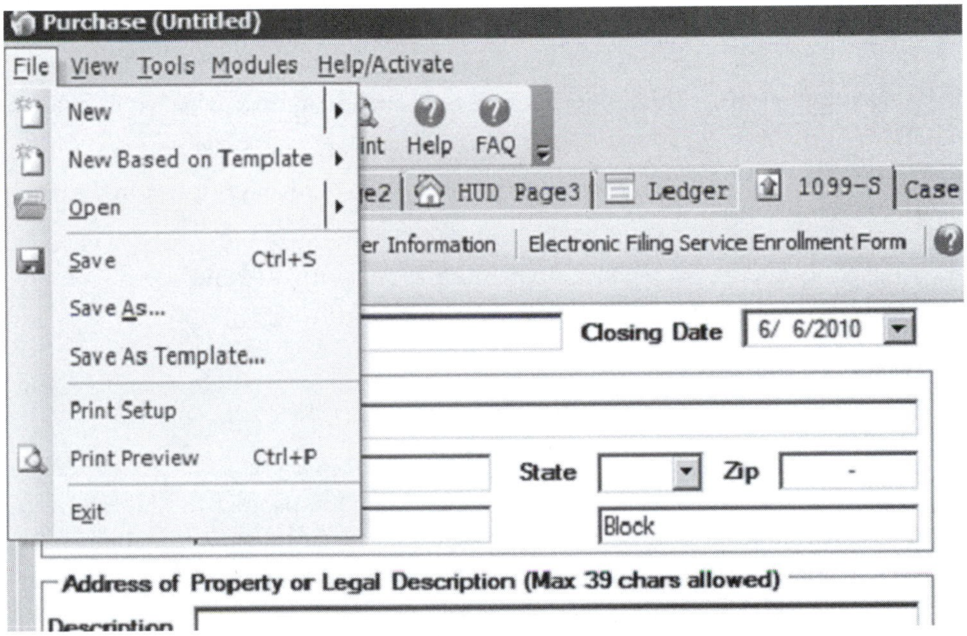

Figure 3-29. HUD-1 software—File tab and submenu

ii. Tools tab

This software can:

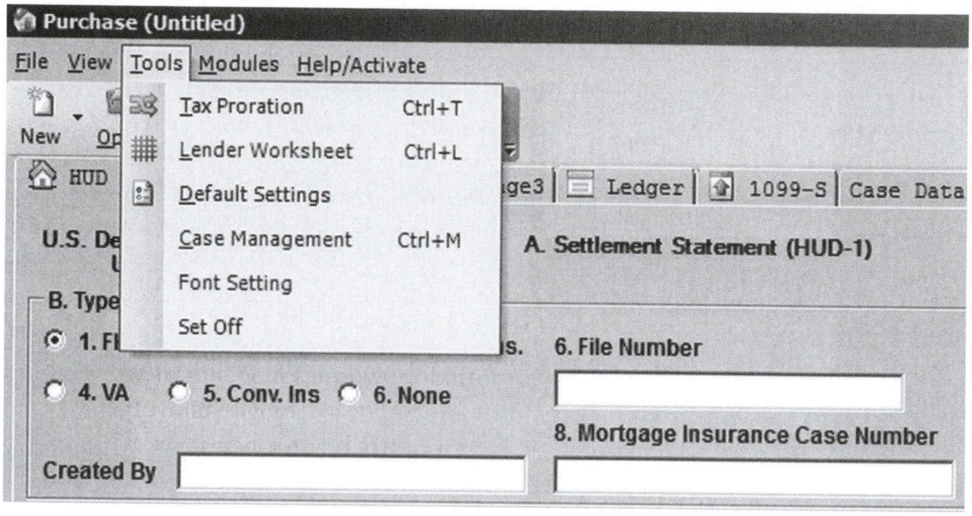

Figure 3-30. HUD-1 software—Tools tab and submenu

▶ Calculate the **tax proration:** all taxes, like city, county, or school, due at the time of the sale;

▶ Generate a lender worksheet with important information, like the identity of all parties to this sale;

▶ Set default settings, like identifying a **settlement agent,** who would coordinate the closing;

▶ Determine set-offs: those expenses related to the closing but not included in the HUD-1; and

▶ Engage in document management, such as making available the documents associated with the closing.

b. Tabs: bottom row

i. HUD-1 pages

This software presents screens that correspond to each page of the HUD-1. The HUD-1 uses a double-column approach to present that information about buyer and seller in parallel to one another. For example, payment of the buyer's deposit to create the contract to purchase the home will show up as an expense in the buyer's column and a gain in the seller's column, as seen in Figure 3-34.

ii. HUD page 1 tab

Critical information about the sale includes:

▶ Whether the federal government provided the loan via an agency, such as the Fair Housing Administration (FHA);

▶ The location of the property;

▶ A proposed closing date;

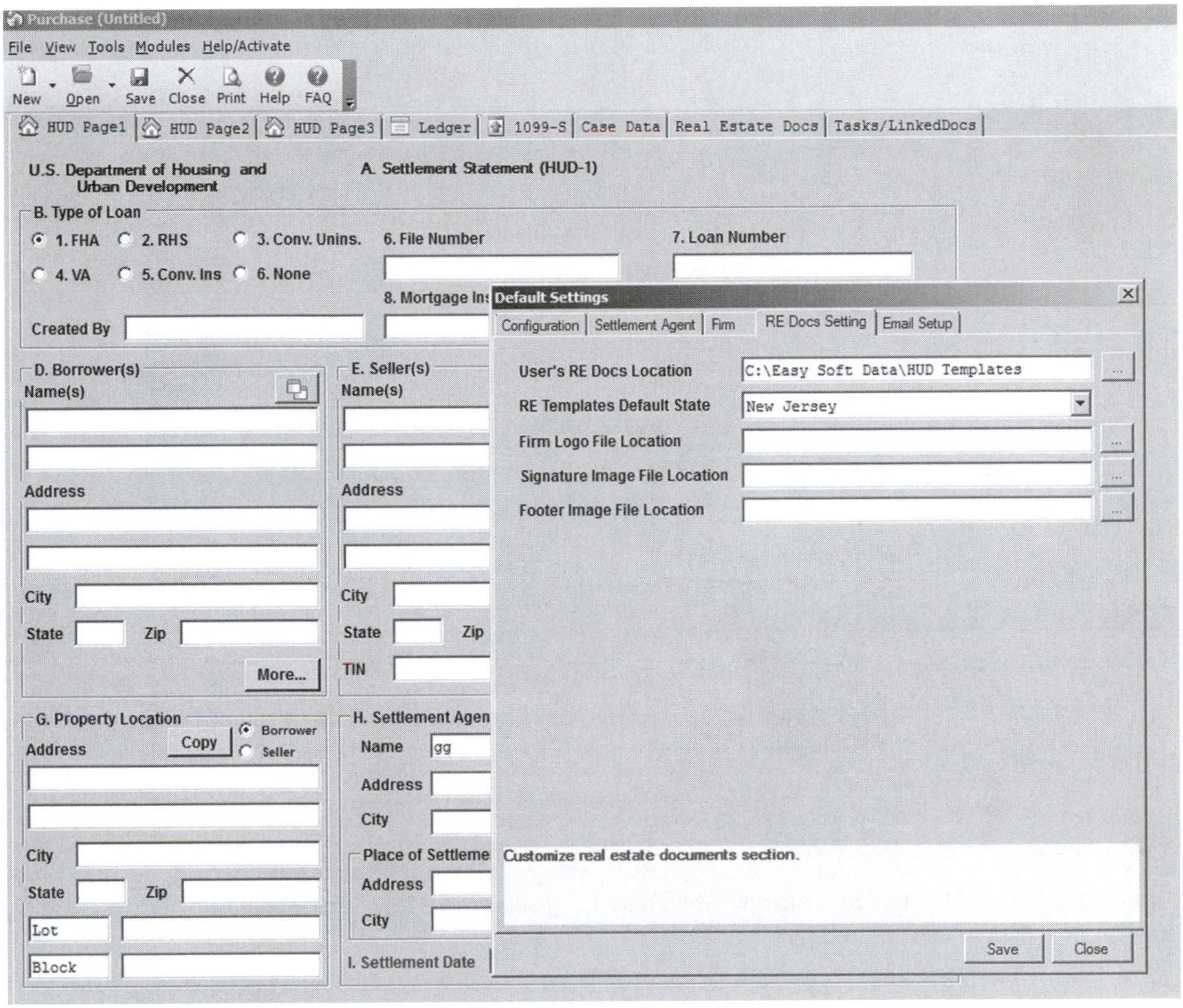

Figure 3-31. HUD-1 software—Toolbar: New Button and submenu, HUD Page 1 tab

▶ A summary of transactions, such as:

  ▷ What the buyer will pay;

  ▷ The price of the property; and

  ▷ Adjustments, like taxes and other assessments, that the seller will pay in advance.

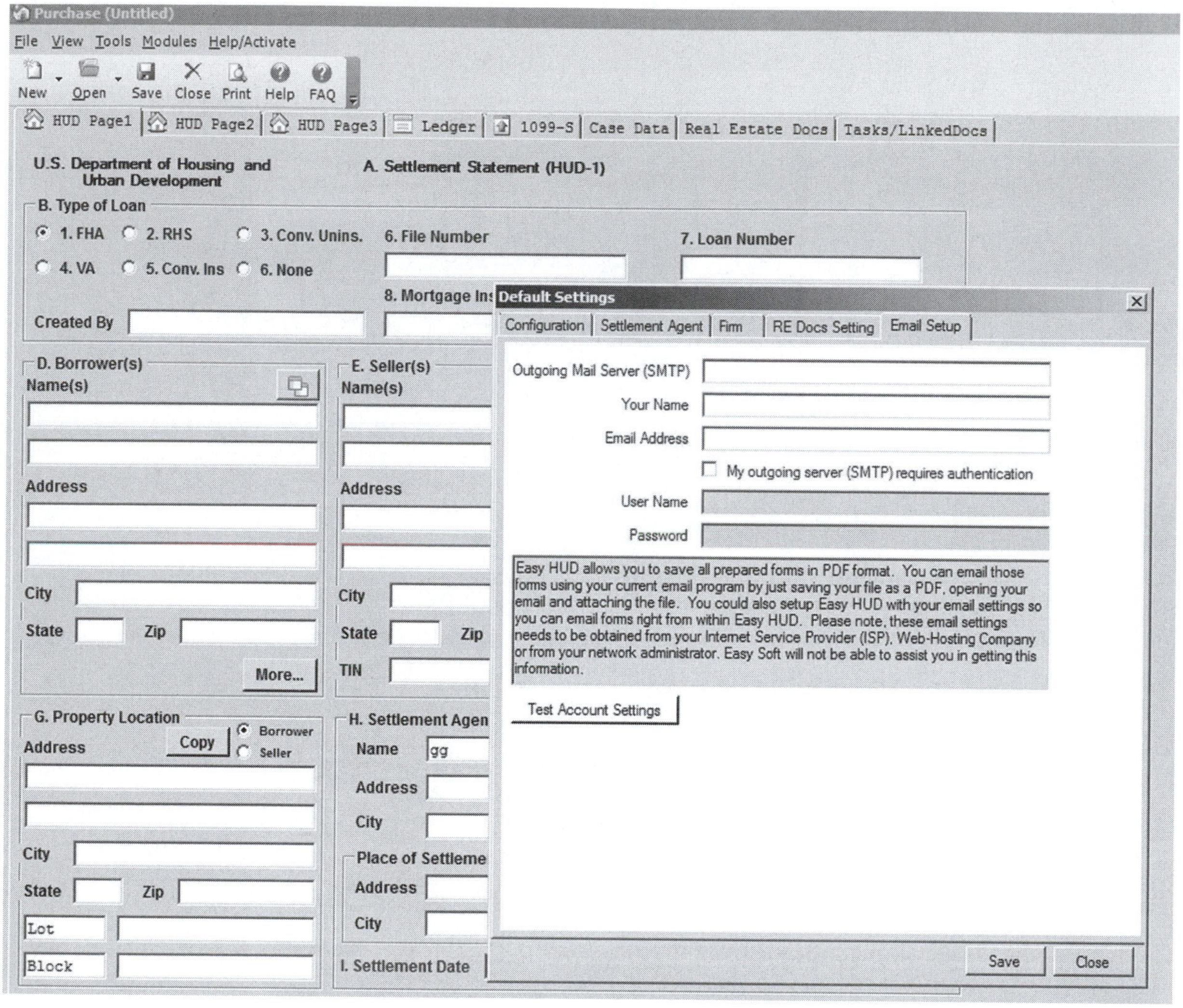

Figure 3-32. HUD-1 software—Toolbar: New Button and submenu, HUD Page 1 tab, Summary of Transactions [Lines 100–120 and Lines 400–420]

▶ Amounts paid by the borrower, including the deposit and the size of the loan;

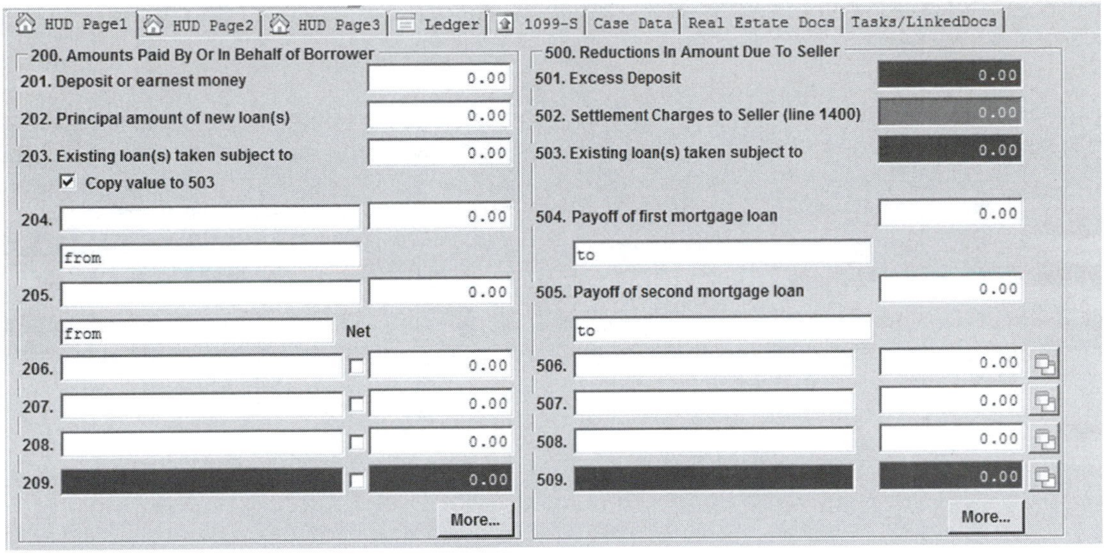

Figure 3-33. HUD-1 software—Toolbar: New Button and submenu, HUD Page 1 tab, Summary of Transactions [Lines 200–209 and Lines 500–509]

[Note: The More buttons, available at the end of each column, make it possible to add information about existing loans on the property.]

▶ Adjustments for items unpaid by the seller, such as outstanding property taxes; and

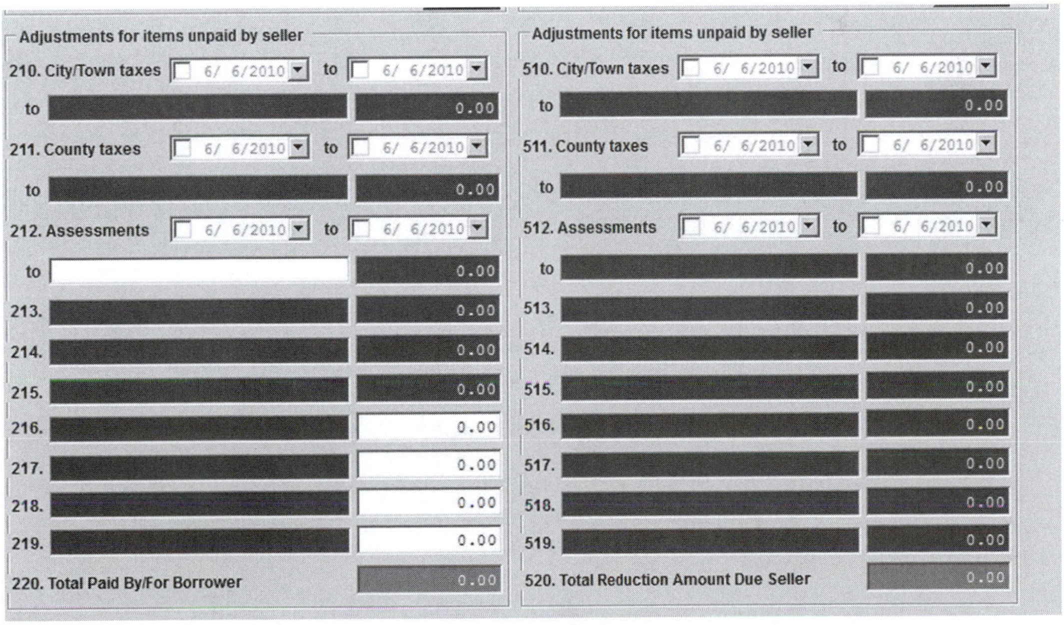

Figure 3-34. HUD-1 software—Toolbar: New Button and submenu, HUD Page 1 tab, Adjustments for Items Unpaid by Seller [Lines 210–220 and Lines 510–520]

▶ Cash settlements, of what the borrower will pay and the seller will receive.

300. Cash At Settlement From/To Borrower		600. Cash At Settlement To/From Seller	
301. Gross amount due from borr. (line 120)	0.00	601. Gross amount due to seller (line 420)	0.00
302. Less amount paid by/for borr. (line 220)	0.00	602. Less amount due to seller (line 520)	0.00
303. Cash From Borrower	0.00	603. Cash To Seller	0.00

Figure 3-35. HUD-1 software—Toolbar: New Button and submenu, HUD Page 1 tab, Cash at Settlement From/To Borrower [Lines 300–303] and Cash at Settlement To/From Seller [Lines 600–603]

iii. HUD page 2 tab

Critical information includes:

▶ Fees paid to buyer and/or seller's **brokers** and how to apportion them, especially when multiple brokers worked on making the sale;

HUD Page1	HUD Page2	HUD Page3	Ledger	1099-S	Case Data	Real Estate Docs	Tasks/LinkedDocs

L. Settlement Charges

700. Total Real Estate Broker Fees

Price $ 0.00   0.000 % = 0.00 ☑ Calculate

Division of Commission (line 700) as follows: (701 % 100.00)

		Net	Paid From Borrower's Funds At Settlement	Paid From Seller's Funds At Settlement
701. $ 0.00 to		☐		
702. $ 0.00 to		☐		
703. Commission paid at settlement to			0.00	0.00
704.	to	☐	0.00	0.00

Figure 3-36. HUD-1 software—Toolbar: New Button and submenu, HUD Page 2 tab, Total Real Estate Broker Fees [Lines 700–704]

▶ Fees related to getting the loan, to:

▷ Secure it, called an origination charge;

▷ Evaluate the property's value objectively, via an appraisal;

▷ Obtain current credit reports, so that the lender knows about the buyer's financial history;

▷ Pay for tax service charges; and

▷ Obtain flood certification, if the property has a known risk of flooding.

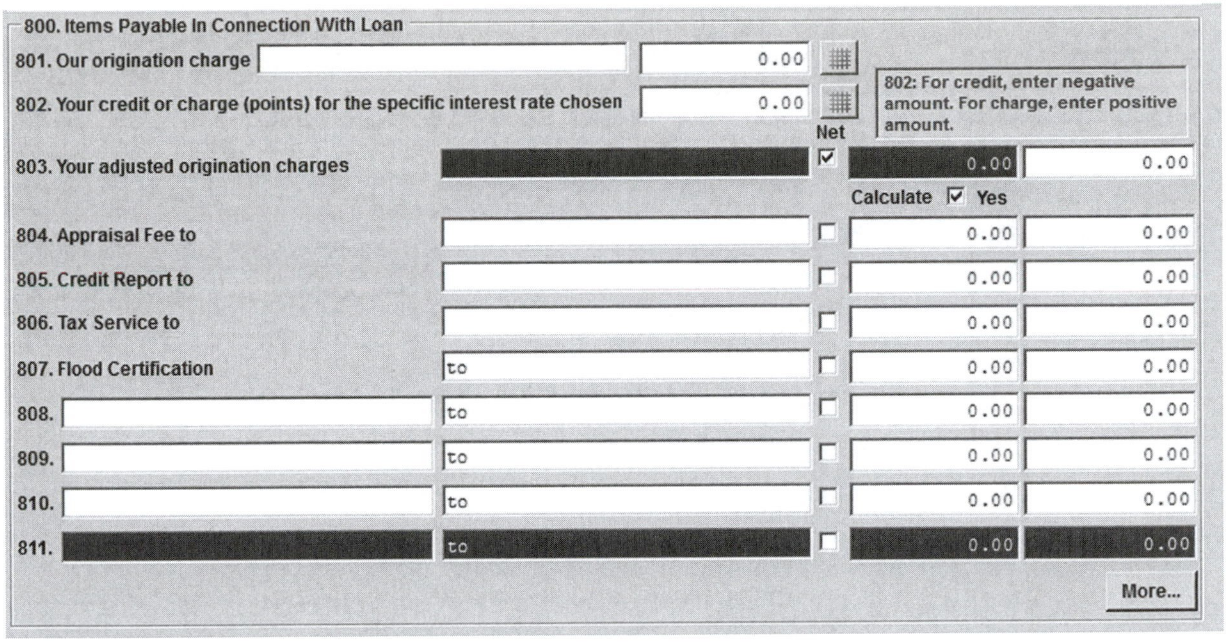

Figure 3-37. HUD-1 software—Toolbar: New Button and submenu, HUD Page 2 tab, Items Payable in Connection with Loan [Lines 800–810]

▶ Items that the lender wants paid in advance, such as:

▷ Interest;

▷ A premium for mortgage insurance, which would pay off the loan if a title dispute subsequently arose; and

▷ A premium for homeowner's insurance.

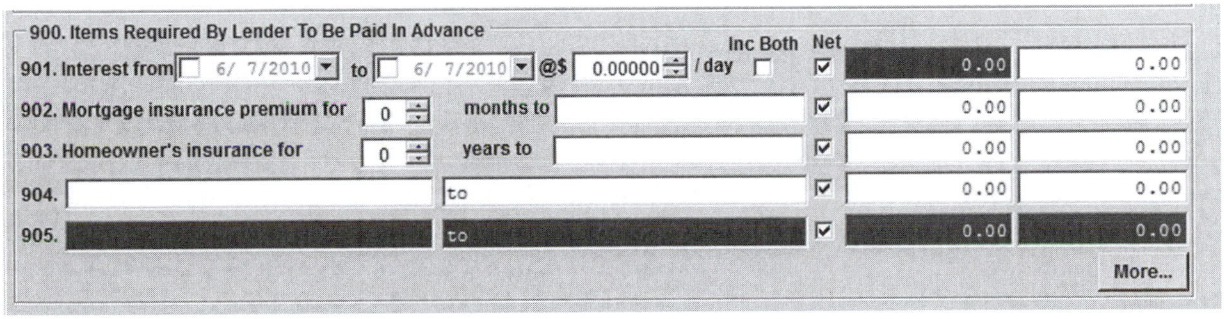

Figure 3-38. HUD-1 software—Toolbar: New Button and submenu, HUD Page 2 tab, Items Required by Lender to be Paid in Advance [Lines 900–905]

▶ Reserves deposited with the lender in an **escrow account.** The lender may require that some of the fees that a new owner will have to pay, like property taxes, be paid ahead of time into this special kind of account so as to be available when those fees become due.

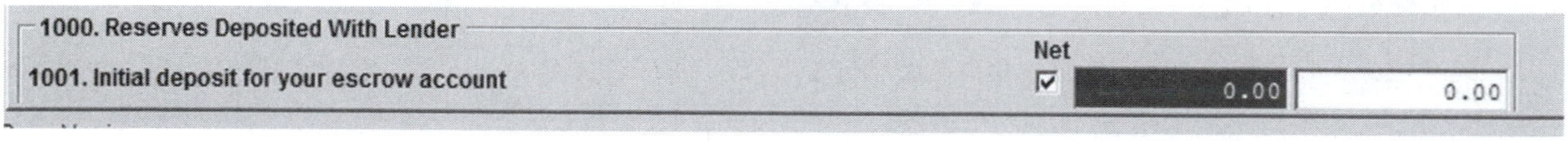

1000. Reserves Deposited With Lender

	Net		
1001. Initial deposit for your escrow account	☑	0.00	0.00

Figure 3-39. HUD-1 software—Toolbar: New Button and submenu, HUD Page 2 tab, Reserves Deposited with Lender [Lines 1000–1001]

iv. HUD page 3 tab

▶ Identifying costs that might change before the closing, broken down into categories, of those that:

▷ Will not change;

▷ Can change; and

▷ May rise no more than 10%.

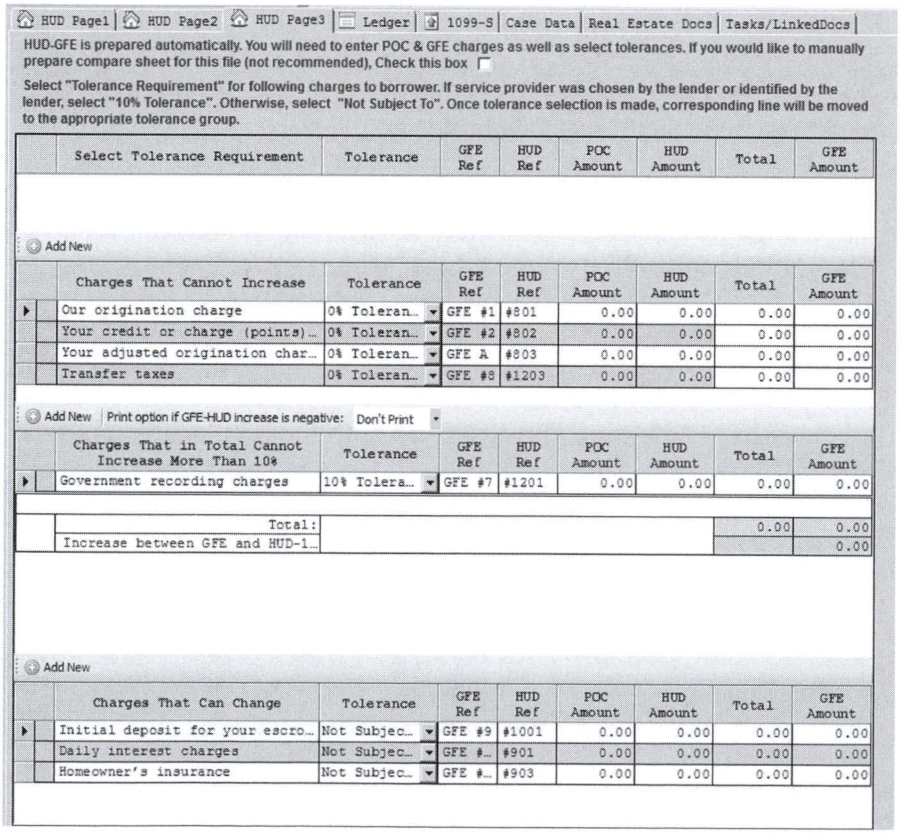

Figure 3-40. HUD-1 software—Toolbar: New Button and submenu, HUD Page 3 tab

▶ Calculating "the bottom line" about the loan, including:

▷ The impact of an increase in the interest rate, when getting an adjustable rate mortgage;

▷ Whether and how the loan balance could change;

▷ The impact of a change of the mortgage insurance rates;

▷ How much of a penalty the borrower may incur by paying off the loan before it is due; and

▷ A breakdown of those items that would be paid out of the escrow account, such as insurance.

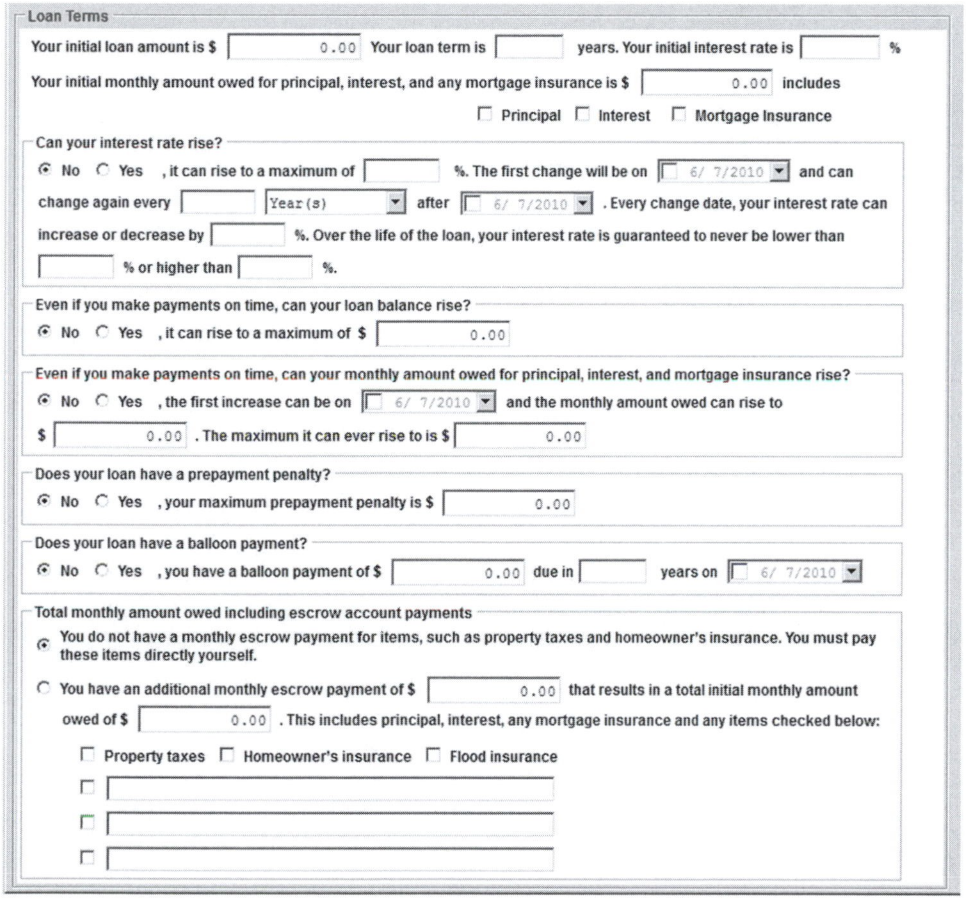

Figure 3-41. HUD-1 software—Toolbar: New Button and submenu, HUD Page 3 tab, Loan Terms submenu

v. Ledger tab

Software might provide a ledger, which would describe all financial transactions associated with a closing.

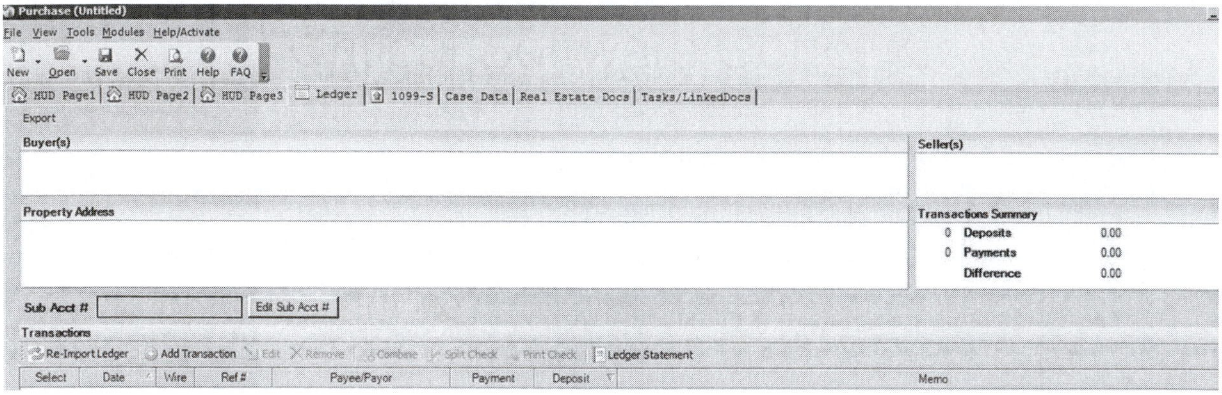

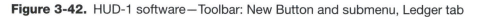

Figure 3-42. HUD-1 software—Toolbar: New Button and submenu, Ledger tab

vi. Form 1099-S tab

Because any transaction that generates income could require the payment of federal taxes, the software can:

▶ Generate the appropriate form, called a 1099-S form;

▶ Import an existing 1099-S form; and

▶ File this document electronically, at least with this software.

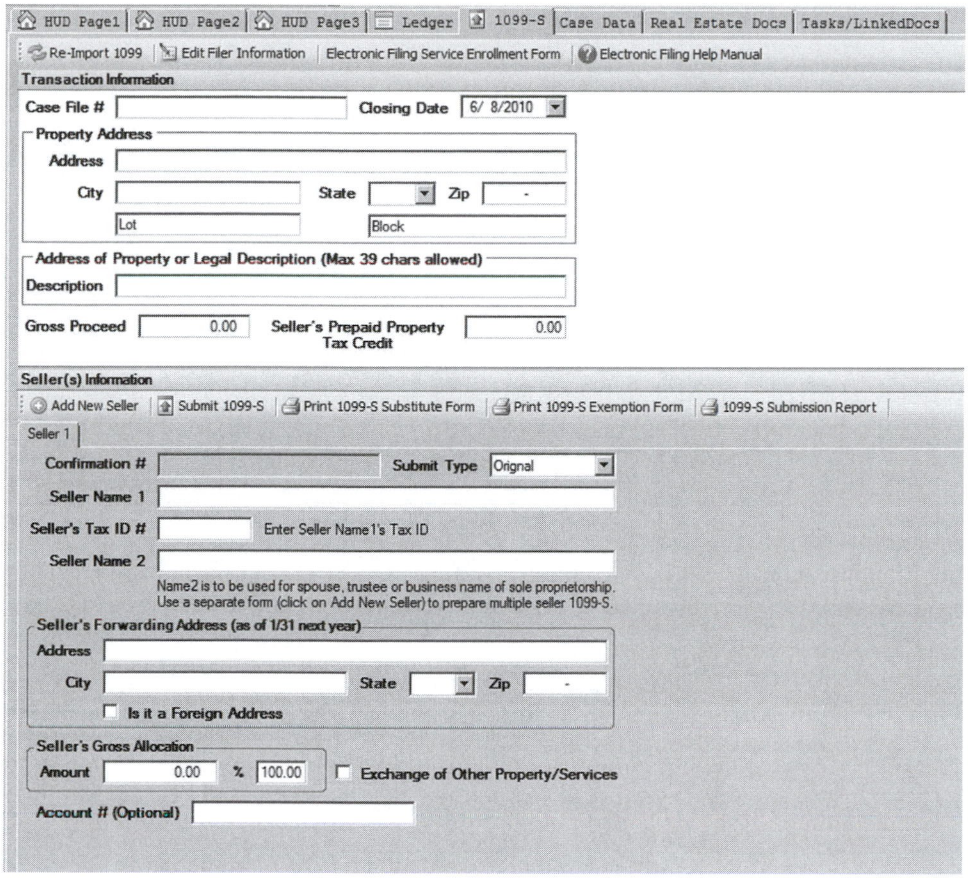

Figure 3-43. HUD-1 software—Toolbar: New Button and submenu, 1099-S tab

vii. Case data tab

On the chance that a law firm does business with the client in the future, like arranging for a sale of the newly purchased property, it might want to record information about the closing, such as:

▶ Buyer information (when a buyer receives the seller's interest in the property, the buyer is the **grantee**).

▶ Seller information, such as the seller's new address upon completion of the sale (when a seller transfers the seller's interest in the property, the seller is the **grantor**);

▶ A description of the property, especially its assessed value, which a community would use when calculating the property taxes;

▶ The amount needed to pay off the mortgage;

▶ Information about all lenders, if this transaction involves more than one lender;

▶ Information about the seller's attorney;

▶ Information about the real estate broker, including the commission a broker gets; and

▶ Any other information that the firm would deem useful, such as who **notarized** the deed.

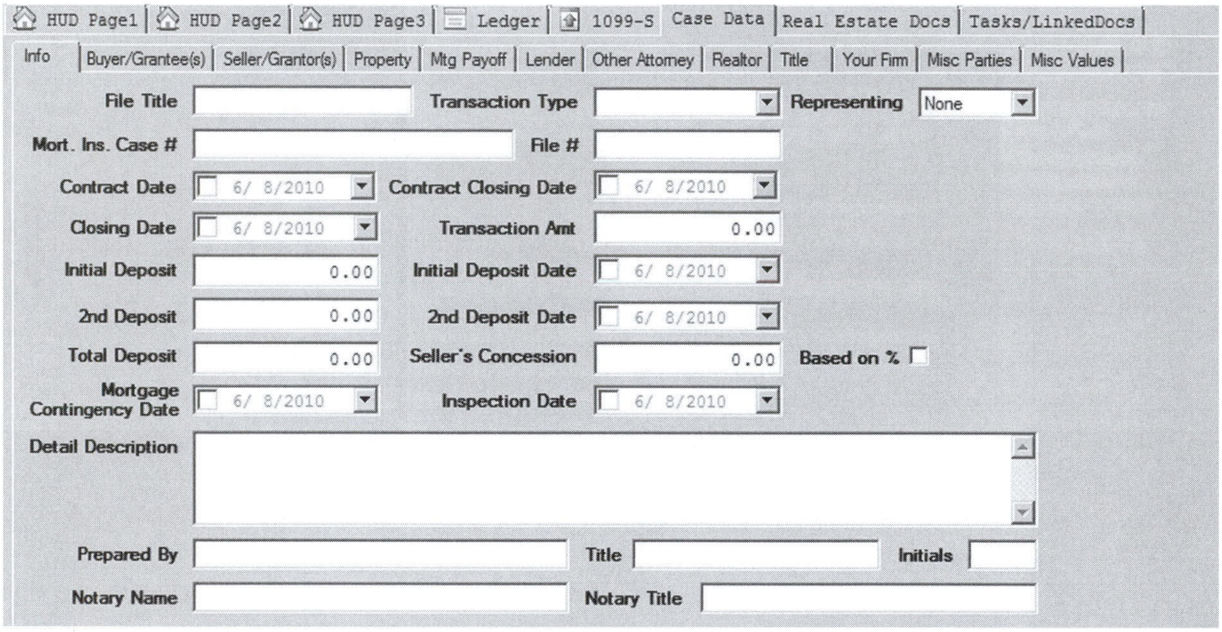

Figure 3-44 HUD-1 software—Toolbar: New Button and submenu, Case Data tab

viii. Real estate documents tab

This might list useful documents, like correspondence sent to all parties to the transaction.

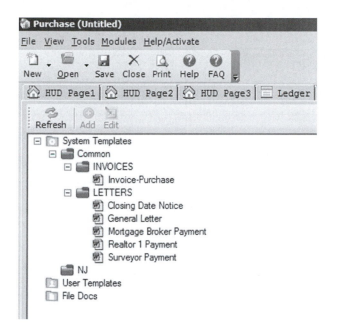

Figure 3-45. HUD-1 software—Toolbar: New Button and submenu, Real Estate Documents tab

ix. Tasked/linked documents tab

Among other options, this tab provides access to an expandable checklist that can be prioritized by deadline, of tasks related to the closing, such as:

▶ Ordering the title search; and

▶ Acknowledging receipt of the **binder** deposit, a sum paid by a prospective buyer to create a binding contract for the purchase of the property.

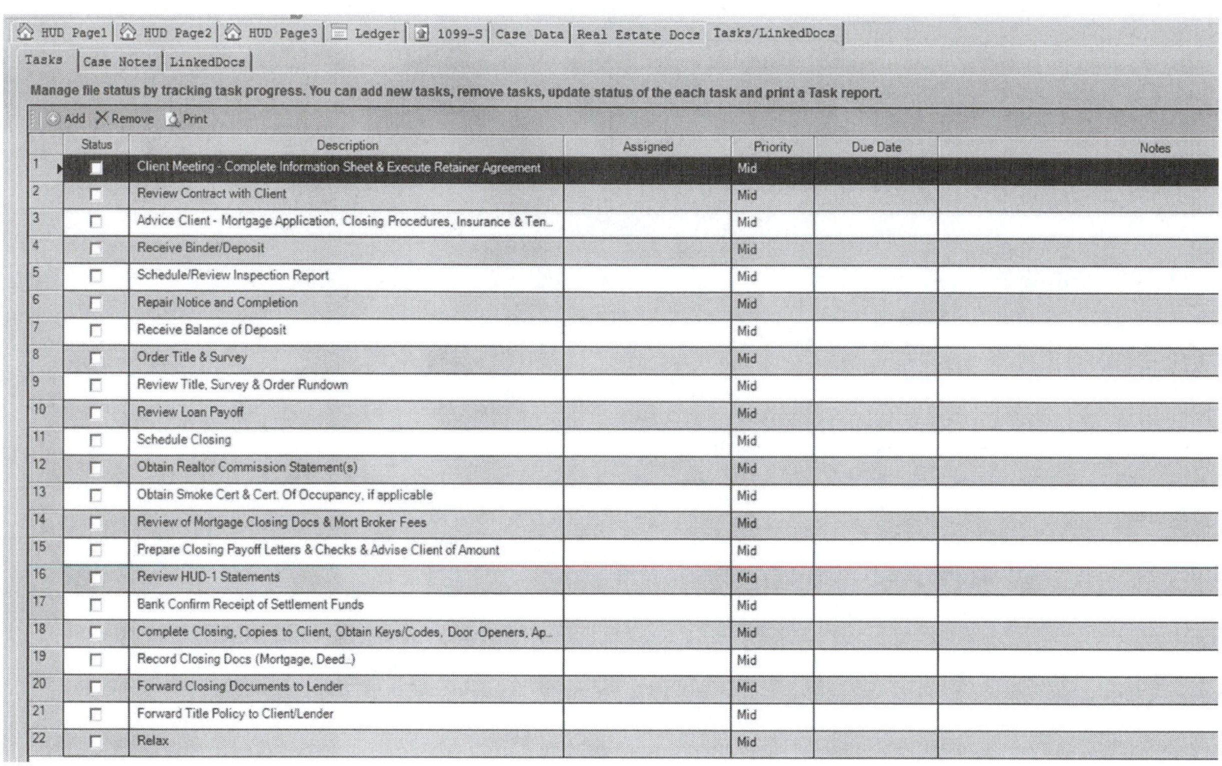

	Status	Description	Assigned	Priority	Due Date	Notes
1	☑	Client Meeting - Complete Information Sheet & Execute Retainer Agreement		Mid		
2	☐	Review Contract with Client		Mid		
3	☐	Advice Client - Mortgage Application, Closing Procedures, Insurance & Ten...		Mid		
4	☐	Receive Binder/Deposit		Mid		
5	☐	Schedule/Review Inspection Report		Mid		
6	☐	Repair Notice and Completion		Mid		
7	☐	Receive Balance of Deposit		Mid		
8	☐	Order Title & Survey		Mid		
9	☐	Review Title, Survey & Order Rundown		Mid		
10	☐	Review Loan Payoff		Mid		
11	☐	Schedule Closing		Mid		
12	☐	Obtain Realtor Commission Statement(s)		Mid		
13	☐	Obtain Smoke Cert & Cert. Of Occupancy, if applicable		Mid		
14	☐	Review of Mortgage Closing Docs & Mort Broker Fees		Mid		
15	☐	Prepare Closing Payoff Letters & Checks & Advise Client of Amount		Mid		
16	☐	Review HUD-1 Statements		Mid		
17	☐	Bank Confirm Receipt of Settlement Funds		Mid		
18	☐	Complete Closing, Copies to Client, Obtain Keys/Codes, Door Openers, Ap...		Mid		
19	☐	Record Closing Docs (Mortgage, Deed...)		Mid		
20	☐	Forward Closing Documents to Lender		Mid		
21	☐	Forward Title Policy to Client/Lender		Mid		
22	☐	Relax		Mid		

Figure 3-46. HUD-1 software—Toolbar: New Button and submenu, Tasked/Linked Docs, Tasks tab

Trusts

Introduction

At law, a **trust** involves a separation of the legal and equitable ownership of real and personal property. The trust owns the property, but the **beneficiary** has the use of the property. For example, if the trust contains money for the beneficiary's college education, the beneficiary has the right to claim that money from the trust to pay for college tuition, but does not control the money. The document for creating the trust contains instructions for a **trustee** about how to manage the property in the trust. At a minimum, a trustee has to keep track of the estate's assets, and of the expenses needed to maintain the property held in trust.

Software

EasySoft LLC's EasyTrust-Accounting software provides an example of the kind of software a trustee would use to keep track of income and disbursements. It is available at http://www.easysoft-usa.com/trust-accounting-software.html. All images taken from this software are copyrighted by the creator of such images and inclusion of such images in this text does not constitute any copyright interest or claim in them. Other sources of software to create trusts include http://legendary willsandtrusts.com/?page_id=247 and Cowles Trust Plus at http://west.thomson .com/products/books-cds/cowles/trust-plus.aspx, among others. This software includes a wizard for setting up basic information that will be used for subsequently generated documents.

Features

This software uses buttons, tabs, and pulldown menus, something quite familiar for those who have used Microsoft's office productivity software.

1. Buttons

Buttons at the top of the page provide quick access to commonly used software features for keeping track of:

Figure 3-47. Trust Accounting software—buttons

▶ How much time a trustee spent managing the trust, for inclusion in a monthly bill for services;

▶ Expenses incurred on behalf of the trust, like filing fees if the trust needs to sue a bank to recover trust funds stolen by a bank employee, or to pay the trustee for services rendered;

▶ Receipts, such as for interest paid by a bank on the trust's money held at that bank; and

▶ A line of credit available to the trust.

2. Tabs

The top toolbar arranges tabs by function, instead of individually, as with buttons.

Easy TimeBill & Trust Accounting
File   View   Tools   Help

Figure 3-48. Trust Accounting software—tabs

a. File tab

This pulldown menu makes it easier to manage trust fund data.

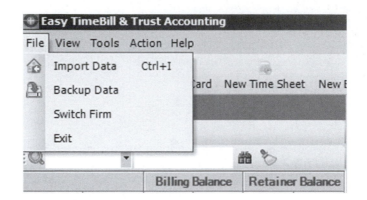

Figure 3-49. Trust Accounting software—File tab: Pulldown menu

b. View tab

Here, the software provides links for useful information, such as:

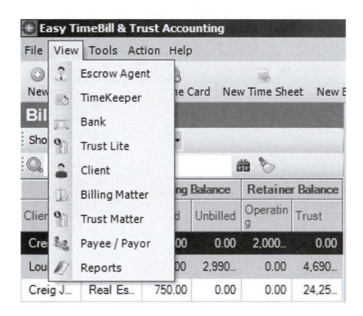

Figure 3-50. Trust Accounting software—View tab: Pulldown menu

▶ Identifying the escrow agent who manages the trust's funds in an escrow account;

▶ A breakdown of time spent managing the trust, broken down by:

▷ Who worked on behalf of the trust;

▷ The nature of the work performed;

▷ Time spent on the activity; and

▷ The rate of compensation for such work.

▶ The bank or banks that have trust fund accounts;

▶ "Trust Lite," for a quick overview of the trust's financial transactions, such as holding a buyer's deposit for the purchase of trust fund property;

▶ "Client," for keeping track of invoices, including a history of when sent, the number sent, a date for payment, and, if needed, the option to "Print Overdue Invoices with Reminder";

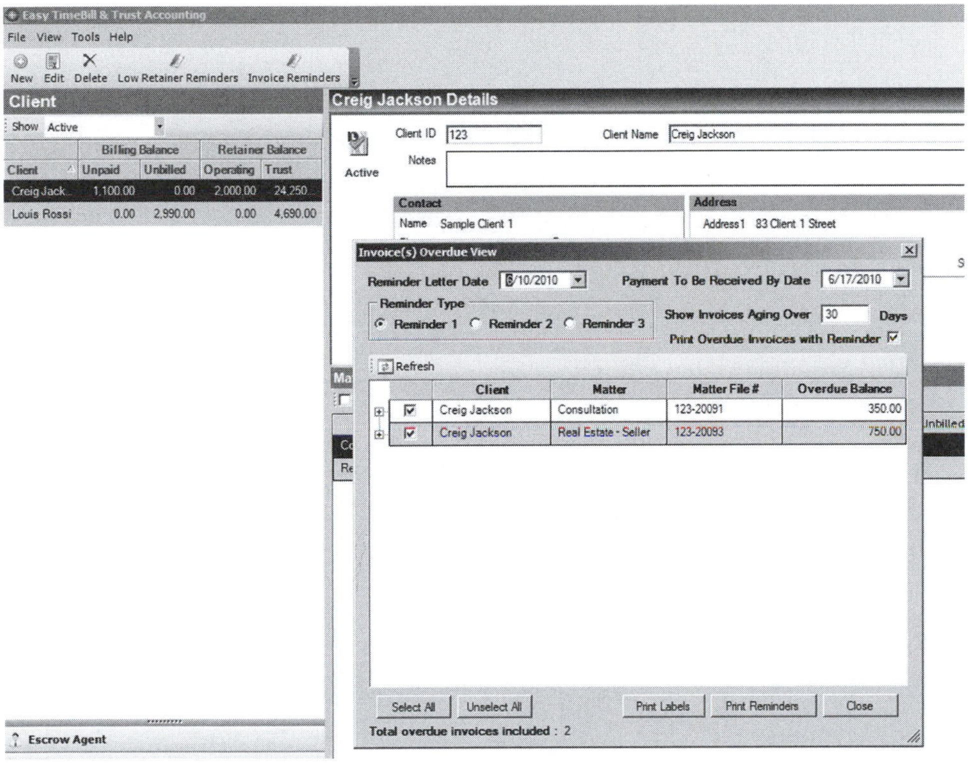

Figure 3-51. Trust Accounting software—View tab: Pulldown menu, Client link, Invoice(s) Overdue submenu

▶ Matters related to billing, such as information provided in the buttons described above;

▶ "Trust Matter," for a detailed overview of the trust's financial transactions;

▶ "Payee/Payor," who received payments from the trust, from a specific account;

▶ Reports, with information about trust fund activity including:

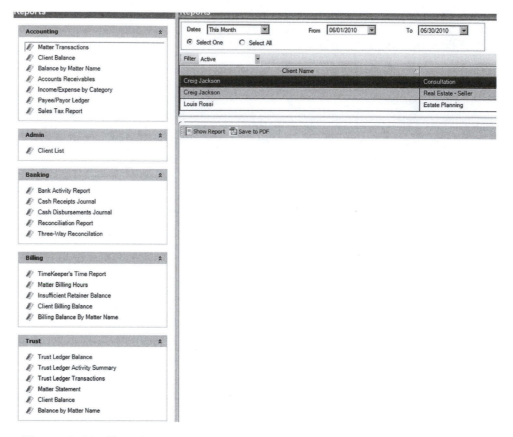

Figure 3-52. Trust Accounting software—View tab: Pulldown menu, Reports link

▷ Accounting, such as:

   ▷ The subject of a transaction;

   ▷ Balances, broken down by subject matter;

   ▷ Accounts receivable, for invoices issued but not yet paid;

   ▷ Income/expenses by category;

   ▷ The payee/payor ledger; and

   ▷ A tax report for sales involving trust property.

▷ Banking, such as a:

   ▷ Record of receipts and disbursements of cash; and

   ▷ Reconciliation report, which tracks all changes to a trust account, by transaction, during a specific time, over multiple accounts.

▷ Billing, including:

   ▷ An account of hours billed; and

▷ A billing balance, all of which can be broken down by subject matter; and

▷ Trust activity as reflected in a ledger, which comprehensively records all financial transactions.

A menu on the left-hand side of the screen also links to these items.

c. Tools tab

This tab, via a pulldown menu, provides options regarding other trust-related matters, such as:

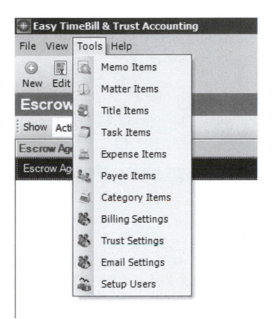

Figure 3-53. Trust Accounting software—Tools tab: Dropdown menu

▶ Memo items regarding trust-related activities like closings, creating a power of attorney (which empowers another to serve as an agent for the trust), and filing an appeal of a tax assessment;

▶ Matter items, regarding leases or litigation, for example;

▶ Title items, a breakdown of services rendered to the trust, broken down by a worker's title, including an **accounts payable** clerk and **accounts receivable** clerk and attorney;

▶ Task items, breaking down services rendered by activity, such as for the drafting of legal documents like an **affidavit** or a **complaint;**

▶ Expense items, regarding non-taxable costs, like:

▷ The cost of a **real estate binder;**

▷ Court costs, such as in the case of litigation;

▷ Copying and printing; and

▷ Telecommunication;

▶ Payee items, for identifying disbursements of fees for services rendered by:

▷ An attorney for the seller in a real estate transaction; or

▷ An office rental management company (which might collect rent for occupying trust property).

▶ Category items, which list expenses by category, such as for utilities or rent;

▶ Billings settings, such as for the generation of invoices; and

▶ Trust settings, regarding information like the defaults used on documents generated from the use of this software.

d. Help tab

As with other software offered by EasySoft LLC, this tab provides the user with access to various kinds of help, including a manual in PDF for using the software.

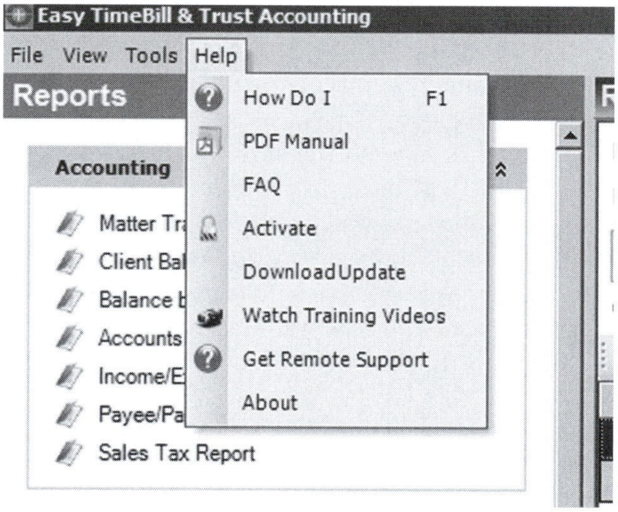

Figure 3-54. Trust Accounting software, Help tab

Wills

The Nature of a Will

A **will** is a legally enforceable document that contains the final wishes of a decedent. To make it enforceable, witnesses must have signed the will, indicating that they had seen the maker of the will sign the document and can subsequently testify if a question arises whether the maker created the will under duress or coercion.

The maker of the will is called the **testator** (for a man) or the **testatrix** (for a woman). The property that the decedent has left is known as the estate. The person identified in the will and charged with the responsibility of managing and distributing the assets of the estate is called an **executor** (for a man) or **executrix** (for a woman).

A person who has left a will is said to have died testate. Absent a will, state law will provide for the distribution of the estate. In this instance, the decedent died **intestate.** A representative who reports to the court about the distribution of the estate, as per state law, is an **administrator,** if male, and an **administratrix,** if female.

Probating an estate involves distributing the estate according to the instructions in the will. If the decedent died without a will, the process is called administration. Many jurisdictions have created a probate court to deal with such matters, among other things.

Software

The following software, offered as an example of what software can do regarding wills, comes from National Lawforms, http://nationallawforms.com/estate/software-last-will-and-testament.asp, copyrighted 2006. Files created by using this software have the suffix .eps.

The software maker has tailored the software to meet the requirements of probate law in each state. For illustrative purposes, the images of the software used here reflect the legal requirements of the Commonwealth of Massachusetts regarding wills. Other sources of this kind of software include http://www.easysoft-usa.com/, www.lawfirmsoftware.com/software/ last_will.htm and http://www.dplprofessionalsolutions.com/will_systems.asp.

All images taken from this software are copyrighted by the creator of such images and inclusion of such images in this text does not constitute any copyright interest or claim in them.

Estate Planning

Estate planning means preparing a will that reflects the client's wishes. Critically, this involves identifying a client's assets. Among other functions, the first screen of the software provides an option to launch a client questionnaire to gather necessary information for the drafting of the will.

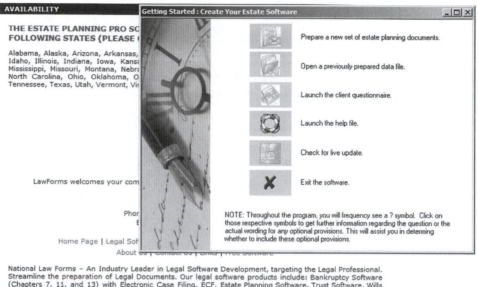

Figure 3-55. National LawForms Last Will and Testament Software—Getting Started screen

The screen that then appears has tabs and pulldown menus familiar to most users of Microsoft software, including File, Edit, and Help.

1. Gathering Data

To generate a will involves gathering critical information, including:

▶ The identity of the maker of the will, as testator or testatrix;

▶ A **conservator** (or guardian) of the estate who will preserve the assets pending the probating of the will;

▶ A personal representative, to serve as an **agent,** with authority to fulfill the maker's instructions regarding ongoing management of property, pending the probating of the will; and

▶ Personal effects, which means any personal property that the decedent had owned.

2. Children

Because children often receive the assets of an estate, identifying these children can have a significant impact. The maker may need to designate in the will a guardian for the care of minor children, and a guardian for management of property in the estate, with instructions about how to distribute it to such minor children once they reach the age of majority.

A child may contest, or challenge, the validity of the will, especially if the maker expressly did not provide for the distribution of the estate's assets to the child, as reflected by the evocative phrase, "I have cut you out of my will." Some states might mandate, however, that any surviving child receive some portion of the estate, regardless of what the will says.

Useful Documents

The software can also generate useful documents, based upon the data gathered, in addition to a will.

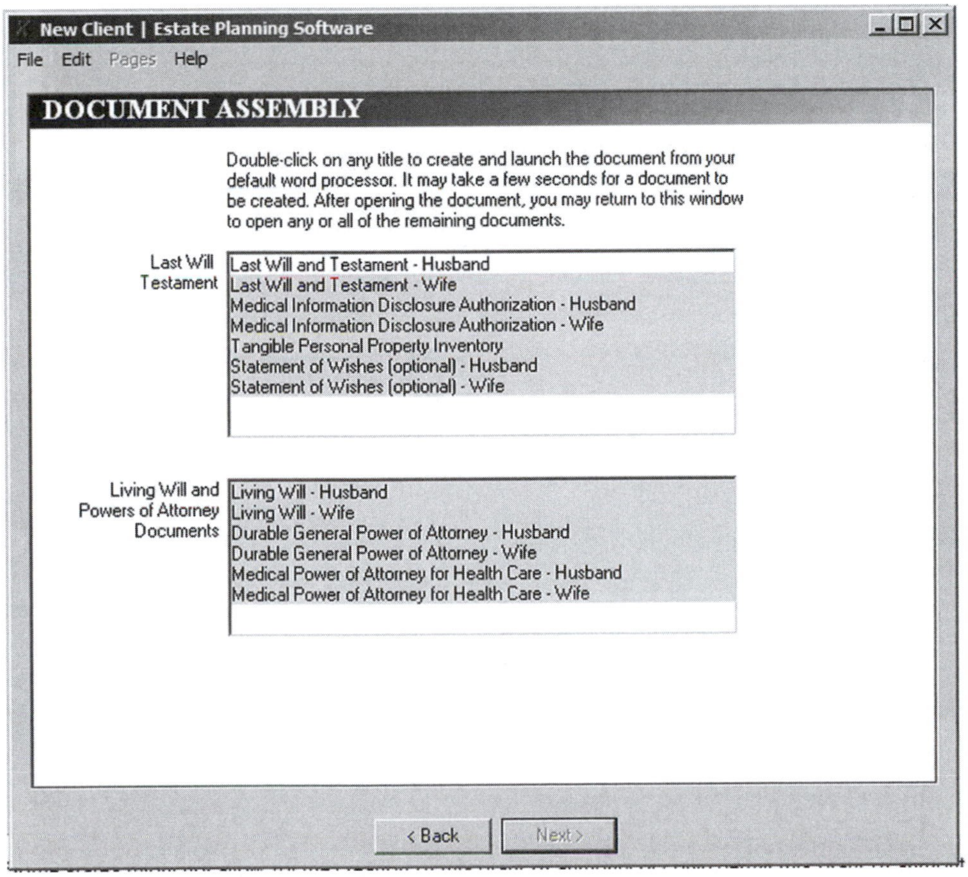

Figure 3-56. National LawForms Last Will and Testament Software—Attorney Information submenu: Document assembly

1. Power of Attorney

Under the law, an agent will act on behalf of the interests of a **principal.** This means that the agent has received a grant of authority to accomplish a goal or goals set forth by the principal. Sometimes the document used to create the agency is known as the power of attorney. Creating an agency could mean that an incapacitated person has someone who will look out for that person's interests during the time of such **incapacitation.**

2. Durable Power of Attorney

A durable power of attorney means that the grant of authority in an agent extends beyond the completion of any specific task.

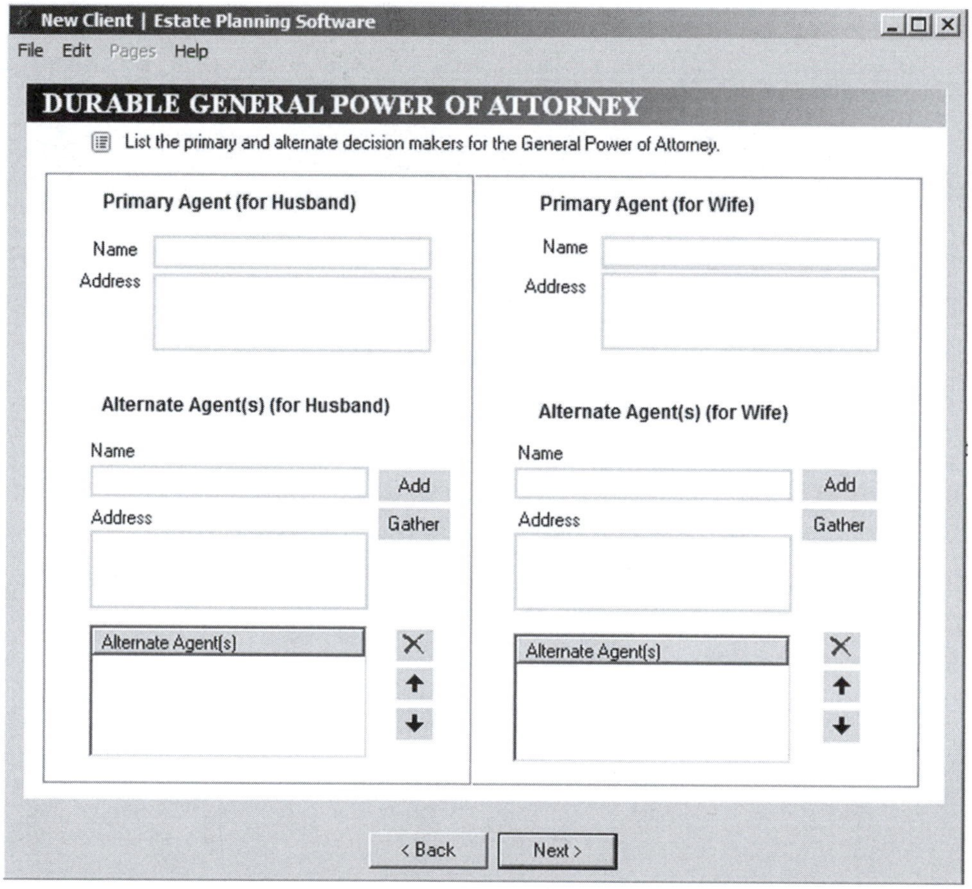

Figure 3-57. National LawForms Last Will and Testament Software—Attorney Information submenu: Durable power of attorney

Not surprisingly, the software asks about the scope of the authority that the principal wishes to vest in the agent. This authority might empower the agent to handle:

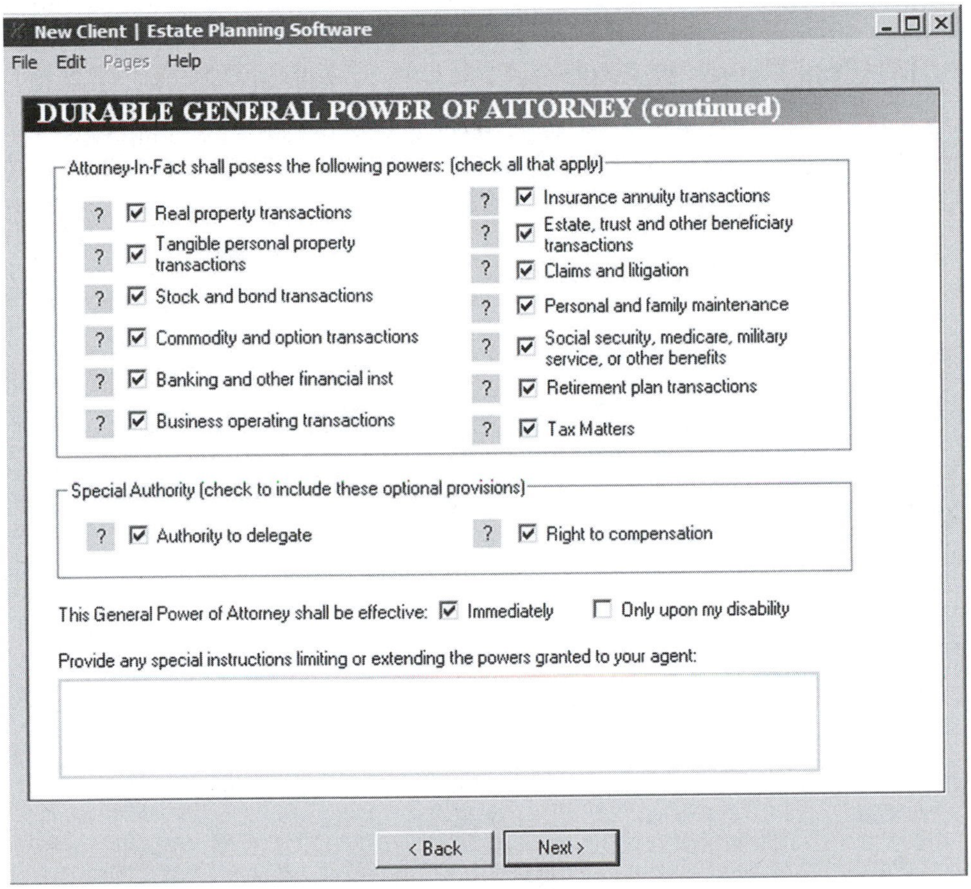

Figure 3-58. National LawForms Last Will and Testament Software—Attorney Information submenu: Durable power of attorney, continued

▶ Real estate transactions;

▶ Personal property transactions;

▶ Stocks and bonds transactions;

▶ Banking and other such financial matters;

▶ Claims and litigation;

▶ Personal and family maintenance;

▶ Retirement plan transactions; and

▶ Tax matters.

Also, the durable power of attorney can empower the agent to:

▶ Delegate authority, by having someone else complete the actions required of the agent; and

▶ Receive compensation for services rendered.

3. Medical Power of Attorney

If permitted under state law, this special type of durable power of attorney, sometimes called a healthcare or medical directive, authorizes an agent to make only medical decisions on behalf of an incapacitated principal, during the period of incapacitation.

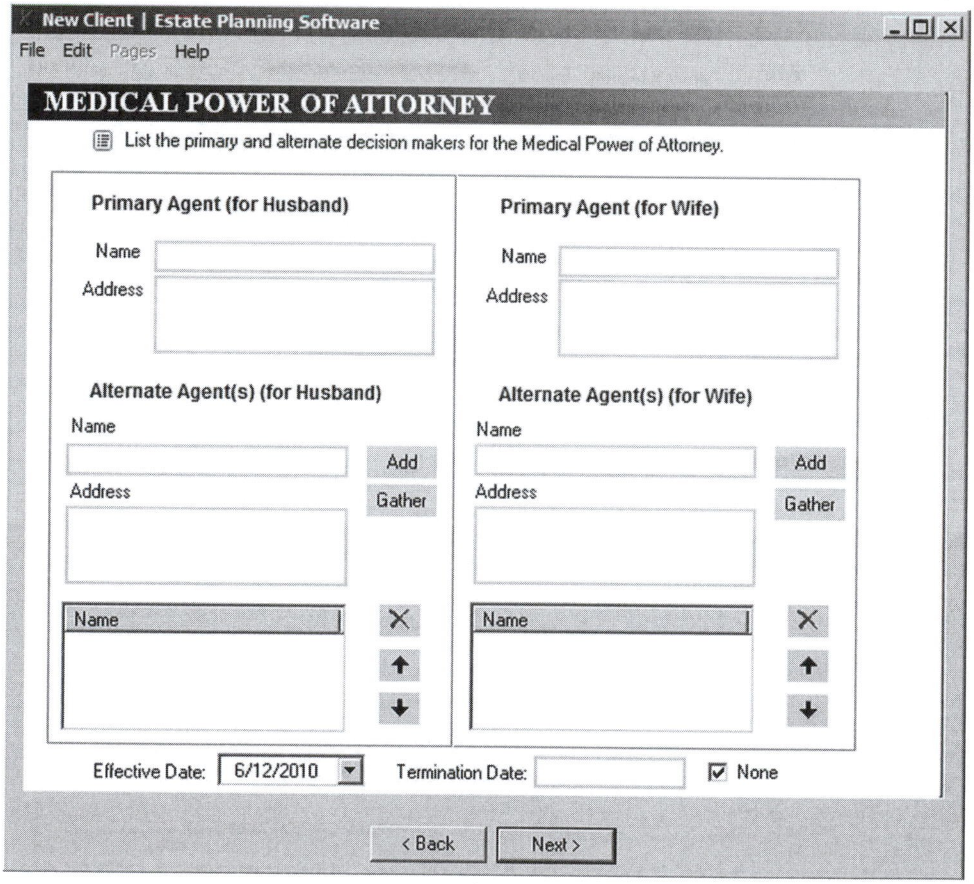

Figure 3-59. National LawForms Last Will and Testament Software—Attorney Information submenu: Medical power of attorney

4. Living Will

Depending on a state's laws, a so-called living will can be another way for an agent to act on behalf of an incapacitated principal. Jurisdictions vary on the terms used for this type of power of attorney.

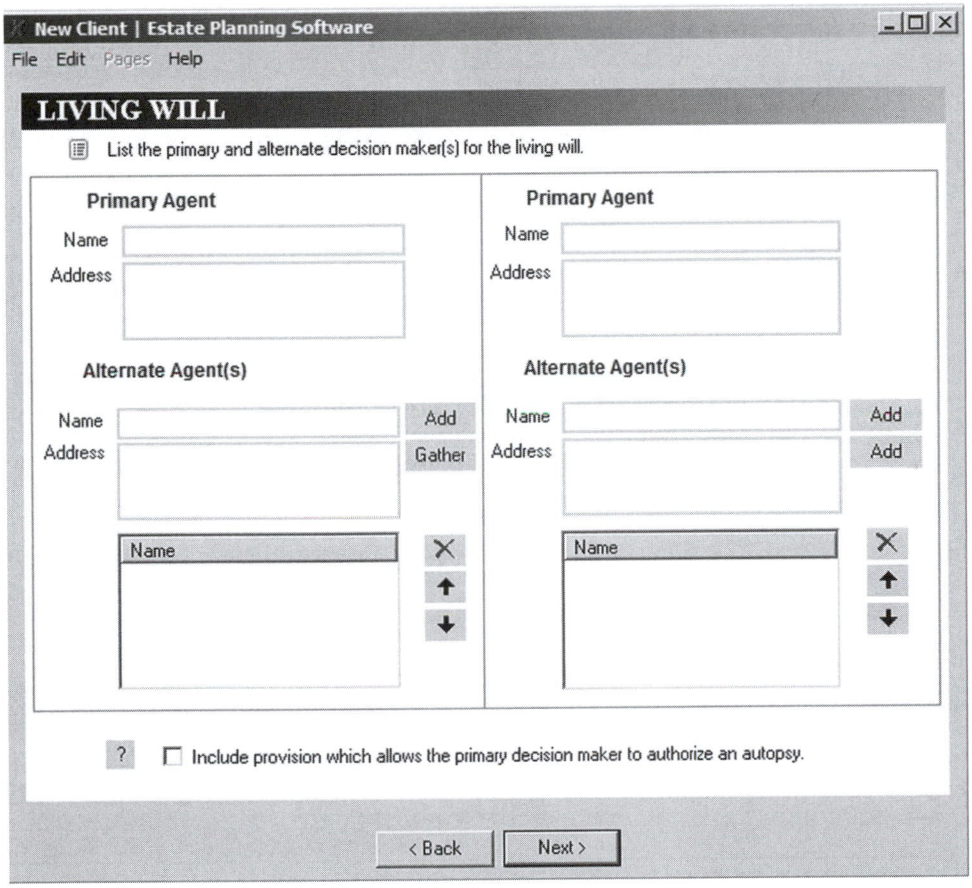

Figure 3-60. National LawForms Last Will and Testament Software—Attorney Information submenu: Living will

Conclusion

Lawyers have an obligation to clients to work efficiently and effectively. Given the complexity of many areas of the law, software can streamline the delivery of services to a client, increasing speed and reducing the chance of mistakes. Topic-specific software typically prompts a user for information to generate a form so that, for example, real estate closing software will complete the HUD-1, a document required under federal law, to complete the sale of property.

Terms

Accounts payable	Contract
Accounts receivable	Corporation
Adjustments	Creditors
Administrator	Creditor matrix
Administratrix	Debtor/petitioner
Affidavit	Deed
Agent	Directors
Alimony	Discharge in bankruptcy
Alternative minimum tax	Dividends
Articles of Incorporation	Docket number
Assets	Durable power of attorney
Assignments	Escrow account
Attests	Estate
Bankruptcy	Executor
Bankruptcy code	Executrix
Beneficiary	Exempt
Binder	Exhibits
Broker	Form 1099-S
Bylaws	Grant
Chapter 7	Grantee
Chapter 11	Grantor
Chapter 13	Guardian
Child support	HUD-1
Closing	Incapacitation
Complaint	Intestate
Conservator	Involuntary petition

Itemized deductions

Lease

Ledger

Liabilities

Lien

Limited liability corporation

Liquidation

Living will

Means test

Medical power of attorney

Meeting minutes

Mortgage

Notarization

Officers

Owner

Pages

Partnership

Payee

Payor

Personal exemptions

Power of attorney

Principal

Probating an estate

Property

Proxy

Real estate

Real estate binder

Registry of deeds

Reorganization

Resident agent

Resolutions

Schedules

Secured loans

Settlement agent

Share

Statements

Stock

Stock options

Stock register

Stockholder

Subchapter S corporation

Tax credits

Tax proration

Tenant

Testator

Testatrix

Title

Title search

Trust

Trustee

Unsecured loans

Voluntary petition

Will

Hypotheticals

1. Complete the bankruptcy form for a voluntary petition of an individual filing under Chapter 7 using the following information.

> Checking account balance $50
>
> House, valued at $378,000, $298,000 due on mortgage; owned since August, 2000
>
> Rental property, valued at $250,000; mortgage of $197,500; occupied by tenant who pays $950/month
>
> Car, 1997 Mazda Protégé, worth $2300, fair market value
>
> Computer, tablet, valued at $250
>
> Computer, desktop, valued at $500
>
> Computer, laptop, valued at $950
>
> Computer monitors (2), valued at $50 each
>
> Laser printer, valued at $45
>
> TV, valued at $750
>
> Household goods, approximately $500
>
> Artwork, Dave Cockrum (2 pieces), $500 each
>
> SEP-IRA, $19,000
>
> Roth-IRA, $46,000
>
> Income
> $500/week from D-U.edu
> $125/week from A-U.edu
> $400/week from B-U.edu
> $85/week from N-U.edu
> $75/week book royalties
> No other sources of income
>
> Debt
> $12,000/year, tuition
> $24,000/year, credit card debt
> $230,000, gambling debt
> $87,000, personal loan
> $176,000, damages in a lawsuit
> $235,000, student loans
> No other outstanding debt/liabilities
>
> Has never filed for bankruptcy before
> No spouse
> Social security number XXX-XX-0277

2. Complete the HUD-1 using the following information.

Buyer:

Cordwainer Smith (M)

Identifies as White; U.S. citizen, not a veteran, not disabled

Age: 54

Highest level of education: Juris Doctor

First-time home buyer

Social security number XXX-XX-0277

Never filed for bankruptcy

$3,000 in savings account

$63,000 in Roth-IRA, SEP-IRA

No other debt or financial obligations

No co-applicant

Monthly living expenses: approx. $2000/month

Current residence: 2154 Cummings Avenue, Unit 3G, Quincy, MA 02171

Two dependents, who reside with buyer: Emil (M), age 13, Jane (F), age 11

Annual income: approx. $80,000, consultant (20+ years); royalties, $200/week

No other source of income

Down payment: $48,000

Property being purchased: 2779 Cummings Avenue, Quincy, MA 02171

Agreed-upon price: $298,000

Able to secure a mortgage of $250,000, at 4%, for 30 years, fixed rate, from

Tesseract Savings and Loan

1958 Aborn Place

Peabody, MA 01960

Telephone: 978-555-5555

Monthly payment: $1350

Monthly escrow: $450

3. Divorce financials

Use the following information to prepare a financial agreement to accompany a divorce settlement.

Payor:

Cordwainer Smith (M) currently married to payee

D.O.B. 04/01/1958

Residence: 2779 Cummings Avenue, Quincy, MA 02171
Homeowner; approx $2,000 monthly mortgage, escrow payments, total
 Annual property tax $3600 (included in escrow)

Two dependents, who reside with payee: Emil (M), age 13, Jane (F), age 11

Annual income: approx. $100,000, licensed psychologist (17 years)
 No other source of income

$43,000 pension
$13,000 Roth-IRA
$7,000 Mutual Fund
Wedding band, $200
Car, 1997 Mazda Protégé, worth $2300, fair market value
Not subject to the Alternative Minimum Tax

Payee:
Jan Harris (F)
D.O.B. 04/01/1960 currently married to payor
Residence: 3124 S. Willard St., Burlington, VT 05401
Homeowner; approx $2,000 monthly mortgage, escrow payments, total
 Annual property tax $3600 (included in escrow)

Two dependents, who reside with payee: Emil (M), age 13, Jane (F), age 11

Annual income: approx. $80,000, consultant (20+years); royalties, $200/
week
 No other source of income
$3,000 in savings account
$63,000 in Roth-IRA, SEP-IRA
Car, 2004 Subaru Forester, worth $4000, fair market value
Wedding band and ring: approx. $2000

Not subject to the Alternative Minimum Tax

Proposed

Child support: Payor to Payee, $1800/month

No alimony

Education expenses, both dependents (private school and/or college fund)
 Payor to Payee, $1000/month

Visitation:
 Two weeks during summer
 One school vacation/year
 Alternating Christmas, December
 Four weekend visits/year

4. Using the estate planning software, prepare a "single revocable living trust," "wills and powers of attorney documents," using the following data and instructions.

   a. For password, use "Demo"

   b. For estate planning documents, select "single revocable living trust"

   c. Attorney information
   Attorney:
   Guay Associates, LLP
   Attorney George Guay
   P.O. Box XX1
   Arkham, MA 01066
   Phone: 617-555-0001
   Fax: 617-555-0002

   d. Grantor: Catullus Family Trust, Arkham, Norfolk County, MA
   Arthur Gordon Pym
   P.O. Box XX2
   Arkham, MA 01066

   Does not have former spouse

   e. Primary trustee/co-trustee: No
   Attorney George Guay
   P.O. Box XX1
   Arkham, MA 01066

   Co-trustee

   f. Successor trustee(s)
   Guay Associates, LLP
   Attorney Emile Guay
   P.O. Box XX1
   Arkham, MA 01066

   Will act jointly with co-trustee

   g. Beneficiaries
   Janine Tym
   P.O. Box XX3
   Arkham, MA 01066

   Relationship: ex-wife
   100%

   Distribution is *per stirpes*

   Beneficiary is not a child of the grantor

   h. Final distribution to beneficiaries
   Distribute immediately

i. Special distributions
Edwin Jarvis
P.O. Box XX4
Arkham, MA 01066

Property: all my scientific equipment

j. Contingent beneficiary: yes
Edward Jarvis
P.O. Box XX4
Arkham, MA 01066

k. Durable general power of attorney
Primary agent:
Guay Associates, LLP
Attorney George Guay
P.O. Box XX1
Arkham, MA 01066

Alternate agent:
Guay Associates, LLP
Attorney Emile Guay
P.O. Box XX1
Arkham, MA 01066

Also:
Guay Associates, LLP
P.O. Box XX1
Arkham, MA 01066

Attorney-In -Fact should have all authority, as well as all special authority, with General Power of Attorney effective immediately.

l. Medical Power of Attorney
Primary Agent:
Guay Associates, LLP
Attorney George Guay
P.O. Box XX1
Arkham, MA 01066

Alternate Agent:
Hamish Blake, MD
P.O. Box XX5
Arkham, MA 01066

Effective immediately, with no termination date

m. Pour over will
Primary Agent:
Guay Associates, LLP
Attorney George Guay

P.O. Box XX1
Arkham, MA 01066

Alternate Agent:
Guay Associates, LLP
Attorney Emile Guay
P.O. Box XX1
Arkham, MA 01066

Guay Associates, LLP
P.O. Box XX1
Arkham, MA 01066

Wishes body to be cremated

No minor children

n. Living will
Primary Agent:
Guay Associates, LLP
Attorney George Guay
P.O. Box XX1
Arkham, MA 01066

Alternate Agent:
Guay Associates, LLP
Attorney Emile Guay
P.O. Box XX1
Arkham, MA 01066

Guay Associates, LLP
P.O. Box XX1
Arkham, MA 01066

Check of the option to allow primary decision maker to authorize an autopsy

o. Document assembly
Click "Generate all documents"

For Living Trust Wizard, designate a folder on a drive, creating all, then close

Now, close the application

5. Using the estate planning software and the password "Demo," prepare a "last will and testament," with all "wills and powers of attorney documents," using the following data and instructions.

a. Attorney information
Attorney:
Guay Associates, LLP
Attorney George Guay

P.O. Box XX1
Arkham, MA 01066
Phone: 617-555-0001
Fax: 617-555-0002

b. Testator
Norfolk County, MA

Eric Blair
P.O. Box XX7
Arkham, MA 01066

D.O.B. April 1, 1960
SSN: 000-00-0000

Provide for child of testator

Daniella Blair
P.O. Box XX8
Arkham, MA 01066

Gender: Female
D.O.B. May 17, 1980

c. Conservator of my property
Attorney George Guay
P.O. Box XX1
Arkham, MA 01066

Alternate:
Guay Associates, LLP
Attorney Emile Guay
P.O. Box XX1
Arkham, MA 01066

d. Guardian of my children
Desdemona Rathbone
P.O. Box XX9
Arkham, MA 01066

Alternate:
Attorney George Guay
P.O. Box XX1
Arkham, MA 01066

e. Personal representative
Attorney George Guay
P.O. Box XX1
Arkham, MA 01066

Alternate:
Guay Associates, LLP
Attorney Emile Guay

P.O. Box XX1
Arkham, MA 01066

f. Trustee of minor children
Attorney George Guay
P.O. Box XX1
Arkham, MA 01066

Alternate:
Guay Associates, LLP
Attorney Emile Guay
P.O. Box XX1
Arkham, MA 01066

g. Personal effects

Body to be cremated

Residence to:
Daniella Blair
P.O. Box XX8
Arkham, MA 01066

Disinherit everyone but:
Daniella Blair
P.O. Box XX8
Arkham, MA 01066

Special gifts:

G. Orwell, all intellectual property

Other directions:

Provide for the annual reading, in a public forum, of the novel, "1984"

No surviving beneficiaries, then give to:

Miskatonic University, English Department
P.O. Box XX10
Arkham, MA 01066

h. Durable power of attorney
Attorney George Guay
P.O. Box XX1
Arkham, MA 01066

Alternates:

Guay Associates, LLP
Attorney Emile Guay
P.O. Box XX1
Arkham, MA 01066

Guay Associates, LLP
P.O. Box XX1
Arkham, MA 01066

Check all items
Make general power of attorney immediately effective

Special instructions:
Attorney-in-Fact needs to secure services of conservator for all intellectual property

i.   Medical power of attorney
Primary Agent:
Guay Associates, LLP
Attorney George Guay
P.O. Box XX1
Arkham, MA 01066

Alternate Agent:
Hamish Blake, MD
P.O. Box XX5
Arkham, MA 01066

Effective immediately, with no termination date

j.   Living will
Primary Agent:
Guay Associates, LLP
Attorney George Guay
P.O. Box XX1
Arkham, MA 01066

Alternate Agent:
Guay Associates, LLP
Attorney Emile Guay
P.O. Box XX1
Arkham, MA 01066

Guay Associates, LLP
P.O. Box XX1
Arkham, MA 01066

Check of the option to allow primary decision maker to authorize an autopsy

k.   Document assembly
Select "Last Will and Testament"
Now, close the application

5. Answer

    b. Testator screen: effective date can vary; could also select child of deceased child of testator, using "Add" button.

    g. Personal Effects screen: can change any of these options, especially special gifts and other directions, as opportunity to explore choices.

    h. Durable Power of Attorney screen: can change any of the options checked; could also vary special instructions.

Practice Management and Case Management Software

4

Objectives

- ▶ Explore the utility of electronic information management.

- ▶ Study the nature of practice management software.

- ▶ Differentiate between front office and back office applications of practice management software.

- ▶ Contrast the functions of practice management software from case management software.

- ▶ Develop an understanding about case management software and how it differs from practice management software.

- ▶ Investigate how case management software can perform, for example, an analysis of a deposition transcript.

- ▶ Understand how a defensible discovery strategy relates to assessing electronically stored information when preparing a response to a request for discovery.

- ▶ Survey software that does one or the other function, or that integrates them.

Introduction

Software that can better manage the services offered by a legal practice and simplify routine business practices can enhance a law firm's productivity.

Critical Software Concepts

The Database

Software for improving the productivity of a law office generally relies upon data, typically kept in a **database.** The database, often stored on a central **server,** organizes data in a series of files, making it accessible to anyone with a connection to the server. A database can contain client-related data, such as:

▶ Contact information;

▶ Who at the firm did what kind of work and when;

▶ Copies of all work done, such as letters, legal memoranda, and briefs; and

▶ Bills for the work done.

In a database, data must be recorded in a particular format, such as name first, then date of initial contact, then type of legal problem. Using a standardized format allows different kinds of software, like for billing or generating tax forms, to process data differently, depending upon the need.

Practice Management Software Versus Case Management Software

Practice management software would encompass all activity done on behalf of the client, from court appearances to billing. **Case management software** would focus narrowly on the client's legal problem and its status, such as getting ready for trial. Practice management software can integrate neatly with case management software. For example, using case management software, a lawyer could file a complaint on behalf of a client. The practice management software could take note of this to set up a preliminary bill for the lawyer's time spent preparing and filing that complaint. Integrating this software could increase efficiency and decrease the likelihood of error, because the practice management software would automatically keep track of the lawyer's time since the lawyer drafted the complaint on the system.

The Nature of Practice Management Software

Practice management software increases the efficiency for performing common business office functions, such as generating correspondence, documents, records of accounting, and data. This can mean harnessing the processing speeds of a CPU through the use of application software, like a spreadsheet.

In addition to automating the process of preparing bills, for example, practice management software could even identify opportunities for increased productivity. By taking note of the types of legal services that a legal practice provides in a month, the firm could launch an Internet marketing campaign, touting the kinds of services that the firm provides.

Front Office and Back Office

Most business offices divide their operations into front office or back office activities. **Front office activities** would deal with all aspects of client contact, such as the gathering of client information or the completing of a client transaction. These activities include:

▶ Time management, especially focusing on deadlines;

▶ Tracking potential conflicts of interest, which can raise ethical issues for a firm;

▶ Document management, for keeping track of documents in a client's case;

▶ Contract management, relating to legally enforceable agreements;

▶ Contact management, critical for remaining connected to client;

▶ Communications management, from phone messages to faxes;

▶ Report management, especially helpful when deciding how to run a legal practice; and

▶ Remote access, for access to a firm's database anywhere outside of the office.

Back office operations involve those business practices common to any business. These include:

▶ Accounting and billing, such as accounts payable and accounts receivable; and

▶ A ledger, which provides a detailed overview of all income and expenses for a business.

1. Front Office Functions

Front office activities focus on managing each client's case.

a. Contact management

Software can work like the old-style Rolodex, which made contact information quick and easy to find. Now, a lawyer or paralegal can more easily transfer a copy of contact information to a smartphone, for example, and can synchronize changes made to the original information. The software can find contacts faster and make it easier to change contact information. In the example from TimeMatters, buttons on the top toolbar make it easy to find and edit contact information.

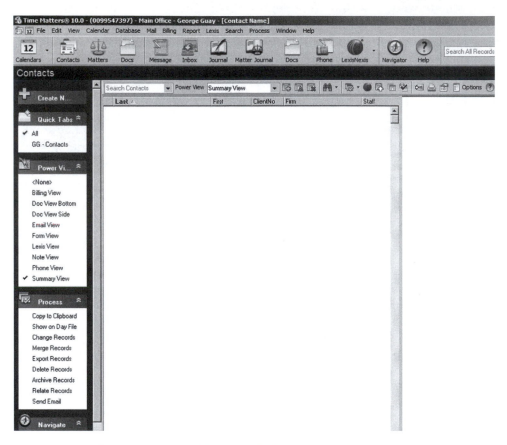

Figure 4-1. TimeMatters—Buttons: Example—Contact

b. Communications management

Having software that records text (like e-mail and instant messages), as well as audio messages, can make it easier to search for messages and copy them to a portable device, like a laptop or smartphone, for later reference. The example from TimeMatters depicts the message management screen that the lawyer or paralegal would see upon clicking the Navigator button, seen in the previous figure.

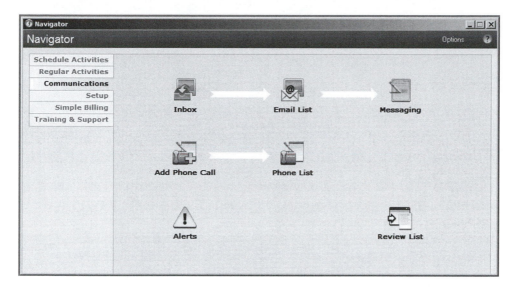

Figure 4-2. TimeMatters—Side toolbar Navigator communications

c. Time management

Time management involves the delivery of services efficiently and effectively. For example, **calendaring software** can keep future appointments organized. A law firm needs good time management software because of several issues typically associated with the practice of law, which are discussed next.

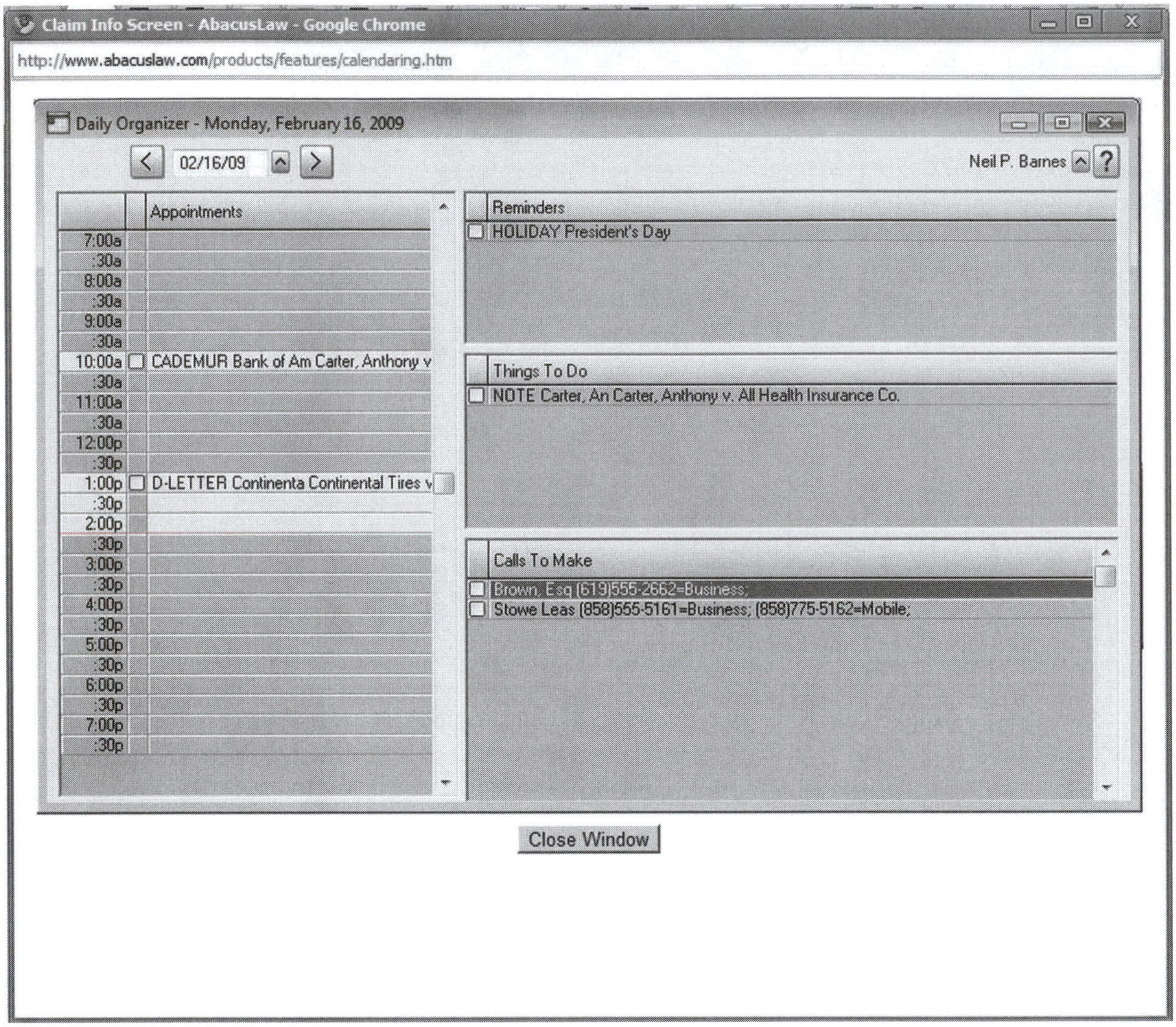

Figure 4-3. AbacusLaw—Daily calendar screen

i. Statutes of limitation

A lawyer must file a complaint about a client's legal problem by a particular time, usually from the date when the problem arose. Failure to do so means that the complaint is barred because of a **statute of limitation,** which requires the timely filing of a claim. Calendaring software should take note of such deadlines, especially to notify a lawyer when that time is approaching for filing a complaint for a client. By issuing such "**ticklers**" the lawyer has advanced notice of an impending deadline.

ii. Tracking

Courts need to keep track of their cases. To manage a large number of cases, some jurisdictions have created schedules, or **tracks,** which establish a timetable for getting the case to trial. Calendaring software, which records and keeps track of the dates that the court has assigned for a client's case on a particular track, makes it easier for a legal practice to meet tracking deadlines.

iii. Docketing

Courts keep track of deadlines created by the parties. For example, a party might serve on an opponent a request for discovery, which might need to be completed in 30 days. The court records such deadlines in a **docket,** to keep track of activities for a specific case. Software that can synchronize with a court docket serves as another way for a legal practice to keep track of developments in a case.

iv. Rules

A lawyer could create rules for the calendaring software so that, for example, new deadlines are automatically generated upon a new development in a case. Parties might set up a negotiation deadline that does not correspond to specific deadlines for a case. They might agree to talk about a settlement in a case in two months, but would not necessarily have needed to do this to comply with the track that the court has assigned to the specific case.

v. Continuing legal education

If a jurisdiction requires lawyers to earn continuing education units, calendaring software could keep a running total of time spent keeping up with these obligations, as well as indicate when a lawyer needs to do more.

vi. Commitments

Calendaring software can generate a timeline to help a lawyer coordinate work commitments at the law firm. For example, it can alert an attorney when a potential scheduling conflict arises.

For a practice, this can produce an overview of the time commitments of every attorney, alerting the firm about a potential need for additional help. The firm would know, for example, when a lawyer plans to take time off for a vacation and would then know how to plan for this.

vii. Coordinating

Calendaring software can:

▶ Allow for the coordination of the schedules of lawyers assigned to a particular case;

▶ Facilitate the efficient use of conference rooms and other meeting places;

▶ Enhance the usefulness of work collaboration software, like Lotus Notes or Novell Groupwise; and

▶ Synchronize a lawyer's calendar across multiple platforms, so that an appointment recorded on a smartphone shows up in the firm's database when the lawyer connects the smartphone to the firm's network.

d. Avoiding conflicts of interest

Lawyers must take care when considering whether to take on a new client, that a potential client's problems will not involve a previous client of the firm. For example, if a client has sued an insurance carrier to recover under the terms of a policy, the firm might not subsequently represent that insurance carrier to respond to a suit about the validity of a denial of a claim. This example, from Tabs3, shows how software might help a firm to determine whether a conflict exists.

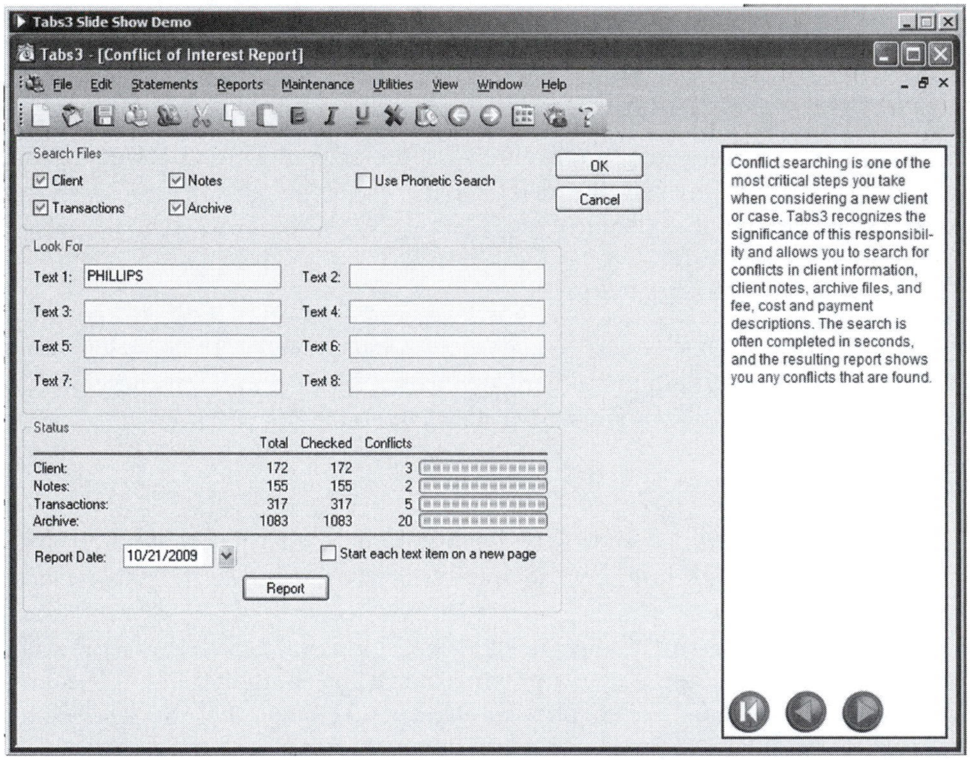

Figure 4-4. Tabs3—Determining whether a potential conflict of interest arises

Practice management software could help identify a potential conflict of interest by looking at:

▶ The legal services provided, such as making a court appearance or preparing an opinion letter;

▶ The nature of a client's problem, such as a divorce or the sale of real estate;

▶ Whether lawyers hired from another firm might have done work related to a new client's business; and

▶ Identifying characteristics, such as names, case names, or dates.

A firm can still take on the new client's business, even though a conflict exists, if it creates a so-called **ethical wall.** This would effectively isolate those who worked on the first case from working on the new client's case, as though a "wall" had been erected.

e. Document management

i. Index

Software might organize data, via an index, according to client, case type, year, or other sorting-related criteria, making it easier to find documents.

ii. Templates

Documents generated for other cases, such as a complaint or request for discovery, could serve as a **template** for when a lawyer or paralegal needs to create similar documents for a new case. Also, using a template can take advantage of the initial review for accuracy done after creating the template and not have to repeat that review with subsequent uses of the template. In addition to using those documents as the basis for creating a template, the software itself might provide templates. Sites like HotDocs, at www.hotdocs.com, from HotDocs Ltd., has automated the process of generating standardized documents from templates.

f. Contract management

Contracts, which are legally enforceable agreements, can create obligations for a law firm and/or a client. Software that keeps track of these obligations can, for example:

▶ Generate a "tickler," a reminder, about an impending deadline;

▶ Automate the modification of a contract, such as when the parties want to extend a deadline;

▶ Organize priorities, through the coordination of payments as specified within the contract; or

▶ Issue bills periodically, per the terms of the contract.

Software might have contract templates which lawyers could use as the starting point for writing up a contract. Using a template can insure that certain standard language, such as the consequences to a party for breaching the contract, will be included.

g. Report management

Reports can help lawyers in a legal practice understand different management concerns regarding the operation of a legal practice. Using an example from TimeMatters, a report could contain:

▶ An overview of cases;

▶ A history of the installation and upgrading of software used in the legal practice;

▶ A description of firm expenses, like rent and insurance, thereby allowing the lawyers to figure out what bills need to be paid first; and

▶ A review of services previously provided, like preparing a will or generating a contract for buying real estate, for use in crafting a marketing strategy.

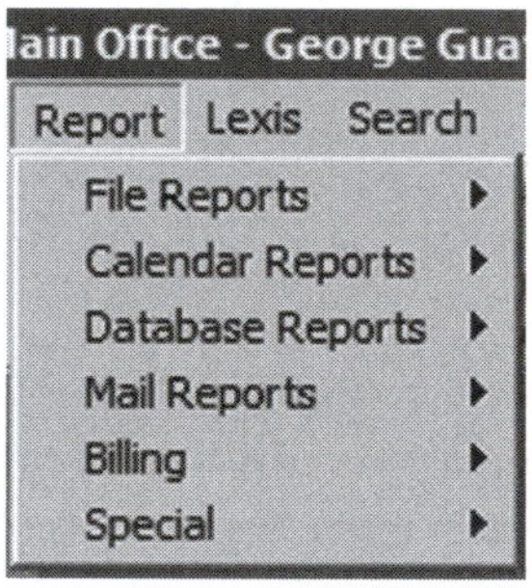

Figure 4-5. TimeMatters—Top toolbar: Pulldown menus, Types of reports

h. Remote access

When out of the office, software can allow an attorney or paralegal to access a firm's database via the World Wide Web, thereby making it easier to work on a client matter. This is known as **remote access.** Because lawyers have an ethical obligation to keep client information confidential, the software needs to have in place safeguards against inadvertent access to or disclosure of such data.

2. Back Office Operations

Back office operations involve those business practices common to any business. To run efficiently, all businesses need to keep track of bills and generate appropriate tax documents. If "front office" involved working with customers in public, then "back office" historically meant the work that customers typically would not see, such as generating bills or keeping track of payments from clients.

a. Accounting and billing

Lawyers have an ethical obligation to account for all of a client's property, including funds and personal property.

i. Client's funds accounts

Lawyers may end up holding funds on behalf of a client, such as payments made by an insurance company to settle a client's personal injury suit, but these are the client's funds, not the lawyer's. The lawyer cannot deduct from those funds any fees for services rendered until the lawyer has presented the bill to the client for review and approval. It follows, then, that accounts holding only clients' funds must be kept separate from any of a law firm's accounts, to avoid the risk of commingling funds.

Clients' funds must be kept in an interest-bearing account, known as an **Interest On Lawyer Trust Account (IOLTA).** Whenever a firm receives funds on behalf of a client, it must deposit them in the IOLTA. A failure to do so could result in a lawyer having to face allegations of violation of an ethical obligation. Therefore, back office software needs to record receipt of funds and their deposit into the correct account for clients' funds.

ii. Billing

The lawyer's ethical obligation to provide timely accounting also means that a firm must generate accurate bills. An easy way to generate an accurate monthly bill would involve using software that records time spent on a client's case when any employee works on a case. Software for generating bills needs to take into account the firm's payment arrangement with the client. For example, a client might be billed:

▶ By the hour;

▶ Under a flat fee;

▶ Contingent upon the client receiving a financial recovery;

▶ For a minimum, periodically billed, fee;

▶ According to a payment plan;

▶ Against a retainer; or

▶ For recurring work by day, week, or month.

b. Ledger

The back office functions of a law firm include keeping a **ledger,** which will keep track of income and expenditures. For example, the PCLaw software packages give the firm options to look at monthly or annual financial transactions.

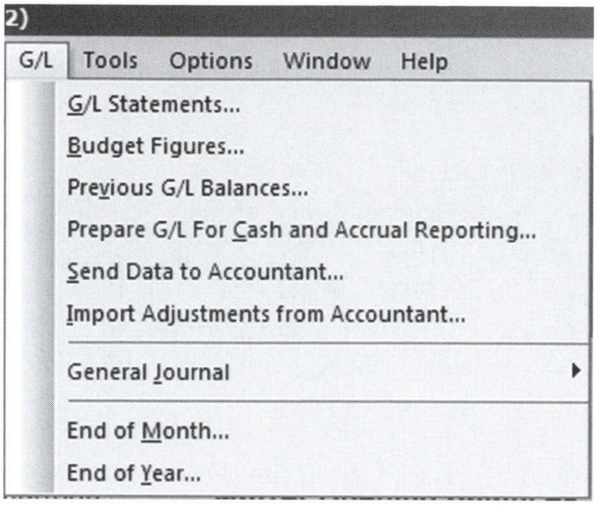

Figure 4-6. PCLaw—Toolbars: General Ledger tab

Such software could make it easy to search for transactions by:

▶ Ledger entry;

▶ Type of transaction;

▶ Subject matter; or

▶ Client.

A ledger would keep track of:

▶ Checks, such as for supplies or for payroll;

▶ State and/or federal payroll taxes, and could generate the federal W-2 income tax forms a firm must issue annually for each employee; and

▶ The amounts and awarding of bonus pay.

The software could:

▶ Keep track of financial transactions for larger firms, for each office, or for the entire legal practice;

▶ Generate reports for intervals, such as weekly or monthly, or by type of legal services provided;

▶ Integrate with widely used bookkeeping software, such as Quicken; and

▶ Facilitate a thorough review of a firm's transactions, when auditing the ledger.

Types of Practice Management Software

1. AbacusLaw

AbacusLaw practice management software, at www.abacuslaw.com, provides these functions, and makes it easy to synchronize computers so that they all contain the same data. For example, a new e-mail sent via a laptop will get copied automatically to a desktop computer, once they are connected for synchronization. The front office features of AbacusLaw include the option to:

▶ Generate the daily calendar of an employee;

▶ Produce forms to fill out, like a complaint;

▶ Create reports from preselected data;

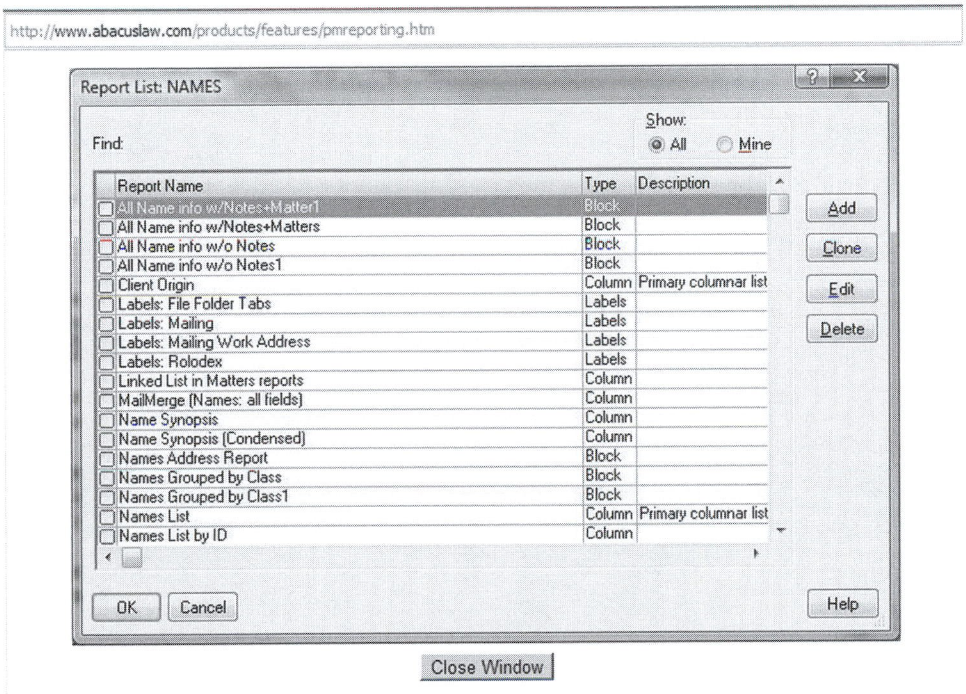

Figure 4-7. AbacusLaw—Report characteristics screen

▶ Record client information; and

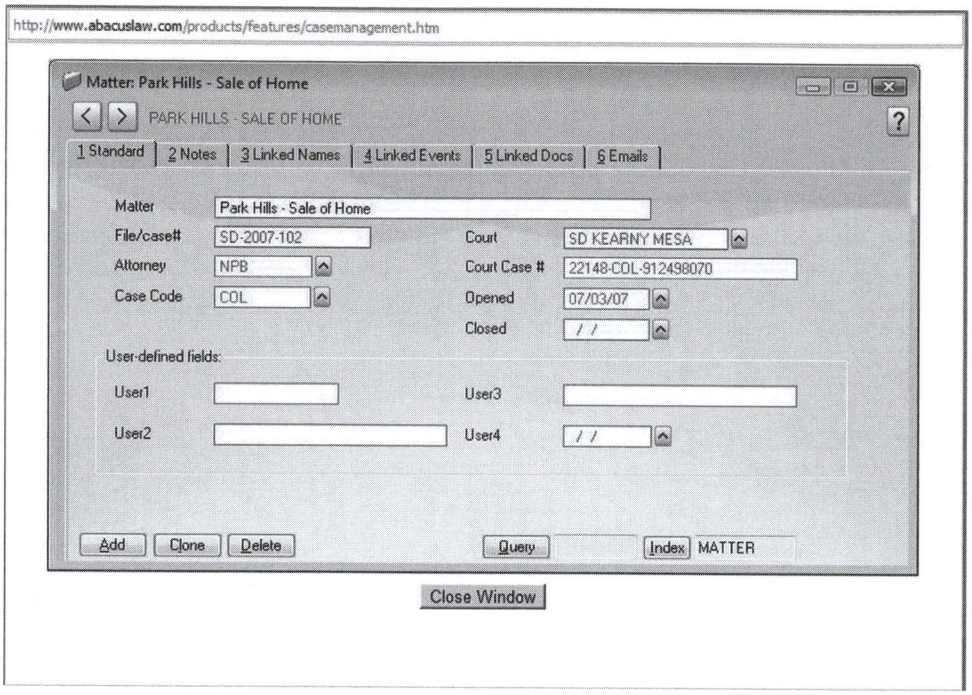

Figure 4-8. AbacusLaw—Client information screen

▶ Provide an overview of all matters related to a case.

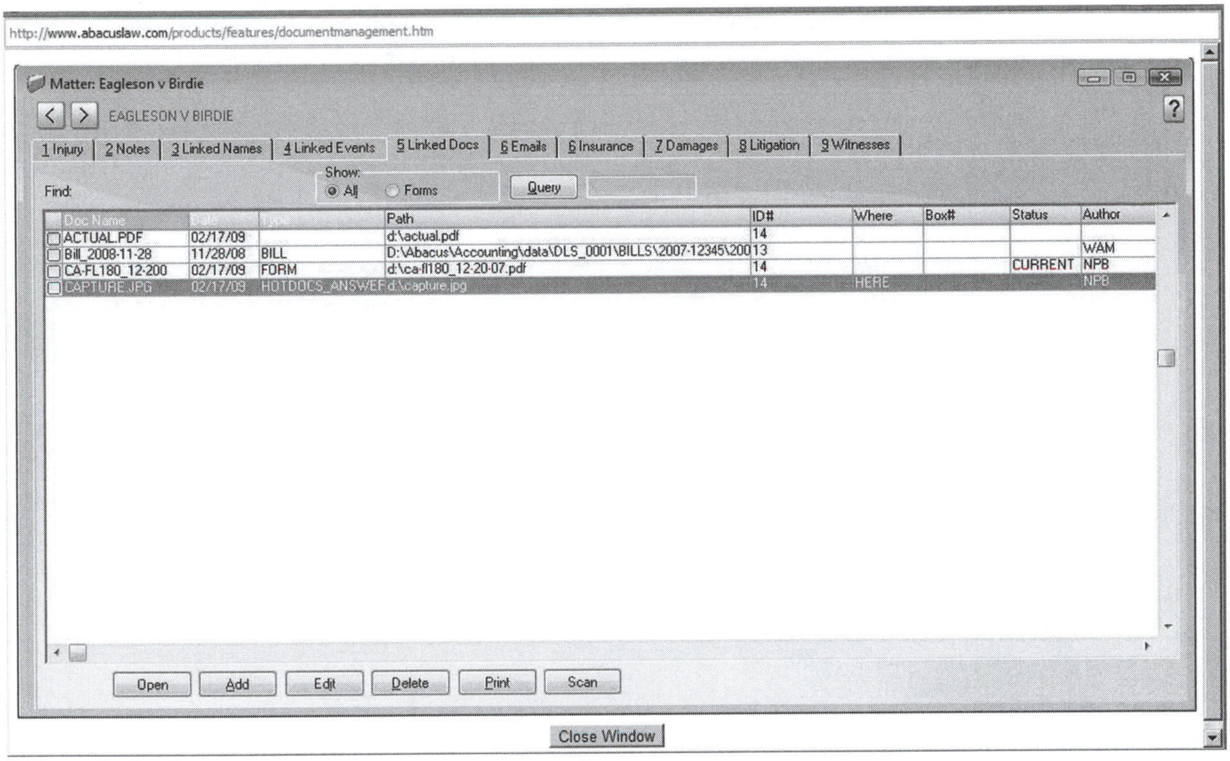

Figure 4-9. AbacusLaw—Client's associated legal matters

Other front office functions available when using AbacusLaw include:

▶ Conflict checking;

▶ Automatic creation of legal documents;

▶ Contact management;

▶ Contract management;

▶ Document management;

▶ Communications management; and

▶ Remote access.

In addition to offering typical back office features, such as keeping track of clients' funds in trust accounts, this software makes it possible for a firm to accept credit card payments and generate 1099 forms, as per federal law, whenever making a payment to a contractor.

2. Amicus Attorney

The robust practice management software offered at www.amicusattorney.com provides a typical array of useful functions. These include front office features, like managing contacts or calendaring, and back office functions, like bill generation and maintaining a ledger. Amicus Attorney comes in different packages, including one designed for a small firm: http://www.amicusattorney.com/products/comparison.html.

Product Comparison Chart

This quick reference chart shows some of the key differences between various 2013 Amicus products:

	Premium Edition	Premium Edition with Billing	Small Firm Edition	Amicus Cloud
Maximum Number of Users	Unlimited	Unlimited	10	Unlimited
Complete Matter Management System	x	x	x	x
Contact Management	x	x	x	x
Calendaring & Docketing	x	x	x	x
Time Tracking & Management	x	x	x	x
Communications Management	x	x	x	x
Notes & Stickies Management	x	x	x	
Favorites	x	x	x	
Library For Knowledge Management	x	x	x	
Document Management	x	x	x	x
Document Assembly	x	x	x	coming soon
Microsoft Word Integration	x	x	x	
Corel WordPerfect Integration	x	x	x	
HotDocs Integration	x	x	x	
Adobe PDF Integration	x	x	x	
Outlook E-mail Integration	x	x	x	x
Outlook Calendar & Contacts Synchronization	x	x	x	x
Ability to Synchronize with Mobile Devices	x	x	x	x
Accounting Product Links & Export Templates	x	x	x	x
CompuLaw Integration	x	x	x	
Custom Fields for Files & Contacts	x	x	x	Files only
File Intake Form	x	x	x	
Conflict Checking	x	x	x	x
Precedents	x	x	x	
Group & Firm-Wide Calendars	x	x	x	x
Relate Email & Documents to Events	x	x	x	
Progressive Priority Levels for Tasks	x	x	x	
Show Adjournments	x	x	x	
Customizable Dashboard	x	x	x	
Workgroup Calendars	x	x	x	x
Merge Templates for Email	x	x	x	
Firm Member Availability	x	x	x	x
Work Offline	x	x	x	
End User Reports	x	x	x	x
Scheduled Backups	x	x	x	
Runs on SQL Server 2008/2008R2/2012	x	x		
SQL Report Authoring	x	x		
Receive Daily Agenda Via Email	x	x		
Many-To-Many Relationships	x	x		

Figure 4-10. Amicus—Chart showing features of versions of Amicus software

	Premium Edition	Premium Edition with Billing	Small Firm Edition	Amicus Cloud
Unlimited Addresses and Phone Numbers	x	x		
Contact Pictures	x	x		
Relate Documents To Contacts	x	x		
Event History Tracking	x	x		
Amicus-Managed Documents (Check-In/Check-Out)	x	x		
Custom Page Designer	x	x		x
Unlimited Custom Fields	x	x		Files only
Custom Records	x	x		
Login From Any Workstation In Your Firm	x	x		x
Connect Over The Internet	x	x		x
Remote Access Capabilities	x	x		x
Citrix / Terminal Services Support	x	x		
Compatible with Amicus Mobile	x	x		
Worldox Integration	x	x		
Dynamic Link With Microsoft Office	x	x		
Sync With Google	x	x		
Firm-Wide Reporting Capabilities	x	x		x
Security Profiles & Record Restrictions	x	x		
Work with Amicus TimeTracker App	x		x	
Work with Amicus Anywhere App	x			
Track Time & Expenses Per Client				x
Easily Generate Bills		x		x
Trust Accounting		x		x
Track Payments		x		x
Manage Trust Accounts		x		x
Track Retainer Balances		x		x
Monitor WIP		x		x
Batch Bill		x		
Send Reminder Statements		x		x
Automatic Backups				x
Pay As You Go				x
Includes Unlimited Support				x
Always Up To Date				x
Billing Alerts		x		

Figure 4-10. (continued)

3. Needles

The practice management software provided by Needles, at www.Needles.com, uses toolbars with links, buttons, and drop-down menus in the style of such features used in the Microsoft Office Suite. For front office activities, it also uses tabs for recording critical client information. Lawyers and paralegals have a number of ways to search for data about clients, such as by:

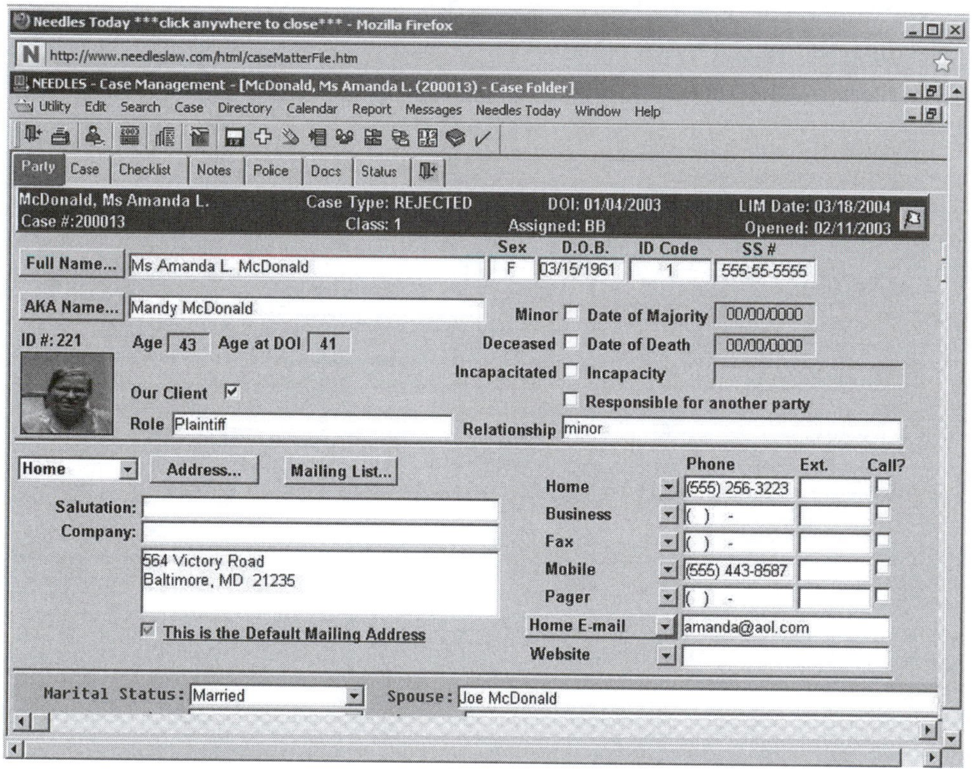

Figure 4-11. Needles—Client information screen

▶ The type of case;

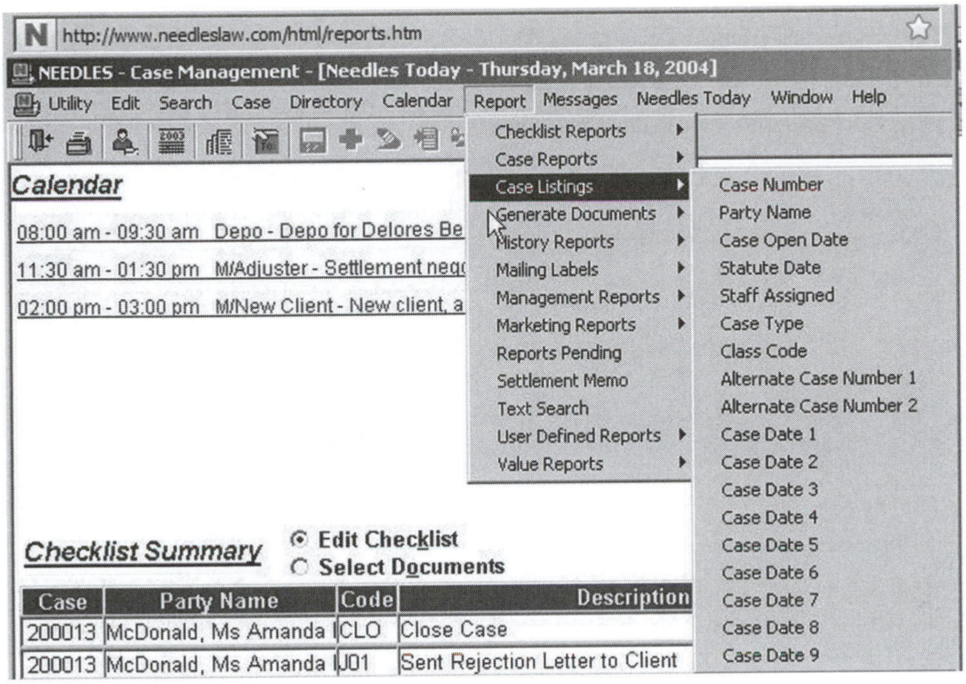

Figure 4-12. Needles—Options for search of cases

▶ Who has worked on a case; and

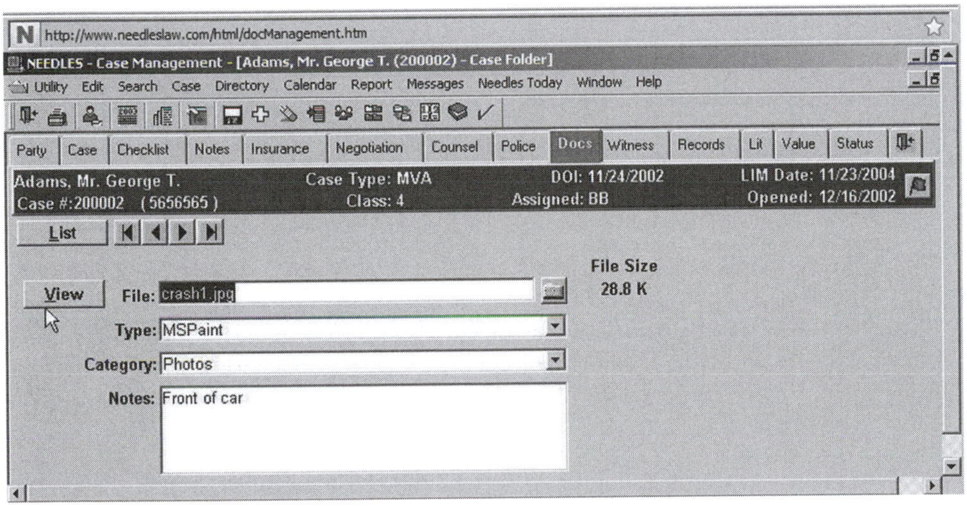

Figure 4-13. Needles—Screen for searching for documents

▶ Per the particular area of the law, such as personal injury or mass tort cases.

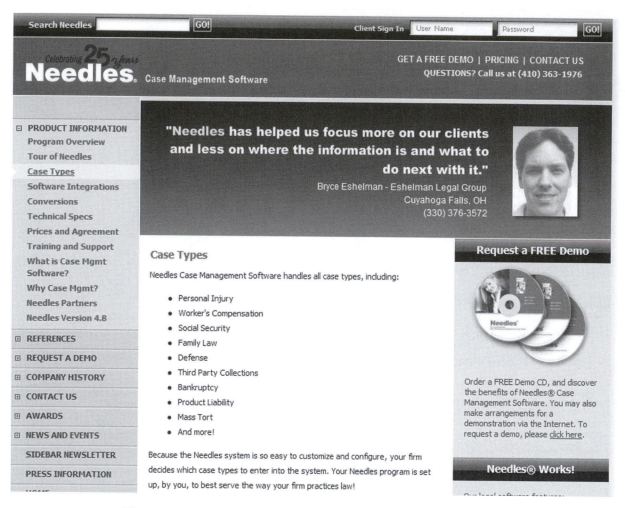

Figure 4-14. Needles—Types of cases that Needles can manage

This software makes it possible to check for conflicts of interest and allows for remote access.

In addition to having a case management application for keeping track of case expenses when preparing a client's bill, it can also integrate with the Lexis-Nexis's back office software package, Juris billing software.

4. Tabs3

Tabs3 practice management software, at www.tabs3.com, has an integrated suite of front and back office functions.

a. Tabs3—Main Task Folder

The default screen for Tabs3, the Main Task Folder, has a toolbar with familiar links, such as View, Window, Help, and File, as well as links to generate reports or statements.

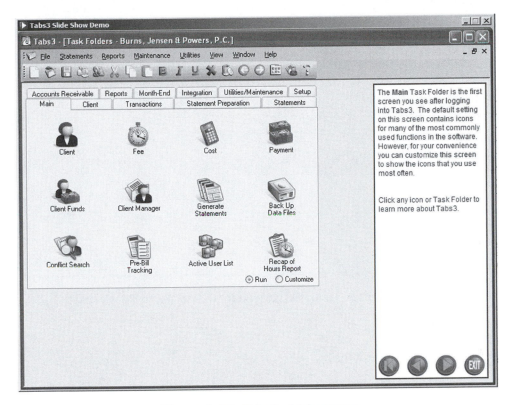

Figure 4-15. Tabs3—Main screen

Via tabs, lawyers and paralegals can perform front office functions, like remote access, and back office functions, such as keeping track of bills that clients have not yet paid, known as **accounts receivables.**

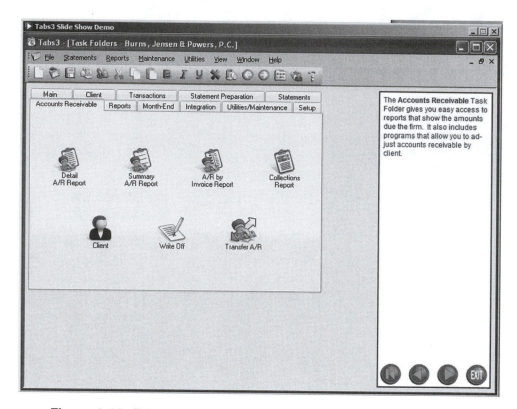

Figure 4-16. Tabs3—Links available under the Accounts Receivable tab

b. Tabs3—PracticeMaster

In addition to providing access to some functions available in the Main Task Folder, the Tabs3-PracticeMaster software makes it possible to create e-mail, make eNotes, and browse the web.

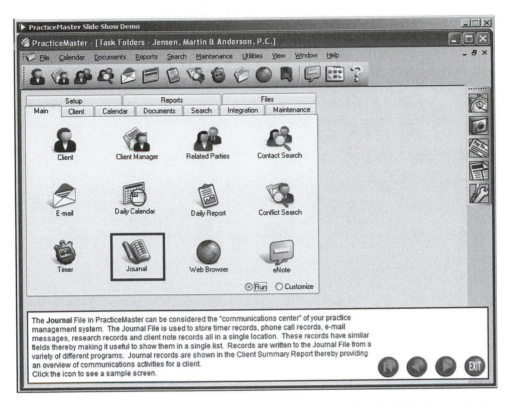

Figure 4-17. Tabs3—PracticeMaster: Links available under the Main Screen tab

c. Tabs3—Financial Software

Tabs3 Financial software concentrates on back office activities, including:

▶ Obtaining access to a general ledger or accounts payable; and

▶ Managing trust accounts, like IOLTA.

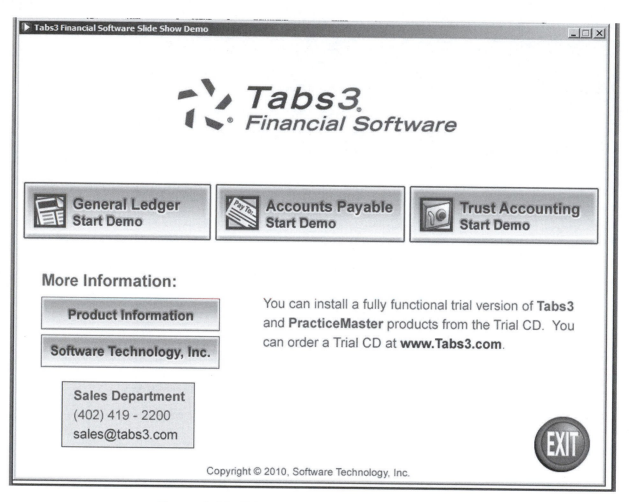

Figure 4-18. Tabs3—Financial Software: First screen

5. Lexis-Nexis Practice Management Software

Lexis-Nexis, famous for its legal research service, also makes practice management software.

a. PCLaw

PCLaw, at http://www.lexisnexis.com/law-firm-practice-management/pclaw/, serves as the umbrella designation for a number of software packages focused on practice management.

The PCLaw package uses a toolbar that has links including:

Figure 4-19. PCLaw—Top toolbar

▶ Tools (focusing specifically on balances or, more generally, on lawyer budgeting); and

▶ Options (relating to administrative functions for using the software).

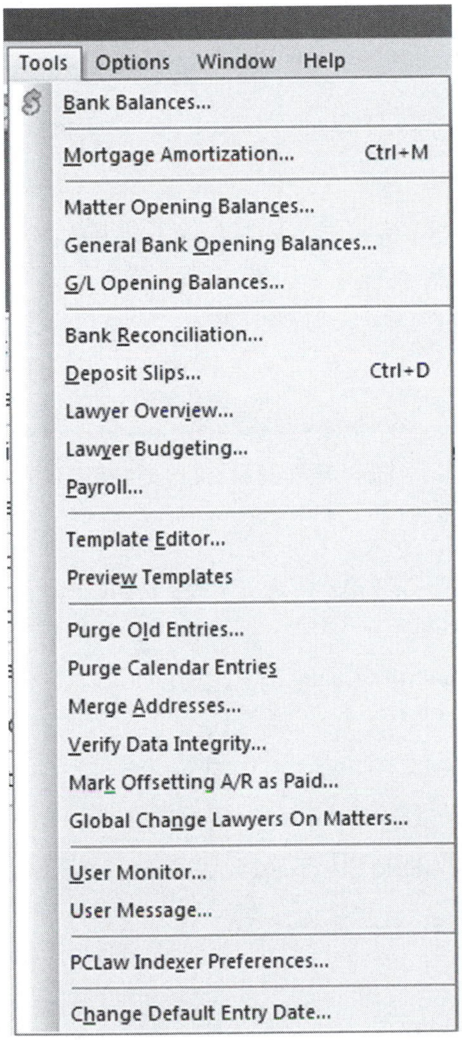

Figure 4-20. PCLaw—Top part of toolbar: Tools tab

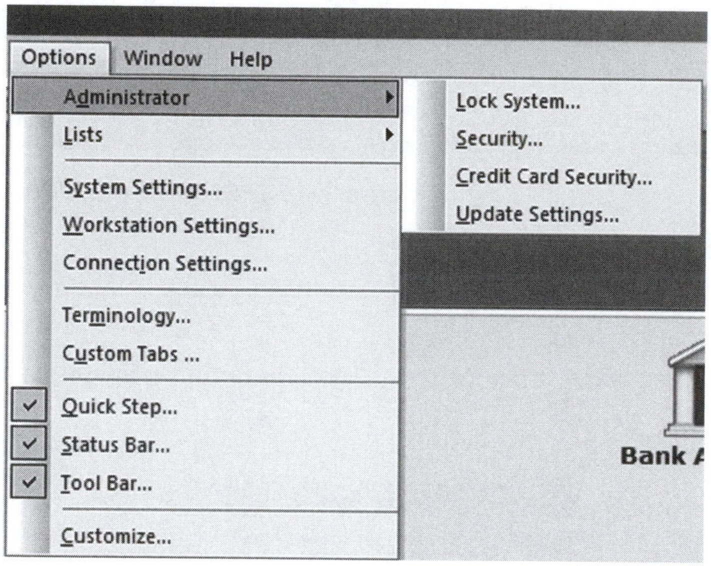

Figure 4-21. PCLaw—Top part of toolbar: Options tab

The toolbar also contains buttons for frequently used actions relating to calendaring and contact management.

Figure 4-22. PCLaw—Bottom part of toolbar: buttons

PCLaw uses a sidebar for links to functions related to the operation of a legal practice. These include:

▶ Daily tasks, like obtaining balances (with access to bank and general ledger accounts, for example);

▶ Accounting (including payroll and trust accounts);

▶ End of month/year (a compilation of summary data);

▶ General setup (including the creation of document templates); and

▶ Training and support (via Lexis-Nexis).

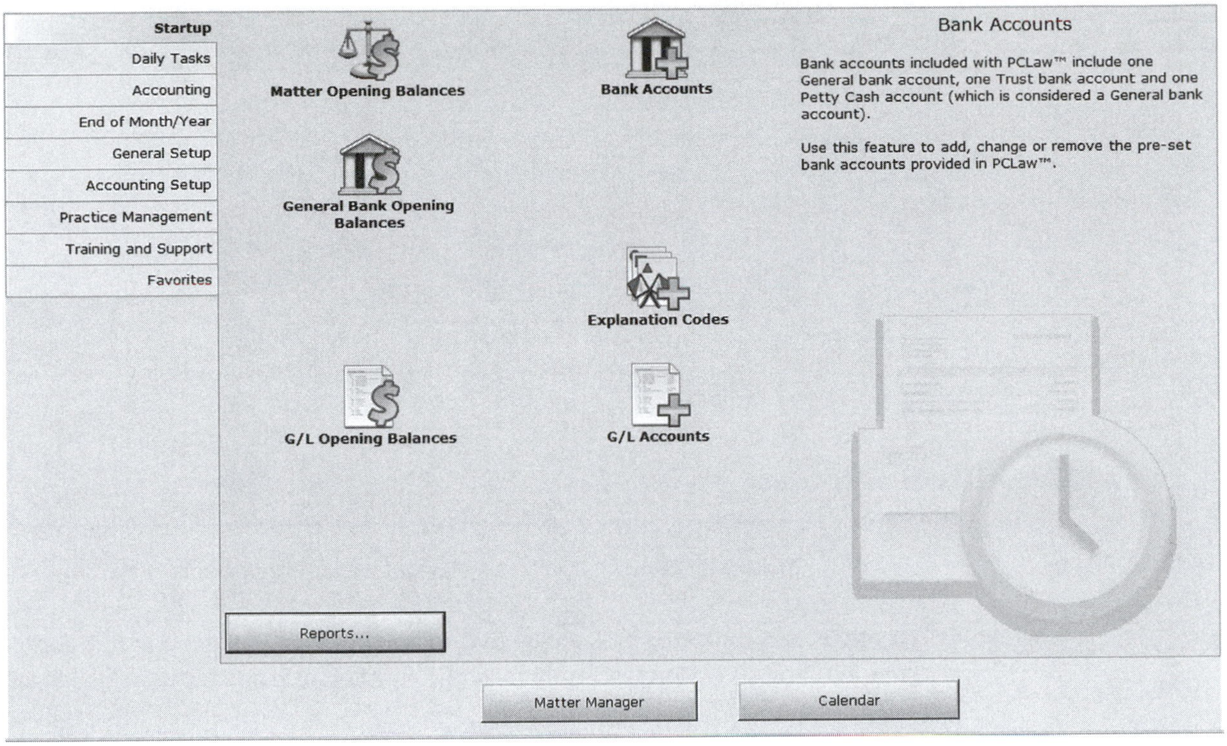

Figure 4-23. PCLaw—Side toolbar: Startup tab

b. TimeMatters

TimeMatters offers features such as:

▶ Navigator, a sidebar menu with tabs that open to a screen with common data management functions, such as tracking activities and managing communications, like the generation of phone lists.

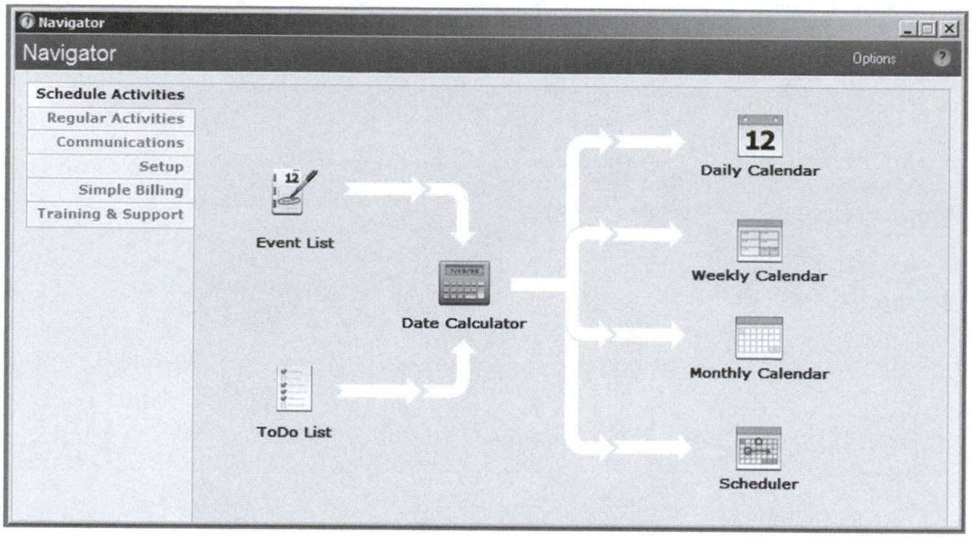

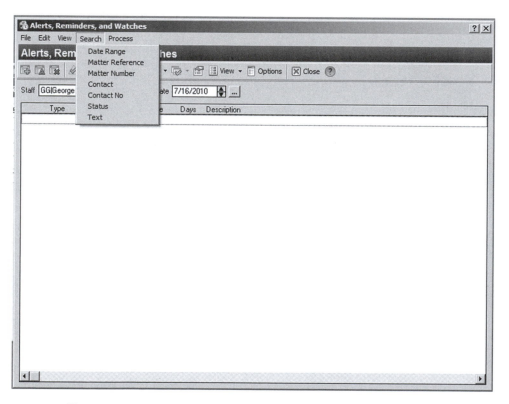

Figure 4-24. TimeMatters—Navigator sidebar options

▶ A toolbar for monitoring business activities and notifying a legal practice about those activities, via alerts, reminders, and watches, such as the status of a legal matter; and

Figure 4-25. TimeMatters—Top toolbar: Search pulldown menu

▶ A toolbar with links and buttons for access to commonly used functions, such as:

  ▷ Database, including a search of an **SQL** database;

  ▷ Lexis, to obtain access to the Lexis-Nexis database; and

  ▷ Search, includes web searches; and

  ▷ Matter Journal, a record of issue of law for which the legal practice represents the client.

Figure 4-26. TimeMatters—Toolbar: Commonly used links and buttons

c. Juris

With a focus on the financial management of a firm, Juris helps a law firm understand some of the implications of operating a legal practice. For example, it can identify potential conflicts of interest.

6. Clio

Available at www.goclio.com, this practice management software uses cloud computing, also known as Software as a Service (SaaS) (as discussed in Chapter 1). Accordingly, it has people available who can quickly and accurately diagnose a software problem. Software upgrades happen on Clio's servers, not on the law firm's. Data backups occur daily off-site. Also, a lawyer or paralegal can obtain access to it via any connection to the web.

    Clio preserves the confidentiality of a law firm's client data by using 256-bit **SSL** (secure sockets layer) encryption (as discussed in Chapter 6). This version generates passwords made up of 256 bits of information, so large that a hacker would need a great amount of computing power to crack it by trying all possible password combinations.

    Clio uses a **dashboard,** a small screen that can reside on a user's screen for quick access, such as for the continuous monitoring of a legal practice's financial health. It provides common front office features, such as:

▶ Calendaring;

▶ Reporting;

▶ Checking conflicts of interest; and

▶ Document management.

Clio offers typical back office features, such as generating bills and running a ledger, as well as the means to manage an IOLTA and take electronic payments via a credit card or the web-based PayPal electronic payment service. It offers an interface for use with smartphones, like the iPhone, or those using the Android operating system. Also, it can synchronize with Microsoft's Outlook e-mail program and Google Apps.

7. ProLaw

ProLaw, the practice management software offered by West Publishing (a Thompson Reuters Company), contains a comprehensive software package at http://www.elite.com/prolaw/front-office/. ProLaw can handle front office or back office functions, as well as integrate general business productivity software like Microsoft Office or Adobe Acrobat.

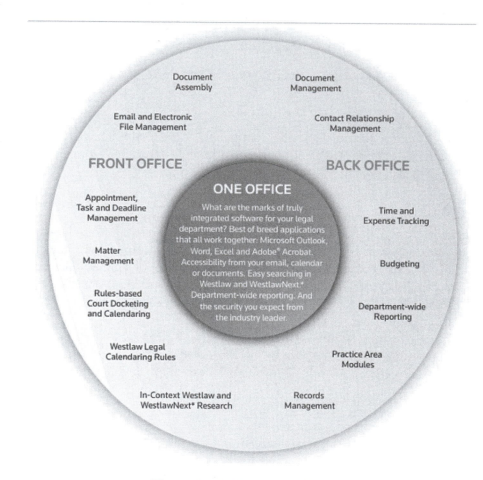

Figure 4-27. Features of ProLaw

a. Front office

Front office functions available through ProLaw include:

▶ Case and matter management, such as creating audit trails, conducting legal research, and providing continuously updated information about practice matters via a dashboard;

▶ Client and contact management, including the tracking of vendors and expert witnesses;

▶ Document management, such as generating an index of litigation-related documents, including documents in different formats, such as a PDF file or a Word document;

▶ Remote access;

▶ Report management;

▶ Time management, including synchronizing calendars on all computing devices; and

▶ Court docketing and calendaring, including synchronizing with groupware, such as IBM Lotus Notes or Novell's GroupWise, and accessing the Westlaw Legal Calendaring Rules.

b. Back office

Notable back office features available with ProLaw include:

▶ Billing, including handling billing rate overrides and determining the status of accounts receivable;

▶ Contingency analysis and disposition, regarding how a legal practice can account for payment to the firm for services only if the legal practice has successfully resolved the client's legal issues;

▶ Integrated accounting, involving payroll, bank reconciliation, and the generation of 1099 forms;

▶ Time and expense tracking;

▶ Budgeting, including how to handle write-offs, which are debts that the firm will no longer seek out for payment;

▶ Collections, regarding payment of outstanding bills; and

▶ Cost recovery, such as billing to a client's account for conducting research on a proprietary database like Westlaw.

Case Management Software

Case management software makes it easier to manage litigating clients' cases because it gives a legal practice an overview of the status of all claims in litigation. Litigation includes several distinct steps, which may include:

▶ Interviewing a client about a legal problem;

▶ Contacting another party to negotiate a settlement to resolve the legal dispute;

▶ Drafting the complaint, to start the litigation process;

▶ Doing research about the law and facts of a case; and

▶ Preparing motions and jury instructions.

This exploration of the case management software will focus on the pre-trial process of discovery. **Discovery** involves the pre-trial exchange of information related to the dispute, by the parties, that can help to resolve the dispute of law. One reason for such an exchange could result in the parties recognizing the benefits to negotiating a settlement instead of taking their chances to win at a trial. Also, agreeing to a settlement would eliminate costs associated with a trial, such as the time lawyers and paralegals would need to prepare for a trial.

Rules of Discovery

The Federal Rules of Civil Procedure (FRCP) contains the guidelines for litigating a civil claim in federal court. The FRCP describes the goals and scope of discovery and the consequences for failing to comply with a valid request for discovery. Because many states have adopted versions of the FRCP, this material looks at discovery from the perspective of the FRCP. Those that do not will still have rules about the discovery process.

Types of Discovery

Discovery includes an array of different types of information related to the legal dispute. For example, if the plaintiff has been injured, the defendant might ask for the plaintiff to see a physician, to assess the nature of the injury. Obtaining that evaluation can help the parties figure out what would be appropriate damages if the defendant should face liability for the injury.

In addition to physical examinations, discovery includes:

▶ Site visits;

▶ Interrogatories, written questions presented to an opposing party; and

▶ Production of documents.

Exemptions from Discovery

Two significant **exemptions** exist to a request for discovery, so that the party receiving the request for data does not have to turn over the requested information. The policy behind one exemption, known as the **attorney-client privilege,** reflects the hope that if clients can speak freely to their attorneys, they can get the best legal advice. Frank discussions between a client and a lawyer can provide the attorney with a better understanding of the case and could lead to a quicker, more satisfying resolution of the legal dispute.

The other exemption involves the so-called **work product doctrine.** Communications within the law firm, made in anticipation of litigation, like a discussion about trial strategy, do not have to be disclosed. Because the adversarial process of litigating a problem would reward the party that best presents a claim in court, keeping confidential how a party plans on winning can lead to a more effective resolution of the problem at trial.

Depositions

1. Nature of the Process

Lawyers for the parties can question the parties, their potential witnesses, and anyone who could have useful information about the claim. This form of discovery is called taking a **deposition.** The person being deposed is known as the **deponent.** A record, known as a **transcript,** is generated.

2. Software

Software can make it easier to look through the transcripts when they are in electronic form. When only a paper transcript exists, however, a firm can use **optical character reading (OCR)** software to scan the content of the paper transcript to convert it into **electronically stored information (ESI).**

Benefits of having software that can review the ESI of a deposition transcript include:

▶ Searchability: as ESI, software can search instantly to find information, like the date when a plaintiff suffered an injury.

▶ Annotation: as with some word processing software, software might allow a reader to enter marginal notes on the electronic version of the transcript, which the reader has identified as significant, such as when a deponent talks about weather conditions.

▶ Index: some software can generate an index of the transcript's contents and even identify the line on a page where information appears. The illustration, taken from DepoSmart, provides a user with options about features that the index could contain.

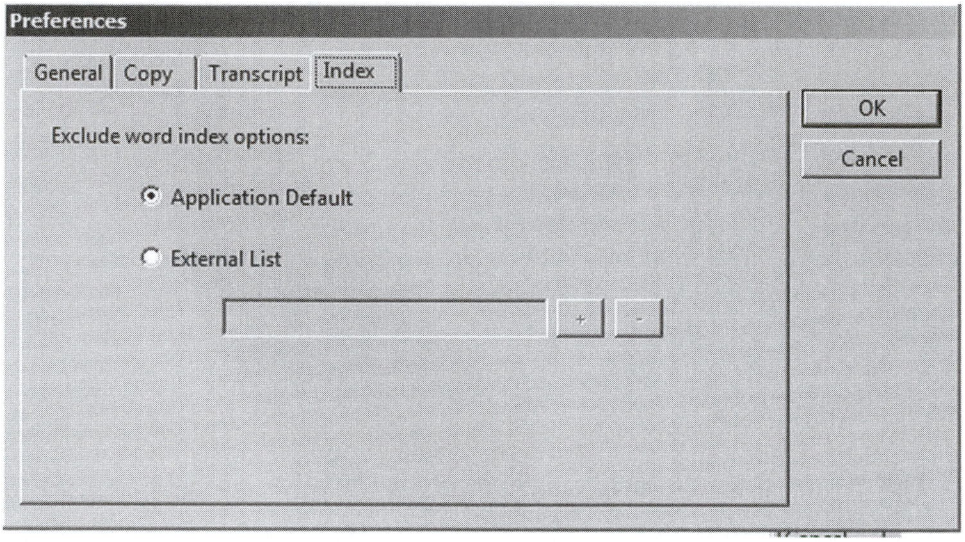

Figure 4-28. DepoSmart—Preferences for generating a deposition summary: Transcript, index

▶ Summarizing: deposition transcripts can run to hundreds or thousands of pages. Software that generates a summary of points made during the deposition can make it faster for a reader to understand what happened during the deposition. In the illustration, DepoSmart provides options such as having questions put into boldface.

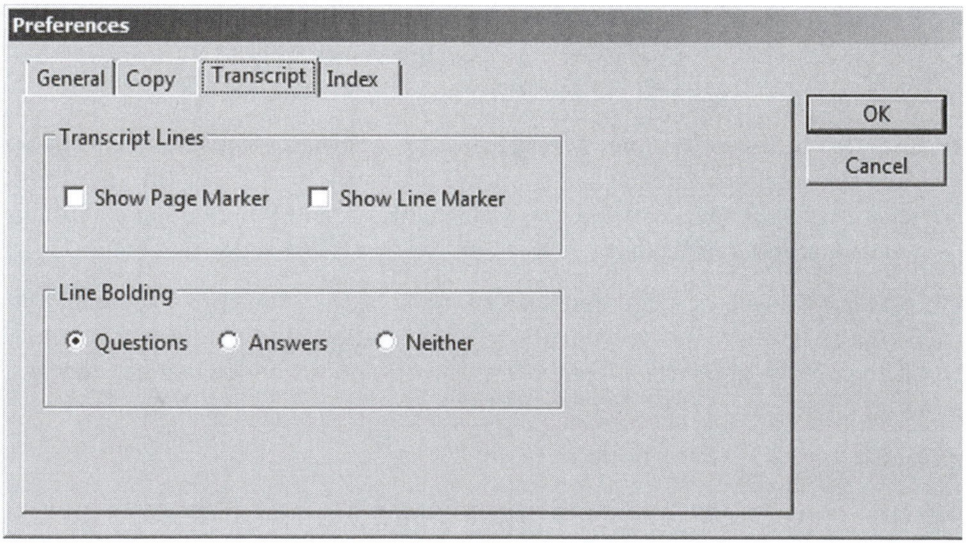

Figure 4-29. DepoSmart—Preferences for generating a deposition summary: Transcript

3. Examples of Software

a. DepoSmart

In addition to the features noted above, DepoSmart, from Clarity Legal Software at www.claritylegalllc, also allows:

▶ The reader to change fonts or to magnify text; and

▶ Multiple readers to look at the same transcript, when stored in a legal practice's database.

The toolbar provides a selection of tabs familiar to users of Microsoft software. Under the Options link, the reader can tell the software how to prepare the summary.

Figure 4-30. DepoSmart—Toolbar

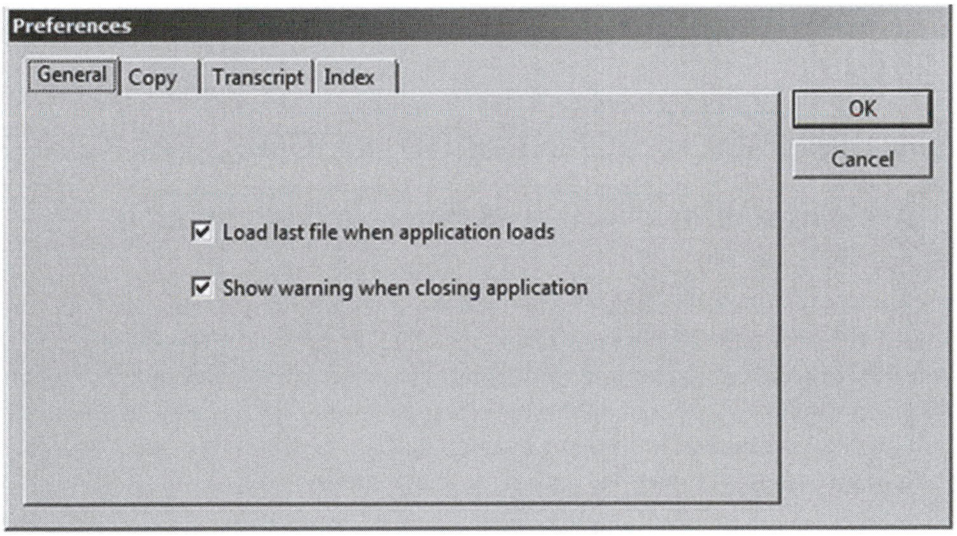

Figure 4-31. DepoSmart—Preferences for generating a deposition summary: In general

b. LiveNote

West Publishing's LiveNote, at http://west.thomson.com/products/services/case-notebook/default.aspx, makes it possible to glean, quickly and efficiently, information from a deposition transcript. Not surprisingly, a user can access this information via other West products, like Westlaw.

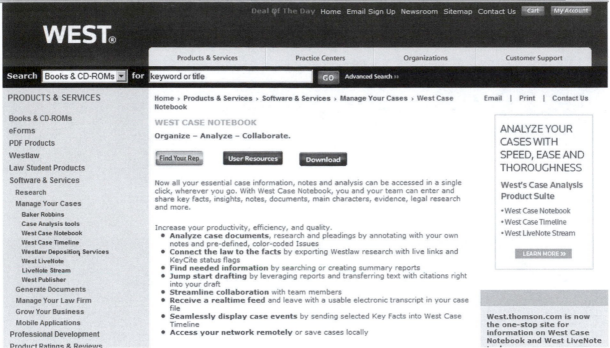

Figure 4-32. LiveNote

Electronically Stored Information

1. Avoiding a Manual Review of Requested Information

Historically, a response to a request for documents would involve a time- and labor-intensive manual review of a client's documents to see what was within the scope of the request. This review would also look to exclude information exempt from discovery. Finally, the last step would involve copying relevant documents and then submitting them to opposing counsel. Conducting a review of electronically stored information, even after having scanned the content of the requested documents, might not involve as much time or expense.

2. Processing Data

The search can go faster because software can quickly review ESI. For example, imagine that the federal Environmental Protection Agency asks that a client turn over all information regarding "chemical discharges," something easily enough and quickly done. But a different issue may arise. To increase the likelihood of fulfilling the request, a paralegal might need to search for more than the phrase "chemical discharge" and search for terms like "waste" or "residue." Software might make this process go faster, but it might not be able to look for those alternative terms or phrases.

3. E-mail

An issue with reviewing e-mail, to see whether it falls within the scope of a request for ESI, might involve the format of the content in e-mail, which the software cannot search. Converting e-mail into a searchable format might increase costs and runs the risk of omitting information, perhaps like the addresses of all recipients.

4. Litigation Holds

An additional complication can arise when trying to comply with a request for discovery because of the way that clients manage their electronic information. Periodically, businesses might destroy ESI because the increased storage costs outweigh the potential benefit of saving the data. A client that is a business might have deleted ten-year-old e-mails since no good reason existed for saving them.

This routine process of purging ESI might present a problem once litigation has started, because some of the ESI might relate to the litigation. Once litigation starts, counsel could ask for a **litigation hold,** which would stop the purging process of a client, at least until the opportunity arose to review the material to determine whether any fell within the scope of the request.

5. Metadata

a. Documents

Electronically generated material often has information encoded in it, generally known as **metadata,** but also called metacontent, that might not seem obvious. Metadata in a Word document, for example, will identify the number of words, lines, and pages. It might reveal who worked on that document and when.

The request for ESI may emphasize data rather than the process used to produce such information. Good legal practice, then, means making sure that only the data requested gets included in a response. One way to review and strip out some or most of the metadata associated with a client's ESI involves a process that some call **scrubbing.** Failure to take reasonable steps to manage metadata might amount to legal malpractice if a court decides that a competent lawyer should have reviewed and removed information outside of the scope of the discovery request.

b. Deduplication

Metadata could make it easier to cull out multiple copies of an e-mail. By looking at metadata, like the **MD5 hash,** a firm could reduce the number of multiple, identical copies that would get turned over. **Deduplication** describes the process of comparing metadata, such as MD5 hash, to eliminate such copies. Comparing metadata can also help to establish what differences may exist between a pair of apparently identical data files.

Defensible Discovery Strategy

That metadata can play a role in preparing an effective response to a request for discovery of ESI raises a potential problem for a court: what did the law firm do to comply with an opponent's request for discovery? The court will need to look at the firm's **defensible discovery strategy**—the strategies and techniques used to review ESI—since having a firm turn over all information to comply with a request could be costly and inappropriate. An acceptable strategy could include using statistically valid sampling or some other type of qualitative methodology for evaluating data. Such an approach could show the court that the law firm took reasonable steps when trying to comply with the discovery request.

1. Preparing a Defensible Discovery Strategy

Such a strategy could include:

▶ Figuring out how to preserve appropriate ESI, for the purpose of implementing a litigation hold;

▶ Creating and implementing a process to sort through the ESI quickly, efficiently, and accurately, and to know when this review has reached the point of completion;

▶ Managing the data produced, such as through the creation of a data map; and

▶ Designing and implementing a way to review the effectiveness of this process, such as generating a list of steps taken, known as an **audit trail.**

2. Inadvertent Disclosure and "Clawback"

If it turns out that a party has inadvertently released privileged or confidential information, the court may review the defensible discovery strategy to determine whether to allow a **clawback,** a recovery of the protected information. The court could allow a clawback without penalty, sparing the law firm that inadvertently released that information from having to pay the costs incurred by opposing counsel to gather and turn back the information. This might critically depend upon whether the inadvertent disclosure happened in spite of the use of a defensible discovery strategy.

3. The Electronic Data Reference Model

One type of defensible discovery strategy involves the **Electronic Data Reference Model (EDRM).**

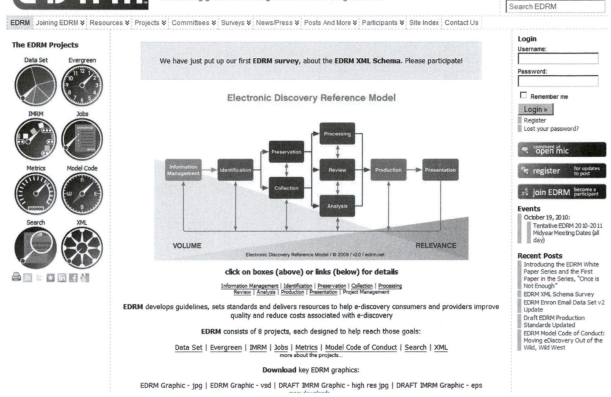

Figure 4-33. EDRM—Chart explaining how the Electronic Data Reference Model works

This approach, as seen at www.edrm.net, has a legal practice set out the steps that it would take when reviewing a client's ESI, in the form of a flow chart. The flow chart, a visual depiction of the strategy that the firm uses, could show how an ongoing review process would produce results that most closely meet the scope of the request for discovery. Using the process depicted in the flow chart might mean that the legal practice recognized a need for engaging in an ongoing process of review to select appropriate ESI, instead of waiting until the end of the search for ESI.

EDGE, from ILSTech, at www.ilstech.com, uses the EDRM model to manage the search for relevant ESI. For example, it sorts through e-mail by looking at the unique MD5 hash generated for each e-mail and simultaneously performs deduplication. EDGE keeps track of decisions made by reviewers, so that if a legal practice needs to defend how it searched through a client's ESI, the law firm can show how it reasonably tried to comply with the request for ESI.

Reviewing ESI

To conduct a defensible discovery strategy, a law firm could get software or have the review done by an outside service.

ESI Review Software

A legal practice can load software on a computer for immediate access. The **scalability** of the software could mean that the law firm would be able to use it on different devices, from a desktop to a smartphone.

1. iCONECT nXT

Among the features available from iCONECT, at http://www.iconect.com, the nXT software package allows a user to:

▶ Sort through documents;

▶ Store the documents in folders; and

▶ Create a log to keep track of what the files contain.

The software can:

▶ Show files in their original format;

▶ Allow the reviewer to annotate the files;

▶ Allow the reviewer to redact files and images, perhaps to protect confidential data; and

▶ Generate a detailed report regarding the level of success in using the selected criteria to gather information.

When reviewing ESI in the form of e-mail, the user can select review criteria to identify a chain of e-mails, relating to a topic, and to a single e-mail in that chain. For example, the defendant is alleged to have sold a car without a critical safety feature. Using this software, the plaintiff's lawyer could track the exchange of e-mails between an engineering department's perspective about a critical safety feature and a marketing department's interest in keeping the price low enough to make it competitively priced.

2. Intella

Intella, from Vound Software, at www.vound-software.com, is ediscovery software that can evaluate ESI. For example, it can provide a visualization of the relationship of data, in the form of a cluster map, such as showing corporate expenses relative to sales.

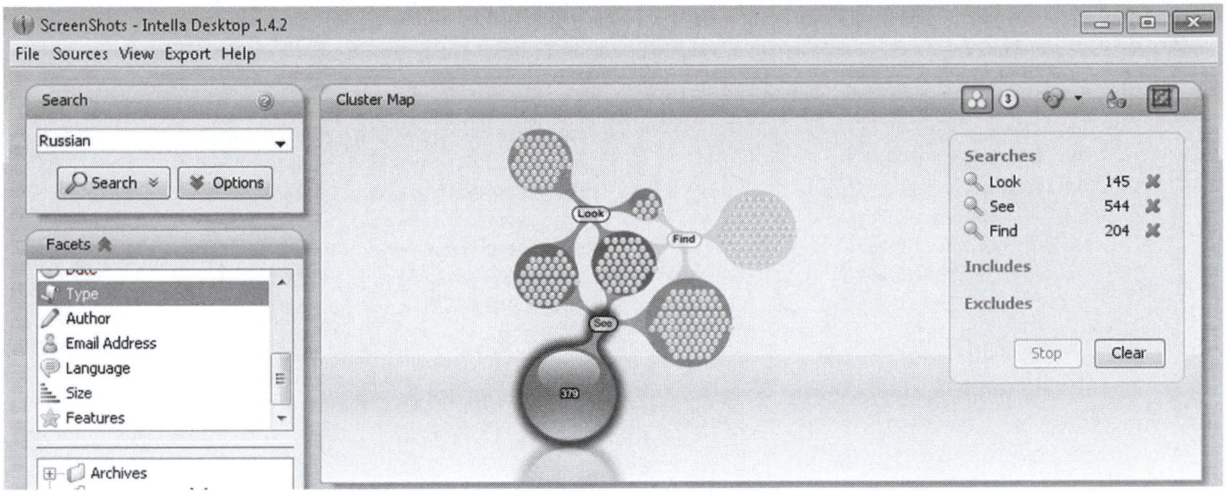

Figure 4-34. Intella—Visualized search depicting associations of data processed

When it detects a relationship among e-mails, like an exchange between the CEO of a corporation and the board of directors about launching an initial public offering of corporate stock, it can depict that visually.

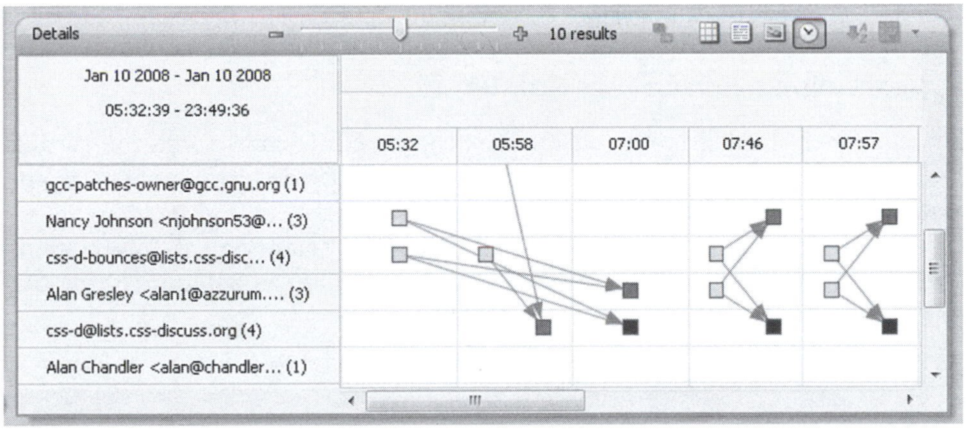

Figure 4-35. Intella—Visual depiction of associations among e-mails in a chain

It can also produce results in a more traditional format, such as a list or thumbnail images.

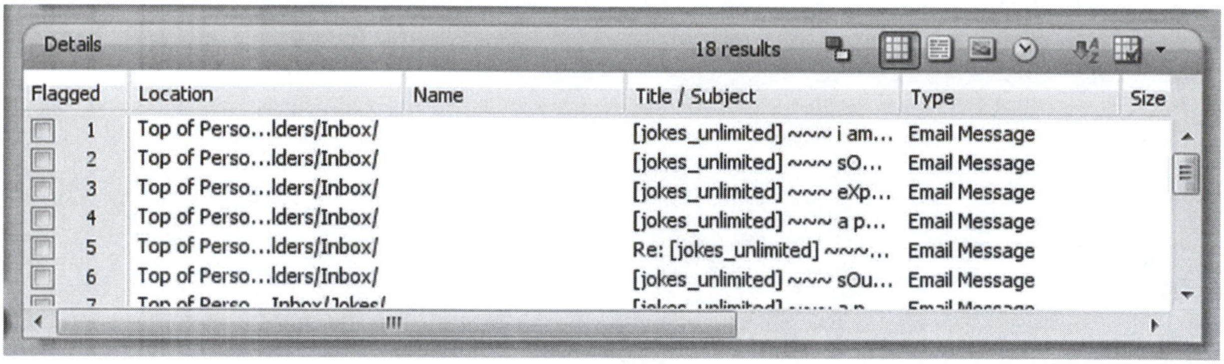

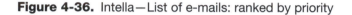

Figure 4-36. Intella—List of e-mails: ranked by priority

Intella can:

▶ Identify all lawyer-client communications, which would be exempt from discovery under the attorney-client privilege;

▶ Use MD5 hash values to do deduplication;

▶ Generate an index, which can include images embedded in documents;

▷ Gain deeper insight into ESI through visualization; and

▷ Export results in a choice of formats for later use in other eDiscovery platforms, investigative products, or reporting.

3. Lexis-Nexis ediscovery Solutions

The ediscovery management software from Lexis-Nexis can handle the sorting of a client's data in response to a request for ESI as part of a comprehensive approach for seeing litigation through to completion.

LAW PreDiscovery software manages ESI by first gathering all information, while preserving metadata. It can then conduct searches in batches, saving the culled information for further review.

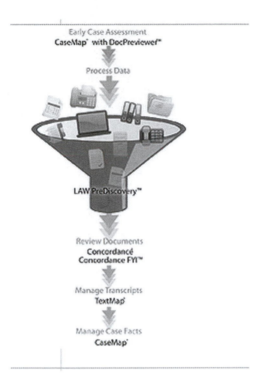

Figure 4-37. Lexis-Nexis—LAW PreDiscovery-funnel: Graphic representing the LAW PreDiscovery searching process

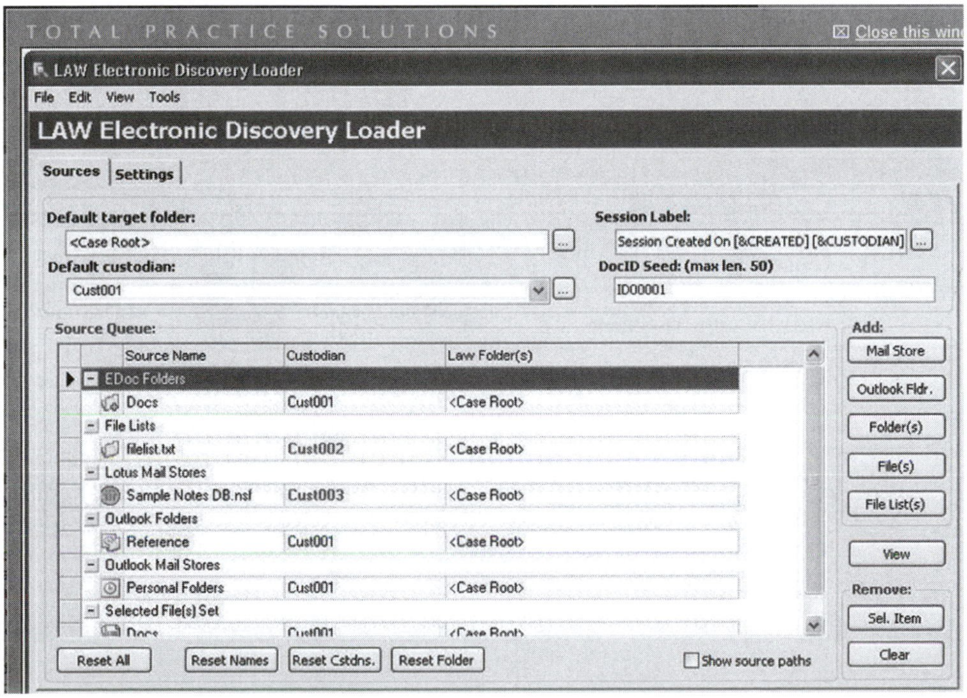

Figure 4-38. Lexis-Nexis—LAW PreDiscovery: Discovery loader

A search of a client's ESI can include documents scanned via optical character reading (OCR) and source material in languages other than English. It can incorporate material drawn from depositions, via TextMap, and from cases, via the CaseMap application.

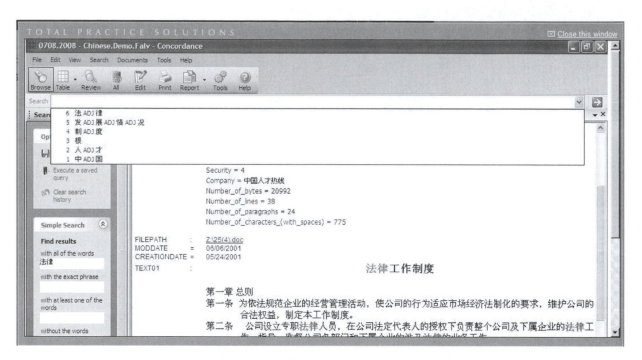

Figure 4-39. Lexis-Nexis—Concordance

4. Masterfile

MasterFile (www.masterfile.biz) addresses the four core stages of the EDRM model described on page 227 for managing, searching and organizing ESI: processing and loading, review, analysis and production. Its case analysis module can chronologically track facts and sort them, using color coding. Any information within MasterFile can be tied to case issues as analysis progresses.

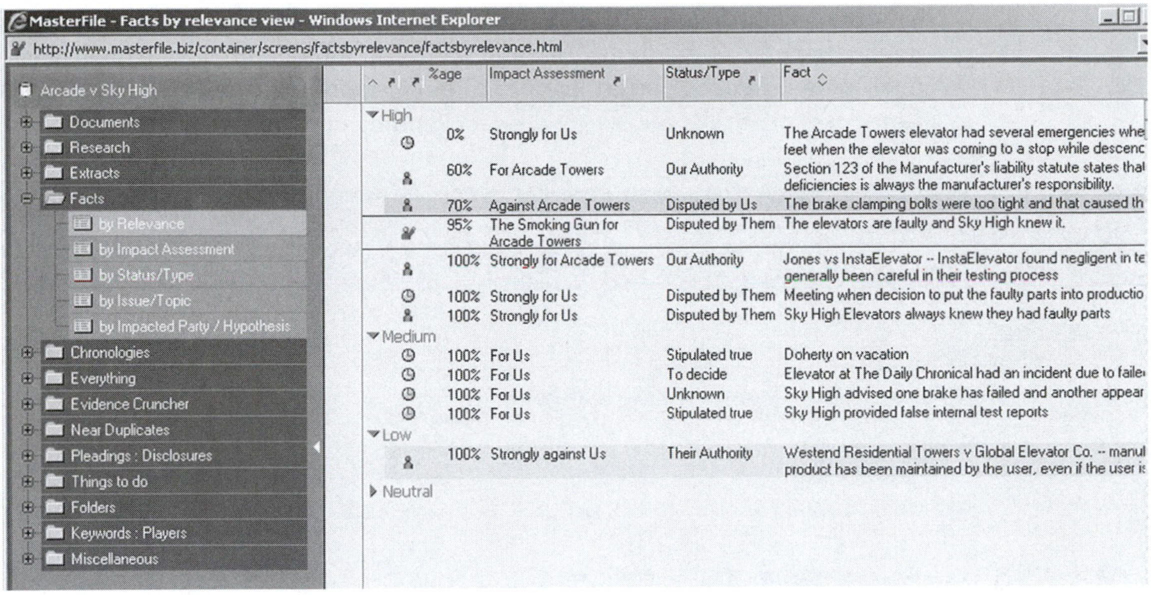

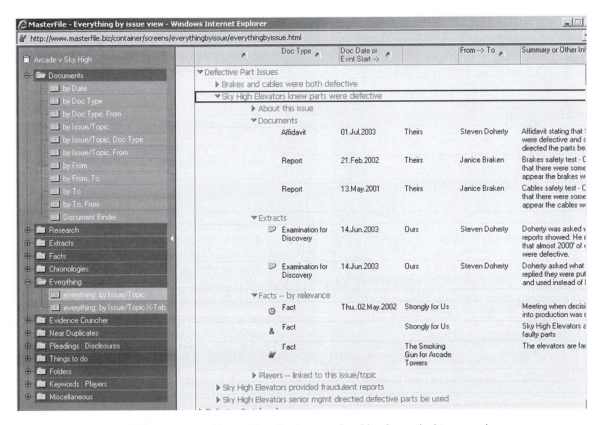

Figure 4-40. Masterfile—Color coding of facts by relevance

Figure 4-41. Masterfile—Data organized in views tied to case issue

One feature makes it possible to organize case information in terms of how it might support an argument. For example, you could identify and explain accounting reports, prepared according to standard accounting procedures, to show that a business client did have a good understanding of its financial health.

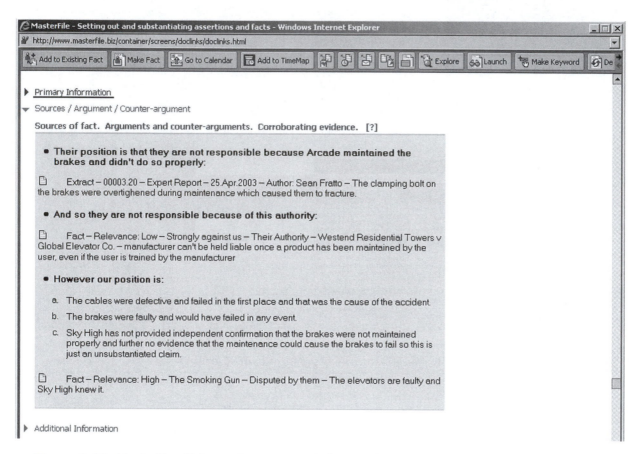

MasterFile's Express Load lets you load ESI including Outlook emails directly. Documents can be found in two or three clicks or searched for. Documents can be produced in PDF and native formats, and tracked with Bates numbers, redactions, and so forth, to meet disclosure requests.

5. Case Logistix

Westlaw's Case Logistix, at http://store.westlaw.com/products/services/westlaw-case-logistix/default.aspx, can sort through ESI via a multiple-review process. For example, a first review of the client data might look for information that would substantially comply with a discovery request. A second, more focused review could look for data to redact, such as that covered by the attorney-client privilege.

A third review could involve quality control. After that, counsel might be ready to turn over the material to comply with the discovery request.

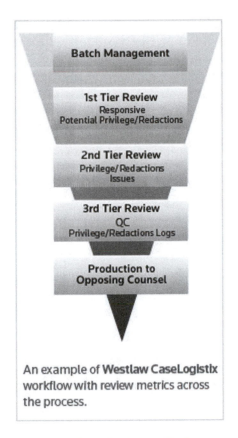

An example of **Westlaw CaseLogistix** workflow with review metrics across the process.

Figure 4-43. Case Logistix—Review process

The law firm can conduct a native review to understand the context of information that the software has identified. This scalable software can conduct searches based upon synonyms and phonic speech. It includes an option to look for embedded content in a tagged image file format (TIFF) file.

Examples of ESI Review Services

A firm might find it easier and cheaper to hire an outside vendor to search through a client's ESI. The vendor would have experience doing such a review and might have better hardware and software to do that review. Of course, the legal practice would need to hire a vendor with impeccable credentials, such as years of experience doing these reviews, a well-earned professional reputation, and evidence of continued training and/or improvement.

1. Categorix

Categorix is a document review litigation service provided by Xerox at http://www.xerox-xls.com/ediscovery/categorix.html. Using statistical measures, the service reviews ESI repeatedly to look at the ratio of relevant data retrieved as a part of the overall amount of data. For example, by calling attention to a particular e-mail, the Categorix service can review ESI for data to determine whether it deserves further attention because of its relationship to the particular e-mail. Using this statistical approach makes it easier for a legal practice to demonstrate that it has used a defensible discovery strategy to satisfy the request for information.

Via a dashboard, the service can show the rate at which it has processed ESI. It can track information, such as when information is transmitted using the FTP (file transfer protocol) method. Also, it can identify who has had custody of the information. This means, for example, that the service can identify the exchange of drafts of a contract for the renovation of a community's downtown and show who has the final draft of the contract.

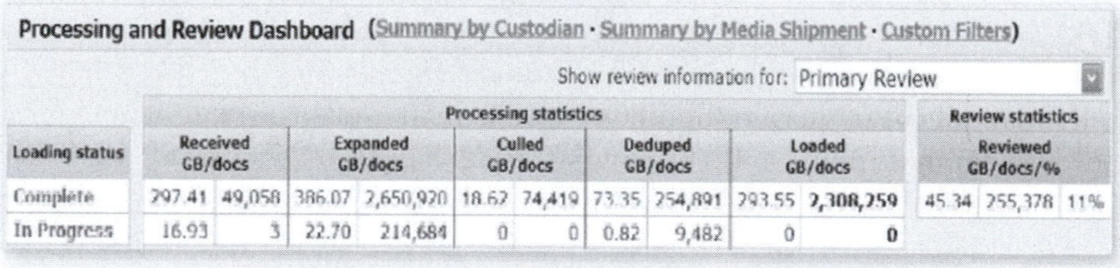

Processing and Review Dashboard (Summary by Custodian · Summary by Media Shipment · Custom Filters)

Show review information for: Primary Review

Loading status	Processing statistics										Review statistics		
	Received GB/docs		Expanded GB/docs		Culled GB/docs		Deduped GB/docs		Loaded GB/docs		Reviewed GB/docs/%		
Complete	297.41	49,058	386.07	2,650,920	18.62	74,419	73.35	254,891	293.55	2,308,259	45.34	255,378	11%
In Progress	16.93	3	22.70	214,684	0	0	0.82	9,482	0	0			

Figure 4-44. Categorix—Processing and review dashboard

2. Daegis ediscovery

The eDiscovery Analytics Consulting service provided from Daegis at www.daegis.com, uses the electronic data reference model (EDRM; see above) to review ESI.

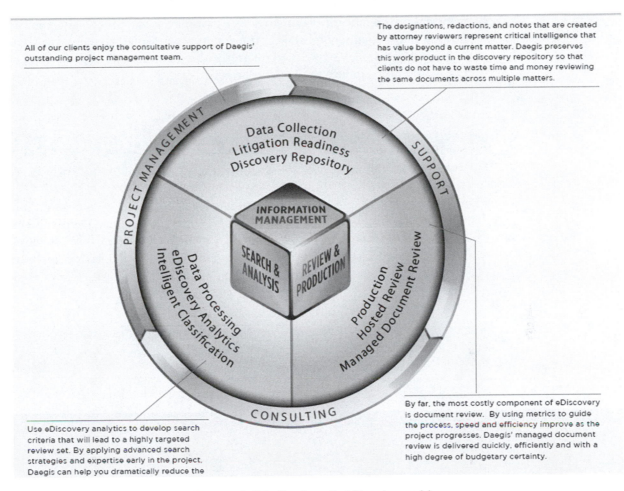

All of our clients enjoy the consultative support of Daegis' outstanding project management team.

The designations, redactions, and notes that are created by attorney reviewers represent critical intelligence that has value beyond a current matter. Daegis preserves this work product in the discovery repository so that clients do not have to waste time and money reviewing the same documents across multiple matters.

Use eDiscovery analytics to develop search criteria that will lead to a highly targeted review set. By applying advanced search strategies and expertise early in the project, Daegis can help you dramatically reduce the

By far, the most costly component of eDiscovery is document review. By using metrics to guide the process, speed and efficiency improve as the project progresses. Daegis' managed document review is delivered quickly, efficiently and with a high degree of budgetary certainty.

Figure 4-45. Services that Daegis provides

The service:

▶ Preserves the integrity of ESI when transferring it from the client;

▶ Uses a single interface to streamline the review process;

▶ Creates an audit trail if the law firm needs to show that it has engaged in a defensible discovery strategy when preparing a response to a request for information;

▶ Can review electronic records from different sources, such as from Lotus Notes, and Microsoft Exchange; and

▶ Can identify significant documents. For example, a law firm might need to provide transaction reports sent to the appropriate regulatory agency to show that a publicly traded client filed quarterly reports on time, if the client faces prosecution for a failure to file those on time.

Conclusion

Many lawyers have found that better time management works to meet multiple demands for their services. Using software tailored to practice management, with its emphasis on running a business, can help a legal practice do high-quality legal work for its clients. Case management software makes it possible for a legal practice to obtain a quick and accurate understanding of a client's case.

Terms

Accounts receivables

Attorney-client privilege

Audit trail

Back office operations

Calendaring software

Case management software

Clawback

Cloud computing

Dashboard

Database

Deduplication

Defensible discovery strategy

Deponent

Deposition

Discovery

Docket

Electronic Data Reference Model (EDRM)

ESI

Ethical wall

Exemptions

Federal Rules of Civil Procedure (FRCP)

Firewall protection

Front office activities

Interest On Lawyer Trust Accounts (IOLTA)

Ledger

Litigation hold

MD5 hash	SQL
Metadata	SSL
Optical character reading (OCR) software	Statute of limitations
Practice management software	Template
Remote access	Ticklers
Scalability	Track
Scrubbing	
Servers	Transcript
Software as a Service (SaaS)	Work product doctrine

Hypotheticals

1. Explain what is involved in crafting a defensible discovery strategy.

2. Based upon the software described in this chapter, evaluate four software packages so that you could recommend to a law firm that it purchase specific software, based upon its ability to handle front office functions. Explain your selection.

3. Based upon the software described in this chapter, evaluate four software packages so that you could recommend to a law firm that it purchase specific software, based upon its ability to handle back office functions. Explain your selection.

4. What features would be critical for evaluating data in a deposition transcript ? Why?

5. **a.** When it comes to reviewing a client's ESI when trying to respond to a request for discovery, which is better: having the software or using SaaS? Why?

   b. Pick one of the types of software packages mentioned in this chapter, for each type, and explain why it would be the best choice in that category. Then, compare any two of the same kind of software, and explain why you think one would be better than the other.

Internet-Based Legal Research

5

Objectives

▶ **Compare** and contrast features of the major, proprietary legal databases, like Lexis-Nexis, Westlaw, and Loislaw.

▶ **Identify** critical functions of a database, such as how to find out about the future treatment of a case, via Lexis-Nexis's Shepard's, Westlaw's KeyCite, or Casemaker's CaseCheck.

▶ **Investigate** what non-proprietary databases, like LII, and search engines, like Google Scholar, have to offer.

▶ **Examine** unique features of a legal database, such as the graphic depiction of the relationship of data in Fastcase or the widget in Loislaw.

Introduction

Conducting legal research at a large legal practice traditionally meant working in the firm's law library, which meant the firm had to pay rent for space to store the law books and to pay for subscriptions to keep those materials up to date. Alternatively, a law firm could rely on a public law library at a courthouse or law school, with access limited to the library's hours of operation.

Electronic research can provide an attorney with instant access to the latest information on the law, without the need for space to store the many volumes needed to have a good quality law library. Additionally, because a client would pay for such research, a need exists to work effectively and efficiently.

This chapter's focus on conducting Internet-based legal research aims to provide an overview of electronic research options rather than to talk about legal research strategies in general, something more fully addressed in a text that examines all types of legal research strategies.

Researching the Law

The Nature of Law

1. Sources of Law

Primary law is "controlling law," the law that a court follows to resolve a legal problem. A court needs to have jurisdiction, which is the legal authority to resolve that problem of law. Most problems involve state law. A state court that has jurisdiction would rule based upon:

▶ Prior court rulings;

▶ A state's constitution;

▶ **Statutes;** and

▶ **Regulations.**

A court in Massachusetts would have the authority to resolve a problem involving that state's law.

While every state will have jurisdiction over problems in that state, the federal government would have jurisdiction over problems of law involving two or more states or problems that involve federal, or national, law. A federal court trial judge might need to decide a case over a copyright dispute, since copyright protections exist under federal law, or interstate commerce, as when someone who lives in Massachusetts makes a purchase of a computer system from a seller in California.

Court rulings from outside of a court's jurisdictional authority do not have binding effect, yet a court could find them especially persuasive because they came about through the application of due process principles. For example, a court in Ohio does not need to follow court rulings from Nevada because those rulings don't apply in Ohio due to lack of jurisdiction. But if an Ohio judge needs to resolve a case of "first impression," something not previously addressed in any previous Ohio case, such as the scope of a new criminal law, the Ohio judge could look at how a court in Arizona ruled regarding the scope of a similar Arizona law.

Secondary law has a persuasive, not controlling, influence. A court might review secondary law when looking for insight about a particular issue of law. Secondary law can include:

▶ **Law reviews** (scholarly publications often published by law schools);

▶ **Treatises** (an exploration of a topic by legal professionals);

▶ Legal encyclopedias, such as the *Corpus Juris Secundum* and *Am.Jur.*2d;

▶ Restatements of law (scholarly treatises about the law, like torts or contracts, put out by the American Law Institute); and

▶ Newspapers about the law.

So, a court might feel that arguments put forth in a law review article about a new tort, for example, for invasion of privacy, make a strong enough case to recognize that such a tort exists in that court's jurisdiction.

2. Common Law

The American legal system is almost completely based upon English **common law.** Centuries ago, judges effectively made law because no elected legislature existed to create law. For example, if everyone in the community agreed that arson was wrong, a judge would rule in a case that arson was a crime. Common law is also known as case law or judge-made law.

English judges understood that their rulings could provide guidance about how to deal with a similar problem in the future. Courts would then need to apply the law consistent with what other judges had decided, earlier and elsewhere, called **following precedent.** Following precedent would reinforce a sense of predictability to the law. If a court in one case, for example, came up with a method for deciding whether a will was properly created, a court in another case involving a dispute over the validity of a will would need to use the same approach as the court in the earlier ruling. If a client has asked a lawyer to prepare a will, the lawyer could rely on the earlier court's opinion for guidance about when a will is valid. The policy that had English judges follow precedent is known by the Latin phrase *stare decisis*.

While the United Kingdom and the United States now have legislatures to make law by enacting statutes, a judge could still create law when deciding whether a prior ruling created precedent that had to be followed in the case before that judge. Also, a court would effectively create law by interpreting a phrase in a statute. For example, the federal Americans with Disabilities Act does not specifically define what a disability is. Instead, courts have had to determine the meaning of the term on a case-by-case basis.

3. Statutes

Not only would legislatures create law by enacting statutes, they had the authority to overrule a court's decision. For example, people can use force in self-defense to end a threat, but only under certain conditions, such as if the person has no opportunity to retreat safely. A court might rule that if the person in the home could safely retreat from the home, then that person needed to retreat instead of using force in self-defense. A legislature might react to that ruling by passing a law that says that even if a person facing the threat of physical harm by a burglar in that person's home could retreat safely from the home, "A man's home is his castle," so that no retreat is necessary before using force in self-defense. This is the "castle doctrine."

4. Regulations

Congress and state legislatures have delegated some of their rule-making and enforcement authority to executive branch offices known as agencies. Agencies use this authority to enact and enforce a type of law known as a **regulation,** because an agency could develop expertise about a specific problem. For example, in the late 1960s, Congress created the Environmental Protection Agency (EPA) and gave the EPA authority to create regulations to set limits on acceptable levels of pollution and the power to enforce those regulations against illegal polluters.

5. U.S. Supreme Court Rulings

The effect of a state court's ruling ended at its borders, but the rulings of the U.S. Supreme Court, which has the final responsibility for interpreting the U.S. Constitution, serve as primary law throughout the country.

Database Versus Search Engine

Researching the law electronically might involve consulting a **database** or using a **search engine.** Both could contain case law or statutes, but they are not the same.

1. Database

With a database, a business has encoded information, like court rulings, in a way to make it easy to search through the information, such as by the name of the case or the law involved in a case. The business could also encode information in those cases according to the business's own unique approach to doing legal research.

For example, the international publisher Thomson Reuters owns the Westlaw database, which contains an exhaustive range of material about the law. When creating the database, it has also encoded information in court rulings with **key numbers,** its proprietary system for classifying points of law in the case. So, if someone wanted to do research on an *in terrorem* clause in a will, that person could start with the legal encyclopedia published by Thomson Reuters, the *Corpus Juris Secundum,* and see that the entry about wills is broken down by key numbers into subsections. Then the researcher could look up those cases that have that specific key number to see what the courts say about having such a clause in the will.

To recoup the cost of creating the Westlaw database, and for keeping it up to date, a researcher needs to pay a fee to use Westlaw or other proprietary databases, like Reed-Elsevier's Lexis-Nexis or Wolter Kluwers's Loislaw. A law firm using the database on behalf of a client would, in turn, charge the client a fee for that use.

2. Search Engine

Search engines will rely only on information from the Internet to create a database. The operators of the search engine might not encode information like Westlaw did when assigning key numbers to points of law made in a case or when providing a link on that point of law to articles from its American Law Reports publications. To subsidize the cost of maintaining the search engine, an operator might need to rely upon revenue from the sale of advertising.

3. Public Databases

a. Agencies

Governmental agencies might have created databases. For example, the Department of Labor has created a database about statutes and regulations involving federal labor laws.

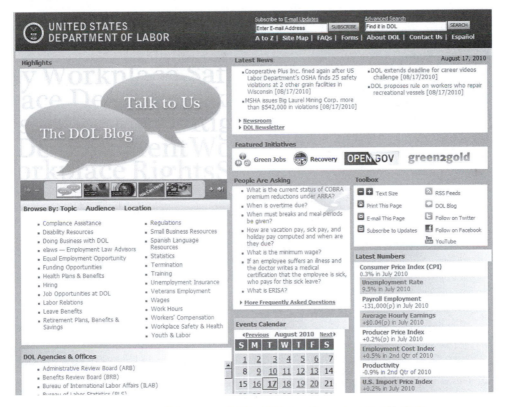

Figure 5-1. Web page—United States Department of Labor

The data available on this free database will have a high likelihood of validity and reliability, since the government created it specifically to inform the public about federal employment law.

b. PACER

Another public database, **PACER (Public Access to Court Electronic Records),** a subsystem of the federal judiciary's Case Management/Electronic Case filing system, contains U.S. District and appellate court rulings. Access fees to this database help to pay for its support and maintenance.

c. Non-profit databases

Cornell University's **Legal Information Institute** database, at http://www.law. cornell.edu, includes federal statutes and rulings, as well as model laws, like the Uniform Commercial Code. This free database will continue to expand its coverage to include state case law and statutes.

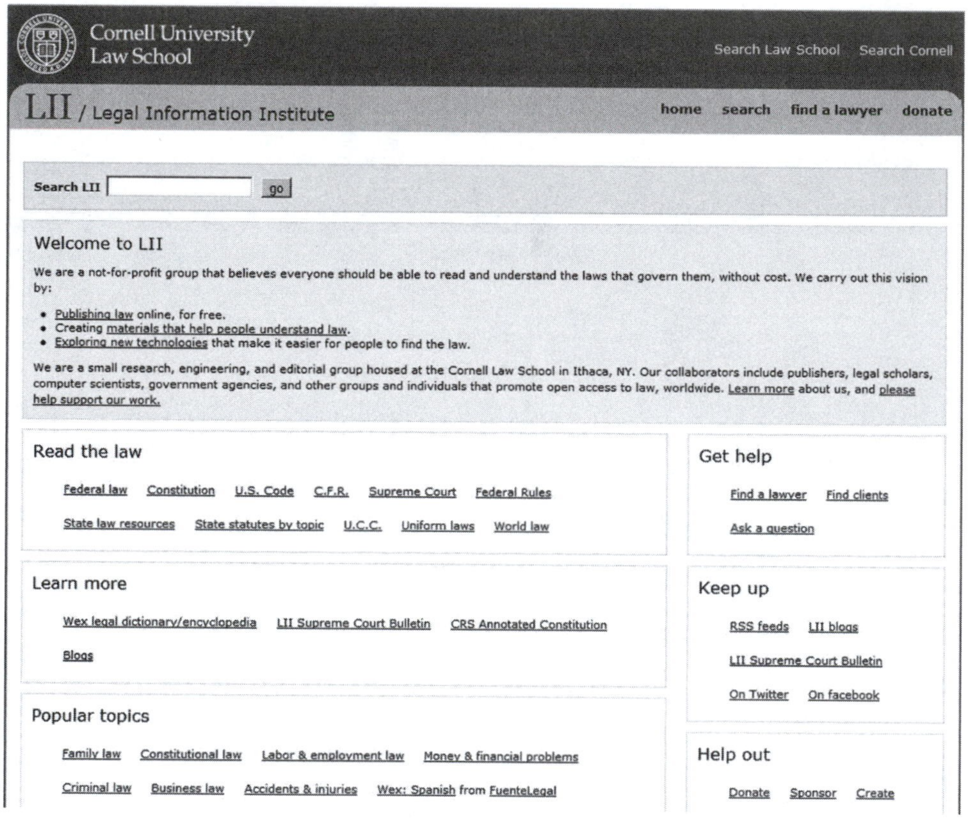

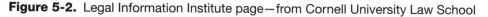

Figure 5-2. Legal Information Institute page—from Cornell University Law School

Lexis-Nexis

Lexis-Nexis, owned and operated by the multinational information business, Reed-Elsevier, offers a range of services involving its proprietary database. One version, typically used at a law firm, uses tabs on a toolbar for selecting different ways to locate information about the law.

Figure 5-3. Lexis—Law office version toolbar

Some colleges and universities subscribe to a version of Lexis-Nexis that does not have such a toolbar.

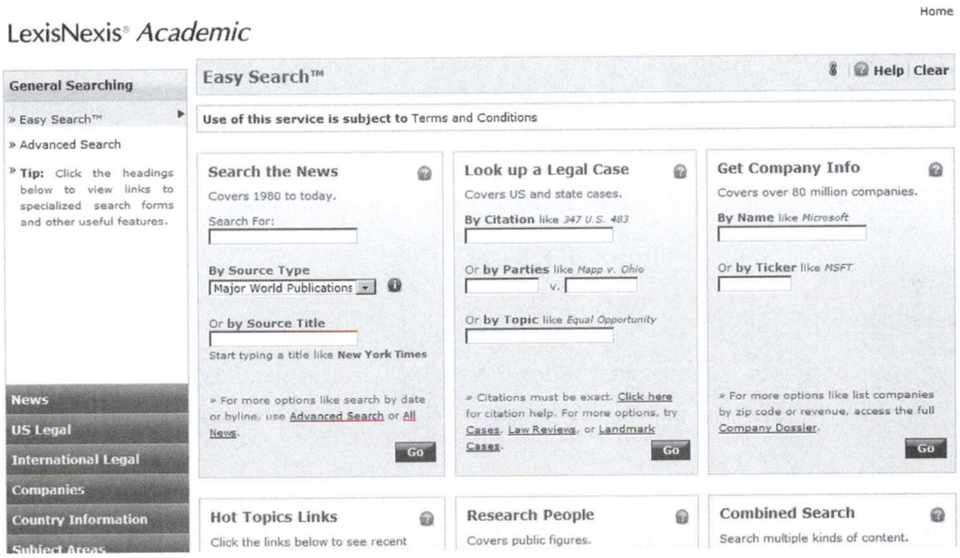

Figure 5-4. Lexis—Academic version

This analysis will focus on the version commonly used in a law firm, starting with tabs on the left.

Conducting Legal Research Using the "McDonald's Cup of Coffee" Case

To explore how this database works, start with the premise that a researcher at a law firm needs to learn about the so-called "McDonald's Cup of Coffee" case. The researcher knows nothing about the case, beyond that it involved a claim in tort law for negligence. In this case, Stella Liebeck successfully sued McDonald's for damages when she spilled very hot coffee on herself and suffered third-degree burns. Lexis-Nexis offers several ways to find out more about the case.

1. My Lexis Tab

Under the My Lexis tab, a researcher can quickly search the database, using the phrase "McDonald's Cup of Coffee Case," selecting as the jurisdiction Federal & State Law Combined, and checking off the Cases box.

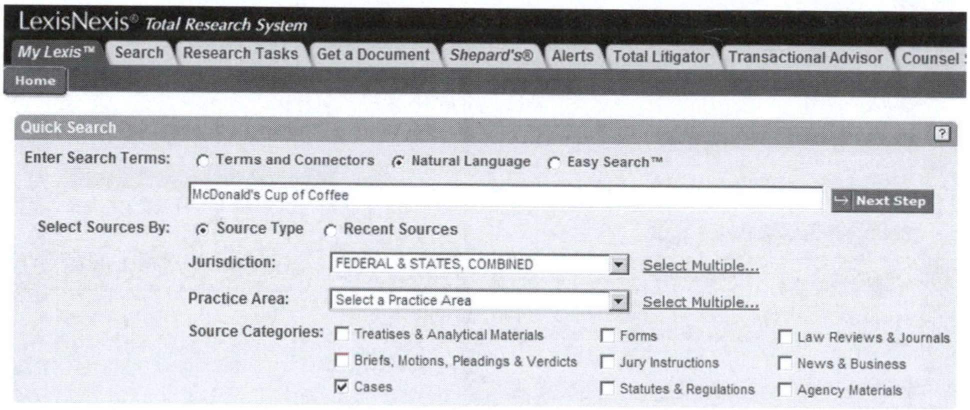

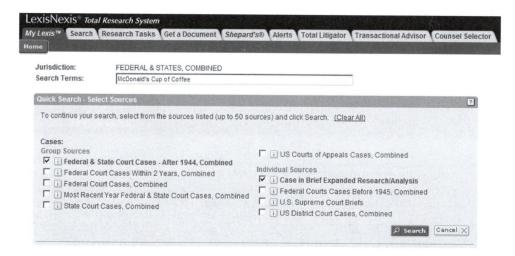

Figure 5-5. Lexis—Quick Search

Clicking the red Next Step button brings the researcher to a screen for selecting specific cases, such as the Federal & State Court Cases After 1944, and an individual **source,** such as Case in Brief Expanded Research/Analysis.

Figure 5-6. Lexis—My Lexis: Quick Search—Select Sources

Clicking the link for Case Law produces a breakdown of cases and briefs by category and sources. The researcher can next examine the listing of 24 cases, sorted by name, for short overview or the full opinion of each case.

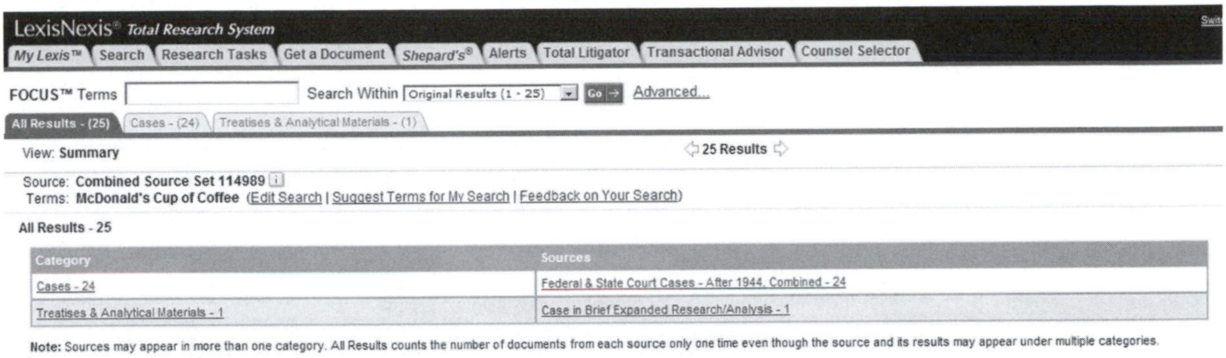

Figure 5-7. Lexis—My Lexis: All Results—25

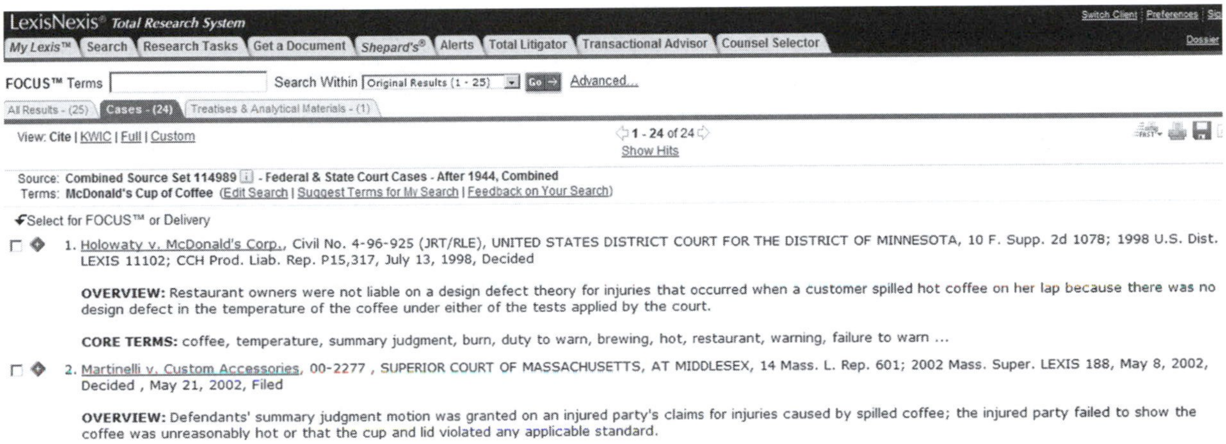

Figure 5-8. Lexis—My Lexis: Cases—24 link

To narrow the search further, a researcher could insert "McDonald's Coffee" in the box next to **FOCUS** Terms, in the upper-left corner of the screen, and click the red Go button. This does not produce the McDonald's case, but does turn up a case that mentions the McDonald's case. By clicking the case name, the researcher gets to the full court opinion in *Greene v. Boddie-Noell Enterprises*, so as to look for a specific mention of the McDonald's case.

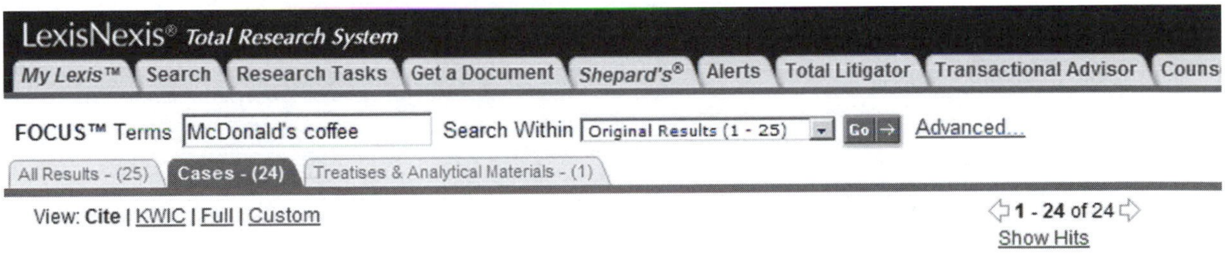

Figure 5-9. Lexis—My Lexis: FOCUS Terms

Both Greene and Blevins testified that they had heard of the "McDonald's coffee **[*418]** case" prior to this incident ¹ and Greene testified that while she was not a coffee drinker, she had been aware that if coffee spilled on her, it would burn her. After the accident, Greene gave a recorded statement to a representative of the defendant in which she stated, "I know the lid wasn't on there good. It came off too easy."

FOOTNOTES

1 On August 17, 1994, a state court jury in Albuquerque, New Mexico, awarded 81-year old Stella **Liebeck** $ 160,000 in compensatory damages and $ 2.7 million in punitive damages, after she was burned by coffee purchased from a drive-through window at a McDonald's restaurant. The trial judge later reduced the punitive damages to $ 480,000, and the parties settled the case before an appeal. According to news reports, Mrs. **Liebeck** contended that for taste reasons McDonald's served coffee about 20 degrees hotter than other fast food restaurants, and in spite of numerous complaints, had made a conscious decision not to warn customers of the possibility of serious burns. The jury's verdict received world-wide attention. *See* Andrea Gerlin, *A Matter of Degree: How a Jury Decided That One Coffee Spill Is Worth $ 2.9 Million,* Wall St. J. Europe, Sept. 2, 1994, *available in* 1994 WL-WSJE 2037634.

Figure 5-10. Lexis—Research Tasks: *Greene v. Boddie-Noell Enterprises*, mention of Stella Liebeck

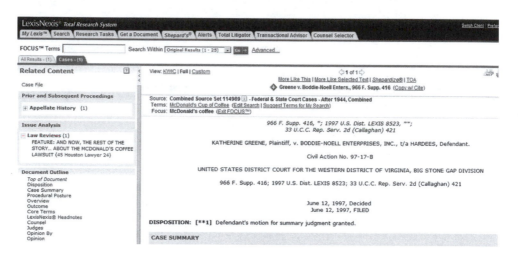

Figure 5-11. Lexis—My Lexis: The top of the full opinion in *Greene v. Boddie-Noell Enterprises*, along with a link to a law review

Toward the left of that case appears a link to a law review article, apparently about the McDonald's case. The article provides much more detail about the case. It also mentions public disbelief over the case, where some have called it a frivolous lawsuit.

More Like This | More Like Selected Text | *Shepardize®* |
45 Houston Lawyer 24 (Copy w/ Cite)

Service: **Get by LEXSEE®**
Citation: **45 Houston Lawyer 24**

✔Select for FOCUS™ or Delivery
☐

45 Houston Lawyer 24, *

Copyright (c) 2007 Houston Bar Association
The Houston Lawyer

July/August, 2007

45 Houston Lawyer 24

LENGTH: 4789 words

FEATURE: AND NOW, THE REST OF THE STORY... ABOUT THE MCDONALD'S COFFEE LAWSUIT

By Kevin G. Cain

Figure 5-12. My Lexis—Law Review article

While doing a quick search of the Lexis-Nexis did not turn up the specific "McDonald's Cup of Coffee" case, it did yield the kind of information that would have told someone with no knowledge of the case that the plaintiff was Stella Liebeck and that the accident happened in New Mexico.

2. Search Tab

A researcher might have more luck finding the actual "McDonald's Cup of Coffee" case using options available on the Search tab, adjacent to the My Lexis tab. The Search tab has several buttons.

a. By Source

i. Option 1—Search

Under the button "By Source," the researcher has two choices. The first brings the researcher to the same screen available under the My Lexis tab.

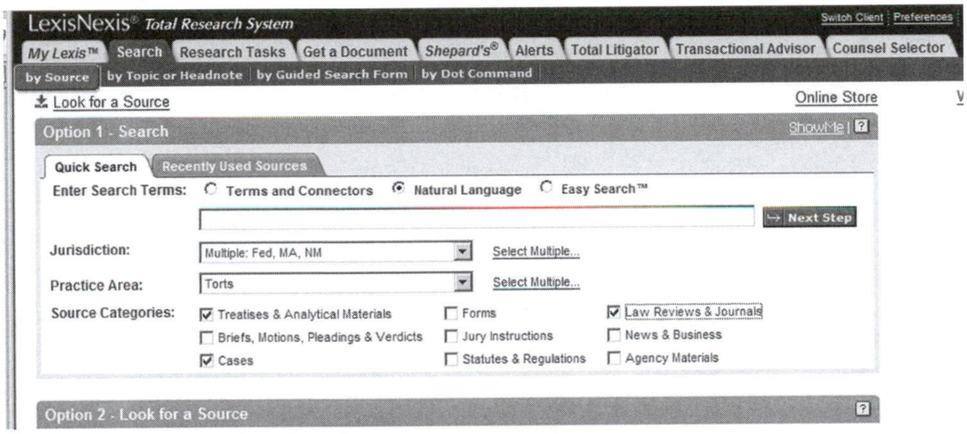

Figure 5-13. Lexis—Search tab: by Source button, "Option 1—Search"

ii. Option 2 - Look for a Source

Toward the bottom of the screen, the researcher will see "Option 2—Look for a Source."

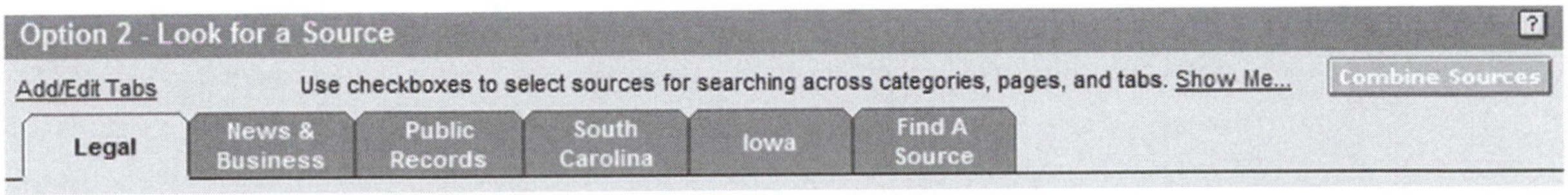

Figure 5-14. Lexis—Search tab: by Source button, "Option 2—Look for a Source"

a. Legal tab
Researchers could start by looking under the Legal tab.

1) Cases—U.S.
Like with the My Lexis search, the researcher could start by looking for cases, under Cases—U.S., and by checking Federal & State Cases, Combined.

Legal	News & Business	Public Records	South Carolina	Iowa	Georgia	Find A Source

Cases - U.S.

☐ Federal & State Cases, Combined ⓘ
☐ Federal Court Cases, Combined ⓘ
☐ State Court Cases, Combined ⓘ
   View more sources

Court Records, Briefs and Filings

☐ All Federal and State Pleadings, Combined ⓘ
☐ All Federal and State Briefs and Motions, Combined ⓘ
☐ U.S. Supreme Court Briefs ⓘ
   View more sources

Expert Witness Analysis, Jury Verdicts & Settlements

☐ Mega Jury Verdicts & Settlements (Including IDEX) ⓘ
   View more sources

Federal Legal - U.S.

☐ United States Code Service - Titles 1 through 50 ⓘ
☐ USCS - Federal Rules Annotated ⓘ
☐ CFR - Code of Federal Regulations ⓘ
☐ FR - Federal Register ⓘ
☐ Federal Agency Decisions, Combined ⓘ
   View more sources

States Legal - U.S.

Area of Law - By Topic

Banking & Financial Services   International Law
Bankruptcy   Labor & Employment
Environment   Litigation Practice & Procedure
Estates, Gifts & Trusts   Patent Law
Foreign Laws & Legal Sources   Securities
Insurance   Taxation
International Arbitration   Trademark Law
   View more sources

50 State Multi-Jurisdictional Surveys

☐ LexisNexis 50 State Surveys, Legislation & Regulations ⓘ
☐ Multi-Jurisdictional Surveys by Topic with Analysis ⓘ

Secondary Legal

Emerging Issues Analysis   Jurisprudences, Restatements and Principles of the Law
Matthew Bender(R)   Tax Analysts
CLE Materials   Forms & Agreements
Jurisprudences, ALR & Encyclopedias   In-House Memoranda
Law Reviews & Journals
   View more sources

Figure 5-15. Lexis—Search tab: by Source button, "Option 2—Look for a Source," Legal tab, Cases—U.S.

2) Area of Law—By Topic
Alternatively, the researcher could search by topic. Clicking the Area of Law—By Topic link to search by topic brings the researcher to this screen. A case that

resulted in damages for a plaintiff because of spilled coffee would involve tort law, which is also known as personal injury law. So, clicking the personal injury link produces this screen.

Option 2 - Look for a Source

Add/Edit Tabs   Use checkboxes to select sources for searching across categories, pages, and tabs. Show Me...   Comb

| Legal | News & Business | Public Records | South Carolina | Iowa | Georgia | New Mexico | Find A Source |

Legal > **Area of Law - By Topic**

Accounting	General Business
Administrative Law	Health Care
Admiralty	Immigration
Alternative Dispute Resolution	Insurance
Antitrust & Trade	International Arbitration
Banking & Financial Services	International Law
Bankruptcy	International Trade
Class Actions	Labor & Employment
Commercial Law	Litigation Practice & Procedure
Commercial (UCC)	Mass Torts and Procedure
Communications	Medical
Constitutional Law & Civil Rights	Medical Malpractice
Construction	Mergers & Acquisitions
Contracts	Military Law
Copyright Law	Municipal Government
Corporate	National Security - Homeland Security
Corporate Counsel	Patent Law
Criminal Law	Pension & Benefits
Cyberlaw & E-Commerce	Personal Injury

Figure 5-16. Lexis—Search tab: by Source button, "Option 2—Look for a Source," Legal tab, Area of Law—By Topic

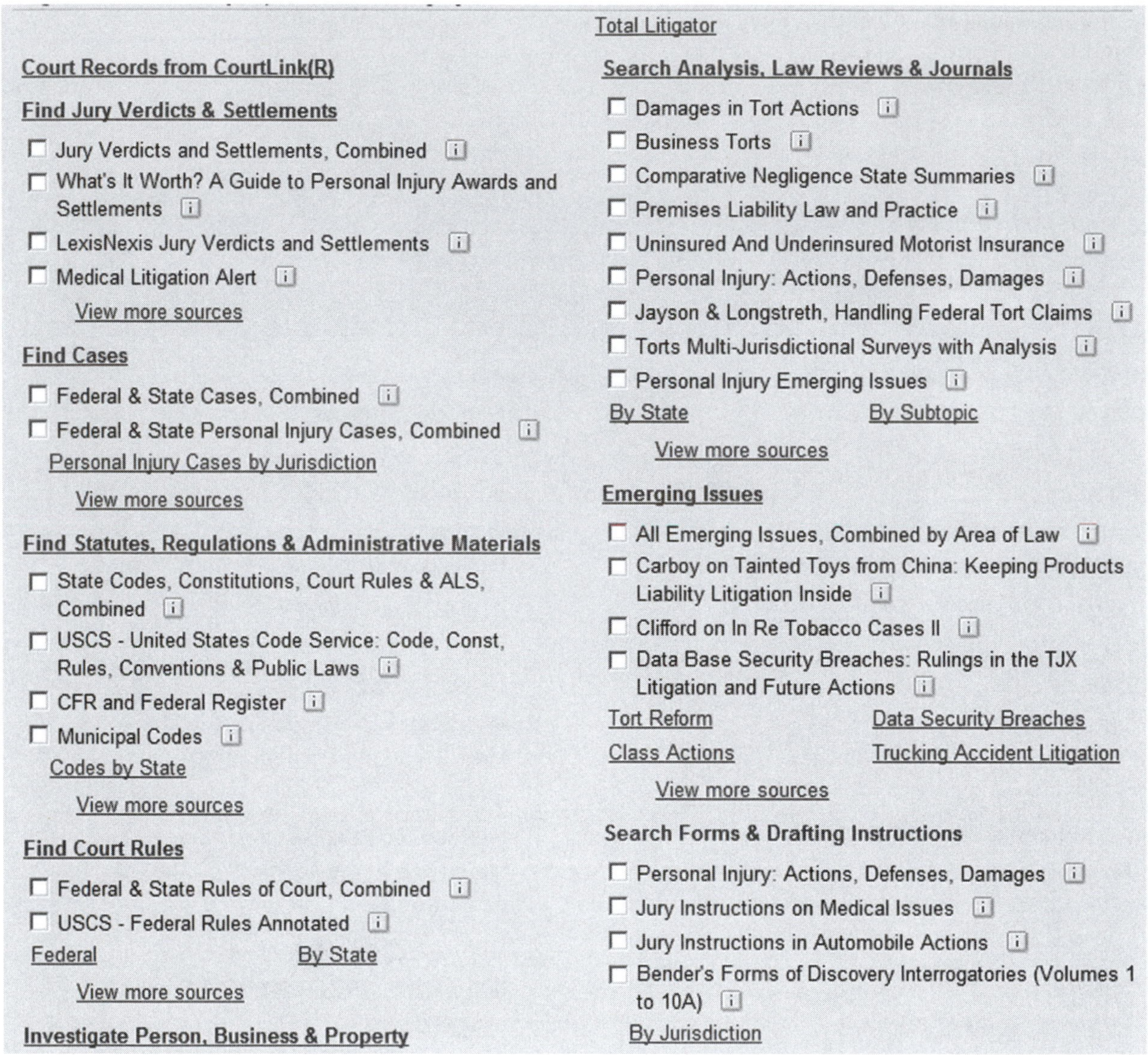

Total Litigator

Court Records from CourtLink(R)

Find Jury Verdicts & Settlements

☐ Jury Verdicts and Settlements, Combined ⓘ
☐ What's It Worth? A Guide to Personal Injury Awards and Settlements ⓘ
☐ LexisNexis Jury Verdicts and Settlements ⓘ
☐ Medical Litigation Alert ⓘ
     View more sources

Find Cases

☐ Federal & State Cases, Combined ⓘ
☐ Federal & State Personal Injury Cases, Combined ⓘ
     Personal Injury Cases by Jurisdiction
     View more sources

Find Statutes, Regulations & Administrative Materials

☐ State Codes, Constitutions, Court Rules & ALS, Combined ⓘ
☐ USCS - United States Code Service: Code, Const, Rules, Conventions & Public Laws ⓘ
☐ CFR and Federal Register ⓘ
☐ Municipal Codes ⓘ
     Codes by State
     View more sources

Find Court Rules

☐ Federal & State Rules of Court, Combined ⓘ
☐ USCS - Federal Rules Annotated ⓘ
Federal   By State
     View more sources

Investigate Person, Business & Property

Search Analysis, Law Reviews & Journals

☐ Damages in Tort Actions ⓘ
☐ Business Torts ⓘ
☐ Comparative Negligence State Summaries ⓘ
☐ Premises Liability Law and Practice ⓘ
☐ Uninsured And Underinsured Motorist Insurance ⓘ
☐ Personal Injury: Actions, Defenses, Damages ⓘ
☐ Jayson & Longstreth, Handling Federal Tort Claims ⓘ
☐ Torts Multi-Jurisdictional Surveys with Analysis ⓘ
☐ Personal Injury Emerging Issues ⓘ
By State   By Subtopic
     View more sources

Emerging Issues

☐ All Emerging Issues, Combined by Area of Law ⓘ
☐ Carboy on Tainted Toys from China: Keeping Products Liability Litigation Inside ⓘ
☐ Clifford on In Re Tobacco Cases II ⓘ
☐ Data Base Security Breaches: Rulings in the TJX Litigation and Future Actions ⓘ
Tort Reform   Data Security Breaches
Class Actions   Trucking Accident Litigation
     View more sources

Search Forms & Drafting Instructions

☐ Personal Injury: Actions, Defenses, Damages ⓘ
☐ Jury Instructions on Medical Issues ⓘ
☐ Jury Instructions in Automobile Actions ⓘ
☐ Bender's Forms of Discovery Interrogatories (Volumes 1 to 10A) ⓘ
By Jurisdiction

Figure 5-17. Lexis—Search tab: by Source button, "Option 2—Look for a Source," Legal tab, Area of Law—By Topic, Personal Injury link

This brings the researcher to a page for creating a search that looks at, for example, just Federal and State Personal Injury Cases, or secondary sources, like law reviews. Or the researcher might want to see whether the database contains information about court records in the "McDonald's Cup of Coffee" case, like pleadings or briefs, by clicking **CourtLink,** in the upper-left corner.

3) Secondary Legal
Searching through secondary sources, like legal encyclopedias or treatises such as the Restatements, could mean obtaining a broader view on the issue. Back at the page under the Legal tab, clicking the Secondary Legal link would produce this screen and offer options to look at different secondary sources.

Legal > Secondary Legal

☐ Combined ALI-ABA Course of Study Materials ⓘ

☐ Combined CLE sources ⓘ

☐ Bar Journals, Combined ⓘ

☐ Combined Legal Newsletters ⓘ

☐ Combined Restatement Rules, Jurisprudences and Law Reviews ⓘ

☐ In-House Memoranda ⓘ

☐ Law Reviews, CLE, Legal Journals & Periodicals, Combined ⓘ

☐ US & Canadian Law Reviews, Combined ⓘ

☐ Combined Canadian Law Reviews ⓘ

☐ US Law Reviews and Journals, Combined ⓘ

☐ Martindale-Hubbell(R) Listings, All ⓘ

☐ Martindale-Hubbell Legal Articles ⓘ

☐ American Jurisprudence 2d ⓘ

☐ American Law Reports (ALR) ⓘ

☐ US Supreme Court Lawyers' Edition 2d Annotations ⓘ

☐ Jurisprudences & Encyclopedias, Combined ⓘ

☐ Martindale-Hubbell(R) Law Digest ⓘ

☐ Restatement Rules, Combined ⓘ

☐ Restatement Annotated Case Citations, Combined ⓘ

Emerging Issues Analysis

Matthew Bender(R)

Mealey Reports

Martindale-Hubbell(R) Law Directory Listings

Multi-Jurisdictional Surveys

Annotations & Indexes

Area of Law Treatises

Bar Journals

Clauses

CLE Materials

Jurisprudences, ALR & Encyclopedias

Law Reviews & Journals

Model Acts & Uniform Laws

Jurisprudences, Restatements and Principles of the Law

Individual ALI-ABA Materials

American Bar Association (ABA)

John Wiley

National Institute for Trial Advocacy

Practising Law Institute

Figure 5-18. Lexis—Search tab: by Source button, Legal tab, Secondary Legal

b. New Mexico tab

The researcher has the option of adding a tab, in addition to "Legal." Because the accident took place in New Mexico, a researcher could add a tab for "New Mexico" to find out more about state law and the case.

| Legal | News & Business | Public Records | South Carolina | Iowa | Georgia | New Mexico | Find A Source |

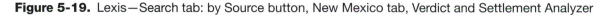

(Remove "New Mexico" tab)

Verdict & Settlement Analyzer

Find Cases

☐ Federal & State Cases, Combined ⓘ

☐ NM Federal & State Cases, Combined ⓘ

☐ NM State Cases, Combined ⓘ

☐ NM Cases, Administrative Decisions & Attorney General Opinions, Combined ⓘ

By Area of Law

View more sources

Find Statutes, Regulations, Administrative Materials & Court Rules

☐ NM - New Mexico Code, Constitution, Court Rules & ALS Combined ⓘ

☐ NM - Michie's Annotated Statutes Of New Mexico ⓘ

☐ NM - New Mexico Administrative Code ⓘ

☐ NM - Michie's Annotated State & Federal Court Rules Of New Mexico ⓘ

☐ NM Agencies & Attorney General Opinions, Combined ⓘ

☐ NM Bill Tracking Reports ⓘ

View more sources

Find Briefs, Motions, Pleadings & Jury Verdicts

☐ All Federal and State Briefs and Motions, Combined ⓘ

☐ All Federal and State Pleadings, Combined ⓘ

Jury Verdicts & Experts

Find Jury Instructions

☐ Modern Federal Jury Instructions ⓘ

View more sources

Search Forms & Drafting Instructions

Search Analysis & CLE Materials

☐ Moore's Federal Practice - Civil ⓘ

☐ Powell on Real Property ⓘ

☐ Modern Estate Planning ⓘ

☐ Damages in Tort Actions ⓘ

☐ Family Law & Practice ⓘ

☐ Appleman on Insurance 2d and Appleman on Insurance Law & Practice ⓘ

☐ Labor and Employment Law ⓘ

View more sources

Health Care Reform Resources

Emerging Issues

☐ All Emerging Issues, Combined by Area of Law ⓘ

Electronic Discovery & Evidence

Search Law Reviews & Journals

☐ New Mexico Law Reviews, Combined ⓘ

☐ New Mexico Law Review ⓘ

☐ Tribal Law Journal ⓘ

☐ US & Canadian Law Reviews, Combined ⓘ

View more sources

Court Records from CourtLink(R)

Access Directories

☐ NM Listings - Martindale-Hubbell(R) Law Directory ⓘ

☐ Legal Dictionaries, Combined ⓘ

View more sources

Public Records

Figure 5-19. Lexis—Search tab: by Source button, New Mexico tab, Verdict and Settlement Analyzer

b. By Topic or Headnote

A researcher could also search by Topic or Headnote. Lexis-Nexis assigns **headnotes** to the court rulings it publishes. These headnotes call attention to critical, topical legal issues in a case. A researcher can just look at the headnotes of a ruling to determine quickly whether it might have critical information about the issue of law in a client's case.

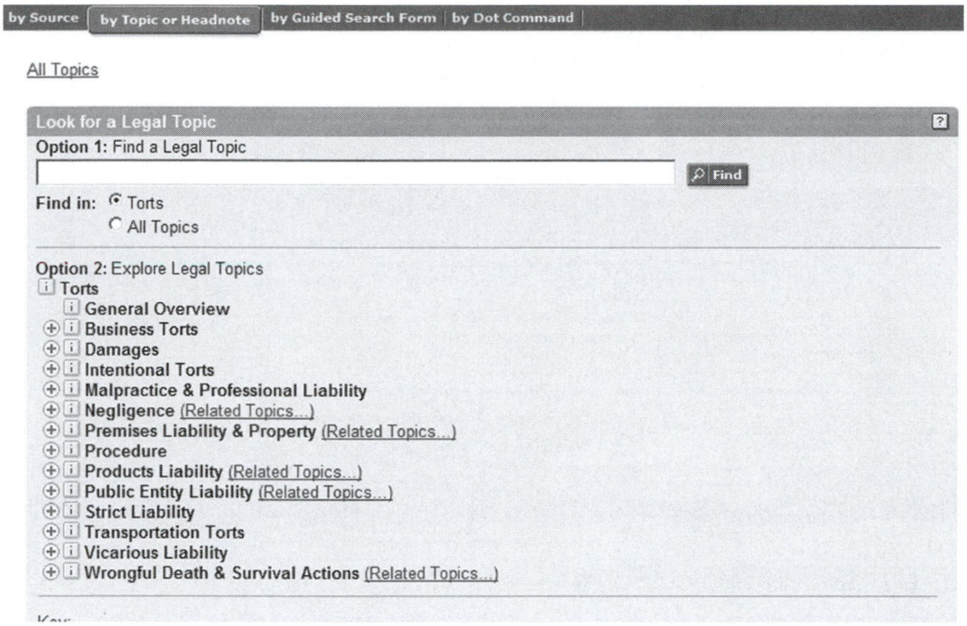

Figure 5-20. Lexis—Search tab: By Topic or Headnote button

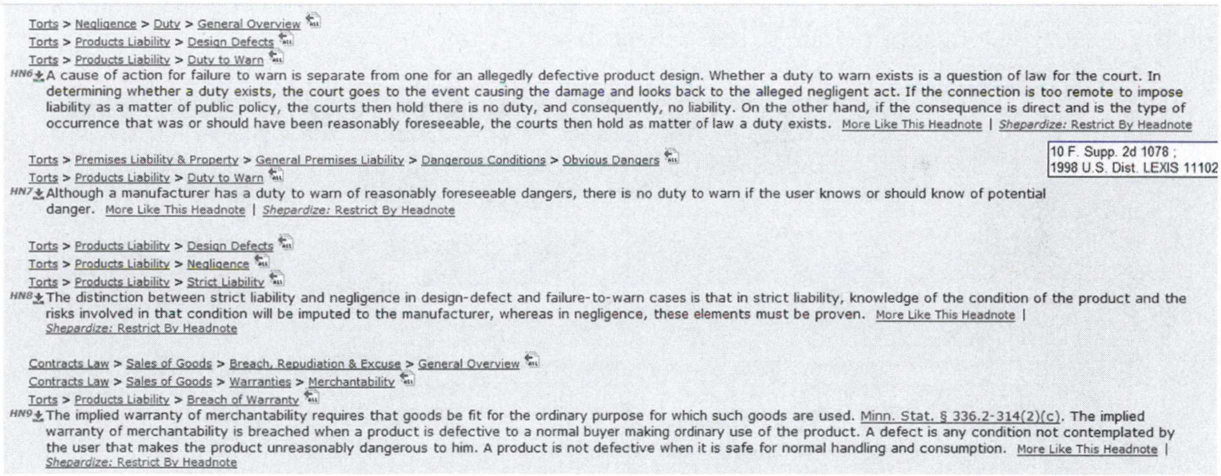

Figure 5-21. Lexis—Example of headnotes: On-line version of a case

One reason that people might know about Ms. Liebeck's personal injury case involves the total damages awarded. News reports stated that Ms. Liebeck received a damages award of $3 million. So, another approach to finding out more about this case could involve focusing on the damages awarded in that case. Subsequent research will reveal that part of the nearly $3 million award involved punitive damages. The researcher could go here to explore the issue in the case in more detail.

Figure 5-22. Lexis—Search by Source: By Topic or Headnote button, Damages link

c. By Guided Search Form

A researcher with limited information about a case could use the Guided Search Form button to obtain results. Clicking the red Go button next to the States Legal leads to a screen where the researcher can insert the phrase "Mc-Donald's Coffee" to produce this screen. In this instance, however, none of the results pertain to the Liebeck case.

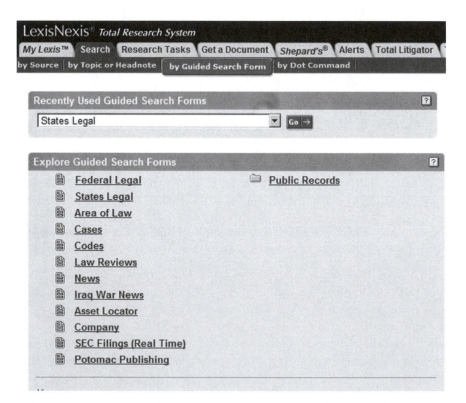

Figure 5-23. Lexis—Search by Source: By Guided Search Form button

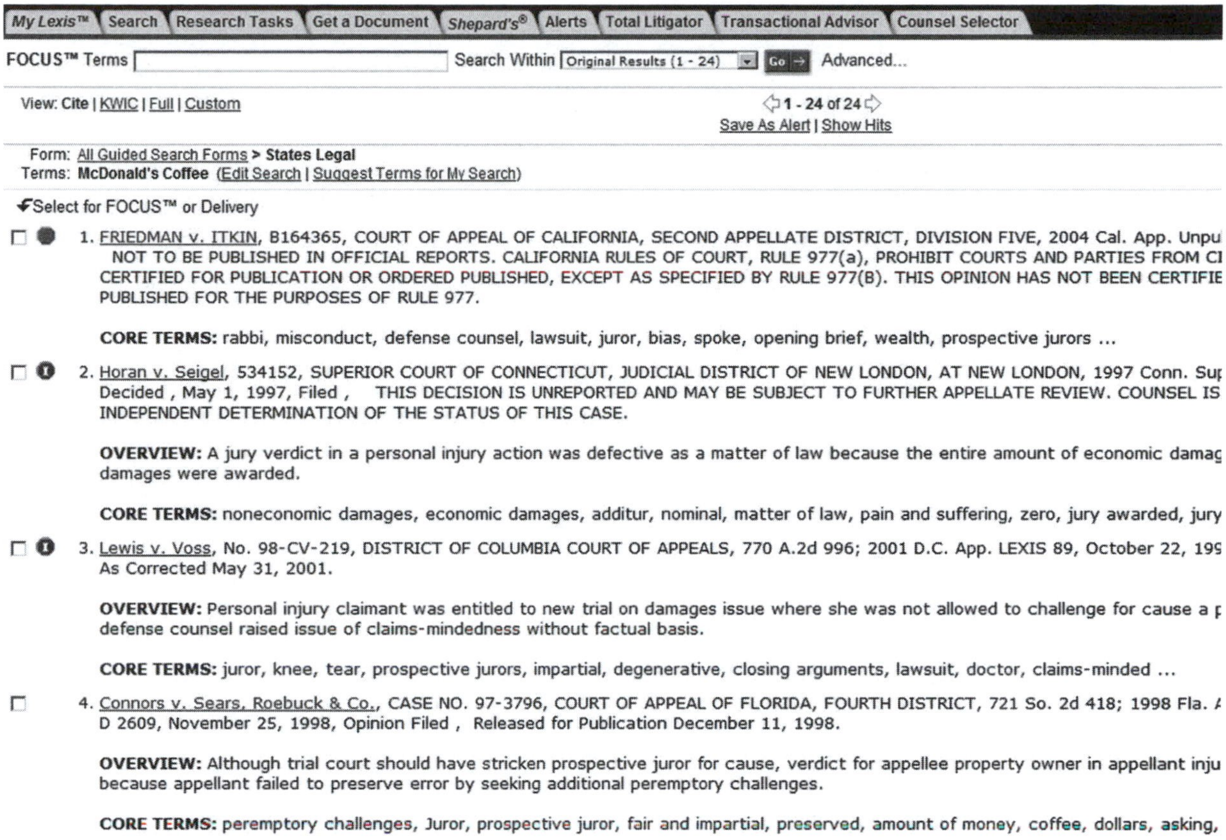

| My Lexis™ | Search | Research Tasks | Get a Document | *Shepard's*® | Alerts | Total Litigator | Transactional Advisor | Counsel Selector |

FOCUS™ Terms [   ]   Search Within [Original Results (1 - 24) ▼] [Go →]   Advanced...

View: **Cite** | KWIC | Full | Custom   ◁ **1 - 24 of 24** ▷
         Save As Alert | Show Hits

Form: All Guided Search Forms **> States Legal**
Terms: **McDonald's Coffee** (Edit Search | Suggest Terms for My Search)

✔Select for FOCUS™ or Delivery

☐ ●   1. FRIEDMAN v. ITKIN, B164365, COURT OF APPEAL OF CALIFORNIA, SECOND APPELLATE DISTRICT, DIVISION FIVE, 2004 Cal. App. Unpu
       NOT TO BE PUBLISHED IN OFFICIAL REPORTS. CALIFORNIA RULES OF COURT, RULE 977(a), PROHIBIT COURTS AND PARTIES FROM CI
       CERTIFIED FOR PUBLICATION OR ORDERED PUBLISHED, EXCEPT AS SPECIFIED BY RULE 977(B). THIS OPINION HAS NOT BEEN CERTIFIE
       PUBLISHED FOR THE PURPOSES OF RULE 977.

       CORE TERMS: rabbi, misconduct, defense counsel, lawsuit, juror, bias, spoke, opening brief, wealth, prospective jurors ...

☐ ❶   2. Horan v. Seigel, 534152, SUPERIOR COURT OF CONNECTICUT, JUDICIAL DISTRICT OF NEW LONDON, AT NEW LONDON, 1997 Conn. Su
       Decided , May 1, 1997, Filed ,   THIS DECISION IS UNREPORTED AND MAY BE SUBJECT TO FURTHER APPELLATE REVIEW. COUNSEL IS
       INDEPENDENT DETERMINATION OF THE STATUS OF THIS CASE.

       OVERVIEW: A jury verdict in a personal injury action was defective as a matter of law because the entire amount of economic damag
       damages were awarded.

       CORE TERMS: noneconomic damages, economic damages, additur, nominal, matter of law, pain and suffering, zero, jury awarded, jury

☐ ❶   3. Lewis v. Voss, No. 98-CV-219, DISTRICT OF COLUMBIA COURT OF APPEALS, 770 A.2d 996; 2001 D.C. App. LEXIS 89, October 22, 199
       As Corrected May 31, 2001.

       OVERVIEW: Personal injury claimant was entitled to new trial on damages issue where she was not allowed to challenge for cause a p
       defense counsel raised issue of claims-mindedness without factual basis.

       CORE TERMS: juror, knee, tear, prospective jurors, impartial, degenerative, closing arguments, lawsuit, doctor, claims-minded ...

☐   4. Connors v. Sears, Roebuck & Co., CASE NO. 97-3796, COURT OF APPEAL OF FLORIDA, FOURTH DISTRICT, 721 So. 2d 418; 1998 Fla. A
       D 2609, November 25, 1998, Opinion Filed , Released for Publication December 11, 1998.

       OVERVIEW: Although trial court should have stricken prospective juror for cause, verdict for appellee property owner in appellant inju
       because appellant failed to preserve error by seeking additional peremptory challenges.

       CORE TERMS: peremptory challenges, Juror, prospective juror, fair and impartial, preserved, amount of money, coffee, dollars, asking,

Figure 5-24. Lexis—Search by Source: Search tab, By Guided Search form button, "McDonald's Coffee" search phrase and results

d. By Dot Command

A researcher could search, under this tab, for case law according to a specific library of law, such as GENFED (for federal law in general) or 7CIR (for appellate court rulings in the federal Seventh Circuit). Westlaw also uses these designations for its libraries. Also, a researcher would have to use certain commands, something that a casual user of the Lexis-Nexis database might find daunting, especially where other, easier to use, search options exist.

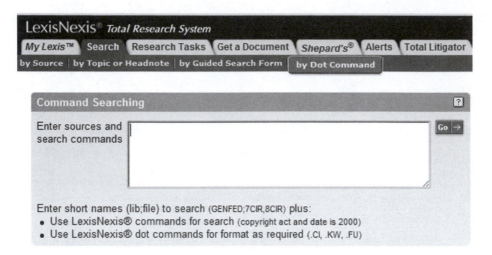

Figure 5-25. Lexis—Search tab: By Dot Command button

e. Summary

Options available under the Search tab allow a researcher to use several strategies for locating information. With time, a researcher might develop the kind of experience to identify a strategy that would lead to the most efficient use of the researcher's time, and the client's money.

3. Research Tasks Tab

Using the Research Tasks tab makes more sense when working with corporate clients instead of a person filing a personal injury litigation claim.

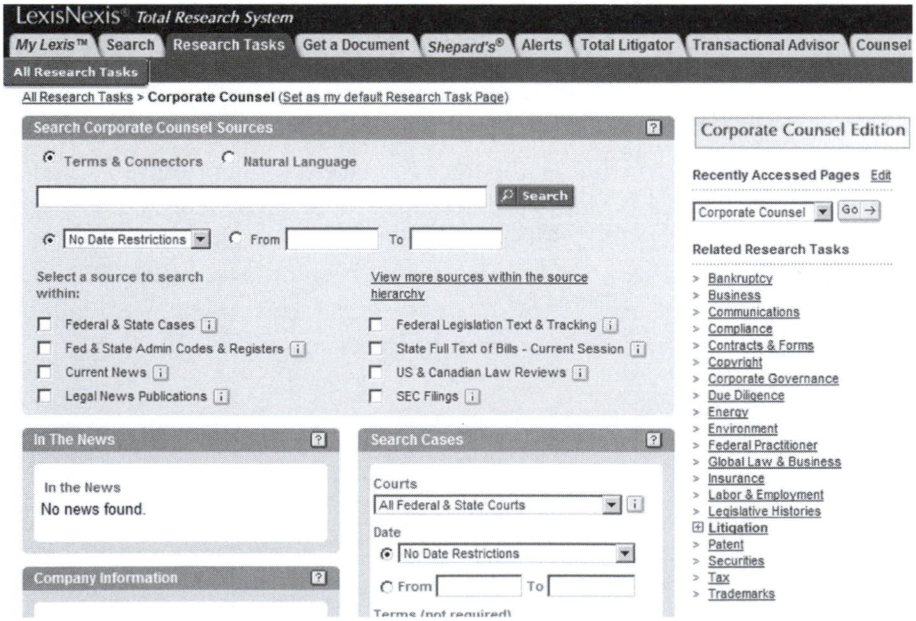

Figure 5-26. Lexis—Research Tasks tab: All Research Tasks button

While searching for Stella Liebeck does not produce that case, it does identify the *Greene v. Boddie-Noell Enterprises* case, mentioned previously. This demonstrates that using a different search strategy can still yield useful results.

Select for FOCUS™ or Delivery

☐ △ 1. McMahon v. Bunn-O-Matic Corp., No. 97-4131, UNITED STATES COURT OF APPEALS FOR THE SEVENTH CIRCUIT, 150 F.3d 651; 1998 U.S. App. LEXIS 14926; CCH Prod. Liab. Rep. P15,298, May 27, 1998, Argued , July 2, 1998, Decided

   OVERVIEW: Coffee maker manufacturer was not liable to a consumer, who was injured by hot coffee after her styrofoam cup collapsed, under theories of a failure to warn or an unreasonably dangerous product caused by a design defect.

   CORE TERMS: coffee, temperature, consumer, cup, hot, warning, burn, beverage, coffee maker, liquid's ...

   ... 80 Ohio St. 3d 1415, 684 N.E.2d 706 (1997), and a suit in New Mexico (**Liebeck** v. McDonald's Restaurants, P.T.S., Inc.) produced a ...

☐ ◆ 2. Greene v. Boddie-Noell Enters., Civil Action No. 97-17-B, UNITED STATES DISTRICT COURT FOR THE WESTERN DISTRICT OF VIRGINIA, BIG STONE GAP DIVISION, 966 F. Supp. 416; 1997 U.S. Dist. LEXIS 8523; 33 U.C.C. Rep. Serv. 2d (Callaghan) 421, June 12, 1997, Decided , June 12, 1997, FILED

   OVERVIEW: In products liability case, patron failed to show that her burns from hot coffee were the result of restaurant's breach of a recognizable standard and, thus, court granted summary judgment in favor of restaurant.

   CORE TERMS: coffee, lid, cup, summary judgment, restaurant, burned, food, hot, spilled, drink ...

   ... New Mexico, awarded 81-year old Stella **Liebeck** $ 160,000 in compensatory damages and $ ...
   ... an appeal. According to news reports, Mrs. **Liebeck** contended that for taste reasons McDonald's served ...

Figure 5-27. Lexis—Research Tasks tab: All Research Tasks button, search results

4. Get a Document Tab

Another research strategy would involve looking for documents related to the Liebeck case, like briefs or pleadings. The researcher would need to have discovered
that the plaintiff in the "McDonald's Cup of Coffee" case is Stella Liebeck to take
advantage of this option. This strategy might make sense if the firm has decided
to accept the client's case and file suit, since the documents could provide a basis
for a litigation strategy.

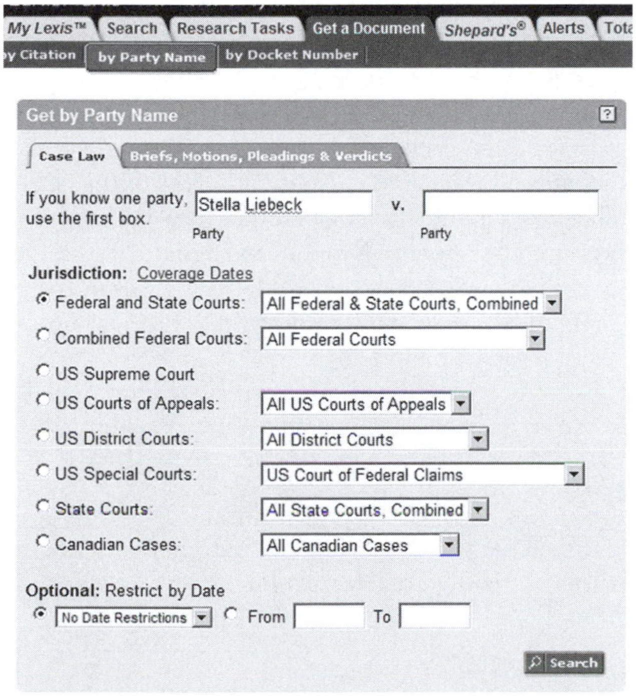

Figure 5-28. Lexis—Get a Document tab: By Party Name button

5. Shepard's Tab

To shepardize a case means using Lexis-Nexis materials to discover how courts have subsequently treated a particular court ruling. This is one way to find out, for example, whether another court has overruled the earlier ruling, thereby greatly diminishing the legal significance of the prior case.

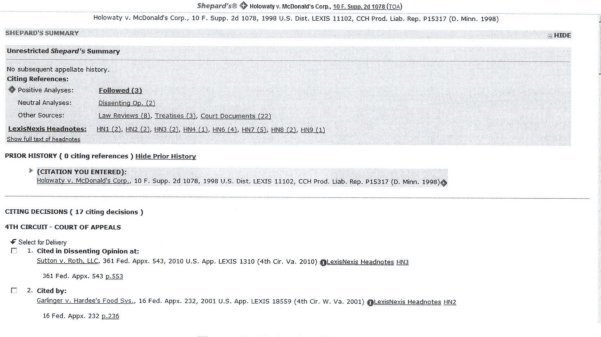

Shepard's® ◆ Holowaty v. McDonald's Corp., 10 F. Supp. 2d 1078 (TOA)

Holowaty v. McDonald's Corp., 10 F. Supp. 2d 1078, 1998 U.S. Dist. LEXIS 11102, CCH Prod. Liab. Rep. P15317 (D. Minn. 1998)

SHEPARD'S SUMMARY   ⊟ HIDE

Unrestricted *Shepard's* Summary

No subsequent appellate history.
Citing References:
◆ Positive Analyses: **Followed (3)**
   Neutral Analyses: Dissenting Op. (2)
   Other Sources: Law Reviews (8), Treatises (3), Court Documents (22)
LexisNexis Headnotes: HN1 (2), HN2 (2), HN3 (2), HN4 (1), HN6 (4), HN7 (5), HN8 (2), HN9 (1)
Show full text of headnotes

PRIOR HISTORY (0 citing references) Hide Prior History

   ▶ **(CITATION YOU ENTERED):**
      Holowaty v. McDonald's Corp., 10 F. Supp. 2d 1078, 1998 U.S. Dist. LEXIS 11102, CCH Prod. Liab. Rep. P15317 (D. Minn. 1998)◆

CITING DECISIONS (17 citing decisions)

4TH CIRCUIT - COURT OF APPEALS

✔ Select for Delivery
☐ 1. **Cited in Dissenting Opinion at:**
      Sutton v. Roth, LLC, 361 Fed. Appx. 543, 2010 U.S. App. LEXIS 1310 (4th Cir. Va. 2010) ❶LexisNexis Headnotes HN3

      361 Fed. Appx. 543 p.553

☐ 2. **Cited by:**
      Garlinger v. Hardee's Food Sys., 16 Fed. Appx. 232, 2001 U.S. App. LEXIS 18559 (4th Cir. W. Va. 2001) ❶LexisNexis Headnotes HN2

      16 Fed. Appx. 232 p.236

Figure 5-29 Lexis—Shepard's tab

Failure to shepardize a case might expose a lawyer to the risk of a lawsuit for professional negligence, called legal malpractice. If a lawyer has written a brief around an important court opinion, a failure to shepardize the case might mean that the lawyer does not discover that the court's ruling was overturned. Because a researcher can shepardize a case with the press of a button, failure to do so could be grounds for a suit for legal malpractice.

Unless the researcher had already discovered the citation for the Liebeck case, this seems like an unlikely place to start research about the case.

6. Alerts Tab

Under this tab, a researcher can obtain updates automatically about a prior search, such as if a case was overturned in a later ruling.

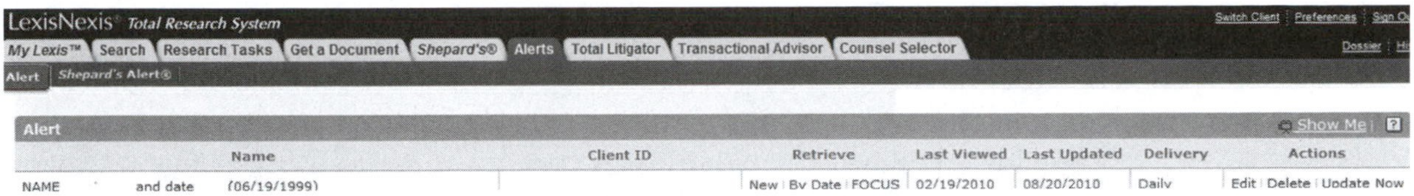

Figure 5-30. Lexis—Alerts tab

7. Total Litigator Tab

The options available under this tab can help a researcher to manage a case, including preparing for trial. For example, using the "Early Case Assessment" button can help a firm to decide whether it wants to represent a new client. This does not seem especially relevant for preliminary research about the Liebeck case.

Figure 5-31. Lexis—Total Litigator tab: Home button

8. Transactional Advisor Tab

A researcher can obtain information about commercial transactions here. This will not help here, since the Liebeck case involves a personal injury suit.

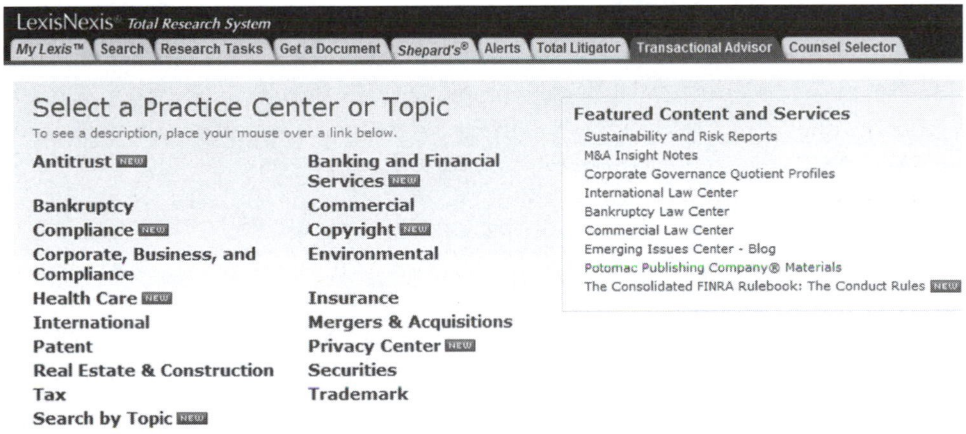

Figure 5-32. Lexis—Transactional Advisor tab

9. Counsel Selector Tab

If a case will require the assistance of a lawyer in another jurisdiction, this feature can make it easier to identify prospective co-counsel because it incorporates the Martindale-Hubbell database, which contains a national list of many lawyers. Or, if a researcher found out who represented Ms. Liebeck, the researcher's firm could contact that firm about its experience litigating this kind of personal injury claim.

Figure 5-33. Lexis—Counsel Selector tab

Innovations

Changes in technology have always sparked innovations with Lexis-Nexis. For example, the business had originally created its own network, with specially designed terminals, to make doing research easier. Not only is the Lexis-Nexis service now accessible via the World Wide Web, but the company has continued to look at integrating technological changes with the service to make it easier to do legal research. Here are a few examples.

1. Lexis for Microsoft Office

Lexis for Microsoft Office makes it possible to do legal research when using Microsoft's Outlook and Word applications. In this example, the Word document is on the left with the Lexis-Nexis interface on the other side. Here, the traditional Word toolbar now has a tab for using the Lexis-Nexis service. Better still, whether using Word or Outlook, all cites are automatically shepardized. As the figure shows, there are at least two cases of questionable utility.

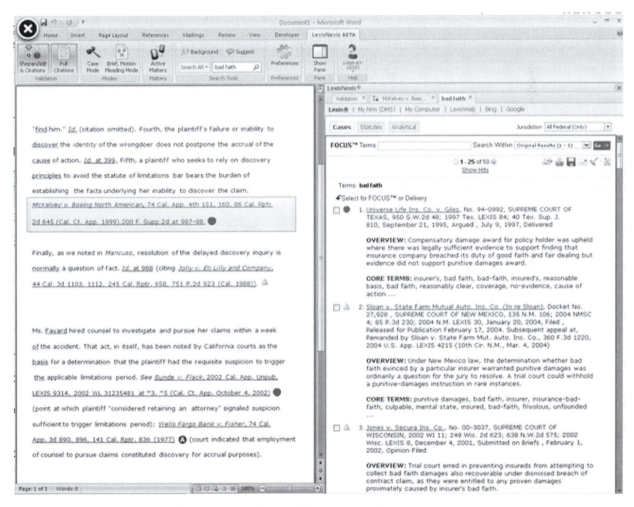

Figure 5-34. Lexis—Word and the Lexis database

2. LexisAdvance for Solos

LexisAdvance for Solos (LAS) uses a "carousel" interface, a feature also used with Google Scholar and WestlawNext, below. It also uses a "Word Wheel," which lists queries similar to the one initiated by the researcher to suggest alternative approaches for conducting a search.

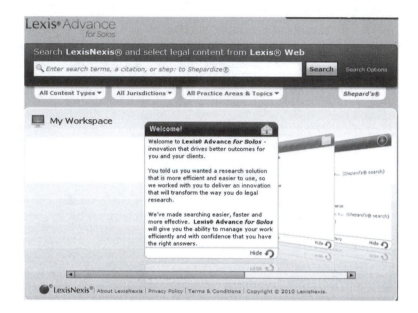

Figure 5-35. Lexis—Lexis Advanced Solos (LAS) interface: "Carousel"

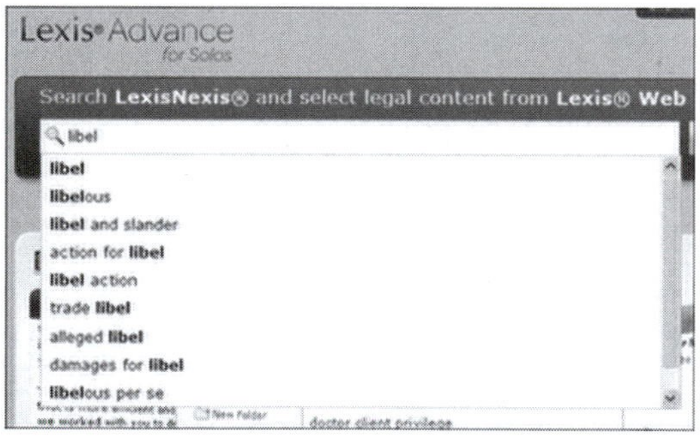

Figure 5-36. Lexis—Screen image of "Word Wheel"

3. LexisONE

Via this link, http://law.lexisnexis.com/webcenters/lexisone, Lexis-Nexis offers free access to appellate state court rulings from the last ten years, with a few exceptions.

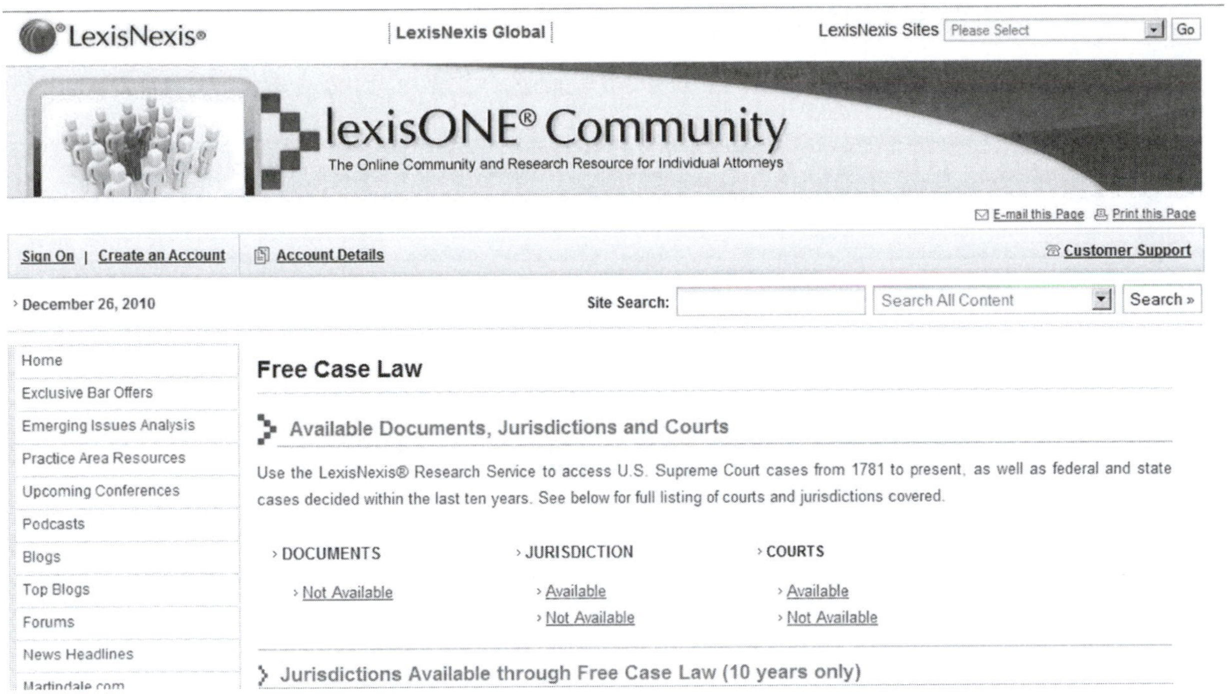

Figure 5-37. Lexis—Free case law option available through LexisONE service

Westlaw

Many consider **Westlaw,** a proprietary database offered by Thomson Reuters, as among the premiere legal subscription services. This exploration of the Westlaw service uses the interface available through academic institutions and will also look for information about the "McDonald's Cup of Coffee" case.

Conducting Legal Research Using Westlaw

1. Search

Clicking on the Law tab at the top of the first page provides a researcher with two options for conducting a search.

a. Basic Search tab

Under the Basic Search tab the researcher needs only to type in the word or phrase. The researcher can limit the scope of the search by a range or preset interval of time.

Search

Advanced Search   Basic Search

Search:	[_____]
AND ▾	[_____]
AND ▾	[_____]
AND ▾	[_____]
NOT	[_____]
Date:	Unrestricted ▾

[Search] **Search Tips**

Use the AND, OR operators between each field to create a more precise search.

Use quotation marks to get an exact match
(e.g.,"war crimes")

Use ! to expand your search
(e.g.,"communicat!")

More Search Tips

Figure 5-38. Westlaw—Search: Basic Search tab

b. Advanced Search tab

i. Using multiple search terms and **Boolean** connectors

Under the Advanced Search tab, the researcher has more control over the search process. Researchers have the option of using Boolean connectors like AND, OR, and NOT to design a better, more focused search by using combinations of multiple search terms. Note: Inclusion of NOT and "obesity" is to eliminate those cases brought against McDonald's on the grounds that the restaurant sold food that contributed to the obesity of its customers.

About | Research Trail | Help (FAQs)

Westlaw

Search

Advanced Search   Basic Search

Search:	McDonald's
AND ▾	cup
AND ▾	coffee
AND ▾	[_____]
NOT	obesity
Date:	Unrestricted ▾

[Search] **Search Tips**

Use the AND, OR operators between each field to create a more precise search.

Use quotation marks to get an exact match
(e.g.,"war crimes")

Use ! to expand your search
(e.g.,"communicat!")

More Search Tips

Select Database(s)

Encyclopedias and Law Reviews
☐ American Jurisprudence 2d | Table Of Contents ⓘ
☐ American Law Reports ⓘ
☐ Journals and Law Reviews Select a State ▾

Cases
☐ All Federal Cases ⓘ
☑ All State Cases ⓘ
☐ State Cases: Select a State ▾
☐ Supreme Court Cases ⓘ

Figure 5-39. Westlaw—Search: Advanced Search tab, McDonald's cup of coffee case search terms

ii. Select database(s)

Beneath that part of the page, the researcher selects different databases to search. If a researcher knows nothing about the "McDonald's Cup of Coffee" case, looking through secondary sources like encyclopedias and law reviews could give the researcher a broad understanding of the problems presented by such a case.

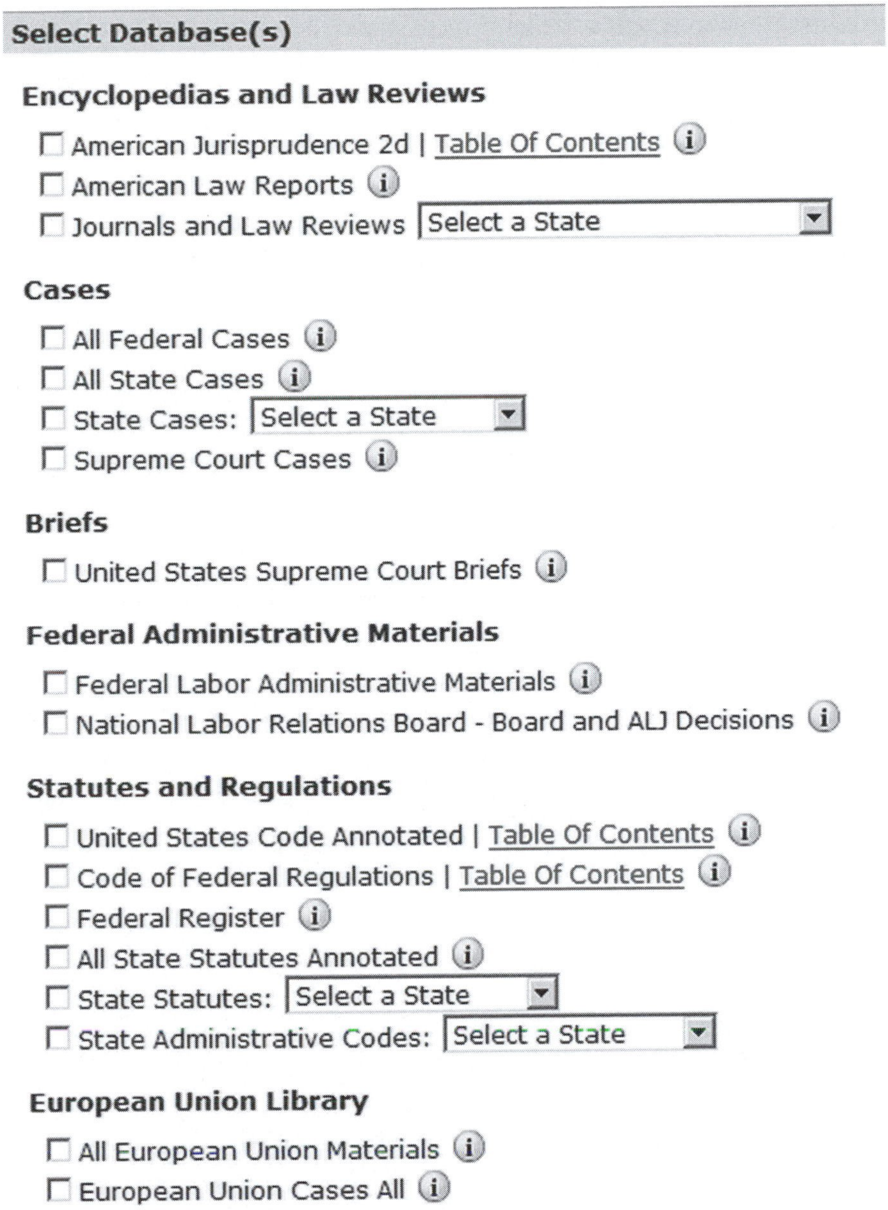

Select Database(s)

Encyclopedias and Law Reviews

☐ American Jurisprudence 2d | Table Of Contents ⓘ
☐ American Law Reports ⓘ
☐ Journals and Law Reviews | Select a State ▾ |

Cases

☐ All Federal Cases ⓘ
☐ All State Cases ⓘ
☐ State Cases: | Select a State ▾ |
☐ Supreme Court Cases ⓘ

Briefs

☐ United States Supreme Court Briefs ⓘ

Federal Administrative Materials

☐ Federal Labor Administrative Materials ⓘ
☐ National Labor Relations Board - Board and ALJ Decisions ⓘ

Statutes and Regulations

☐ United States Code Annotated | Table Of Contents ⓘ
☐ Code of Federal Regulations | Table Of Contents ⓘ
☐ Federal Register ⓘ
☐ All State Statutes Annotated ⓘ
☐ State Statutes: | Select a State ▾ |
☐ State Administrative Codes: | Select a State ▾ |

European Union Library

☐ All European Union Materials ⓘ
☐ European Union Cases All ⓘ

Figure 5-40. Westlaw—Search: Advanced Search tab, Select Database(s)

a. Encyclopedias and law reviews; AmJur2d

The legal encyclopedia that Thomson Reuters publishes, **American Jurisprudence 2d,** has served as one of the major research works in American law for decades because of its broad range of topics. Clicking the Table of Contents link on the right opens up a list of topics in the legal encyclopedia.

Figure 5-41. Westlaw—Search: Advanced Search tab, AmJur2d table of contents

b. American Law Reports (ALR)

The researcher could look at the American Law Reports, which offers annotated articles on specific topics. Looking here produces these results. The two articles do not seem to be about the infamous case because one is too old and the other is too broad.

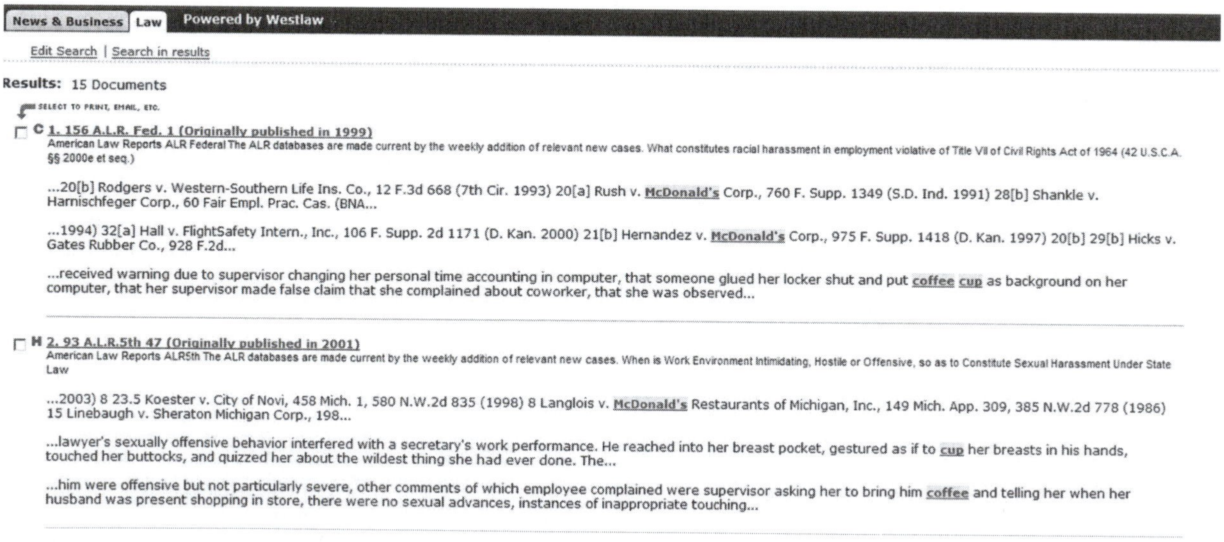

Figure 5-42. Westlaw—Search: Advanced Search tab, Search of ALR for the McDonald's cup of coffee case

c. Journals and law reviews

Journals and law reviews could have commentary regarding this notorious case, but this search yields too many documents to review individually.

News & Business	Law	Powered by Westlaw

Edit Search | Search in results

Results: 243 Documents

SELECT TO PRINT, EMAIL, ETC.

☐ **1. 101 Trademark Rep. 805**
The Trademark Reporter May-June, 2011 International Annual Review The Eighteenth Yearly Review of International Trademark Jurisprudence EDITOR'S NOTE

...Province filed an application to register SHAOLIN MEDICINAL CLINIC in Chinese characters and SHAOLIN MEDICINE in English for instant noodles, **coffee**, rice boxes, and tea. In September 2006, the Chinese Trademark Office (TMO) rejected the application on the ground that use...

Figure 5-43. Westlaw—Search: Advanced Search tab, Results of search through journals and law reviews

Inserting "McDonald's" in the box that appears after clicking on the Search in Results link yields 243 cases.

News & Business	Law	Powered by Westlaw

Edit Search in results | Cancel Search in results

Locate Results: 20 of 243 Documents

SELECT TO PRINT, EMAIL, ETC.

☐ **4. 17 Ann. Surv. Int'l & Comp. L. 185**
➡ Annual Survey of International and Comparative Law Spring, 2011 U.S. PUNITIVE DAMAGES BEFORE GERMAN COURTS: A COMPARATIVE ANALYSIS WITH RESPECT TO THE C

...the defect. [FN15] One famous example of the award of punitive damages is the 1994 product liability lawsuit Liebeck v. **McDonalds**

Figure 5-44, Westlaw—Search: Advanced Search tab, Results using Search in Results

Most significantly, entry 58 yields the case name and, importantly, the case citation: *Liebeck v. McDonald's Rest.*, No. CV-93-02419, 1995 WL 360309 (D.N.M. Aug. 18, 1994).

☐ **C 58. 86 Or. L. Rev. 533**
➡ Oregon Law Review 2007 Article HOW TO MANUFACTURE A CRISIS: EVALUATING EMPIRICAL CLAIMS BEHIND "TORT REFORM" John T. Nockleby

...461, 494 (2006)[FN163] . See American Tort Reform Association, http://www.atra.org/ (last visited Jan. 7, 2008).[FN164] . See Liebeck v. **McDonalds** Rest., No. CV-93-02419, 1995 WL 360309 (D.N.M. Aug. 18, 1994)[FN165] 174 Cal. Rptr. 348 (Cal. Ct. App...

Figure 5-45. Westlaw—Search: Advanced Search tab, Result 58

d. Cases

1) Searching
Putting in the phrase "McDonald's cup of coffee in state cases," because federal courts may not typically handle such claims, produces these results.

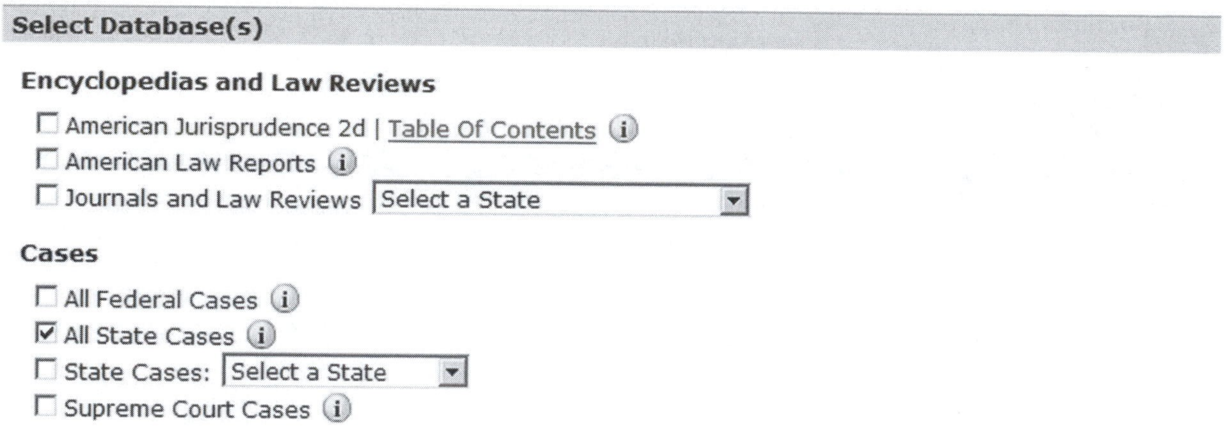

Select Database(s)

Encyclopedias and Law Reviews

☐ American Jurisprudence 2d | Table Of Contents ⓘ
☐ American Law Reports ⓘ
☐ Journals and Law Reviews | Select a State ▾ |

Cases

☐ All Federal Cases ⓘ
☑ All State Cases ⓘ
☐ State Cases: | Select a State ▾ |
☐ Supreme Court Cases ⓘ

Figure 5-46. Westlaw—Search: Advanced Search tab, Select Databases, Cases, All State Cases

2) Search in results

Having 65 cases to review may require further refinement of the search and that is possible when using the Search in Results link. Entering in "burns" produces nine cases.

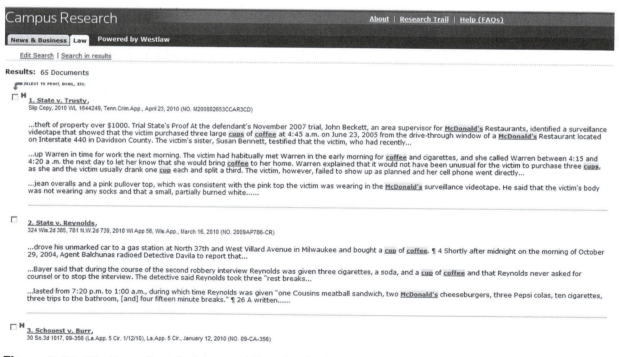

Figure 5-47. Westlaw—Search: Advanced Search tab, Select Databases, Cases, All State Cases, Results of search for McDonald's cup of coffee case

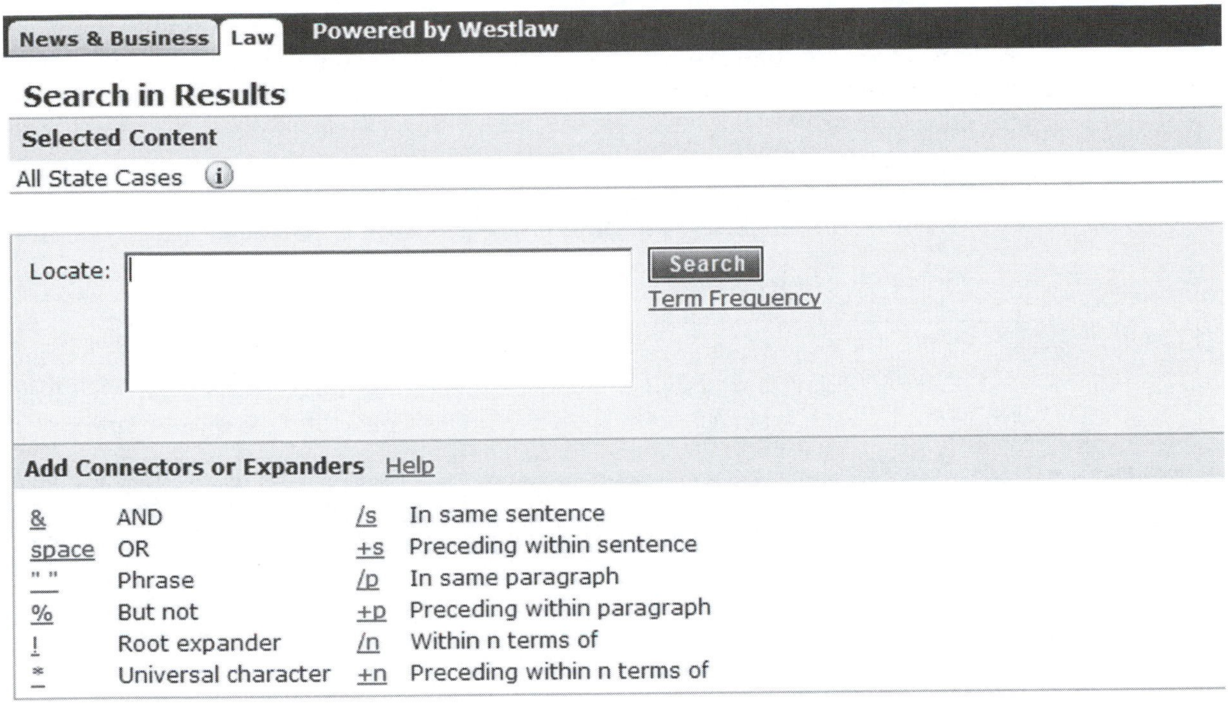

| News & Business | Law | **Powered by Westlaw** |

Search in Results

Selected Content

All State Cases ⓘ

Locate: [   ]   **Search**
                                  Term Frequency

Add Connectors or Expanders Help

&	AND	/s	In same sentence
space	OR	+s	Preceding within sentence
" "	Phrase	/p	In same paragraph
%	But not	+p	Preceding within paragraph
!	Root expander	/n	Within n terms of
*	Universal character	+n	Preceding within n terms of

Figure 5-48. Westlaw—Search: Advanced Search tab, Select Databases, Cases, All State Cases, Search in Results link page

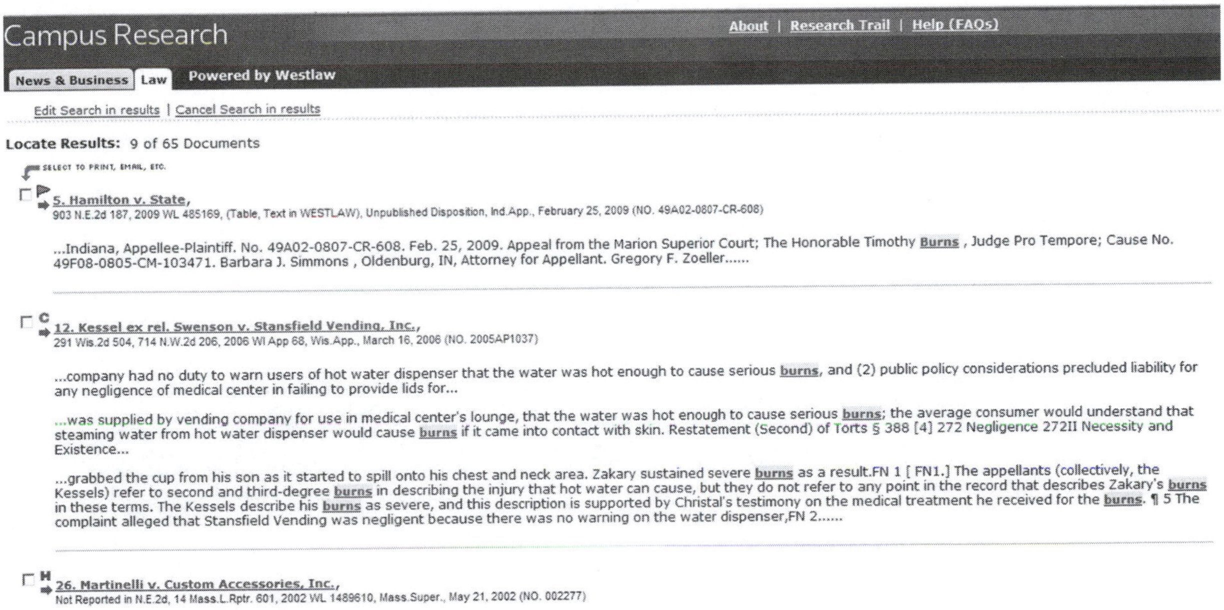

Campus Research   About | Research Trail | Help (FAQs)

| News & Business | Law | **Powered by Westlaw** |

Edit Search in results | Cancel Search in results

Locate Results: 9 of 65 Documents

SELECT TO PRINT, EMAIL, ETC.

☐ **5. Hamilton v. State,**
903 N.E.2d 187, 2009 WL 485169, (Table, Text in WESTLAW), Unpublished Disposition, Ind.App., February 25, 2009 (NO. 49A02-0807-CR-608)

...Indiana, Appellee-Plaintiff. No. 49A02-0807-CR-608. Feb. 25, 2009. Appeal from the Marion Superior Court; The Honorable Timothy **Burns** , Judge Pro Tempore; Cause No. 49F08-0805-CM-103471. Barbara J. Simmons , Oldenburg, IN, Attorney for Appellant. Gregory F. Zoeller......

☐ **12. Kessel ex rel. Swenson v. Stansfield Vending, Inc.,**
291 Wis.2d 504, 714 N.W.2d 206, 2006 WI App 68, Wis.App., March 16, 2006 (NO. 2005AP1037)

...company had no duty to warn users of hot water dispenser that the water was hot enough to cause serious **burns**, and (2) public policy considerations precluded liability for any negligence of medical center in failing to provide lids for...

...was supplied by vending company for use in medical center's lounge, that the water was hot enough to cause serious **burns**; the average consumer would understand that steaming water from hot water dispenser would cause **burns** if it came into contact with skin. Restatement (Second) of Torts § 388 [4] 272 Negligence 272II Necessity and Existence...

...grabbed the cup from his son as it started to spill onto his chest and neck area. Zakary sustained severe **burns** as a result.FN 1 [FN1.] The appellants (collectively, the Kessels) refer to second and third-degree **burns** in describing the injury that hot water can cause, but they do not refer to any point in the record that describes Zakary's **burns** in these terms. The Kessels describe his **burns** as severe, and this description is supported by Christal's testimony on the medical treatment he received for the **burns**. ¶ 5 The complaint alleged that Stansfield Vending was negligent because there was no warning on the water dispenser,FN 2......

☐ **26. Martinelli v. Custom Accessories, Inc.,**
Not Reported in N.E.2d, 14 Mass.L.Rptr. 601, 2002 WL 1489610, Mass.Super., May 21, 2002 (NO. 002277)

Figure 5-49. Westlaw—Search: Advanced Search tab, Select Databases, Cases, All State Cases, Refinement of search, Search term "burns"

While doing this produces an unintended result—because "burns" turns out to be the name of the judge, as in the first, eighth, and ninth case—a more sophisticated search might eliminate these results. Of the remaining, only one seems like the case. Yet, this involved hot coffee from a Dunkin' Donuts restaurant, so it is not the right case.

e. Statutes and Regulations; United States Code Annotated (USCA)

Perhaps the case involves federal law, which would mean looking through the United States Code Annotated (USCA). Under the heading of Statutes and Regulations, as seen in Figure 5-40, checking off the United States Code Annotated and clicking the adjacent Table of Contents link brings the researcher to a web page with federal law broken down by the sections of the USCA, known as Titles.

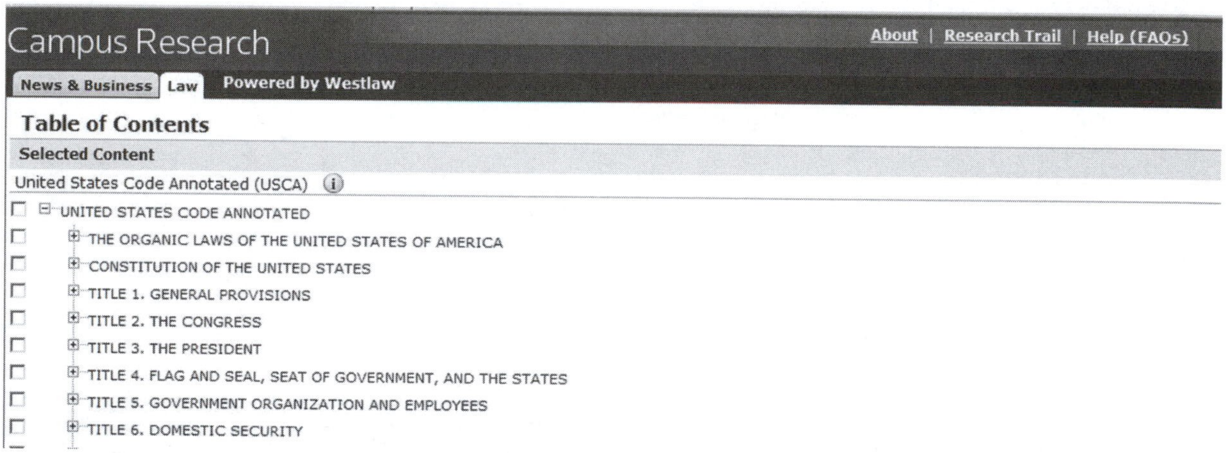

Figure 5-50. Westlaw—Search: Advanced Search tab, Select Databases, Statutes and Regulations, the United States Code Annotated, Table of Contents link

1) Popular Name Table

If the case had involved a well-known federal law, like the Clean Air Act, clicking on the Pop. Name Table link to the right of the screen would produce that citation after entering that law's name.

Figure 5-51. Westlaw—Search: Advanced Search tab, Select Databases, Statutes and Regulations, the United States Code Annotated, Table of Contents link, Pop. Name Table page

2) *50 State Surveys*

If a researcher has had no success because the case did not involve federal law, clicking the adjacent 50 State Surveys link brings the researcher to categories of law, under the Resources heading. A researcher can create a survey, an overview of a particular area of the law, with the "McDonald's Cup of Coffee" case, that would involve at least tort law.

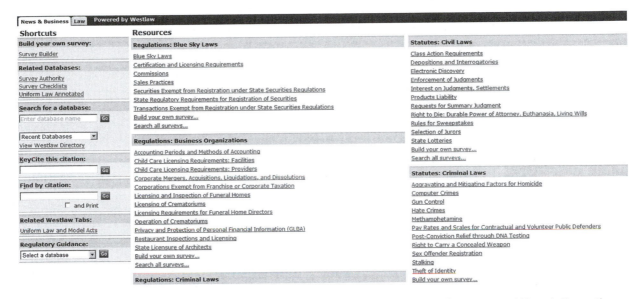

Figure 5-52. Westlaw—Search: Advanced Search tab, Select Databases, Statutes and Regulations, the United States Code Annotated, Table of Contents link, the 50 State Surveys page

3) *Survey Builder*

Under the Shortcuts heading, a researcher can create an overview of law in a jurisdiction. Clicking the Survey Builder link leads to the Survey Builder page, where a researcher can tailor a search to a particular area of a state's law. For example, a researcher who wants to find out about selling corporate securities in Massachusetts, which involves Blue Sky laws, would get this screen, then could further narrow the scope of the results.

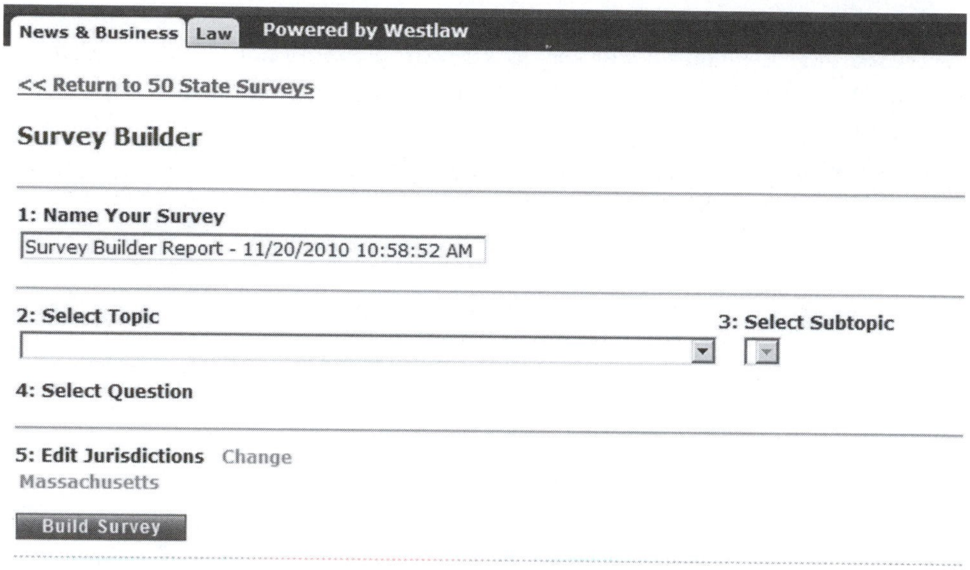

Figure 5-53. Westlaw—Search: Advanced Search tab, Select Databases, Statutes and Regulations, the United States Code Annotated, Table of Contents link, the 50 State Surveys link, Survey Builder page

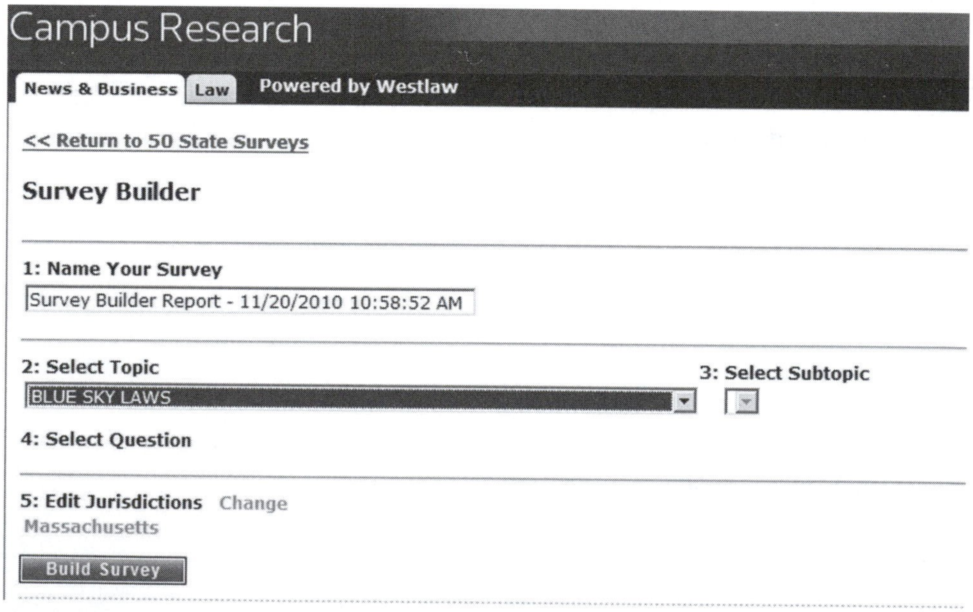

Figure 5-54. Westlaw—Search: Advanced Search tab, Select Databases, Statutes and Regulations, the United States Code Annotated, Table of Contents link, the 50 State Surveys link, Survey Builder page, Select Topic Blue Sky Laws in Massachusetts

4) Survey Authority

A researcher can create an overview of topics in the law using the Survey Authority link. Accordingly, a researcher could create a topical survey on tort law.

News & Business | **Law** | **Powered by Westlaw**

- Survey Authority
  - Business Organizations
    - ANTI-BRIBERY AND ANTI-CORRUPTION PROVISIONS
    - CONVERSION OF PARTNERSHIP TO AN LLC
    - INDEMNIFICATION OF OFFICERS, DIRECTORS, EMPLOYEES AND AGENTS
    - INTERNATIONAL SERVICE OF PROCESS
    - LIQUIDATION: TAX CONSEQUENCES
    - LIQUIDATION: DEBTS AND CREDITOR RIGHTS
    - PREVENTIVE MEASURES FOR DATA SECURITY
    - REORGANIZATION AND RESTRUCTURING: DEBTS AND CREDITOR RIGHTS
    - SECURITY BREACH
    - SECURITY OF PERSONAL HEALTH CARE INFORMATION
  - Employment Law
    - OFFSHORING: LABOR & EMPLOYMENT/DATA PRIVACY
    - OFFSHORING: TAXATION
  - Environmental Law
    - GREENHOUSE GAS EMISSIONS
    - STATE RENEWABLE PORTFOLIO STANDARDS
  - Financial Services
    - SUBPRIME LENDING
  - Insurance
    - SUITABILITY REQUIREMENTS WHEN SELLING LIFE INSURANCE POLICIES AND ANNUITIES
  - Intellectual Property
    - INFRINGEMENT OF COPYRIGHTS, PENALTIES
    - INFRINGEMENT OF PATENTS: CIVIL AND CRIMINAL PENALTIES
    - INFRINGEMENT OF TRADEMARKS: CIVIL AND CRIMINAL PENALTIES
    - INTERNATIONAL PRIORITY OF PATENTS
  - Litigation

Figure 5-55. Westlaw—Search: Advanced Search tab, Select Databases, Statutes and Regulations, the United States Code Annotated, Table of Contents link, the 50 State Surveys link, Survey Authority page

2. Shortcuts

Researchers have the option, under this heading, to do quick and simple searches.

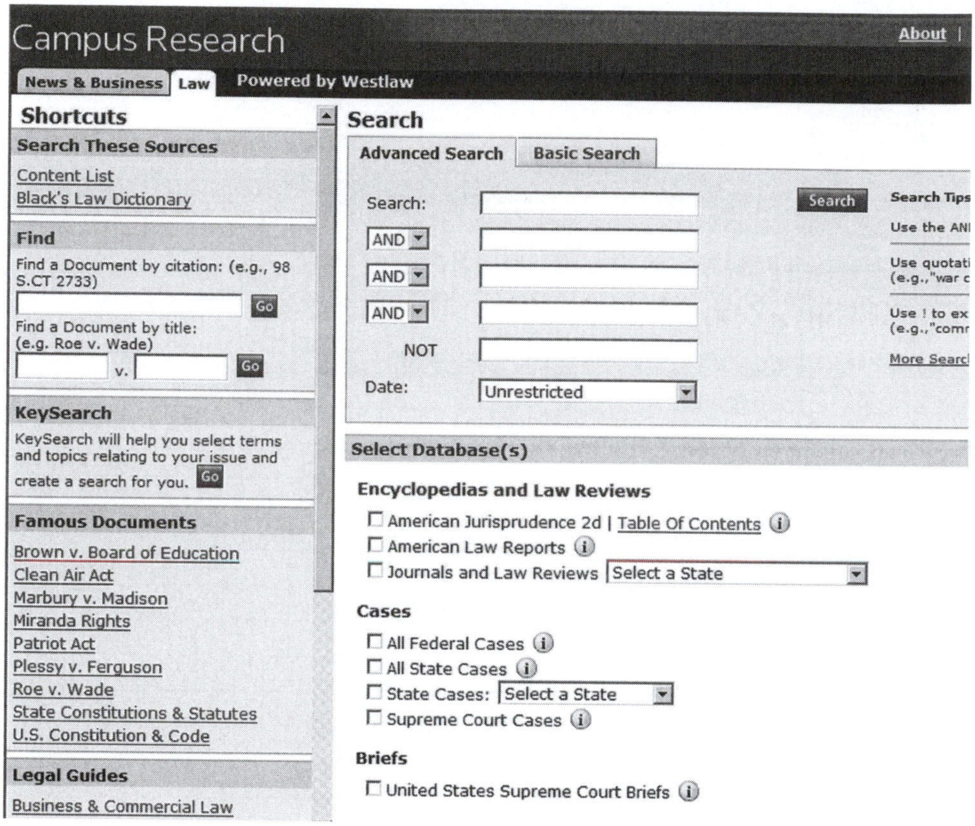

Figure 5-56. Westlaw—Shortcuts

a. Search These Sources

i. Content List link

The Content List link provides links to the same databases available on the Search side to the right, as seen in Figure 5-57, but in a different sequence.

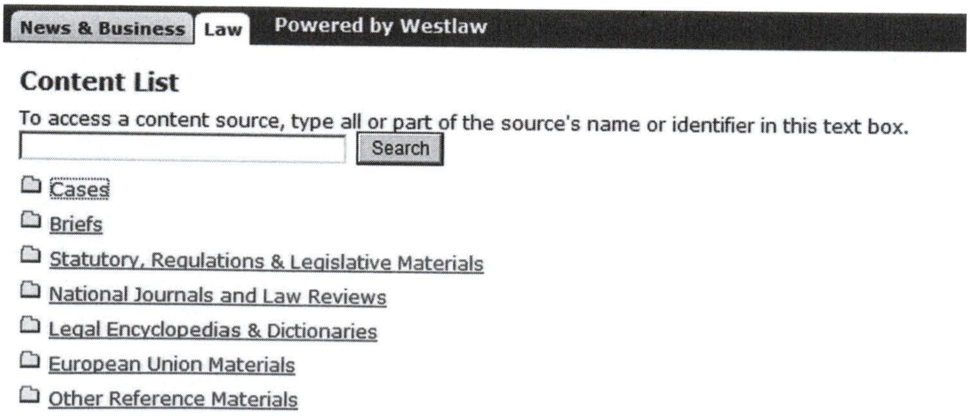

Figure 5-57. Westlaw—Shortcuts: Search These Sources box, Content List link

ii. Black's Law Dictionary link

The Black's Law Dictionary link provides quick access to definitions of concepts in the law.

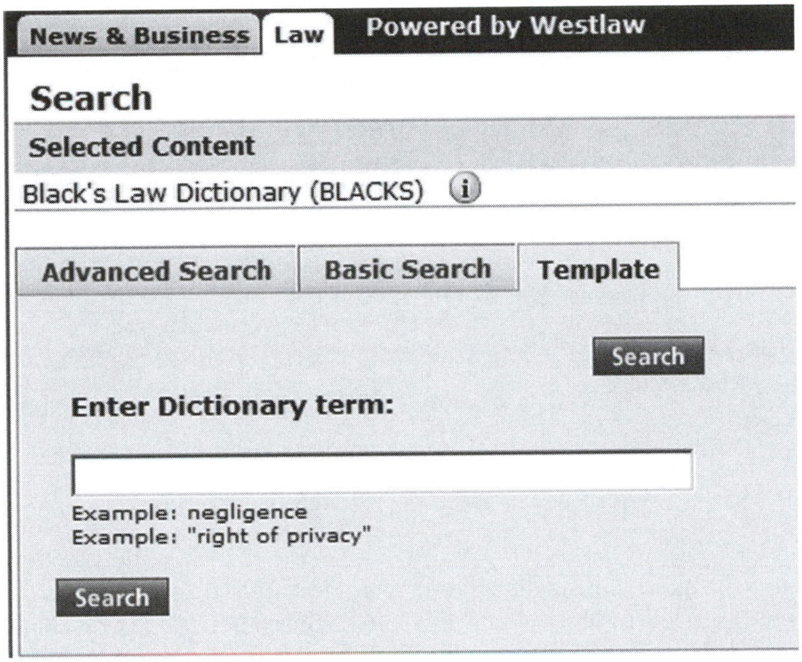

Figure 5-58. Westlaw—Shortcuts: Search These Sources box, Black's Law Dictionary link

b. Find

i. Using the Find box

With this box, a researcher needs only to plug in a party's name, although having a defendant's name would considerably narrow down the scope of that search. In the "McDonald's Cup of Coffee" case, prior research determined that Stella Liebeck had suffered injury because of burns caused by spilling the extremely hot coffee from McDonald's.

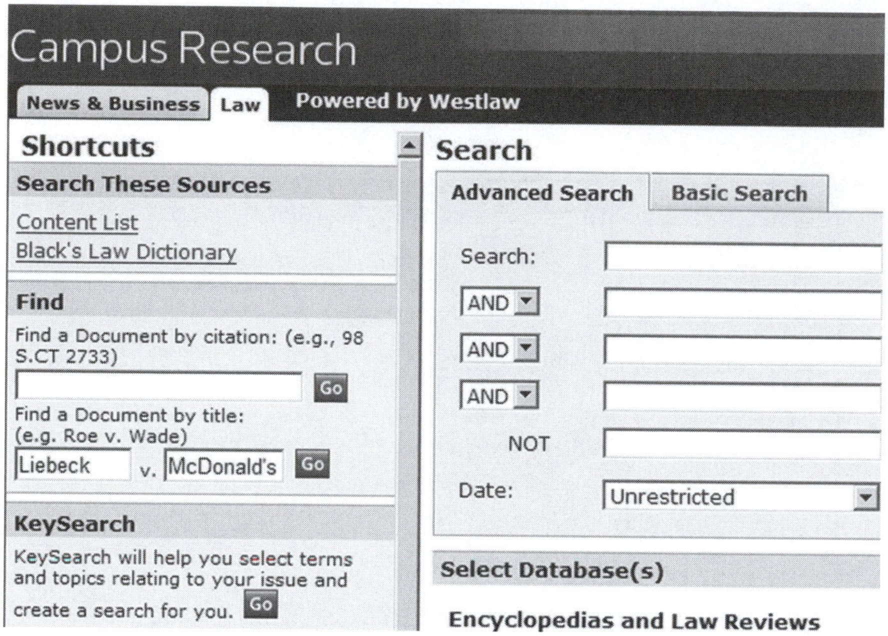

Figure 5-59. Westlaw—Shortcuts: Find box

Hitting the blue Go button produces immediately helpful results. Clicking on the red flag in the upper-right corner reveals that this trial court ruling was followed up with an entry of a settlement by the parties, three months later.

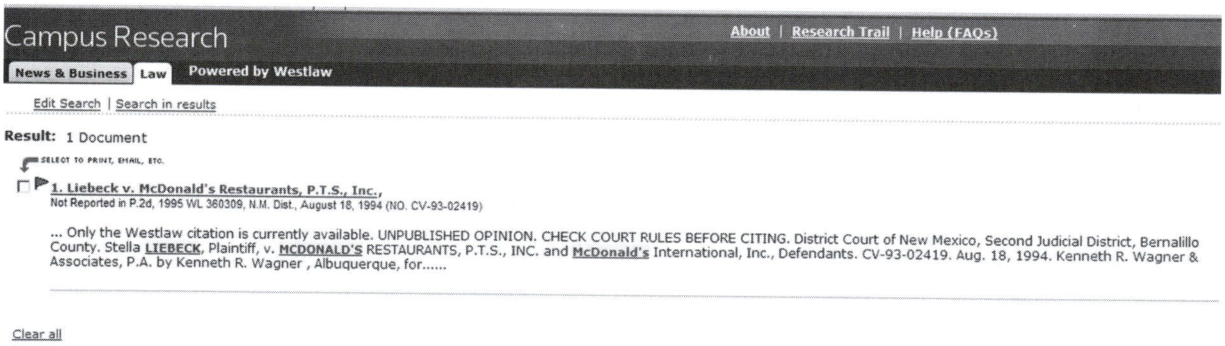

Figure 5-60. Westlaw—Shortcuts: Find box, Liebeck v. McDonald's results

Clicking on the case name produces the entry of judgment for Stella Liebeck on some of her claims, but not on all of them, based upon a jury's findings. Note that under finding 4, the court called attention to a reduction in an award in damages by 20 percent for Ms. Liebeck, based upon how much her actions helped to bring about her injuries.

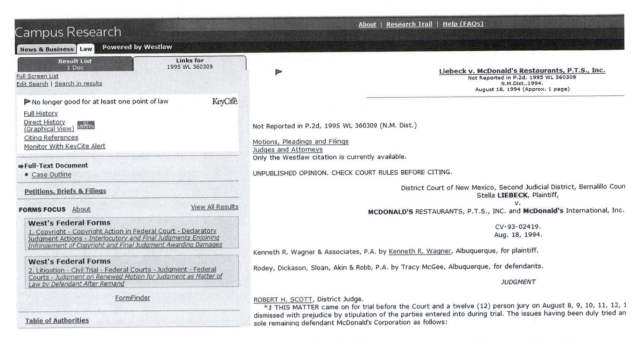

Figure 5-61. Westlaw—Shortcuts: Find box, Liebeck v. McDonald's results, Clicking on case name screen

ii. The Full History link

By clicking on the Full History link on the left side of the screen, the researcher not only sees the sequence of actions taken by the court, but also has access to documents such as pleadings and reports by expert witnesses. So, if the reason for having looked up the "McDonald's Cup of Coffee" case was to figure out the likelihood of success if a new client came in, claiming similar injuries, then having the documents submitted by the expert witnesses provides their insights. It also identifies them, if the firm needs to hire them to testify at a trial. This subscription, however, does not allow for access to such documents.

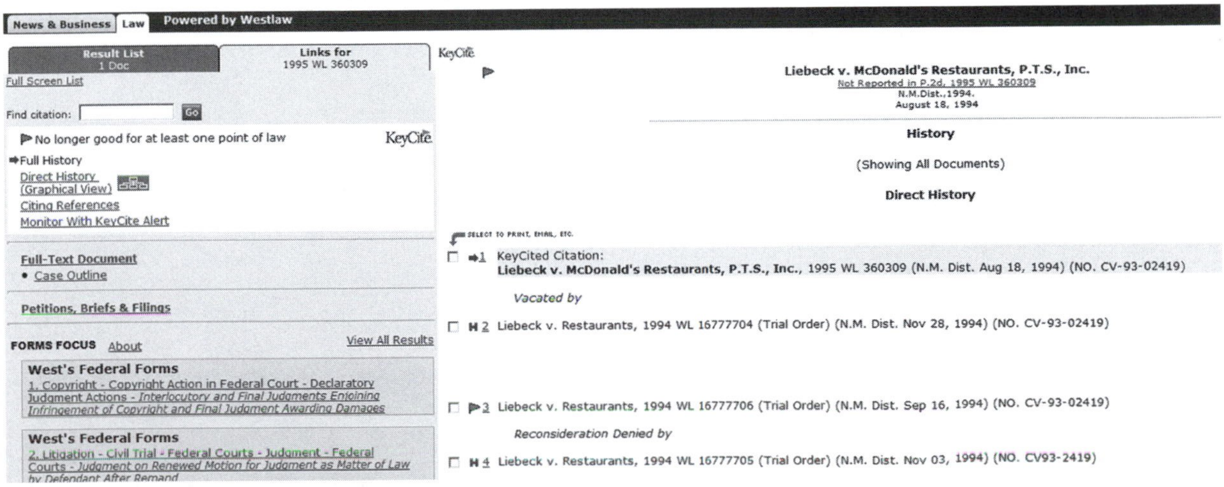

Figure 5-62. Westlaw—Shortcuts: Find box, Liebeck v. McDonald's results, Full History link, page

iii. The Direct History (Graphical View) link

Below the Full History link, the Direct History (Graphical View) link connects to a map of how the Liebeck case proceeded.

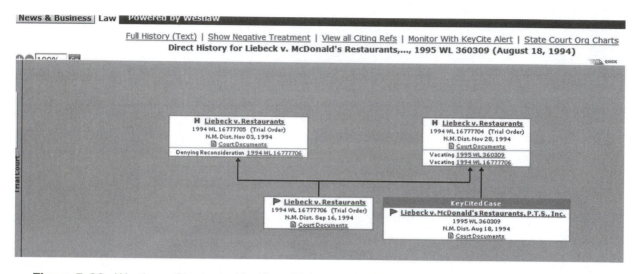

Figure 5-63. Westlaw—Shortcuts: Find box, Liebeck v. McDonald's results, Direct History link, page

iv. The KeyCite Alert link

Below these links, the researcher can elect to receive a **KeyCite Alert,** which will issue upon a mention of the case in subsequent proceedings. This subscription does not provide the KeyCite Alert service.

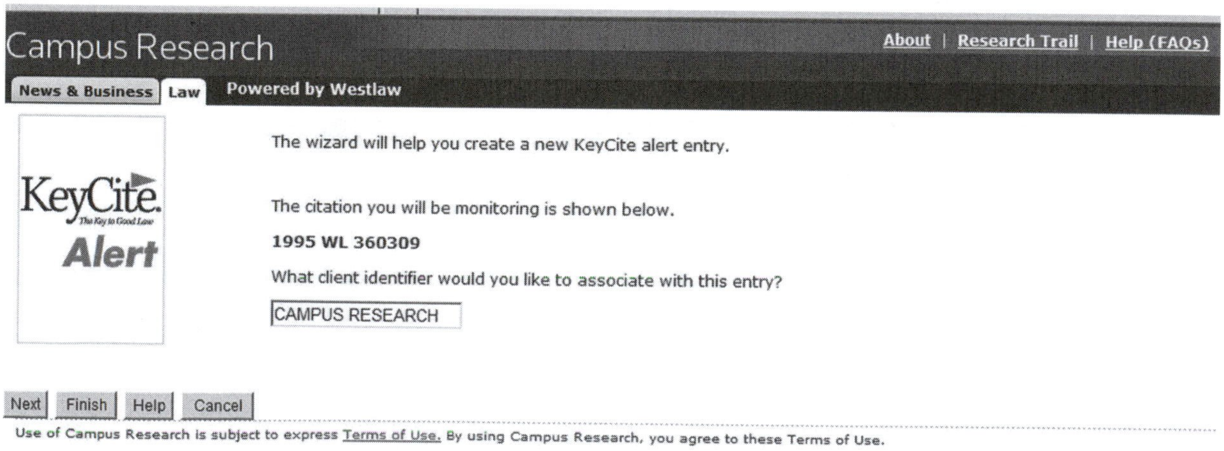

Figure 5-64. Westlaw—Shortcuts: Find box, "Liebeck v. McDonald's" results, Monitor with KeyCite Alert link, page

c. Key search

Using the Key system, from AmJur2d and the ALR series, can make it easier to conduct research by looking at a topic. Clicking the Go button shows the researcher a range of topics.

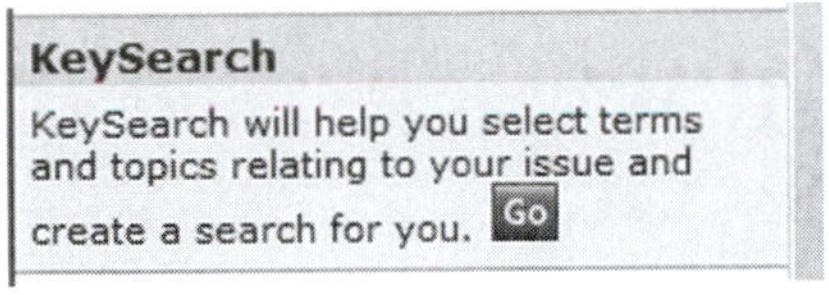

KeySearch

KeySearch will help you select terms and topics relating to your issue and create a search for you. [Go]

Figure 5-65. Westlaw—Shortcuts: Key Search box

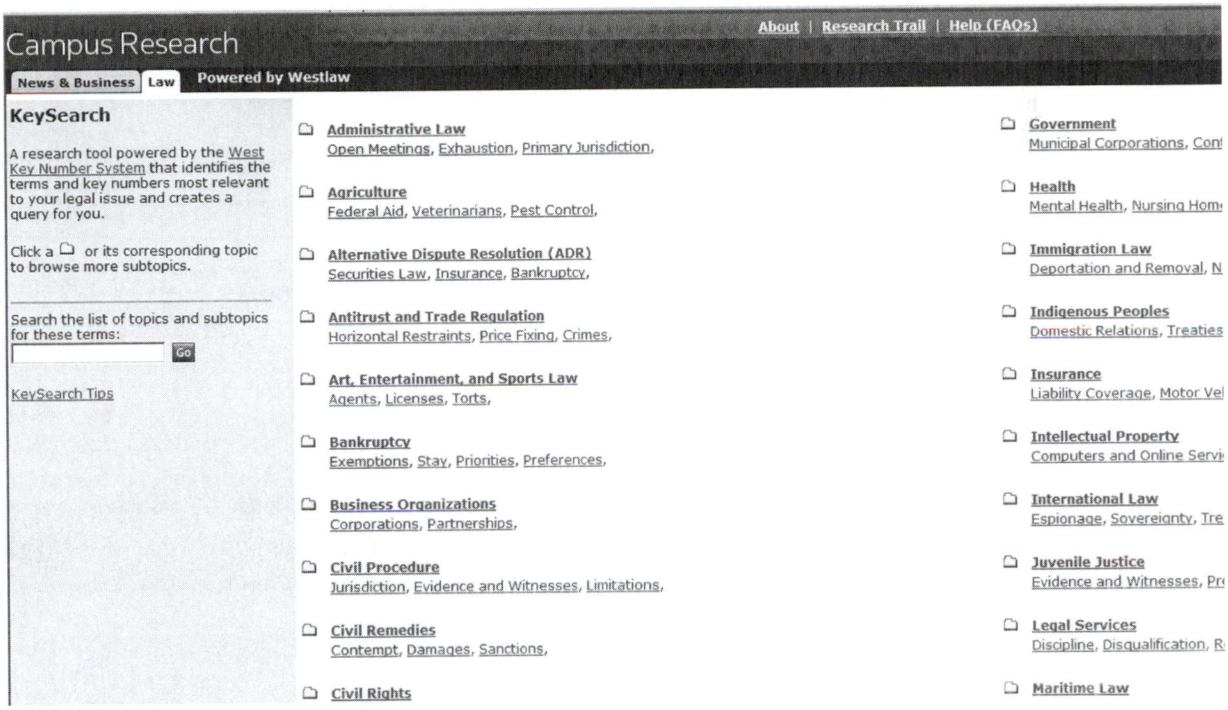

Figure 5-66. Westlaw—Shortcuts: Key Search box, topics

3. Research Trail Link

On the main Westlaw page, at the top, a link entitled "Research Trail" appears. This link goes to a record of the research steps taken by a researcher. For example, clicking the link produces a record of a search for information about the "McDonald's Cup of Coffee" case.

Figure 5-67. Westlaw—Research Trail link

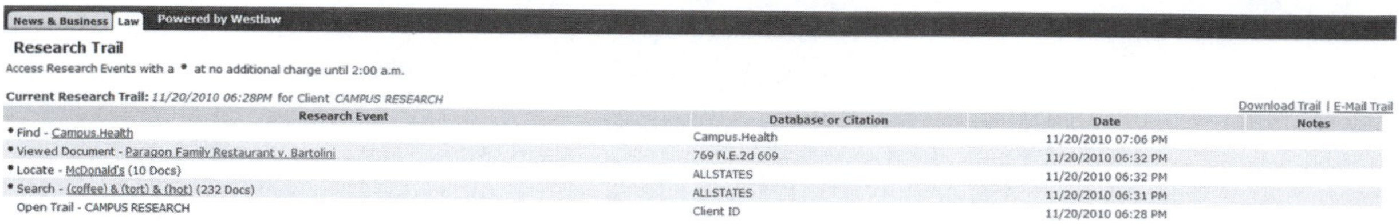

Figure 5-68. Westlaw—Research Trail link: Research Trail page

The researcher can download this record to figure out what other steps to take when conducting a search that, to this point, has not yielded useful results.

4. KeyCite

Westlaw also has available KeyCite, a service to check whether a court has followed or overruled another court's ruling. It corresponds to the Shepard's service provided by Lexis-Nexis.

WestlawNext

1. A Different Interface with Familiar Features

West Publishing has recognized that researchers will feel more at ease using an interface similar to the one available when conducting Internet-based research. The design of WestlawNext provides the researchers with an easy-to-use, intuitive interface. This kind of interface puts the researcher in charge instead of requiring a researcher to learn how to use a database's distinct interface.

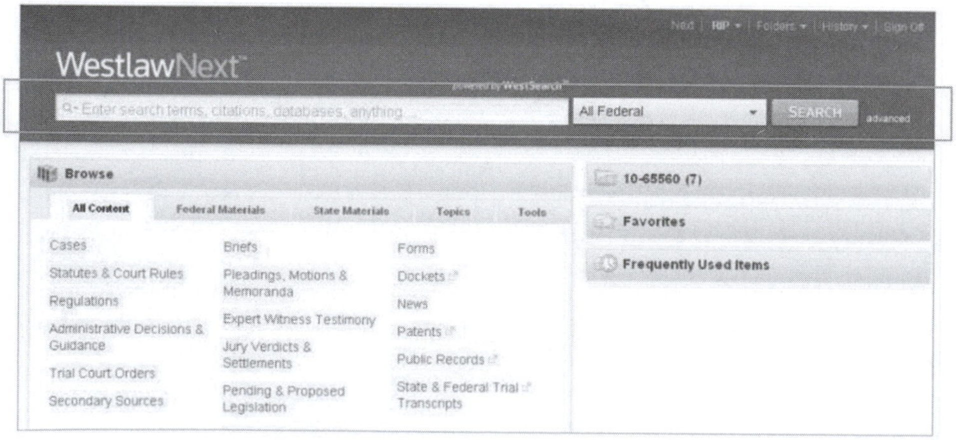

Figure 1. Home page

Figure 5-69. Westlaw—WestlawNext: home page

A free app exists that tailors access to WestlawNext features expressly for the iPad. WestlawNext Mobile allows a researcher to use WestlawNext content via a smartphone like BlackBerry or iPhone, devices using the Android operating systems, as well as browsers like Safari and Opera.

2. Sharing

Researchers may share the results of a search, identifying recipients of the results by the role each plays, such as a researcher or a contributor.

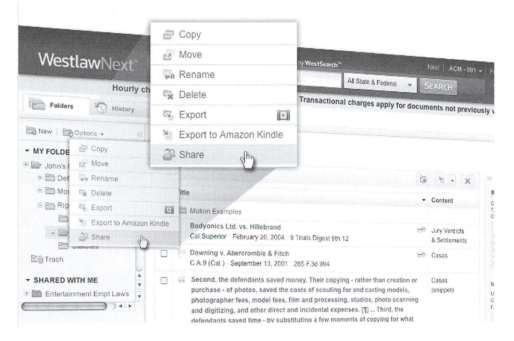

Figure 5-70. Westlaw—Example of how to share results of a search using WestlawNext

3. Features

Features of WestlawNext include:

▶ Westlaw's KeyCite function, for subsequent treatment of a case;

▶ Case Summaries, tied in to West Publishing's proprietary Key Number taxonomy;

▶ A dashboard:

  ▷ For quick access to commonly used features, such as ranking results by relevance;

  ▷ Which highlights relevant portions; and

  ▷ For inserting notes, akin to the attachable, adhesive-backed notes common to an office environment.

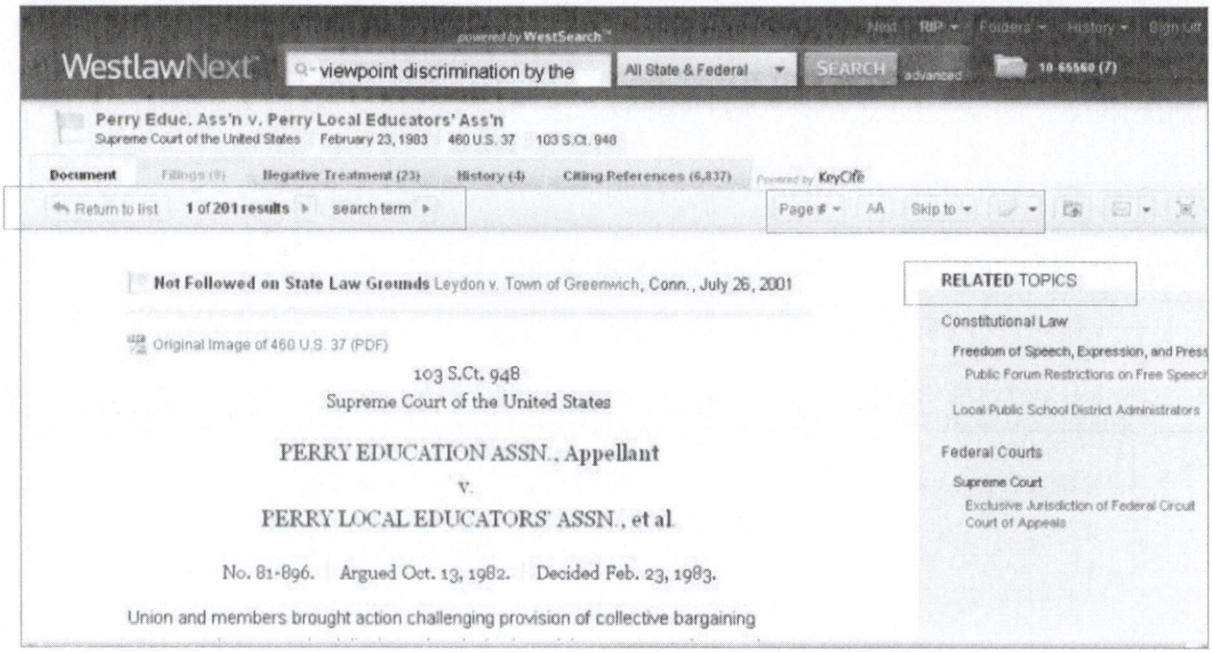

Figure 5-71. Westlaw—WestlawNext: Ability to insert notes in search results produced using WestlawNext

▶ A means for putting a case cite into one of the leading legal citation formats, such as *The Bluebook*; and

▶ Obtaining access to previously conducted searches.

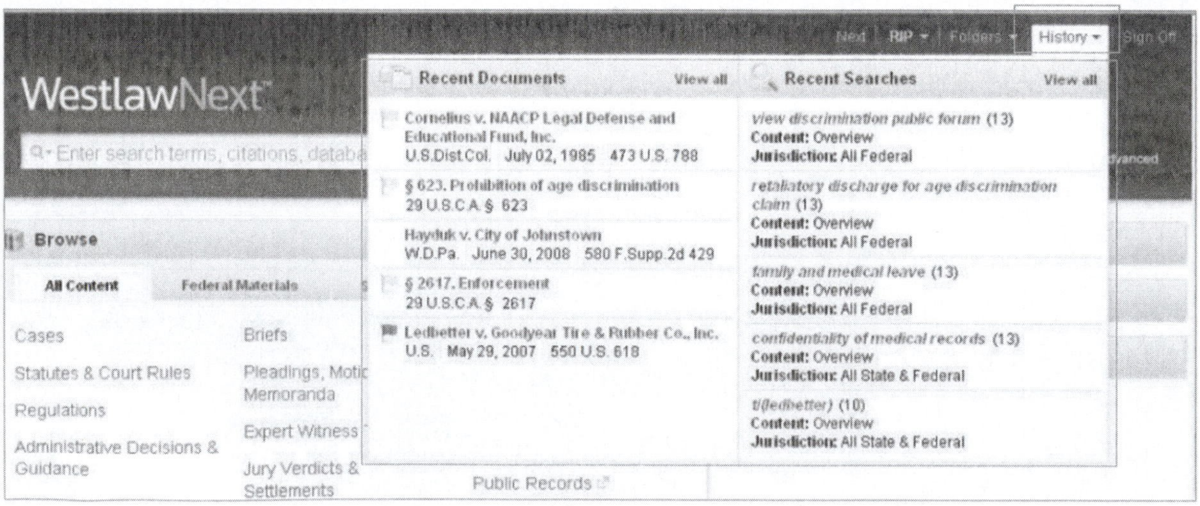

Figure 5-72. Westlaw—WestlawNext: History of recent searches

Loislaw

Loislaw, at www.loislaw.com, is a legal database created by the publishers of this text, Wolters Kluwer. It offers a range of sources, beyond federal and state laws, including public records like UCC-1 filings (which relate to borrowing for the purchase of business equipment) and corporate public records.

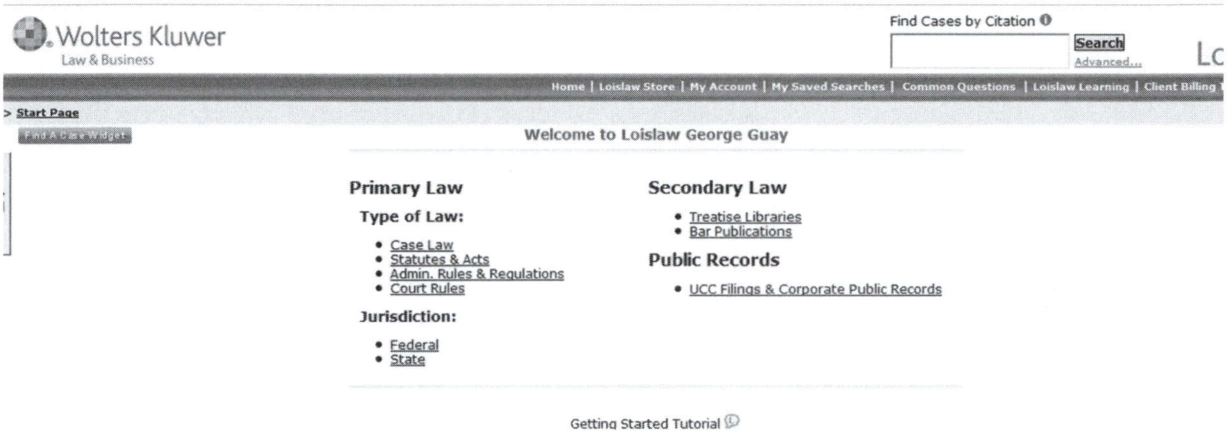

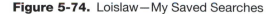

Figure 5-73. Loislaw—Home page: Loislaw

The exploration of this site is via the Loislaw Online Legal Research Paralegal Prepaid Access Pass, which provides unlimited research access for four months, the length of a traditional college semester. A researcher can also purchase unlimited access to the database.

Also, the exploration of the features available on Loislaw will use the McDonald's "Cup of Coffee" case.

Links

Along the top, toward the right side of the screen, links include:

▶ My Saved Searches, where a researcher can save up to five previous searches, with this version;

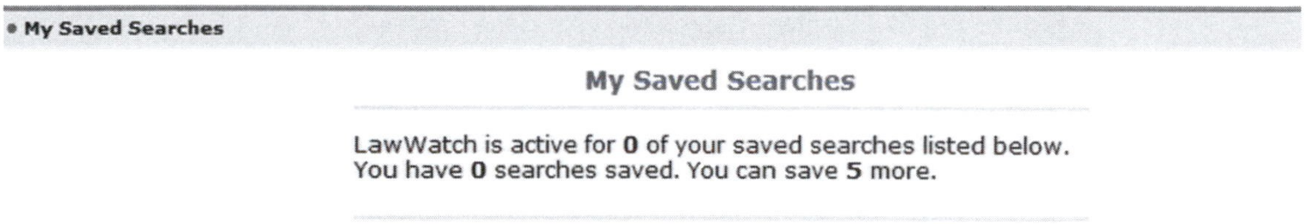

Figure 5-74. Loislaw—My Saved Searches

▶ Loislaw Learning, which includes links to tutorials; and

▶ Client Billing Timer link, for keeping track of time spent on a client's case.

Research Resources

1. Primary Law

As seen in Figure 5-73, a researcher has access by jurisdiction to primary law, case law, statutes, and administrative rules and regulations, including those under the federal system, which would include the Federal Register.

One strategy could involve searching for the actual court ruling. Using the Search All States link, however, produces too many cases for a researcher practically to review. So, using the Search within a Search button and the phrase "Product Liability" can dramatically reduce the number to review. Result 12 would bring the researcher the following result, although not the actual case name.

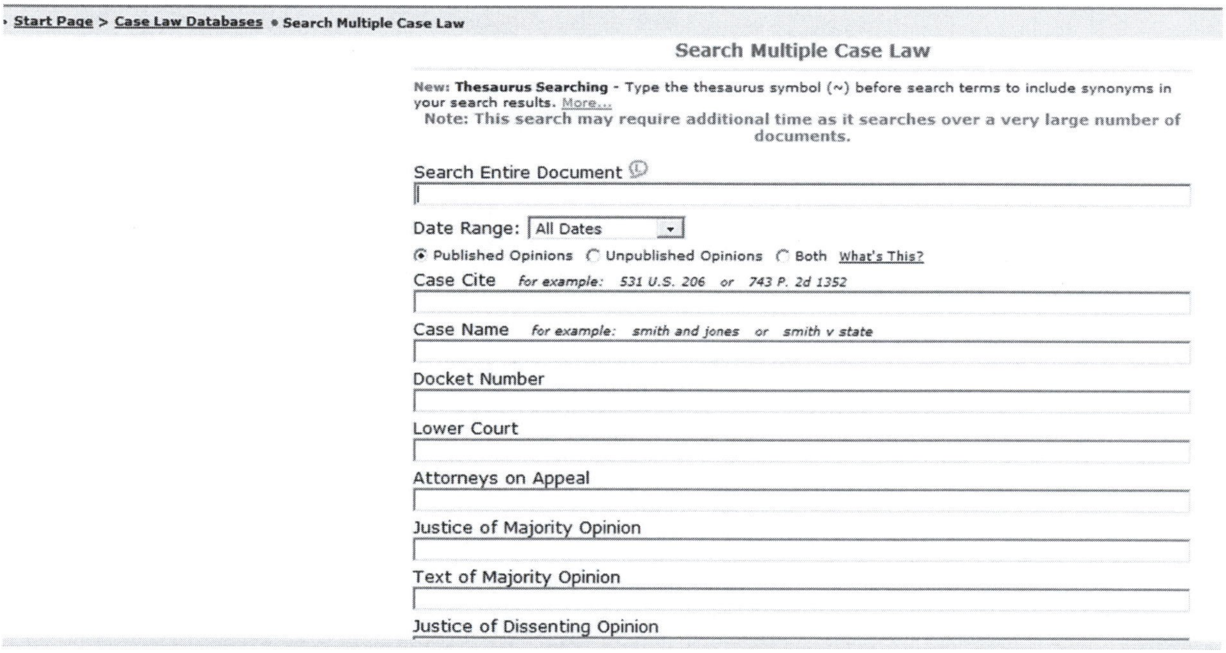

Figure 5-75. Loislaw—Search Multiple Case Law page

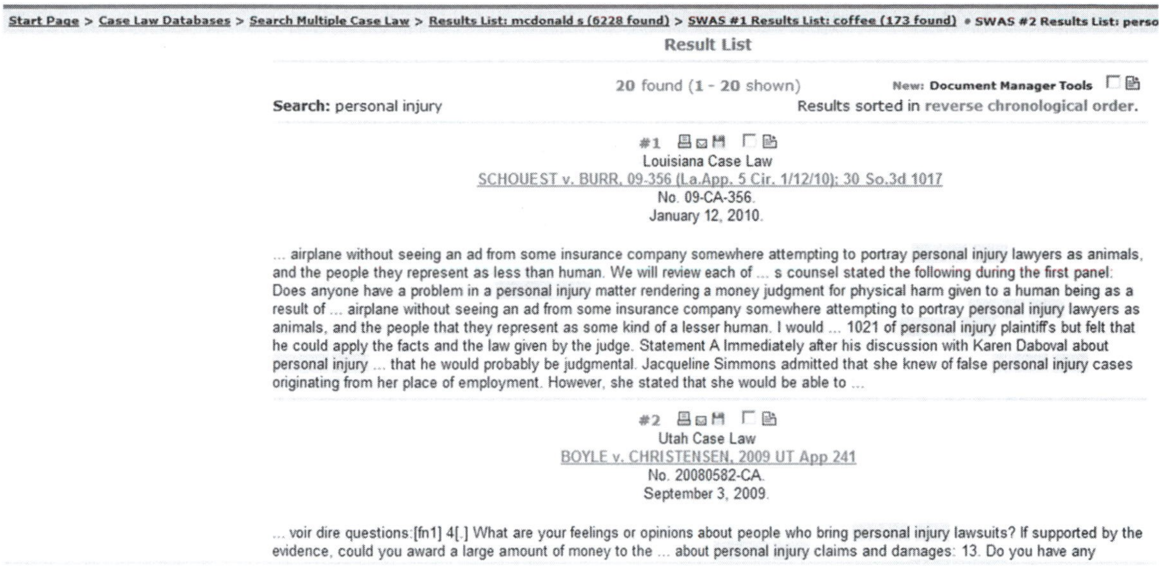

Result List

20 found (1 - 20 shown)   New: Document Manager Tools

Search: personal injury   Results sorted in reverse chronological order.

#1
Louisiana Case Law
SCHOUEST v. BURR, 09-356 (La.App. 5 Cir. 1/12/10); 30 So.3d 1017
No. 09-CA-356.
January 12, 2010.

... airplane without seeing an ad from some insurance company somewhere attempting to portray personal injury lawyers as animals, and the people they represent as less than human. We will review each of ... s counsel stated the following during the first panel: Does anyone have a problem in a personal injury matter rendering a money judgment for physical harm given to a human being as a result of ... airplane without seeing an ad from some insurance company somewhere attempting to portray personal injury lawyers as animals, and the people that they represent as some kind of a lesser human. I would ... 1021 of personal injury plaintiff's but felt that he could apply the facts and the law given by the judge. Statement A Immediately after his discussion with Karen Daboval about personal injury ... that he would probably be judgmental. Jacqueline Simmons admitted that she knew of false personal injury cases originating from her place of employment. However, she stated that she would be able to ...

#2
Utah Case Law
BOYLE v. CHRISTENSEN, 2009 UT App 241
No. 20080582-CA.
September 3, 2009.

... voir dire questions:[fn1] 4[.] What are your feelings or opinions about people who bring personal injury lawsuits? If supported by the evidence, could you award a large amount of money to the ... about personal injury claims and damages: 13. Do you have any

Figure 5-76. Loislaw—Search within a Search of Result List for search for McDonald's case

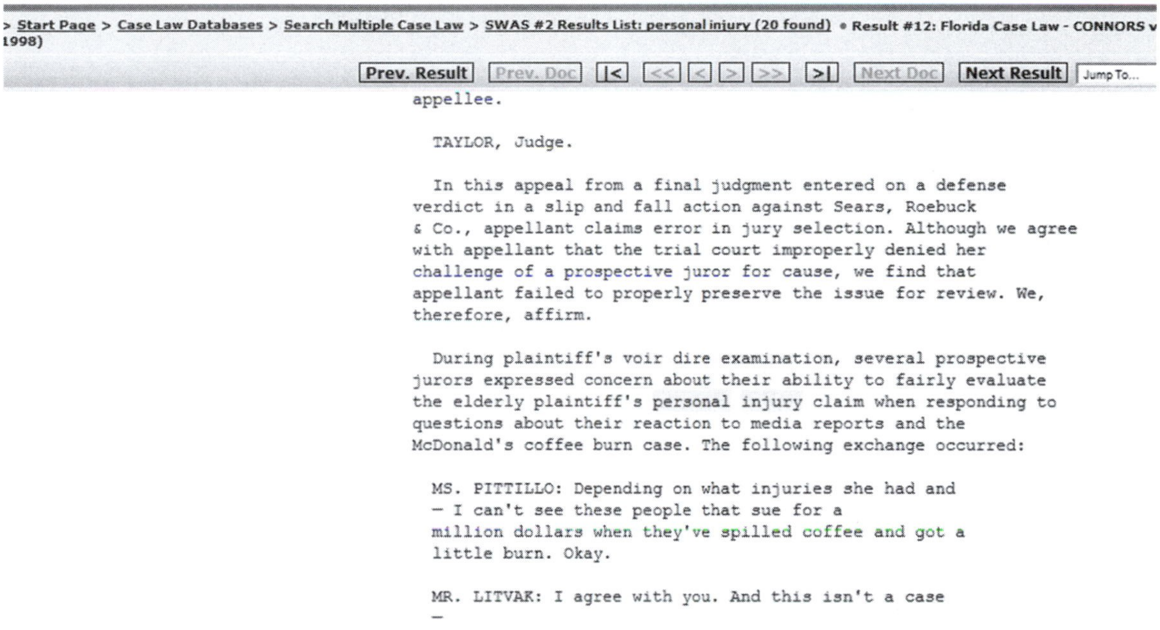

Prev. Result | Prev. Doc | |< | << | < | > | >> | >| | Next Doc | Next Result | Jump To...

appellee.

TAYLOR, Judge.

In this appeal from a final judgment entered on a defense verdict in a slip and fall action against Sears, Roebuck & Co., appellant claims error in jury selection. Although we agree with appellant that the trial court improperly denied her challenge of a prospective juror for cause, we find that appellant failed to properly preserve the issue for review. We, therefore, affirm.

During plaintiff's voir dire examination, several prospective jurors expressed concern about their ability to fairly evaluate the elderly plaintiff's personal injury claim when responding to questions about their reaction to media reports and the McDonald's coffee burn case. The following exchange occurred:

MS. PITTILLO: Depending on what injuries she had and — I can't see these people that sue for a million dollars when they've spilled coffee and got a little burn. Okay.

MR. LITVAK: I agree with you. And this isn't a case —

Figure 5-77. Loislaw—Results of search 12, with search term highlighted

2. Secondary Law

For secondary law, Loislaw provides access to:

▶ Treatises can provide contemporary thinking on a topic of law, an especially helpful feature regarding a case of first impression. So, using the Employment Law Library could provide information about a new employment statute, or using the Aspen/CCH Bankruptcy Case Reporter (a proprietary database) could provide updates about bankruptcy law, especially court rulings; and

Figure 5-78. Loislaw—Treatise Libraries page

▶ Bar publications, materials issued by a bar association which often provide insights on a topic that the researcher has just started to research.

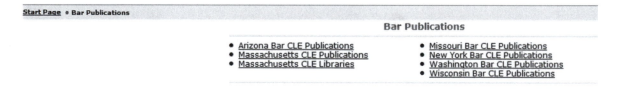

Figure 5-79. Loislaw—Bar Publications page

If a researcher knew that the "McDonald's Cup of Coffee" case involved a large damages award, the Loislaw Treatise Libraries' Personal Injury Law Library might be a good place to start. Using the Search within a Search button and the term "Coffee" yields these highlighted results.

Start Page > Treatise Libraries ● Product Liability Law Library

Product Liability Law Library

Search All Databases　　　　　　　　　　　　　　　　　　　Clear All Databases

☐ Forms & Checklists ▢　　　　　　　　☐ Product Liability Desk Reference ▢
☐ The Preparation of a Product Liability　☐ Product Warnings, Defects and Hazards ▢
　　Case, Third Edition ▢　　　　　　　☐ Scientific Evidence and Experts
☐ Product Liability Case Digest ▢　　　　　　Handbook ▢
　　　　　　　　　　　　　　　　　　☐ Malingering and Deception in Litigation ▢

Figure 5-80. Loislaw—Product Liability Law Library: page

Start Page > Treatise Libraries > Product Liability Law Library > Search Product Liability Law Databases > Results List: mcdonald s (4 found) ● SWAS #1 Results List: coffee (3 found)

Result List

3 found (1 - 3 shown)　　　　　　　　New: **Document Manager Tools** ☐ ▣

Search: coffee　　　　　　　　　　　　　　　　　　Results sorted by score.

#1 - $

▢ **Product Liability Case Digest**
▢ **Consumer Products**
▤ Food and Drink

... D. Minn. 1998). Plaintiff was burned after purchasing coffee at the restaurant. The coffee spilled while she was riding in her car. The coffee was brewed at 190 degrees and kept at 180 degrees. The ... holding that coffee was not defective and risk of plaintiff's injury was open and obvious, thereby relieving defendants of duty to warn. The court also found no breach of implied warranty. New Jersey ... 966 F. Supp. 416 (W.D. Va. 1997). Plaintiff was burned by hot coffee purchased from a fast-food restaurant drive-thru window. The coffee spilled after the driver of the vehicle handed it to her. Court ... coffee was unreasonably dangerous and therefore could not recover. No evidence was presented regarding the heat of the coffee or safety of the cup to show that applicable standards were breached ...

#2 - $

▢ **The Preparation of a Product Liability Case, Third Edition**
▢ **Part I Overview of a Product Liability Case**
▢ **Chapter 2 Strict Liability**
▢ **§ 2.07 Failure to Warn and Marketing Defects**
▢ **§ 2.07[E] Types of Failure-to-Warn Cases**
▤ § 2.07[E][2] Adequacy of the Warning

... coffee are generally apparent to the public. In addition, because of the obvious benefits of hot coffee, most courts that have addressed the issue have determined that one who is burned by hot coffee ... may not shift the costs of these burns to coffeemaker manufacturers or distributors of hot coffee.[fn156] Similarly, dangers and risks that are generally known to a particular trade or profession do ...

#3 - $

▢ **Product Liability Case Digest**
▢ **Consumer Products**
▤ Appliances and Furnishings

Service Corp., 61 Md. App. 23, 484 A.2d 652 (1984). Thermos bottle exploded or imploded when coffee and milk were poured into it. Expert testimony was not required to show that product was

Figure 5-81. Loislaw—Search within a Search of results

Loislaw Widget

A button in the upper-right corner of the Loislaw home page makes it possible for a researcher to use a **widget.** The Loislaw Widget allows the researcher to customize a search portal to an **intranet** or a Microsoft Sharepoint website. Anyone with access to that intranet or Sharepoint website would have access to the Loislaw widget.

Loislaw Widget *A customizable, importable, search portlet*

What's a widget?

A widget is a fully functional search portlet you can customize and place on your intranet, extranet, or sharepoint website. **Loislaw Widgets** are search utilities offered free of charge to subscribers.

Loislaw Find A Case Widget makes it easy to retrieve a case from within your firm's portal or intranet. The Widget can be customized to match your design template and if you wish, you can private brand it. You cho search methods to include: by citation, by case name and/or by keyword. In addition, you can include links to the Loislaw advanced case search template as well as to the multi-cite template.

Getting Started

- Visit the **Getting Started** page for instructions, help, tips, and how to get started creating your customized **Loislaw Find A Case Widget**.
- Or dive right in using the **Loislaw Widget Generation Page** to generate any **Loislaw Widget**.

Widget Samples

Here are a few Loislaw Find a Case Widget Samples:

Figure 5-82. Loislaw—Loislaw Widget page

By creating a widget, a researcher can tailor a search according to certain attributes. Using "McDonald's" yields a great number of cases. Note that the second case is an unpublished opinion, which attests to the sweep of the Loislaw database.

Loislaw Widget Generation Page

Creating and importing a **Loislaw Widget** is an easy three step process.

- Step 1 offers a selection of options to customize the display and function of the Widget to your needs.
- Step 2 allows you to preview your Widget and run test searches.
- Step 3 details how to download the Widget and import it into your environment, such as your website, intranet, or sharepoint site.

If you have questions or require assistance, please **Contact Us**, or visit the **Getting Started** page for more instructions, help, and tips.

1. **Configure The Widget**

Note: Hover over the ⍰ icons for help tips.

Figure 5-83. Loislaw—Loislaw Widget Generation page

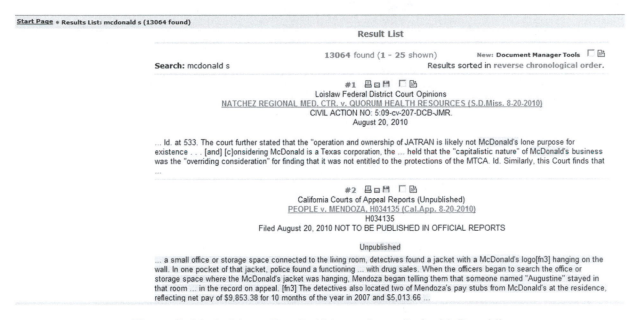

Figure 5-84. Loislaw—Results List search results for McDonald's

Using the Search within a Search button can narrow down the amount of cases to a number that a researcher feasibly could review. The second document offers some especially useful information, such as the state where the injury occurred. Clicking on the link for the case yields the following, including the docket number for the Liebeck case: No. D-202-CV-9302419.

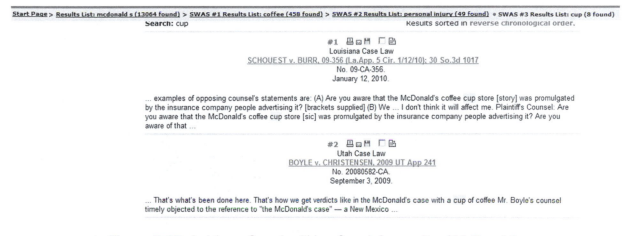

Figure 5-85. Loislaw—Search within a Search for results of McDonald's

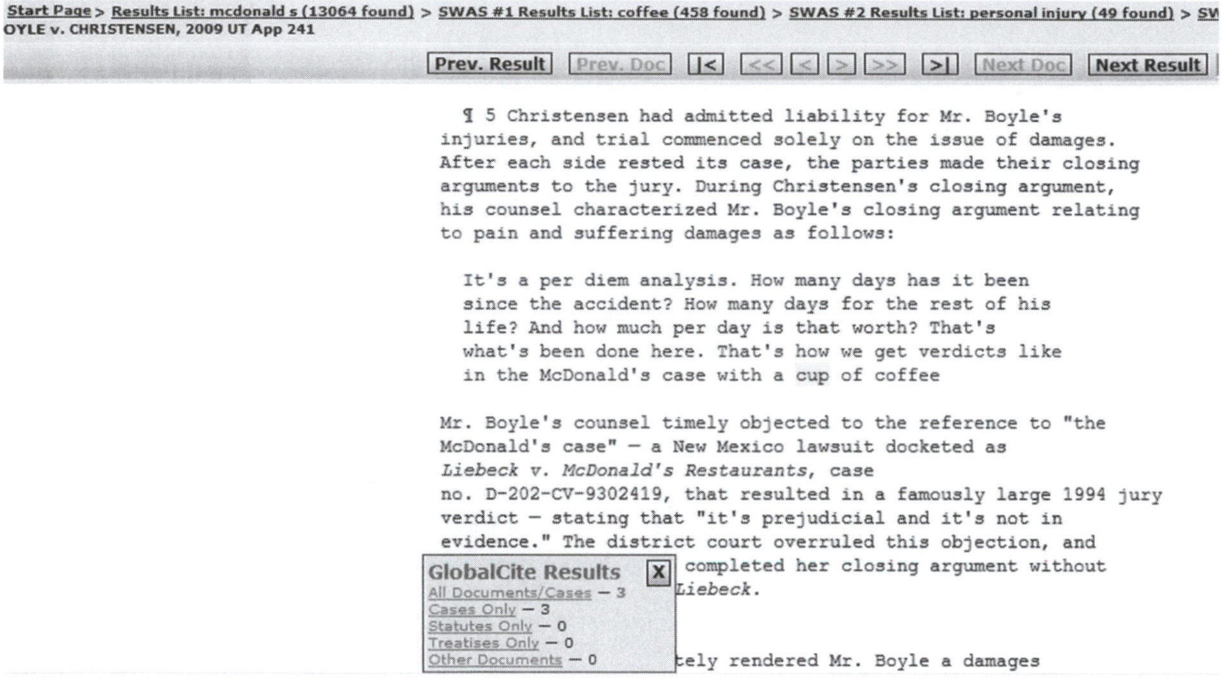

Start Page > Results List: mcdonald s (13064 found) > SWAS #1 Results List: coffee (458 found) > SWAS #2 Results List: personal injury (49 found) > SW
OYLE v. CHRISTENSEN, 2009 UT App 241
Prev. Result
Prev. Doc
|<
<<
<
>
>>
>|
Next Doc
Next Result
¶ 5 Christensen had admitted liability for Mr. Boyle's injuries, and trial commenced solely on the issue of damages. After each side rested its case, the parties made their closing arguments to the jury. During Christensen's closing argument, his counsel characterized Mr. Boyle's closing argument relating to pain and suffering damages as follows:
It's a per diem analysis. How many days has it been since the accident? How many days for the rest of his life? And how much per day is that worth? That's what's been done here. That's how we get verdicts like in the McDonald's case with a cup of coffee
Mr. Boyle's counsel timely objected to the reference to "the McDonald's case" — a New Mexico lawsuit docketed as Liebeck v. McDonald's Restaurants, case no. D-202-CV-9302419, that resulted in a famously large 1994 jury verdict — stating that "it's prejudicial and it's not in evidence." The district court overruled this objection, and
completed her closing argument without
Liebeck.
tely rendered Mr. Boyle a damages
GlobalCite Results
X
All Documents/Cases — 3
Cases Only — 3
Statutes Only — 0
Treatises Only — 0
Other Documents — 0

Figure 5-86. Loislaw—Results of search: New Mexico law

Public Records

The document called the UCC-1 contains information about corporate financing. With some financing, the borrower grants the lender the authority to take property purchased with the loan if the borrower fails to make a loan payment. Here, the researcher can look for liens, created by the filing of the UCC-1, on any business's property, which could matter if the researcher needs to find assets to satisfy a judgment.

Start Page
CT Lien Solutions
Professional People.
Perfected Results.
Products & Services ›
Resources ›
About Us ›
Contact Us ›
Account Status ›
CT Lien Solutions – Exceeding your expectations every day.
With over 30 years of expertise, count on us to deliver the same fast, accurate services with the flexibility and reliability you expect in even the most challenging times.
More»
iLien
User ID:
Password:
LOG IN»
Forgot your password?
Need Help? Call 1.800.833.5778

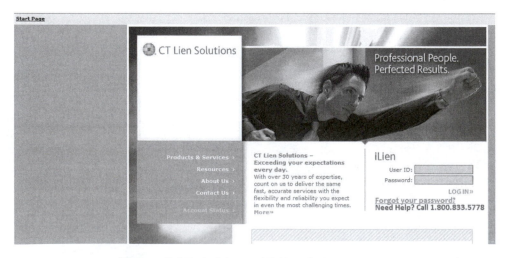

Figure 5-87. Loislaw—CT Lien Solutions page

Fastcase

Fastcase, a subscription-based legal research site, at www.fastcase.com, offers a broad array of information about federal and state law. Significantly, this research service ranks results, much like how the Google search engine presents results. It also graphically depicts research results in terms of relevance. A researcher can obtain access to the service on a desktop computer, an iPad, or an iPhone.

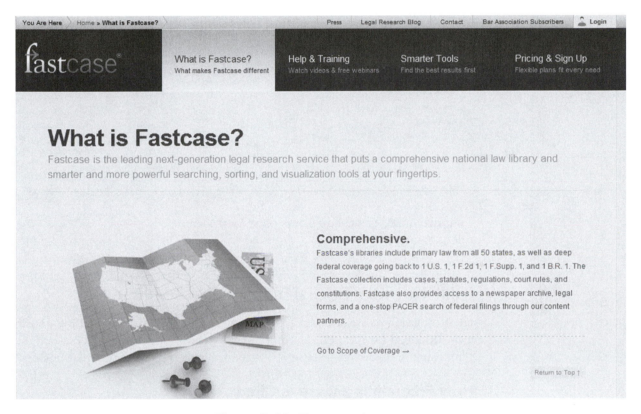

Figure 5-88. Fastcase—home page

When a user logs into Fastcase, the start page offers the user a streamlined graphic interface, one that a researcher can modify so as to have more control over a search. The researcher has the option to search case law quickly and has detailed help options.

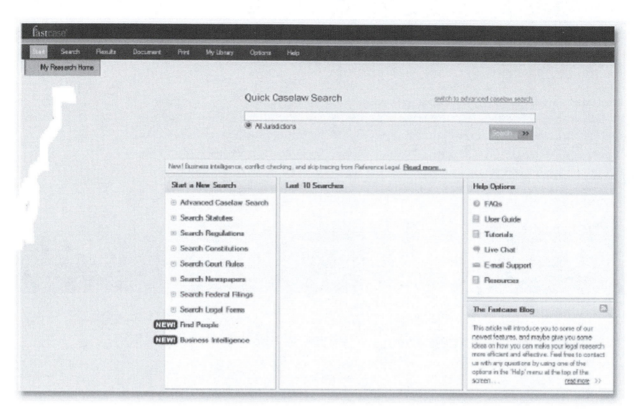

Figure 5-89. Fastcase—Home page for a search

Graphic Representation of Results

Visual information makes it easier to recognize certain kinds of associations in the content produced by a search. Graphic imagery can produce spatial connections with information, to convey a sense of the nature and strength of the relationships.

1. How Frequently a Case Is Cited

In this example, which graphically reflects the relationship among different cases produced by a search, the year serves as the X-axis and the level of relevance is the Y-axis.

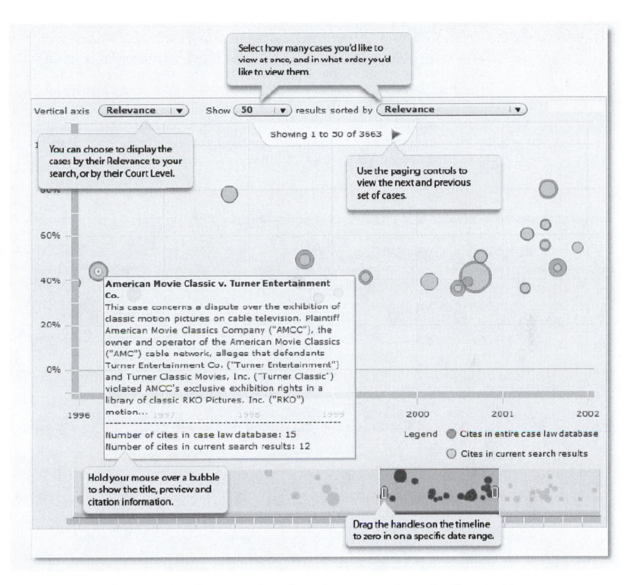

Figure 5-90. Fastcase—Search results expressed as a timeline graphic

For each circle, the area in gold represents the number of times a case was cited in current search results. The gray represents the number of times a case was cited in the entire database. The researcher could also distribute this information according to the time of citation to a case, along a timeline.

2. By Court Level

A researcher could choose to look at the court level, whether trial or appellate, of an opinion found during the search. With these results, the X-axis is the year of the ruling and the Y-axis, the level of the court. The gold shows how frequently a case was cited in other cases, while the gray shows how often the case was cited. In this example, the U.S. Supreme Court seems to have frequently talked about tort law and product liability from the mid-1980s to the mid-1990s. State courts have also talked about the topic, but not as frequently, during that time.

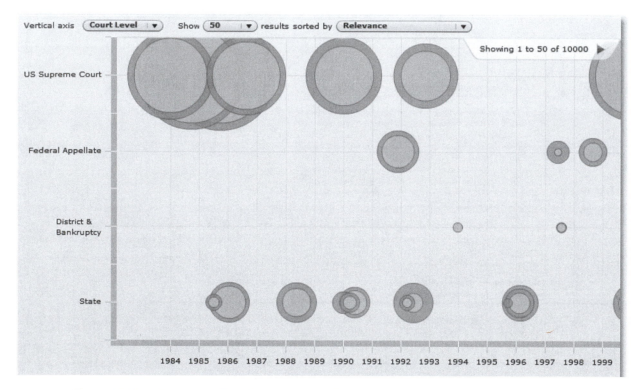

Figure 5-91. Fastcase—Timeline results for Fastcase search: looking at the court level

a. Forecite

The unique **Forecite** feature automatically identifies seminal cases which otherwise went undetected in the original keyword search, increasing the chances of finding a court ruling that has a material impact on the research process.

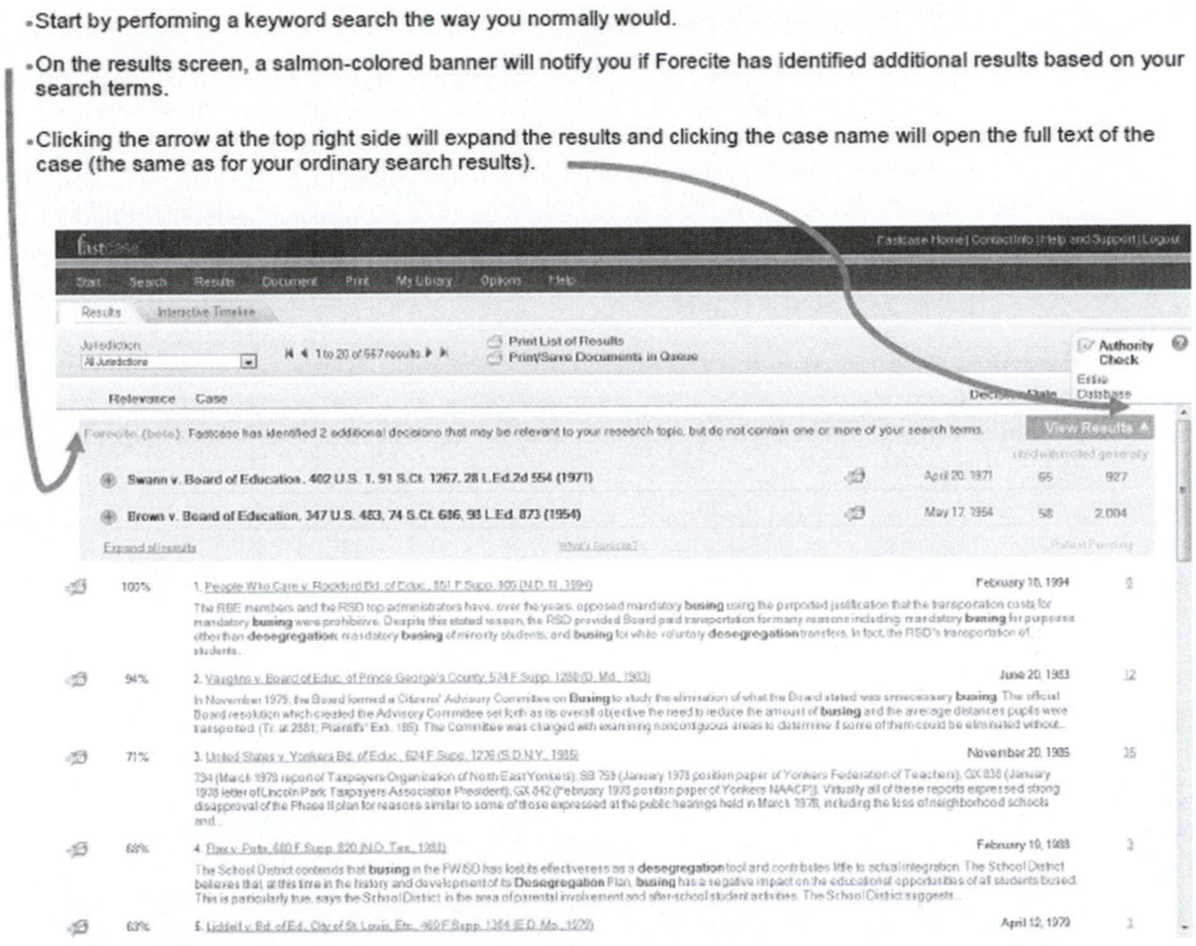
•Start by performing a keyword search the way you normally would.
•On the results screen, a salmon-colored banner will notify you if Forecite has identified additional results based on your search terms.
•Clicking the arrow at the top right side will expand the results and clicking the case name will open the full text of the case (the same as for your ordinary search results).
Print List of Results
Print/Save Documents in Queue
Authority Check
Relevance
Case
View Results
Swann v. Board of Education, 402 U.S. 1, 91 S.Ct. 1267, 28 L.Ed.2d 554 (1971)
Brown v. Board of Education, 347 U.S. 483, 74 S.Ct. 686, 98 L.Ed. 873 (1954)

Figure 5-92. Fastcase—Forecite: graphic and explanation of how Forecite works

b. AuthorityCheck

This service also contains **AuthorityCheck,** a feature that operates like Lexis-Nexis's Shepard's or Westlaw's KeyCite, to report on the subsequent treatment of a case.

c. App

Recognizing a trend, Fastcase offers researchers a free iPhone app. This would suggest that it will produce an app for the operating systems of other smartphones, such as Google's Android.

d. Report of Current Opinions (RECOP)

In collaboration with the Public.Resource.org site, Fastcase issues a free weekly release of all federal and state appellate court opinions, called the **Report of Current Opinions (RECOP).** This service thereby provides a researcher with an easy way to keep current on court rulings.

Casemaker

Casemaker, at www.casemaker.us, differs from other legal research databases because state bar associations created and maintain this service. Members of a state bar association could pay reduced rates to use this service, which might even be included as part of the bar association's membership fee. These savings could then be passed along to clients.

Figure 5-93. Casemaker—Home page

Casemaker seems to cover law since at least the 1960s, and further back in many instances. Its CaseCheck feature presents the subsequent treatment of a case, like with Shepard's and KeyCite. CasemakerDigest provides summaries of case law within days of the release of the court's ruling.

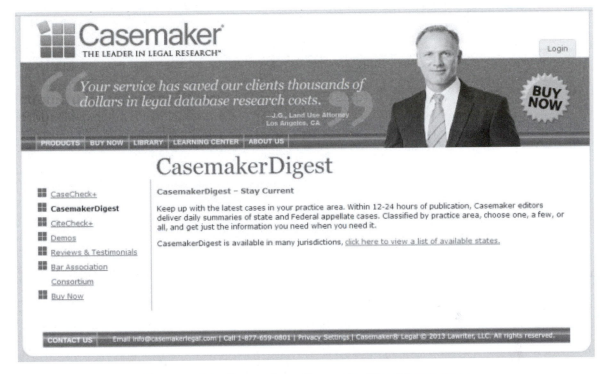

Figure 5-94. Casemaker—CasemakerDigest home page

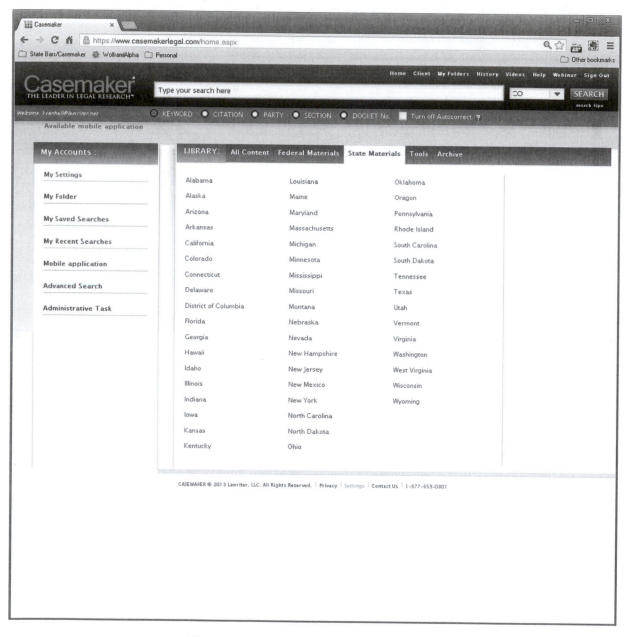

Figure 5-95. Casemaker—State Materials

Google Scholar

Google, the very popular search engine site, also offers **Google Scholar,** at http://scholar.google.com/schhp?hl=en, a free way to conduct on-line legal research.

○ Articles (☑ include patents) ○ Legal opinions and journals

Stand on the shoulders of giants

Go to Google Home - About Google - About Google Scholar

Figure 5-96. Google Scholar—Google Scholar home page

For example, typing the phrase "McDonald's Cup of Coffee" yields this screen. Perhaps coincidentally, this query immediately generated the full case name and cite.

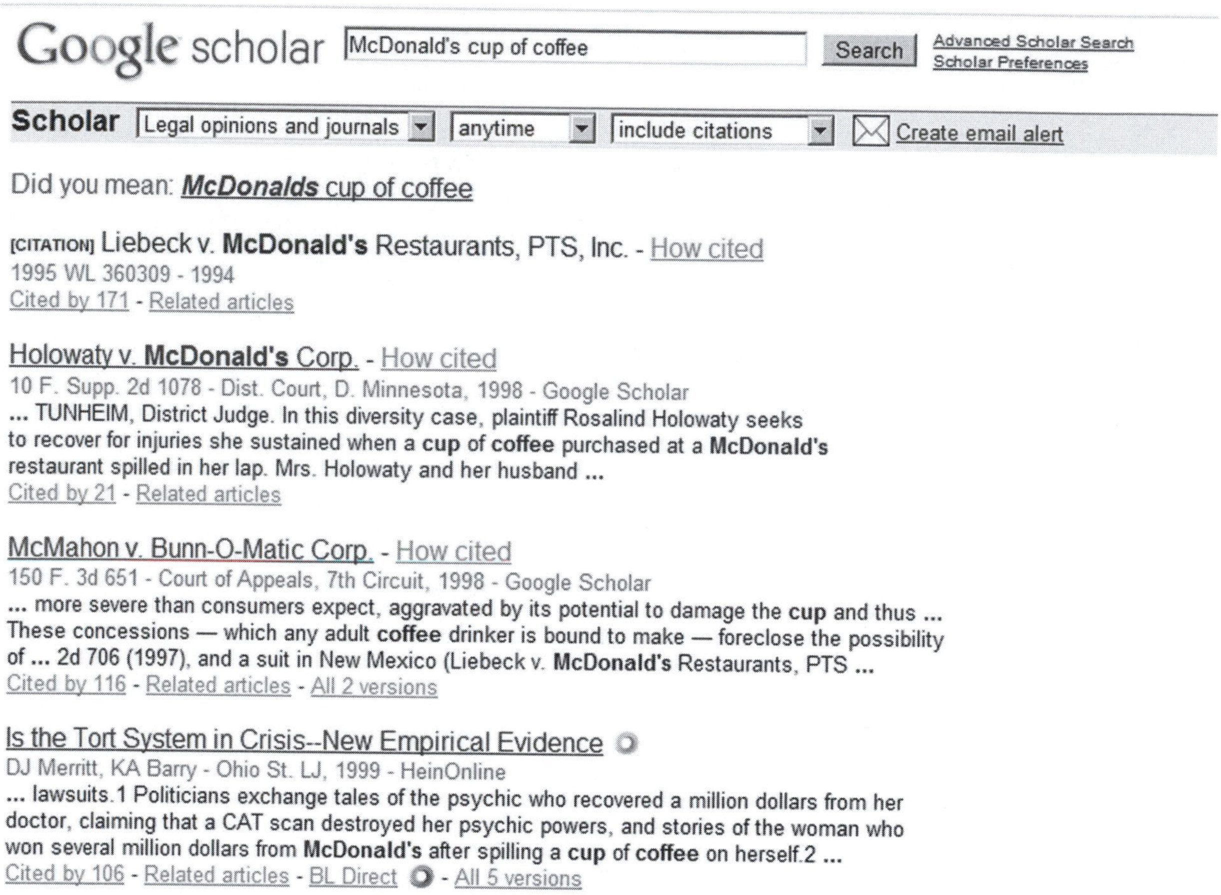

Google scholar | McDonald's cup of coffee | Search | Advanced Scholar Search
Scholar Preferences

Scholar | Legal opinions and journals ▾ | anytime ▾ | include citations ▾ | ☒ Create email alert

Did you mean: **_McDonalds_** cup of coffee

[CITATION] Liebeck v. **McDonald's** Restaurants, PTS, Inc. - How cited
1995 WL 360309 - 1994
Cited by 171 - Related articles

Holowaty v. **McDonald's** Corp. - How cited
10 F. Supp. 2d 1078 - Dist. Court, D. Minnesota, 1998 - Google Scholar
... TUNHEIM, District Judge. In this diversity case, plaintiff Rosalind Holowaty seeks
to recover for injuries she sustained when a **cup** of **coffee** purchased at a **McDonald's**
restaurant spilled in her lap. Mrs. Holowaty and her husband ...
Cited by 21 - Related articles

McMahon v. Bunn-O-Matic Corp. - How cited
150 F. 3d 651 - Court of Appeals, 7th Circuit, 1998 - Google Scholar
... more severe than consumers expect, aggravated by its potential to damage the **cup** and thus ...
These concessions — which any adult **coffee** drinker is bound to make — foreclose the possibility
of ... 2d 706 (1997), and a suit in New Mexico (Liebeck v. **McDonald's** Restaurants, PTS ...
Cited by 116 - Related articles - All 2 versions

Is the Tort System in Crisis--New Empirical Evidence ○
DJ Merritt, KA Barry - Ohio St. LJ, 1999 - HeinOnline
... lawsuits.1 Politicians exchange tales of the psychic who recovered a million dollars from her
doctor, claiming that a CAT scan destroyed her psychic powers, and stories of the woman who
won several million dollars from **McDonald's** after spilling a **cup** of **coffee** on herself.2 ...
Cited by 106 - Related articles - BL Direct ○ - All 5 versions

Figure 5-97. Google Scholar—Results of search for "McDonald's Cup of Coffee" case

The How Cited link shows how others have used this case, which might provide a researcher with an understanding of a case's broader cultural impact. Under the Related Documents box, to the bottom and right of the graphic, a searcher could obtain links to law reviews which specifically address the research topic.

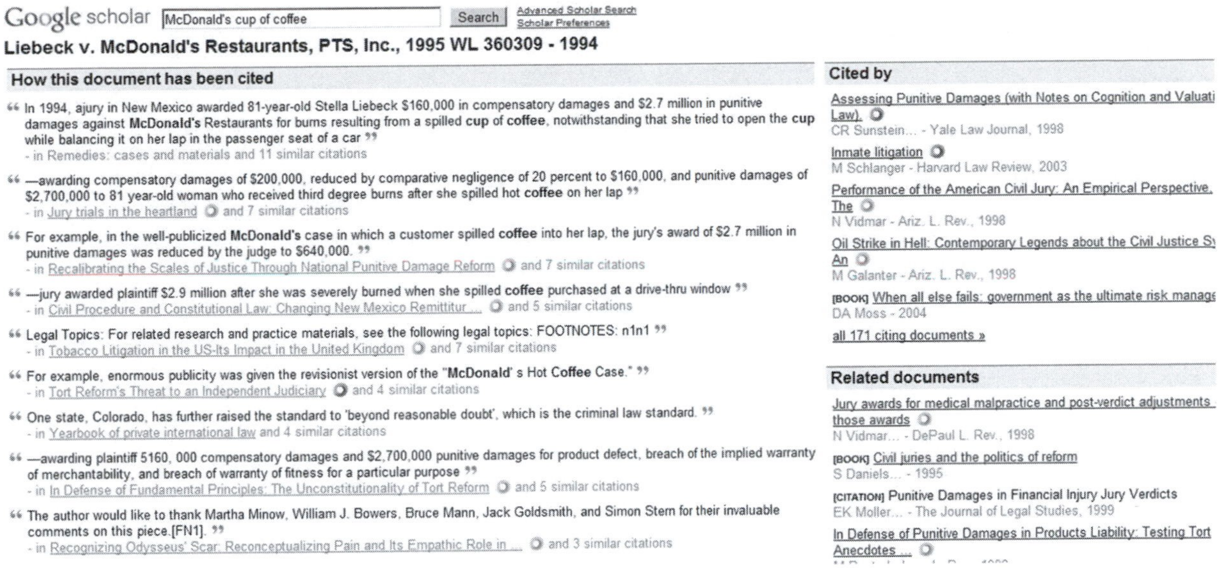

Figure 5-98. Google Scholar—Regarding subsequent use of a case

The Cited by 171 link and Related Articles link provide access to scholarly articles about the case.

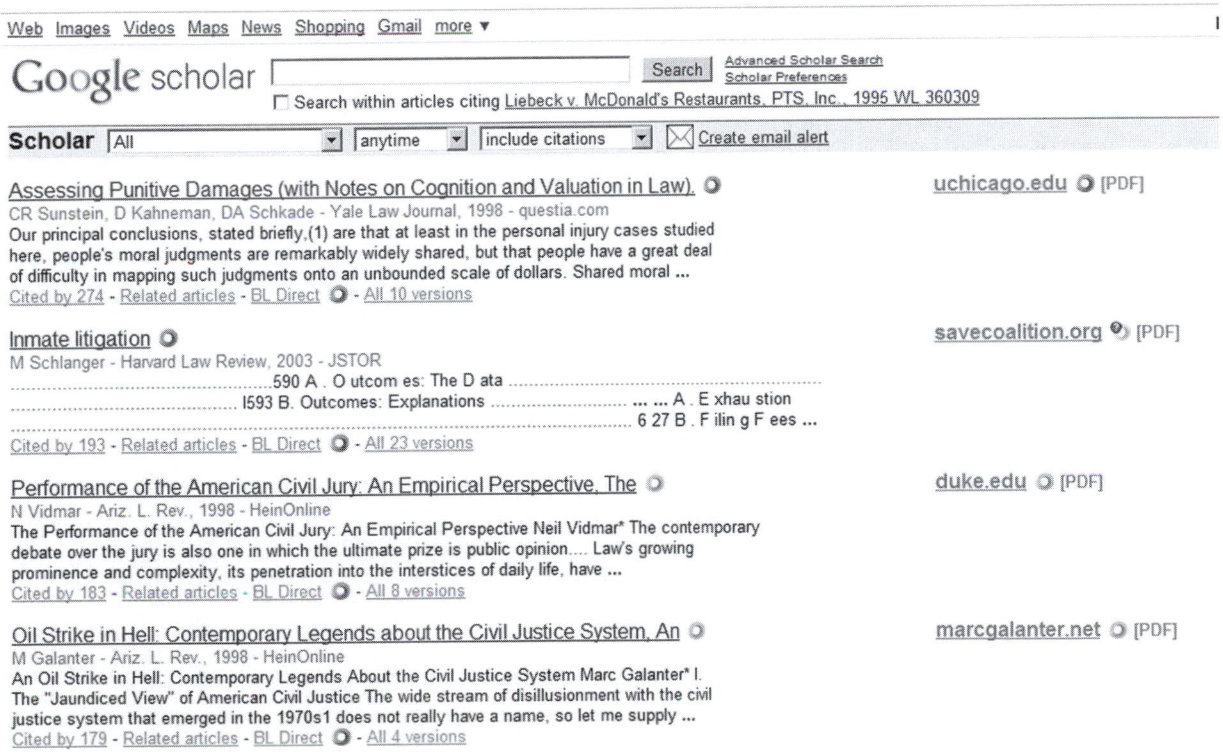

Figure 5-99. Google Scholar—Search results of scholarly articles

Google scholar [ ] Search Advanced Scholar Search
Scholar Preferences

Scholar Results **1** - **10** of about **101** related to <u>Liebeck v. McDon</u>

[CITATION] Liebeck v. McDonald's Restaurants, PTS, Inc. - <u>How cited</u>
1995 WL 360309 - 1994
<u>Cited by 171</u> - <u>Related articles</u>

<u>Jury awards for medical malpractice and post-verdict adjustments of those awards</u> ○   <u>duke.edu</u> ○ [PDF]
N Vidmar, F Gross, M Rose - DePaul L. Rev., 1998 - HeinOnline
JURY AWARDS FOR MEDICAL MALPRACTICE AND POST-VERDICT ADJUSTMENTS OF THOSE
AWARDS Neil Vidmar, Felicia Gross, & Mary Rose* The civil jury continues to be at the center
of an ongoing debate about a tort crisis and the need for "tort reform."1 While some of this ...
<u>Cited by 114</u> - <u>Related articles</u> - <u>BL Direct</u> ○ - <u>All 10 versions</u>

[BOOK] <u>Civil juries and the politics of reform</u>
S Daniels, J Martin - 1995 - books.google.com
Stephen Daniels and Joanne Martin have analyzed patterns in jury verdicts in a number of substantive
legal areas, including medical malpractice, products liability, and punitive damages, against
the background of the larger political and academic debate over tort reform. Civil Juries ...
<u>Cited by 222</u> - <u>Related articles</u> - <u>All 2 versions</u>

[CITATION] Punitive Damages in Financial Injury Jury Verdicts   <u>192.5.14.110</u> ○ [PDF]
EK Moller, NM Pace, SJ Carroll - The Journal of Legal Studies, 1999 - UChicago Press
<u>Cited by 62</u> - <u>Related articles</u> - <u>BL Direct</u> ○ - <u>All 24 versions</u>

<u>In Defense of Punitive Damages in Products Liability: Testing Tort Anecdotes with Empirical Data</u> ○
M Rustad - Iowa L. Rev., 1992 - HeinOnline
Introduction: Punitive Damages and Products Liability- Anecdotes, Half-Truths, and False Allegations
.... I. The Debate Over Punitive Damages in Products Liability .... II. Empirical Studies
of Punitive Damages in Products Liability ..... 24 A. Prior Research ....
<u>Cited by 209</u> - <u>Related articles</u> - <u>BL Direct</u> ○ - <u>All 4 versions</u>

Figure 5-100. Google Scholar—Related Articles link

Advanced Scholar Research allows for the use of Boolean search connectors.
Further refinements on this kind of search involve the Scholar Preferences link.
The researcher can also tailor the search to look only at one state's case law.

<u>Web</u> <u>Images</u> <u>Videos</u> <u>Maps</u> <u>News</u> <u>Shopping</u> <u>Gmail</u> <u>more</u> ▼
Google scholar **Advanced Scholar Search**

Find articles	with **all** of the words	[ ]
	with the **exact phrase**	[ ]
	with **at least one** of the words	[ ]
	without the words	[ ]
	where my words occur	anywhere in the article ▼
Author	Return articles written by	[ ]
		e.g., "PJ Hayes" or McCarthy
Publication	Return articles published in	[ ]
		e.g., J Biol Chem or Nature
Date	Return articles published between	[ ] — [ ]
		e.g., 1996
Collections	**Articles and patents**	

○ Search articles in all subject areas (☐ include patents).

Figure 5-101. Google Scholar—Advanced Scholar Research feature

At this time, Google Scholar does not provide the option to look for subsequent treatment of a case in the way of Shepard's or KeyCite.

Conclusion

Legal research makes it possible for a legal practice to function. While many in the legal profession will know of the on-line legal research services such as those provided by Lexis-Nexis, Westlaw, and Loislaw, others exist which can offer a wide range of features and options. All aim to make it faster and more efficient to conduct legal research in an economical manner, to serve the interests of the client.

Terms

50 State Surveys

Alerts

American Jurisprudence 2d (AmJur2d)

American Law Reports (ALR)

AuthorityCheck

Black's Law Dictionary

Boolean

Casemaker

Code of Federal Regulations

Common law

Counsel Selector

CourtLink

Database

Direct History

Dot Command

Fastcase

Federal Register

FOCUS

Forecite

Full History

GlobalCite

Google Scholar

Guided Search Form

Headnotes

Intranet

KeyCite

KeyCite Alert

Key numbers

Law reviews

Legal Information Institute

Lexis-Nexis

Lexis Advance for Solos

Lexis for Microsoft Office

LexisONE

Loislaw

PACER (Public Access to Court Electronic Records)

Popular Name Table

Precedent

Primary law

RegulationPlus Index

Regulations

Report of Current Opinions (RECOP)

Research Trail

Search engines

Secondary law

Shepard's

Source

Stare decisis

Statutes

Table of Authorities

Total Litigator

Transactional Advisor

Treatise

Uniform Commercial Code

Uniform Law and Model Acts

United States Code Annotated

WestlawNEXT

WestlawNext Mobile

Widget

Hypotheticals

1. A new client has hired the firm with an eye to filing a divorce. The primary reason for a divorce involves the blatant infidelities of the client's spouse. Although the client has tried to file a complaint for adultery against the spouse, the local prosecutor has claimed that more pressing crimes demanded attention. But one of the lawyers in the firm remembers that an obscure tort corresponds to the crime of adultery.

    a. What steps will you take to find out what that obscure tort is, using Lexis-Nexis, Westlaw, or Loislaw?
    b. What are the elements of the tort; that is, what will the lawyer need to show, by a preponderance of evidence, to win a civil suit based on that obscure tort?
    c. After you've identified the tort and found its elements, what steps will you take to find out whether your jurisdiction has enacted a heart balm statute, using Lexis-Nexis, Westlaw, or Loislaw?
    d. What did you discover in that search about such a statute?

2. Adverse possession involves a claim of ownership in the land of another. It can happen, but only under certain specific circumstances.

   a. Find out whether your jurisdiction allows for adverse possession as a way to gain ownership of land, using Lexis-Nexis, Westlaw, or Loislaw.
   b. What conditions must be met for someone to gain valid ownership of land by adverse possession?
   c. Then, what does someone claiming ownership of land by adverse possession in your jurisdiction need to do to get a court to grant ownership formally, via a request to quiet title, using Lexis-Nexis, Westlaw, or Loislaw?

3. A lawyer has asked you to investigate a new trend in conducting electronic discovery, which involves the use of computerized review search software, known as predictive coding, and computer-assisted coding. The lawyer believes that a federal court magistrate judge has allowed for the use of this software in a case from February 2012.

   a. Describe the steps needed to find the case, using Lexis-Nexis, Westlaw, or Loislaw.
   b. What did the magistrate judge specifically say about predictive coding?

4. Over the past few decades, sharp differences of opinion have arisen regarding the sweep of the protections provided in the Second Amendment to the U.S. Constitution. Using only the Legal Information Institute site, identify the case where the U.S. Supreme Court ruled that:

   a. Second Amendment rights apply to the federal government
   b. Second Amendment rights apply to state government.

5. Assume that, as an assignment, you are to find a tort law case in Massachusetts. It involves a slip-and-fall claim involving the accumulation of snow, within the last decade or 15 years, that dramatically changed the law.

   a. Describe at least three features, in Lexis-Nexis, that you would use to find the case. If feasible, answer the same question for Westlaw. If feasible, answer the same question using Loislaw.
   b. Describe the steps needed to find such a case, using only Google Scholar.

Telecommunications and Data Management

6

Objectives

▶ **Study** the nature and workings of the types of networks that a legal practice most likely would have.

▶ **Differentiate** among Internet-related methods of communication, such as Voice Over Internet Protocol (VOIP), and technology, such as smartphones.

▶ **Explore** the security issues associated with any form of telecommunications.

▶ **Examine** issues about ethics related to telecommunications.

Introduction

Telecommunications no longer just involves a telephone, but now includes Internet-based communications, smartphones, and e-mail. Even as law firms rely on networks to transmit data, they need to remain mindful of the ethical obligation to preserve the confidentiality of client information.

Telecommunications

Networks

Whether in a legal practice, or through the Internet, the creation and use of networks has enhanced the productivity of law firms. The size of a network may present distinct issues for effective data transmission. A way of gauging how much traffic a web-based network can handle is to measure **bandwidth.** This describes the rate for data transfer and usually is expressed in terms of bits per second. It might not take much bandwidth to send a client letter on a network, but would likely take much more when transmitting all case law gathered in support of a brief to the court. A larger batch of data would take more time to arrive at the destination. Networks typically will have a computer that acts as storage that everyone on the network can access, called a **server.**

1. Intranet

An **intranet** is a network accessible to a limited number of users, such as people who work in a law firm. It could also connect those users to the Internet, although security measures could protect it from unauthorized access. Larger computer networks might require the setting up of **hubs,** which will serve as transfer points for information, and the use of repeaters, to offset the loss of quality of data transmitted over long distances.

a. Local Area Network (LAN)

A **local area network (LAN)** generally describes a small network. Computers in that network may be connected via **coaxial cables,** wiring designed specifically to handle computer-based traffic, and shielded so as to minimize loss of signal strength and to reduce interference from other sources. Most computers have built-in **Ethernet** ports, for connecting coaxial cable to the network.

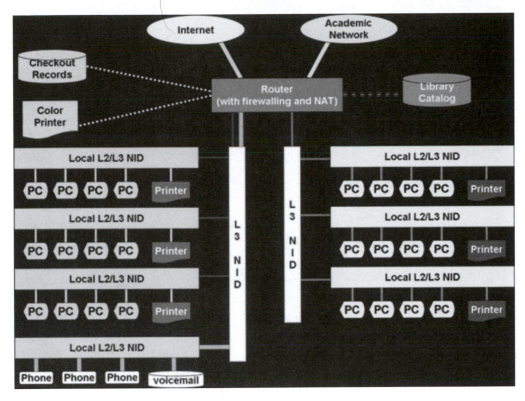

Figure 6-1. LAN network illustration
Source: Hcberkowitz

b. Wireless Local Area Network (WLAN)

A **wireless local area network (WLAN)** can accomplish all that a LAN can without using cables. For example, with a **peer-to-peer network,** computers connect only to one another wirelessly. In this way, lawyers in court could exchange data just between the computers that they are using.

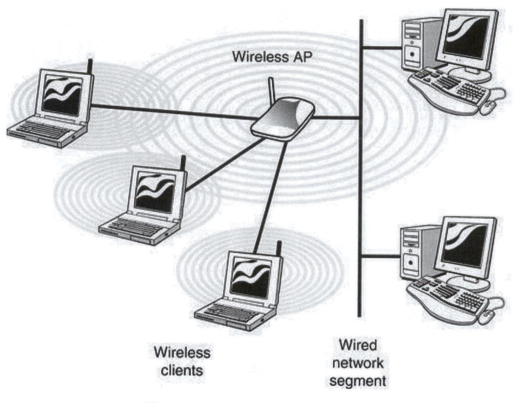

Figure 6-2. WLAN network illustration
Source: RedEagle/Wikimedia Commons

i. Router

Larger networks would rely on a wireless router. A router is a transmitter and receiver that directly connects to the Internet via a cable. The range of access to a router depends upon its capacity to send and receive data wirelessly. For purposes of security, a legal practice should prevent the wireless router from broadcasting the **Service Set Identifier (SSID),** the router's name. This means that a **hacker** will have one less piece of information to use when trying to crack a router's firewall.

ii. Wi-Fi

A common type of WLAN is known as Wi-Fi. Schools, businesses, and libraries have found that offering free Wi-Fi access can serve the public. For example, a coffee shop could offer free Wi-Fi as a way of drawing in customers. Typically, the web page at a business that provides free Wi-Fi access may include a disclaimer regarding the level of security available to users. This would acknowledge the obvious, that using unsecured communication channels can leave users vulnerable to hacking. A law firm that has set up and uses Wi-Fi may have an ethical obligation to secure it against hacking.

c. Wireless Personal Area Network (WPAN)

A **wireless personal area network (WPAN)** connects devices in a small area, like around a user's body. One way to create a WPAN involves using the **Bluetooth** technology, available on most computers. The convenience of setting up such small networks quickly and easily has meant that a lawyer can engage in hands-free communication via a cordless headset.

Figure 6-3. Bluetooth
Source: Wikimedia Commons

d. Virtual Private Network (VPN)

A variation on this idea, a **virtual private network (VPN),** could make secure data transmissions through the use of a process called **tunneling.** Tunneling establishes a unique connection between a computer and a receiver, often by using layers of security protocols or encryption. Setting up a VPN with a public Wi-Fi router can make communications between the computer and wireless router less susceptible to hacking.

e. Firewalls

Hardware firewalls, usually a router that allows only those with passwords to connect to a network, typically protect a LAN at the point that it connects to the Internet. Software firewalls might protect a single computer and may not provide the same level of security as a hardware firewall.

Firewalls with more advanced levels of security might also note when applications, like **file transfer protocol (FTP),** are used, since the use of such an application might mask efforts to find unsecure points of entry to a network. Firewalls also can evaluate the sequence of **data packets** transmitted to see whether a message contains the kind of data that could mask an effort to compromise the security of a computer.

2. Internet

The vast network of computers of the World Wide Web, which contains the Internet, uses **websites** as primary "locations" for the point of connection. A piece of software, the browser, makes it possible to connect to websites on the Internet. Examples of browsers include Firefox, Google's Chrome, Microsoft's Internet Explorer, and Apple's Safari.

a. The home page

Clicking on a computer's browser software will open a home page, that is, the default destination on a computer that a browser always starts on. Some browsers have an icon of a home, so that clicking on it brings the user back to the home page.

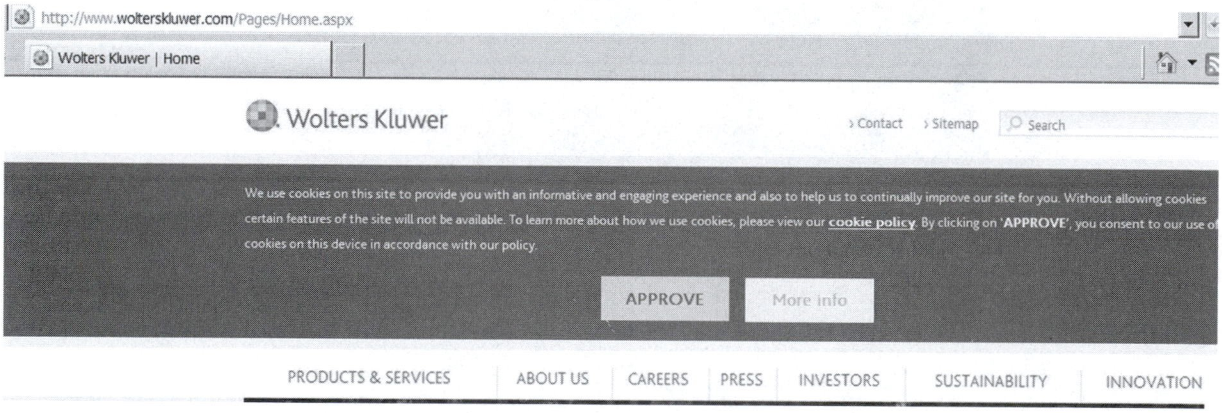

Figure 6-4. Wolters Kluwer home page

b. Web pages

Websites contain web pages, the documents of the Internet. The uniform resource locator, or **URL,** serves as the address for a website. Web pages may allow users to go to another website or elsewhere on a website with the click of a link. A link contains **hypertext,** the computer code for guiding the browser to the destination associated with the link. The custom has been to identify a link by underlining words, in a color different from that of the text: www.wolterkulwers. com. By putting the browser's pointer on the link, a small box opens to reveal the URL contained in the link.

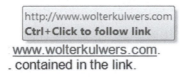

http://www.wolterkulwers.com
Ctrl+Click to follow link
www.wolterkulwers.com.
. contained in the link.

Figure 6-5. URL box

i. HTTP and HTTPS

A web page whose URL starts with WWW or HTTP runs the risk of not providing a secure connection, which could allow for a kind of electronic eavesdropping. HTTP, which stands for **hypertext transfer protocol,** is the computer code that contains the rules for transferring information over the Internet.

http://www.

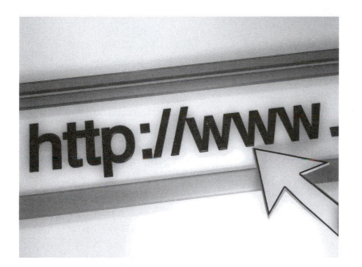

Figure 6-6. HTTP in URL box
Source: Salvatore Vouno – freedigitalphotos.net

That risk diminishes if the URL for the site starts off with HTTPS, which indicates that the site's server has in place certain security protocols. HTTPS means that the website is using **Secure Sockets Layers (SSL),** which decreases the risk of interception because it uses different levels, or layers, of protection.

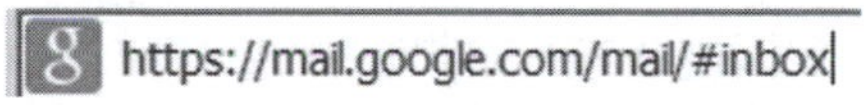
https://mail.google.com/mail/#inbox

Figure 6-7. HTTPS in URL box
Source: Vlastni screenshot/Wikimedia Commons

3. Security

While the vast network of computers of the Internet makes it easier to communicate, using the Internet can come with a cost: websites might not have an adequate level of security for keeping information confidential. This poses a significant problem for a legal practice, which has an ethical obligation to preserve the confidentiality of client information.

a. Security certificate

Upon arrival to a website, browsers may automatically look for its security certificate, which describes basic security measures used for that website. The browser could alert the user to the absence of such a certificate, or that the website uses an outdated one, so that a user can decide whether to continue to use that website.

b. Encryption

Encryption involves the coding of information so that only someone that uses that code, or key, can access the information. A common method for encrypting digital information involves an **algorithm,** a formula for generating numbers for use as keys. One type of encryption uses public and private keys: numbers generated by an algorithm. An algorithm's effectiveness increases as it generates longer numbers because these would be harder to guess. A sender will encrypt data for transmission using a public and a private key, and will then disclose the public key. After having sent the private key to the recipient, the recipient needs to use both keys to decrypt the information.

c. Cookies

Each time a user directs a browser to a site, the site may automatically load simple software onto the user's computer, called a **cookie.** Allowing a site to store a cookie could, for example, speed up the loading of graphic images used on that site. But cookies could also track a user's web browsing, gathering information that the cookie's owner might use for marketing, perhaps by learning about other sites that a user visits. Most browsers allow for the blocking of cookies, but doing that could mean losing access to a site. One compromise might involve deleting cookies after using a site, while another would mean periodically purging a computer of all cookies.

d. Pop-up blockers

Advertising that automatically appears when visiting a website is called a pop-up. While not necessarily malware, pop-ups distract and annoy. Increasingly, web browsers have a feature to block these from appearing.

4. Voice Over Internet Protocol (VOIP)

Technology exists to make telephone conversations over the Internet. This involves using **Voice Over Internet Protocol (VOIP).** VOIP translates speech into data packets, to take advantage of the Internet's capacity to send data packets over numerous routes simultaneously. Because a law firm will already have paid for such access to the Internet, it can use VOIP and eliminate the expense for having a traditional telephone hookup.

VOIP service providers usually charge a flat rate for their service. Among others, **Skype** offers a low-cost approach to VOIP communications by not charging for calls made within the Skype network and charging a modest fee for calls to landlines or mobile telecommunication devices.

Phones using VOIP generally will not support the placing of 911 calls because servers that transmit a VOIP signal are scattered throughout the world. E911 can provide a VOIP with emergency services, so long as the caller has associated a phone number with a particular location.

VOIP service providers can offer a Caller ID service, but it works differently than with a traditional telephone system. This leaves VOIP Caller ID vulnerable to **spoofing,** which involves feeding false Caller ID information to trick a person into taking the call and possibly disclosing confidential information.

5. Videoconferencing

A law firm might want to set up an Internet-based teleconferencing network. For example, a service like **Webex** would set up a special destination on the Internet for the communications to go through, obviating the need for specialized, and potentially costly, video equipment. A business could pay a regular subscription fee for the service or could pay on a per-call basis. Skype users can also engage in video conferencing, although such communications might not match the quality of specialized video-conferencing technology.

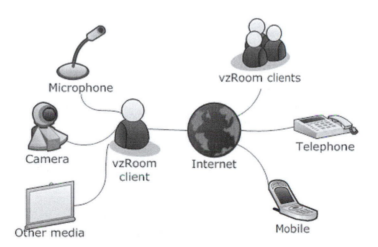

Figure 6-8. Videoconferencing over the Internet
Source: alantypoon/Wikimedia Commons

E-mail

E-mail involves the electronic transmission of information via a computer network, akin to the process of using the U.S. Postal Service to convey information, such as in a letter. Software, such as Microsoft's Outlook and Mozilla's Thunderbird, make such transmissions possible. Microsoft's Outlook might integrate with other applications. For example, Lexis-Nexis makes it possible to coordinate the use of Outlook with a search when using Lexis for Microsoft Office, as mentioned in Chapter 5.

1. Risks

Law firms face risks with e-mail that could compromise the security of all of a firm's computers. These can include:

▶ Unwanted junk e-mail (called **spam,** after a skit by the comedy troupe Monty Python's Flying Circus that made fun of the many uses of this spiced meat product) may merely take up valuable space on the hard drive of a computer. Many types of e-mail software now have spam filters, designed to automatically remove some e-mail, typically coming from an unknown sender.

▶ Fraud, where a type of e-mail may aim to defraud the recipient. For example, an e-mail will supposedly come from a former government official from another country, who needs the help of the recipient to obtain access to funds held in a bank. According to this fraudulent e-mail, known as a "Nigerian 419" letter, all the recipient has to do is to send monies to handle some bureaucratic hurdles. In return, the recipient will receive 10 percent of the funds held at a bank that the sender does not have access to. Even though this may be a new type of fraud, the old adage, "If it's too good to be true, then it's not!" applies.

▶ Compromising the computer's security. **Phishing** involves sending unsolicited e-mail, perhaps containing an enticing offer, with an **attachment** bearing a computer **virus,** designed to subvert a computer's security. Viruses and other **malicious software,** also known as **malware,** such as **spyware** and **Trojans,** can make data stored on a computer or network accessible. This could violate an ethical obligation to keep confidential client information or it could co-opt the computer for surreptitious use by the malware creator, perhaps to create a network for launching a **Denial of Service (DoS)** attack on a website. Having **antivirus software,** especially the kind that can receive automatic updates, can cut down on the risks of infection by a virus.

2. Confidentiality

a. Ethical obligations

According to the **American Bar Association (ABA)** Rule 1.6, as adopted by many states, lawyers in that practice have an ethical obligation to keep the client information confidential. Comment 17 to ABA Model Rule 1.6 (a) talks about how a lawyer, when transmitting confidential information, needs to take reasonable precautions to safeguard against accidental disclosure.

b. Statutes and obligations

A state could impose a duty of care on any business to safeguard confidential client information. A breach of that duty of care could amount to a violation of tort law in negligence. The federal government imposes such a duty on business. The law also requires the keeper of that information to notify the information's owner when a security breach has occurred.

Intercepting electronic communications without authority likely amounts to a violation of the Electronic Communications Privacy Act (18 USC Chapter 119, §§2501 *et seq.*). This federal statute provides the national government with the authority to investigate and to prosecute efforts to intercept such communications.

c. Encryption

Encrypting e-mail could also protect against the accidental disclosure of client information if an e-mail is accidentally sent to the wrong recipient. What about unencrypted e-mail? The ABA's Standing Committee On Ethics And Professional Responsibility addressed this issue directly, in Formal Opinion No. 99-413 (Formal Opinion No. 99-413, 1999). The Committee determined that some forms of communication, such as ordinary mail or a fax, also carried a risk of interception, however unlikely. It concluded that e-mail security had to match the level of security used with ordinary mail or a fax.

Advances in technology in the decade since the issuance of this opinion might increase the possibility of illegally intercepting e-mail. Even modest security measures like encrypting the data could reduce the likelihood of the disclosure of client information. Absent special circumstances, such as the sensitive nature of the information, this does not mean that the lawyer has to employ special security measures. Of course, if a client requires greater security measures, then the lawyer needs to implement such measures.

Smartphones

If cellphones provided practitioners with greater flexibility for communicating, smartphones exceed them by also offering more resources. Smartphones have more computing power, to the point that they can fairly be characterized as handheld or mobile computers.

1. Operating Systems (OS)

Much like with a personal computer, the CPU of a smartphone requires an operating system tailored to its processing capabilities. Several types of OS exist, such as:

▶ Apple iPhone OS: Apple has created an operating system with many of the features of the Macintosh OS X, called iOS. This means that the Apple smartphone, the iPhone, can wirelessly connect with other Apple devices seamlessly. The success of Apple's iOS became obvious because of the explosive development of software applications that took advantage of the iPhone's processing power.

▶ Google's Android: Google's Android OS, like Apple's iOS, is built around the Linux OS kernel. Unlike the iOS, Google has made Android open-source, so that developers have an easier time of making applications that will run on Android. This has resulted in the creation of nearly as many applications for Android as for Apple's iOS.

Seen as a competitor to the iOS, Android even has the capacity to use software that the iOS won't run. For example, Adobe's Flash software (often used to create animations) works on Android but not on iOS.

2. Applications (Apps)

A market has developed for software that can fully use the technological features of smartphones. Such software is typically referred to as an **app (application).** Smartphones may come with apps loaded on them or might obtain them via a download.

Legal service/software providers have recognized the potential inherent in apps. Lexis-Nexis offers apps at http://www.lexisnexis.com/mobile/ and West Publishing offers apps at http://legalsolutions.thomsonreuters.com/law-products/law-books/ebooks-apps/mobile-apps. Others, like Fastcase, offer a free smartphone app. Not surprisingly, these and other apps may be part of a practice's subscription to any of these legal content and service providers.

3. Common Features

Smartphones will typically have the following preloaded features:

▶ Maps: the software of a smartphone has to identify its location to figure out where to direct or receive a call. This also can tell a user about his or her position on a map, making it possible to obtain directions via the smartphone. A lawyer who travels to different courts might especially like this feature.

▶ Office productivity: a smartphone may have the capacity to use common business office productivity software, yet the size of the handheld device may make it difficult to do data entry, like with a laptop. At worst, a lawyer would at least be able to obtain and use an app to read a downloaded document like a court opinion.

▶ Internet connectivity: since smartphones typically have the capacity to connect to the Internet, they could also serve as mobile **hotspots,** a means for a laptop user to connect to the Internet via Wi-Fi. So, a lawyer or paralegal could more easily find data stored on the legal practice's server, such as legal research done on a client's case, by using the cellphone as a mobile hotspot for a laptop, instead of trying to do the legal research via a smartphone's browser.

▶ Graphic interface: an appealing feature on some smartphones involves having a **capacitive,** or touch, screen. A user may open and close programs with a stroke of a finger, eliminating the need to maneuver a browser arrow. Some smartphones, however, do have a small, built-in track ball.

▶ Bluetooth: as with cellphones, smartphones may have Bluetooth capacity. Like any wireless network, activating the Bluetooth technology on a smartphone can make it vulnerable to hacking. Newer versions provide differing levels of security, but a user should turn off the Bluetooth function on a smartphone when not in use.

▶ Keyboard: a smartphone could include a miniature keyboard, thereby making it easier to send a text (**SMS**) message. This process sometimes is identified as instant messaging (IM). Or the user could call up the image of a miniature keyboard, so that with a capacitive screen, a paralegal could type in search terms when using a search engine. It may also have the capacity to connect to a larger scale keyboard, perhaps via a Bluetooth connection.

Figure 6-9. A smartphone with full keyboard
Source: Wikimedia Commons

▶ Storage: smartphones will have enough space to store documents. Via a cable, they then might work like a Flash drive.

4. Battery Life

As with laptops, the battery life of a smartphone can pose an issue. But, most will have a setting that automatically shuts off the smartphone at some point. In addition to having the capacity to recharge the batteries of smartphones via wall sockets, some smartphones might also have the capacity to recharge directly from a computer, via a **USB** cable.

5. Cellular Wireless Standards: 3G and 4G

Many cellphones currently use the 3G (G stands for generation) data transmission standard. This makes it possible to read documents stored on a server, but would not be fast enough to view a video as it loaded into the smartphone. Newer smartphones use 4G, which some consider to be the equivalent of broadband for smartphones because of the speed and the volume of data that can be transmitted.

6. Firewalls

Smartphones, like laptops and desktop computers, often will have the option for erecting a software firewall. Firewall protection on a smartphone might involve layering types of data, thereby increasing the number and kinds of barriers that someone trying to hack into the device would encounter.

Data Management

Issues regarding the lawyer's obligation to keep data confidential go beyond telecommunication and into data management.

Passwords

Passwords stand as the first line of defense against unsanctioned access to data.

a. Complexity

The ideal password should be easy to remember but difficult to guess. Passwords that might be difficult to guess should not use words, names, or commonly used identification information, such as Social Security numbers. One common strategy for generating passwords that a hacker cannot easily guess includes the use of numbers and symbols. A user could substitute a letter with one of the symbols on a keyboard, such as pa$$word, or use a number for a letter, like turnsty1e. Doing both can increase the difficulty that a hacker would face when trying to guess a password, such as pa$$worD*1!.

b. Updates

To enhance the effectiveness of passwords, the manager of a computer network might require all users to change passwords periodically, destroying the value of old passwords. Frequent changes could also frustrate efforts by former employees to gain unauthorized access to a network.

Retention

A firm might want to craft a policy about how long it will keep copies of data like e-mail, since storing data can quickly demand a lot of storage space. This policy might focus on the retention of certain kinds of e-mail, like modifications to the contract that created the lawyer-client relationship, as opposed to messages that confirm an appointment with a client.

VOIP and Voice Mail

Saving audio conversations made over the Internet, via VOIP, also raises ethical issues regarding proper storage. For example, a firm might use encryption with VOIP communications, which will withstand almost all efforts at cracking the encryption. Where feasible, preserving voice mail messages, at least by using passwords, could also make it easier for a legal practice to fulfill its ethical obligations.

Disposal of Equipment

Given an obligation to preserve client confidentiality, a law firm might have an obligation to dispose of client information, when permitted, in a secure manner. For example, deleted files from a permanent storage media can be recovered. Reformatting a disk drive can make the recovery of data even more difficult, but not impossible. A firm might find it easier to consult with a specialist to achieve safe disposal of a client's confidential information kept on a hard drive.

a. Remote Access

In 2011, the thief of a laptop encountered some of the risks inherent in stealing a computer. The laptop's owner, who possessed top-notch programming skills, was able to access the laptop remotely, once the thief connected it to the Internet. The owner used the laptop's camera to get a picture of the thief and notified the thief about the laptop's capacity to identify its location. The thief surrendered the laptop, although not before doing an impromptu dance routine, a portion of which accompanied the television news broadcast of the story about the thief.

Owners might install software that allows the user to lockdown the device remotely and/or eliminate data remotely, denying the thief the benefits of the crime. Services might allow the owner to have a laptop disclose its location by activating global positioning software, facilitating the recovery of the stolen device.

Conclusion

No legal practice could effectively function without telecommunication, involving the use of networks, e-mail, and smartphones. Law firms have an ethical obligation to keep client communication safe, no matter its nature, which could mean using passwords and properly disposing of data, where appropriate.

References

(n.d.). Massachusetts Rules of Professional Conduct Rule 1.6: Confidentiality of Information, retrieved from http://www.lawlib.state.ma.us/source/mass/rules/sjc/sjc307/rule1-6.html.
(1999). Formal Opinion No. 99-413, from
https://www.lexis.com/research/retrieve?_m=8a63d3f69b859c0b80f096a45965d1d4&csvc=fo&cform=searchForm&_fmtstr=FULL&docnum=1&_startdoc=1&wchp=dGLbVtz-zSkAb&_md5=2adbaa4666661dbea18338aed5d739b1

Terms

Algorithm	Data packets
American Bar Association (ABA)	Denial of Service (DoS) attack
Antivirus software	E-mail
App (application)	Encrypts
Attachment	Ethernet
Bandwidth	File transfer protocol (FTP)
Bluetooth	Firewall
Browser	FireWire
Capacitive screen	Hacker
Coaxial cable	Home page
Cookie	Hotspot

HTTPS

Hubs

Hypertext

Hypertext transfer protocol (HTTP)

Instant messaging

Intranet

Local area network (LAN)

Malicious software (malware)

Network

Operating system (OS)

Peer-to-peer network

Phishing

Pop-up blockers

Router

Secure sockets layers (SSL)

Security certificate

Servers

Service set identifier (SSID)

Skype

Smartphones

SMS (short message service)

Spam

Spyware

Telecommunications

Trojans

Tunneling

USB (universal serial bus)

Uniform resource locator (URL)

Virtual private network (VPN)

Virus

Voice Over Internet Protocol (VOIP)

Webex

Web pages

Websites

Wi-Fi

Wireless local area network (WLAN)

Wireless personal area network (WPAN)

Hypotheticals

1. Describe the apps available through Lexis-Nexis and WestLaw. Then identify three features of each that you would find to be most useful. Presume that you have access to all platforms, such as an iPhone or a smartphone that uses the Android OS.

2. Describe the ethical concerns that a legal practice needs to keep in mind when engaging in electronic communication.

3. Describe at least three levels of security mentioned in this chapter. Identify, from that trio, the one that provides the greatest level of security, then explain why.

4. If asked why a law firm would need to purchase software to protect against malware and attacks on the integrity of a network's computer, what points should be raised?

5. Identify different characteristics of at least five types of networks mentioned in this chapter.

▶ Glossary

50 State Surveys: a feature offered by Westlaw that allows a researcher to create a search of a select group, for example, case law and statutes.

Access: Microsoft's database software.

Accounts payable: debts that have been accounted for on the creditor's account and for which invoices may have been issued.

Accounts receivable: debts for which invoices have been issued but payment has not been received.

Adjustments: under tax law, transfers of payment, as from a pension account.

Administrator: a man with the responsibility for distributing the estate of someone who died without a will.

Administratrix: a woman with the responsibility for distributing the estate of someone who died without a will.

Affidavit: a legal document that functions as sworn testimony and for which false statements can result in a charge of perjury.

Agent: someone authorized to act for another, who is known as the principal.

Alerts: a feature offered by Lexis-Nexis that provides updates on prior searches.

Algorithm: a mathematical formula; in computers, may be used to generate public and private keys.

Alimony: in a divorce settlement, money paid by one ex to the other for personal care and maintenance.

Alternative minimum tax: a tax that under federal tax law must be paid even if deductions and credits reduce the tax burden to zero.

American Bar Association (ABA): an organization that recommends rules and guidelines for the ethical conduct of lawyers.

American Jurisprudence 2d (AmJur2d): a legal encyclopedia published by West Publishing.

American Law Reports (ALR): annotated articles on specific topic from Westlaw; tied in via the Key Search system to AmJur2d.

Antivirus software: software designed to prevent viruses (also known as malware) from lodging on a computer.

Application: software that typically performs a particular function, such as word processing; sometimes abbreviated as app.

Articles of Incorporation: documents that must be filed before a corporation can be recognized as a legal entity.

Assets: items of value, including tangible property, like land, and intangible property, like copyrights or patents.

Assignments: the transfer of rights to something owned or possessed.

Attachment: a file that accompanies an e-mail message; opening attachments of e-mail from unknown senders may compromise the security of a computer by releasing a virus.

Attests: a statement that swears to the accuracy of a document, often with an acknowledgment that false attestation could result in a charge of perjury.

Attorney-client privilege: protects from disclosure communication between a lawyer and a client, except when the client makes a credible threat of violence.

Audit trail: a list of steps taken when sorting through electronically stored information during discovery.

AuthorityCheck: a feature offered by Fastcase that performs the same function as Lexis-Nexis Shepard's and Westlaw's KeyCite.

Back office operations: practices common to business, such as generating bills.

Bandwidth: the capacity of an Internet connection to carry information.

Bankruptcy: a legal proceeding in which the petitioner has more debts than assets and seeks help under federal law to discharge the debts.

Bankruptcy code: the federal laws that address the bankruptcy process.

Basic information operating system (BIOS): a type of software that makes it possible to load an operating system on a computer.

Beneficiary: one who receives a benefit, such as from a trust.

Binder: in real estate, an initial payment that demonstrates a buyer's intent to purchase a property.

Black's Law Dictionary: a legal dictionary published by West Publishing.

Blacklining: a way of indicating changes to a previous version of a document.

Bluetooth: a type of connectivity software commonly used to set up a small wireless network.

Boolean: search connectors such as *and*, *or*, and *not*, that a researcher uses during a search.

Broker: a person who arranges the sale of property; in the context of real estate transactions, sometimes represents the buyer.

Browser: software that makes it possible for a user to go to different websites on the Internet.

Buttons: graphic images that can activate a function, like copy or delete.

Bylaws: rules for the daily operation of the corporation.

Cache: a limited-capacity storage unit that contains frequently used software or data.

Calendaring software: keeps track of appointments and court appearances.

Cell: the smallest unit of operation in spreadsheet software like Excel.

Capacitive screen: a touch screen.

Case management software: focuses narrowly on the type of case and its status, such as getting ready for trial.

Casemaker: a legal research database created and maintained by state bar associations.

Central processing unit (CPU): the component of the computer where processing of information happens; metaphorically, the brain of a computer.

Chapter 7: the provision in the bankruptcy code that a debtor or petitioner refers to when seeking liquidation.

Chapter 11: the provision in the bankruptcy code that a debtor or petitioner refers to when seeking reorganization of business debts.

Chapter 13: the provision in the bankruptcy code that a debtor or petitioner refers to when seeking reorganization of individual debts.

Child support: payments for the care of a minor child.

Clawback: a request to a court to retrieve information that should not have been handed over in discovery.

Clip art: simple graphics that come with Microsoft Word.

Closing: a real estate transaction transferring interest from the seller, who provides the deed, to the buyer, who provides something of value, typically money.

Cloud computing: another way of describing software as a service (SaaS), in which software and data are stored on the server of a host. For example, a user of the Google Docs application, available through Google's Chrome browser, can store documents on a Google server.

Coaxial cable: wiring for computer-based communications designed to minimize loss of signal strength and interference from other sources.

Code of Federal Regulations: the compilation of all federal regulations.

Common law: law made by a judge, either in the absence of a lawmaking body to do so or through interpretation of other laws or court rulings; also known as case law or judge-made law.

Compact disc (CD): a storage medium in which information is written on a plastic-enclosed metal disk using a laser. CDs provide greater storage capacity than floppy disks.

Complaint: a document filed to initiate a lawsuit.

Conservator: a person responsible for managing a deceased person's property until the probating of an estate is complete; some jurisdictions talk about a guardian of the property instead of a conservator.

Contract: a legally binding agreement.

Cookie: software that stores information about the websites visited by a computer and helps the web page load faster on subsequent visits.

Counsel Selector: a feature offered by Lexis-Nexis listing lawyers in another jurisdiction.

CourtLink: a feature offered by Lexis-Nexis for obtaining records from a case.

Copyright: a type of intellectual property law that protects a creator's interest in receiving compensation for use of their work.

Core: a cluster of transistors that serve as a central processing unit.

Corporation: a business entity created primarily under state law that has a legal identity separate from that of its owners or creators, thereby limiting their exposure for corporate liability.

Creditors: in bankruptcy law, those to whom the debtor or petitioner owes money.

Creditor matrix: in bankruptcy law, the part of the petition for a discharge that contains information about creditors.

Dashboard: a small screen on a user's screen for quick access to features of software.

Data packet: a basic unit of information for communication via e-mail or the Internet.

Database: a series of files, often stored on a central server, that provides everyone in a firm with a single source for information.

Debtor/petitioner: in bankruptcy law, the person who has filed the petition for bankruptcy.

Deduplication: a process of reviewing electronically stored information to cull identical data kept in multiple locations.

Deed: the document indicating ownership interest in real property; also known as the title.

Defensible discovery strategy: strategies and techniques a legal practice uses to review information in a request for discovery; used because searching every piece of electronic information could be costly and lead to mistakes.

Defragmentation: bringing together fragments of software or data scattered on a hard drive.

Denial of Service (DoS) attack: an attack that sends many requests from many computers to overwhelm a server's capacity.

Deponent: a person being deposed.

Deposition: an out of court session in which questions are put to parties, witnesses, and others who might have information about a lawsuit.

Digital video disk (DVD): a storage medium that writes information on a plastic-enclosed metal disk using a laser and containing greater capacity than compact disks.

Directors: in corporate law, those people whom stockholders have elected to implement policy for running the corporation.

Direct History: a feature offered by Westlaw in which a researcher can obtain graphic representation of the history of activities associated with a case.

Discharge in bankruptcy: where creditors receive some payment on outstanding debts in exchange for the debtor obtaining relief from debts, allowing for a fresh start.

Discovery: information about a lawsuit or crime exchanged between parties before trial; it includes, for example, depositions and requests for information.

Diskette: a removable magnetic storage medium consisting of thin layers of plastic embedded with magnetized particles; no longer a common form of storage media because of limited data storage capacity; also known as floppy disks.

Dividends: moneys paid out by the corporation for each share.

Docket: the court's record of activity in a case.

Docket number: the unique number that a court assigns to a specific case.

Dot Command: a feature offered by Lexis-Nexis to tailor a search, such as by topic, like federal law, or by jurisdiction, like the Seventh Circuit Court of Appeals.

Driver: software that makes it possible for a computer to activate and use installed peripherals like a printer.

Durable power of attorney: a power of attorney that lasts beyond the completion of a specific task.

Electronic data reference model (EDRM): a type of defensible discovery strategy that involves filtering information repeatedly to identify information that should be turned over due to a request for discovery.

E-mail: electronic mail; a type of software that provides for private communication.

Encrypts: translates coded information that only someone with the code can read.

End user licensing agreement (EULA): a type of license usually granted to someone who has purchased software and describes the limited rights that the purchaser acquired.

Escrow: an account created during the sale of real property in which money is kept for future payments of taxes or insurance.

ESI: electronically stored information.

Estate: in bankruptcy, all of the debtor's assets; with a will, what the decedent owned at the time of death.

Ethernet: a designation for a local area network.

Ethernet port: an outlet that connects a computer for high-speed Internet access or to a wired network.

Ethical wall: a process undertaken by a legal practice to isolate those in the practice who had worked on another case that is in conflict with that of a new client.

Executor: a man responsible for distributing a deceased person's estate as per a legally valid will.

Executrix: a woman responsible for distributing a deceased person's estate as per a legally valid will.

Exempt: in bankruptcy law, property not included in the debtor/petitioner's estate because, as a matter of policy, the debtor/petitioner should not be stripped completely of all assets for living.

Exemptions: instances when a party does not have to provide information in a request for discovery; includes attorney-client privilege and the work product doctrine.

Exhibits: documents included with the filing of the plan for the discharge in bankruptcy.

Fastcase: a subscription-based legal research site that depicts search results in graphic form.

Federal Rules of Civil Procedure (FRCP): rules for conducting a civil trial.

Federal Register: a journal of regulations proposed by federal agencies; often published daily by the government.

File transfer protocol (FTP): another way of conveying information via the Internet.

Firewall protection: software or hardware used to protect a networked computer from hijacking of its functionality or data.

FireWire: a type of outlet for connecting devices to an Apple computer or device.

Flash drive: portable solid-state memory that connects to the computer via a port; sometimes called a jump drive or a thumb drive.

FOCUS: a feature offered by Lexis-Nexis that narrows the scope of a search.

Forecite: a feature offered by Fastcase that identifies important cases that otherwise might have gone undetected in a keyword search.

Form 1099-S: a tax form filed with the federal government for a transaction that generates income not involving wages.

Front office activities: deals with all aspects of client contact.

Full History: a feature offered with Westlaw with which a researcher can look at the docket of a case.

GlobalCite: a feature offered by Loislaw that identifies cases where another case is mentioned.

Google Scholar: a free way to conduct on-line legal research; offered by Google.

Grant: in the context of the sale of real property, the transfer of ownership.

Grantee: in the context of the sale of real estate, the one who purchases land.

Grantor: in the context of the sale of real estate, the seller.

Graphic user interference (GUI): the images on a computer screen that make it possible for a user to use software graphically.

Guardian: in some states, a person with an obligation to care for the children of a decedent or the management of property for the benefit of children.

Guided Search Form: a feature offered by Lexis-Nexis that uncovers information about a case, such as the name of a party.

Hacker: someone who wants to use or damage another's computer without permission of the computer's operator.

Hard drive: a computer's primary large-capacity data storage unit.

Headnotes: a feature in cases stored on the Lexis-Nexis database that breaks down a ruling according to important points; linked with other Lexis-Nexis print and electronic resources.

Home page: the default destination on which a browser starts when opened.

Hotspot: a Wi-Fi router.

HTTPS: as indicated at the beginning of the URL for a site, a form of HTTP with an additional level of security.

Hubs: communications devices used to facilitate telecommunications over a network.

HUD-1: a form the federal government requires when selling real property when the buyer has borrowed money for the purchase.

Hyperlink: a method of connecting web pages or sections in a web page.

Hypertext: a programming language used to create and edit web pages.

Hypertext transfer protocol (HTTP): rules related to transmitting information over the Internet.

Incapacitation: a time when a person cannot make sound decisions and that may necessitate the appointment of someone to look out for that person's interests.

Inkjet printer: a type of printer that uses a tiny nozzle to spray ink on a medium, like paper.

Instant messaging: real-time text-based communication via computer, distinct from e-mail or e-mail via the Internet.

Interest On Lawyer Trust Accounts (IOLTA): a type of client's funds account in which interest generated on a client's money held by a law firm that may be sent to a government agency to fund services such as for paying lawyers who represent indigent clients.

Intestate: when someone has died without a will.

Intranet: a network set up with limited access, typically inside a business that might not have access to the Internet.

Involuntary petition: a petition filed by a creditor to initiate a bankruptcy process against a debtor/petitioner.

Itemized deductions: in tax law, costs that can reduce the amount of income tax a person owes.

Kernel: with open-source software, the part that contains the functionality of the software.

KeyCite: a service available with Westlaw that checks whether a court has followed or overruled another court's ruling, for example. It corresponds to the Shepard's service provided by Lexis-Nexis.

KeyCite Alert: a feature offered with Westlaw that provides updates on prior searches.

Key numbers: a way to encode information by assigning designations to identify legal topics; used with West Publishing products, for example, to the AmJur2d.

Laser printer: a type of printer that uses the xerography process of quickly baking patterns of toner powder onto a medium such as paper.

Law reviews: scholarly law publications often published by law schools.

Lease: a right spelled out in a contract to possess and use land for a fixed period of time. The one who provides the lease is the lessor, also called the landlord, and the recipient, the lessee, is often called the tenant.

Ledger: a central accounting document that records debts and obligations so as to determine the present value of a transaction or business.

Legal Information Institute (LII): a free public database of federal and some state laws.

Lexis Advance for Solos: an iteration of the Lexis-Nexis database that uses a "carousel" style interface and a Word Wheel to suggest alternative approaches for conducting a search.

Lexis for Microsoft Office: an iteration of the Lexis-Nexis database that incorporates Microsoft's Outlook and Word applications.

Lexis-Nexis: a proprietary legal database service owned and operated by Reed-Elsevier.

LexisONE: a service offered by Lexis-Nexis for free access to appellate state court rulings from the last ten years.

Loislaw: a proprietary legal database service owned and operated by Wolters Kluwer.

Liabilities: debts or obligations.

Lien: a legal interest filed against property and based on outstanding debt. If property that has a lien on it is sold, the person who filed the lien is paid. A mortgage is a type of lien.

License: legal authority to use a patent or other form of property; usually limited in scope.

Limited liability corporation: a type of corporation with obligations and benefits different from a typical corporation.

Linux: an open-source operating system.

Liquidation: in bankruptcy law, a plan for a debtor/petitioner to pay off creditors with all available assets and obtain a complete discharge from the debts.

Litigation hold: because of litigation or pending litigation, a request to temporarily halt the normal process of deleting data files done by a business to reduce storage costs.

Living will: a type of durable power of attorney in which the agent can make decisions on behalf of an incapacitated principal. In some jurisdictions, it is equivalent to a medical power of attorney. If jurisdictions have both, one may relate to making medical decisions in general and the other about whether to terminate life support.

Local area network (LAN): a network of coaxial cables that connects designated devices.

Mac: short for Macintosh, a personal computer created by Apple.

Macro: a very simple computer program.

Malicious software (malware): software that would use a computer in a way that the operator of the computer would not otherwise want the computer used.

MD5 hash: a type of metadata that can be used to facilitate deduplication.

Means test: in bankruptcy law, a way to determine if debt exceeds assets by a stated amount, qualifying the debtor/petitioner for a discharge of the debt.

Medical power of attorney: a type of power of attorney in which the agent is empowered to make medical decisions on behalf of an incapacitated principal; not available in all states.

Meeting minutes: a record of actions taken in a meeting involving a corporation.

Metadata: electronically generated material with encoded information that might not typically be obvious.

Microprocessor: the computer chip or chips involved in calculations and operations; the "brains" of the computer.

Monitor: the graphic interface that makes it possible to use a computer.

Mortgage: when borrowing to purchase property, the purchaser gives the lender a mortgage. If the borrower fails to make a loan payment, the mortgage provides the lender with the authority to seize and auction the property to recover whatever amount remains due on the loan.

Motherboard: the plastic board embedded with wires that connect components in a personal computer.

Mouse: a computer peripheral that makes it easier for a user to move the cursor on a computer's monitor.

Netbooks: a portable computer that typically weighs a few pounds, often with no hard drive and a small screen.

Network: computers connected to one another.

Notarization: attestation by a third party that people who signed a document proved their identities at the time of signing.

Notebooks: a portable computer that typically weighs less than five pounds.

Officers: in corporate law, those who fulfill specific functions related to the functioning of the corporation, such as president or treasurer.

Open source: a type of software that is not copyright protected so that any may use it.

Operating system (OS): the primary software used to take advantage of a personal computer's processing power; creates the electronic environment in which applications run.

Optical character reading (OCR) software: scanning software that can translate the written word into electronically stored information.

Outlook: Microsoft's e-mail software.

Owner: in the context of real estate law, the entity with an unqualified right to use the land, including to allow another to use the property for a fee.

PACER (Public Access to Court Electronic Records): a federally operated fee-based database that contains U.S. District Court and appellate court rulings.

Pages: documents that must be included with the filing of a plan for the discharge in bankruptcy.

Partnership: a type of business organization in which all members share management.

decisions, and gains and losses, although many variations on this type of business entity exist.

Patches: small computer codes often used to correct a flaw in software, such as a particular vulnerability to hacking attempts.

Payee: one who receives payments.

Payor: one who makes payments.

Peer-to-peer network: a type of *ad hoc* network typically connecting two computers.

Personal exemptions: according to tax law, amounts not included in the taxable income of a person.

PC: a type of personal computer, pioneered by IBM.

Peripherals: equipment used with a computer to enhance its productivity, such as a printer or scanner.

Phishing: a hacking strategy that uses unsolicited e-mails.

Pivot table: a proprietary application of Microsoft, designed for handling and presenting data.

Ports: points to connect peripherals or other external devices to a computer.

Popular Name Table: a feature offered with Westlaw that allows for a search based on, for example, the popular name of a statute.

Pop-up blockers: software that prevents the uploading and displaying of ads on a computer.

Power of attorney: the authority empowering an agent to act on behalf of a principal.

Practice management software: keeps track of activity on behalf of a client, from court appearances to billing. It uses hardware and software to increase the effectiveness of those functions traditionally performed by any law practice, organization, or agency.

Precedent: prior court rulings in a jurisdiction that courts generally need to follow when issuing a ruling in a new case.

Primary law: also known as controlling law. It means that a jurisdiction's court rulings, statutes, and regulations are binding within that jurisdiction.

Principal: grants authority to an agent so that the agent will act on behalf of and consistent with the wishes of the principal.

Printer: an output device that creates paper copies (also called hard copies) of information from a computer.

Probating an estate: the process of carrying out a will's instructions, which must be monitored and approved by a court.

Property: a type of asset; divided into real property (real estate) or personal property (everything else).

Protected document format (PDF): a type of word processing document format.

Proxy: an authorization to cast a vote on behalf of the owner of stock, weighted according to the amount of stock owned by a shareholder.

Random access memory (RAM): a type of short-term storage unit installed on a computer's motherboard connected to the central processing unit.

Real estate: another term for real property; land.

Real estate binder: a contract that buyer and seller make to sell property for a set amount by a specified date.

Redlining: a way of indicating changes from a previous version of a document; used interchangeably with blacklining.

Registry of deeds: a public building where copies of deeds are kept; title searches take place here and sometimes closings.

RegulationPlus Index: a feature offered with Westlaw to narrow a search of regulations.

Remote access: Software that allows an attorney or paralegal to obtain access to a firm's database when out of the office.

Regulations: the types of rules created by governmental agencies.

Reorganization: in bankruptcy law, a plan for a debtor/petitioner to pay some or all debts according to a schedule, subject to the approval of the bankruptcy court judge.

Research Trail: a feature offered with Westlaw that allows a researcher to retrace steps taken when conducting a search.

Ribbon: a way of organizing a collection of buttons; often, at the top of a page.

Read-only memory (ROM): a longer-term storage unit of electronic information installed on a computer's motherboard connected to the CPU.

Report of Current Opinions (RECOP): from Fastcase, a weekly release of all federal and state appellate court opinions; published in collaboration with Public. Resource.org site in 2011.

Resident agent: a representative in a state for purposes of accepting a complaint against a corporation that does business there.

Resolutions: decisions determined by vote of the stockholders about action a corporation must take, for example, an increase in the salaries of officers.

Router: a device that facilitates telecommunications over the Internet.

Scalability: the ease with which software can work well on multiple platforms, such as on the iPhone and the iPad.

Scanner: a computer peripheral that works like a photocopier and scans hard copy, translating it into electronic file format.

Schedules: in the context of a petition in bankruptcy, documents that must be included with a plan for the discharge in bankruptcy.

Scrubbing: stripping metadata associated with a client's electronically stored information.

Search engines: information gathered from the Internet; will not be encoded in the way that information on a database is.

Secondary law: any statement of or about law outside of the jurisdiction's authority; it will not have the binding force of law.

Sector: the smallest unit of storage on a hard drive.

Secure sockets layers (SSL): a type of security protocol intended to reduce the risk of unauthorized access to information.

Security certificate: information associated with a website that a user would need to assess how safe a site is for that user to visit.

Secured loans: a financial arrangement whereby a lender retains the option to force the sale of personal property to recoup any amount outstanding on the loan used to purchase the personal property when the purchaser fails to make a loan payment.

Server: a computer typically connected to the Internet, used to store data and software; a critical component to SaaS.

Service set identifier (SSID): a unique identifying number assigned to devices that use microprocessors.

Service packs: a group of patches often used to correct numerous flaws or vulnerabilities in software.

Settlement agent: a person who coordinates the activities involved in a closing.

Share: an ownership interest in a corporation; often used interchangeably with "stock."

Sheet: the Excel equivalent to a page in Word or a slide in PowerPoint.

Shepard's: a service offered by Lexis-Nexis that describes the subsequent treatment of a case, including when it has been cited or overturned. It corresponds to the KeyCite service provided with Westlaw.

Short message service (SMS): a rudimentary, typed, electronic communication method; often called a text message.

Skype: a type of Voice Over Internet Protocol (VOIP) service.

Slide: the basic unit in a slideshow.

Smartphones: cellphones that commonly have a small video screen and greater processing power; sometimes, they have a miniature keyboard.

Software as a Service (SaaS): a way of using software stored on the server of a host, which also might be the creator of the software; accessible via the Internet; sometimes used as a synonym for cloud computing.

Source: encoded information broken down by jurisdictions, practice areas, or search categories.

Spam: unwanted e-mail.

Spreadsheet software: a type of software that makes it easy to conduct a range of computations, such as those calculated in the course of operating a business.

Spyware: malware intended to secretly monitor activity on a computer.

Stare decisis: Latin for "follow precedent"; a practice by which a judge in a current case must issue rulings consistent with that of a judge in a previous case when substantial similarity exists between the facts and the laws involved.

Statements: in bankruptcy law, questions that the debtor/petitioner must answer before obtaining a discharge in bankruptcy.

Statute of limitations: a law that requires the timely filing of a claim by a set deadline.

Stock: an ownership interest in a corporation, which generally determines what voting rights a stockholder has in a corporation; often used interchangeably with "share."

Statutes: legislatively created laws.

Stock options: where someone can buy shares at a fixed price by a specific date.

Structured query language (SQL): a database format, often associated with Microsoft software.

Suite: a bundle of software, often dedicated to a common goal, such as office productivity.

Stock register: a corporate document that keeps track of who owns what shares in a corporation.

Stockholder: one who owns stock; synonymous with shareholder.

Subchapter S corporation: a type of corporation with obligations and benefits different from a typical corporation.

Synchronization: a process that involves making sure that an exact copy of data on one device exists on another.

Table of Authorities: a list of cases cited in a brief.

Tablet: a type of portable computer that typically weighs less than a pound, typically with no hard drive or keyboard and a screen smaller than that used with a laptop.

Tabs: a type of graphic used for sorting functions, akin to the tabs on a manila folder.

Tax credits: under tax law, credits that reduce the amount of tax owed.

Tax proration: the proportional amount of annual taxes owed on a property at the time of closing.

Telecommunications: a means of electronically communicating.

Template: a blank document that has the proper formatting for generating a type of document.

A template for a complaint would include such information as where the case is being filed.

Tenant: has a possessory interest in land; rights are superior to everyone else in the world except the owner's.

Testator: a man who makes a will.

Testatrix: a woman who makes a will.

Thumbnails: small graphic representations of pages in the documents.

Thunderbird: Mozilla's e-mail software.

Tickler: reminder of impending deadlines or other forthcoming events.

Title: the document that represents the ownership interest in real property; also known as a deed.

Title search: researching of the chain of ownership of real property to confirm that the owner and the owner's predecessor's had a valid legal interest in the property.

Total Litigator: a feature offered by Lexis-Nexis for finding litigation-related materials.

Toolbar: a way of organizing buttons and links.

Track: a schedule issued by the court for the resolution of a complaint.

Transcript: a written record of questions and answers in a deposition.

Transactional Advisor: a feature offered by Lexis-Nexis to obtain information about commercial transactions.

Treatise: a publication that explores a topic of law.

Trojans: a type of malware that appears innocuous but conceals programming granting unauthorized use of a computer.

Trust: a form of ownership in which the legal owner is different from the equitable owner. A trustee manages the trust property (estate) and is the legal owner, and a beneficiary is the equitable owner and receives the benefits of the operation of the trust.

Trustee: in bankruptcy, the person appointed by the court to oversee the reconciling of debtor/petitioner's assets with debts to achieve a discharge in bankruptcy; with a trust, the person with the obligation to manage the trust property.

Tunneling: a way of establishing a unique connection between a sender and receiver, often using layered forms of security, including protocols or encryption.

Uniform Commercial Code (UCC): a type of model law intended to facilitate commercial transactions; adopted by each state.

Uniform Law and Model Acts: a feature offered with Westlaw that allows a researcher to search proposed laws.

Uniform Resource Locator (URL): the "address" of a web page.

United States Code Annotated: a compilation of federal statutes.

USB (universal serial bus): a type of standard connector often used with devices that work with the Microsoft platform.

Unsecured loans: loans in which the lender does not retain the option to force the sale of property purchased with loan funds if the borrower fails to make a loan payment; these tend to receive a lower priority when it comes to paying off the full amount of the loan when the borrower has filed a bankruptcy petition.

Utilities: software that maintains the functionality of the computer, such as battery use or disk management.

Virtual private network (VPN): a type of small network with very limited access.

Virus: a type of malware, often conveyed in e-mail or an attachment to e-mail.

Voluntary petition: the filing of a bankruptcy petition by a debtor/petitioner.

Voice over Internet protocol (VOIP): a way of transmitting speech over the Internet by translating it into data packets.

Webex: a service that provides Internet-based teleconferencing.

Web pages: the documents of a website, usually linked to one another.

WestlawNEXT: a service offered by West Publishing that uses a more intuitive-to-use interface and provides the same features of Westlaw.

WestlawNext Mobile: a service offered by West Publishing that allows for conducting a search of that database from a smartphone.

Widget: from Loislaw, allows the researcher to customize a search portal for an intranet or a Microsoft Sharepoint website.

Will: a legally enforceable document that contains the final wishes of a deceased person.

Wizard: a piece of software that offers step-by-step guidance to use features of the software, such as compressing a file using WinZip.

Workbook: a collection of Excel sheets.

Work product doctrine: protects from disclosure communications made in anticipation of litigation, like a discussion about trial strategy.

Index